THE LONGMAN COMPANION TO
CENTRAL AND EASTERN EUROPE SINCE 1919

LONGMAN COMPANIONS TO HISTORY

General Editors: Chris Cook and John Stevenson

The following Companions to History *are now available*:

Renaissance Europe, 1390–1530
Stella Fletcher

The European Reformation
Mark Greengrass

The Tudor Age
Rosemary O'Day

The Stuart Age, 1603–1714
John Wroughton

Britain in the Eighteenth Century, 1688–1820
Jeremy Gregory and John Stevenson

European Nationalism, 1789–1920
Raymond Pearson

European Decolonisation
Muriel E. Chamberlain

The Middle East since 1914
(Second Edition)
Ritchie Ovendale

America, 1910–1945
Patrick Renshaw

Nazi Germany
Tim Kirk

Britain since 1945
Chris Cook and John Stevenson

Germany since 1945
Adrian Webb

The European Union since 1945
Alasdair Blair

Imperial Russia, 1695–1917
David Longley

Napoleonic Europe
Clive Emsley

Britain in the Nineteenth Century, 1815–1914
Chris Cook

The Labour Party, 1900–1998
Harry Harmer

Russia since 1914
Martin McCauley

Britain, 1914–45
Andrew Thorpe

America, Russia and the Cold War, 1914–1998 (Second Edition)
John W. Young

Formation of the European Empires, 1488–1920
Muriel E. Chamberlain

The Conservative Party Since 1830
N.J. Crowson

THE LONGMAN COMPANION TO

CENTRAL AND EASTERN EUROPE SINCE 1919

Adrian Webb

Longman

An imprint of **Pearson Education**

London · New York · Toronto · Sydney · Tokyo · Singapore · Hong Kong · Cape Town
New Delhi · Madrid · Paris · Amsterdam · Munich · Milan · Stockholm

Pearson Education Limited

Head Office:
Edinburgh Gate
Harlow CM20 2JE
Tel: +44 (0)1279 623623
Fax: +44 (0)1279 431059

London Office:
128 Long Acre
London WC2E 9AN
Tel: +44 (0)20 7447 2000
Fax: +44 (0)20 7240 5771
Website: www.history-minds.com

First published in Great Britain in 2002

© Pearson Education Limited 2002

The right of Adrian Webb to be identified as Author of this Work has been
asserted by him in accordance with the Copyright, Designs and Patents Act 1988.

ISBN 0 582 43732 6

British Library Cataloguing in Publication Data
A CIP catalogue record for this book can be obtained from the British Library

Library of Congress Cataloging in Publication Data
A CIP catalog record for this book can be obtained from the Library of Congress

10   9   8   7   6   5   4   3   2   1

Typeset in 10/12pt New Baskerville by Graphicraft Limited, Hong Kong
Printed in Malaysia, LSP

The Publishers' policy is to use paper manufactured from sustainable forests.

For Miss T. T.

Acknowledgements

It is a particular pleasure to record my thanks to Professor Bruce Graham of the University of Sussex who both encouraged me to write this book and gave valuable comments on some of the text. Any remaining errors of fact or interpretation are, of course, strictly my responsibility. I must also offer my sincere thanks to Dr Chris Cook and Dr John Stevenson, the series editors for their advice, friendship and support.

I am indebted to the staffs and resources of the libraries of the University of Sussex and the West Sussex County Library, Chichester and, not least, to the staff of Pearson Education for their continuing assistance and patience.

Above all, though, I must thank my wife, Valerie, for her selfless advice, criticism and technological expertise over a very long period of time.

CONTENTS

INTRODUCTORY NOTES:
THE SCOPE OF THIS BOOK

Dividing history into periods is notoriously artificial, but by any historical standard 1919 marked a new beginning in central and eastern Europe. Politically, it had been largely divided for at least two centuries, and in many areas for much longer, between the competing empires of Austria, Germany, Russia and Turkey (see map). In 1917, however, the Russian Empire had been defeated by Germany. That German victory was overtaken the following year by the defeat of Austria-Hungary, Germany and Turkey which marked the end of the First World War in November 1918. This defeat of all the imperial powers created a vacuum unparalleled before or since in which the political system could be completely reordered in accordance with the nationality principle. Poland and Lithuania returned to the map of Europe as sovereign states. Czechoslovakia and Yugoslavia appeared for the first time, Estonia and Latvia for the first time as independent entities. Further east, Georgia and the Ukraine briefly enjoyed autonomy (see map).

If the timescale of this book is easy to justify, its geographical limits are very much harder. This is to no small degree because the terms 'Central' and particularly 'Eastern' Europe have been used to describe subjective perceptions rather than objective geographical realities. Before 1919, Central Europe was broadly understood as the territory of the Austro-Hungarian Empire ruled from Vienna, and Eastern Europe as the territory of the Russian Empire ruled from St Petersburg. The Balkans, comprising the independent states of Bulgaria, Montenegro, Romania and Serbia, together with substantial tracts of the Austro-Hungarian and Turkish Empires, formed a third grouping. The new and enlarged states established in 1919 sought to give themselves a more western orientation, but their ambitions enjoyed a mixed response. For their German-speaking neighbours, most of them remained essentially subordinate, colonial peoples and, under Hitler, they could be swept aside in the creation of a new German *Lebensraum* in the east stretching far into what had become the Ukrainian and Caucasian Republics of the Soviet Union. For the British and the French, Eastern Europe comprised the states between Germany and the Soviet Union, whose prime interest, particularly for the French, was their presumed role as allies in the event of another German attack in the west. Embarrassing as it may be to recall now, they were identified primarily with romantic revolutionaries, Ruritanian monarchs with colourful mistresses and 'being troublesome'. Chamberlain was merely being truthful when he declared that 'Czechoslovakia is a far away country of which we know nothing'.

After 1945, 'Eastern Europe' was the term adopted virtually universally to describe the Soviet bloc until its demise in 1990. The term, however, normally excluded the Soviet Union itself. It also ignored the anomaly that Prague is west of Vienna. This new 'Eastern Europe' was again as much a theatre as a real place, with Berlin at centre stage. Few of its governments recognised any responsibility for national actions taken during the Second World War. Even the Austrians, who had contributed Hitler, had been the victims of Nazism. It was now the scene of the struggle between east and west, between good and evil, between light and darkness, between communism and democracy: the assessment depending on the standpoint of the speaker. It was appreciated only slowly that the bloc was far from monolithic.

Its dissolution in 1990 permitted the restoration of a more diversified image. Some definitions became easier, others harder. German unification effectively moved East Germany from 'East' to 'West'. The 'Visegrad' group of Czechoslovakia, Hungary and Poland emerged as the nucleus of a new 'Central Europe', associated in varying degrees with both Austria and the former Yugoslav republic of Slovenia. 'Eastern Europe' came increasingly to mean the Balkans, really south-eastern Europe, while Eastern Europe in the geographical sense implicitly meant the states which had emerged from the dissolution of the Soviet Union in 1991, and which, with the exception of the Baltic states, are now grouped in the Commonwealth of Independent States (CIS).

In order to give this book some coherence against such shifting sands, it has been decided to focus on an 'Eastern Europe' defined as the 1945–90 Soviet bloc, including Albania and also Yugoslavia with whose history it was intimately involved. (Readers particularly interested in East Germany are referred to the present author's *Longman Companion to Germany since 1945*.) That focus is complemented by considerable attention to Austria whose history between 1919 and 1938, and to some extent since 1990, is an integral part of the history of central and eastern Europe. Reference to Greece is restricted to the limited number of occasions when it directly affected developments in its northern neighbours. That is not to imply that Greece is unimportant, merely that its inclusion would introduce so many considerations particular to itself, notably Cyprus and tension with Turkey, that this book might become unwieldy.

The countries now independent but formerly part of the Soviet Union are largely excluded in view of their very different history up to 1991. (Russia itself since 1914 is covered by Martin McCauley's companion volume in this series.) It is appreciated that their exclusion creates some anomalies, and they are accordingly covered in outline in the Glossary in an attempt to meet this difficulty.

GEOGRAPHICAL EQUIVALENTS

The names under which most central and easten European places are now normally known to English speakers are the names in the national language, but that was much less the case in earlier decades. Moreover, political and linguistic boundaries have remained in a state of flux. Again, many names have been changed and then changed back, with the rise and fall of political ideologies. The text of this book normally adopts the name which would have been in use at the time in question, with the current name in brackets where it seems appropriate. Older or foreign sources may follow different conventions and the following list is designed to help the reader accordingly. Major cities and features with established English names such as Belgrade, Prague and Warsaw have been excluded.

Current name	Equivalent name
Alba Iulia (Romanian)	Gyulafehérvar (Hungarian)
Bratislava (Slovak)	Pressburg (German)
České Budějovice (Czech)	Budweis (German)
Cheb (Czech)	Eger (German)
Chisinau (Romanian)	Kishinev (Russian)
Cieszyn (Polish)	Těšín (Czech), Teschen (German)
Cluj (Romanian)	Kolozsvar (Hungarian)
Durrës (Albanian)	Durazzo (Italian)
Dubrovnik (Serbo-Croat)	Ragusa (Italian)
Gdánsk (Polish)	Danzig (German)
Kaliningrad (Russian)	Königsberg (German)
Karlovy Vary (Czech)	Carlsbad (German)
Lviv (Ukrainian)	Lvov (Russian), Lwow (Polish), Lemberg (German)
Márianské Lázně (Czech)	Marienbad (German)
Montenegro (extraterritorial Italian)	Crna Gora (Serbo-Croat)
Oradea Mare (Romanian)	Nagyvarad (Hungarian)
Plzeň (Czech)	Pilsen (German)
Rijeka (Serbo-Croat)	Fiume (Italian)
Sazan (Albanian)	Saseno (Italian)
Shkodër (Albanian)	Scutari (Italian)
Sopron (Hungarian)	Oedenburg (German)
Szczecin (Polish)	Stettin (German)
Tirgu Mures (Romanian)	Marosvasarhely (Hungarian)
Trento (Italian)	Trent (German)
Vilnius (Lithuanian)	Wilno (Polish), Vilna (Russian)
Vlorë (Albanian)	Valona (Italian)
Wroclaw (Polish)	Breslau (German)
Zadar (Serbo-Croat)	Zara (Italian)
Zagreb (Serbo-Croat)	Agram (German)

POLITICALLY INSPIRED NAME CHANGES

The Communist period saw the widespread renaming of towns and streets in honour of Communist heroes, although Stalin was rapidly expunged, except in Georgia, after Khrushchev's denunciation in 1956. Most reverted rapidly after 1990, and Kaliningrad is the only important exception at the time of writing (2001). The more important changes are listed below.

Traditional name	Communist name
Bazardjik	Tolbukhin
Chemnitz	Karl-Marx-Stadt
Dunaujvaros	Sztalinvaros
Eisenhüttenstadt	Stalinstadt
Oneşti	Gheorghe Gheorghiu-Dej
Pernik	Dimitrovo
Podgorica	Titograd
Shumen	Kolarovgrad
Varna	Stalin
Zlin	Gottwaldov

Street name changes are far too numerous to be recorded here, but it should be noted that there has been considerable resistance in eastern Germany to total change. Marx and Engels are felt by many to be part of the national heritage and worthy of continuing commemoration. Karl-Marx-Allee (once Stalinallee) in East Berlin is likely to remain.

PERSONAL NAMES

As with geographical names, English-language sources now usually quote foreign personal names in the form native to the speaker. That used to be much less the case and there are still some exceptions, particularly when familiar forenames such as Peter are involved. This book normally prefers the native form in the interests of consistency, e.g. Franz-Josef rather than Francis-Joseph and Karl rather than Charles, for the last two emperors of Austria-Hungary, and Beneš rather than Benesh for the second Czechoslovak president.

The transliteration of names from the Cyrillic to the Latin alphabet has its own difficulties. Transliterations from the Bulgarian and the Ukrainian now tend to be simpler if slightly less exact, and 'ch' is preferred to 'tch', '-ev' to '-eff', and 'y' to 'j'. Serb names however are now normally given in the parallel Croat spelling rather than transliterated in accordance with Western norms. Bulgarian names (like Russian ones) are, therefore, pronounced broadly as an English speaker would expect, Serb ones are not. This book follows modern practice throughout so that the same name does not appear in two different forms in the same volume.

A BRIEF GUIDE TO PRONUNCIATION

It would clearly be impossible to give a detailed guide to the pronunciation of all the central and eastern European languages, and it is hardly necessary, but the following notes may help those unfamiliar with them to approach the names of places and people with more confidence and to recognise them when they are pronounced by a native speaker. Cassettes are readily available for more detailed study.

The great majority of the region's languages, including Bulgarian, Czech, Macedonian, Polish, Russian, Ruthenian, Serbo-Croat, Slovak, Slovene and White Russian, belong to the slavonic group and are closely related. Only Polish, which, with French and Portuguese, is one of the few European languages to have developed nasal vowels, is significantly different. Different spellings can, therefore, mask very similar sounds or linguistic relationships. Czech *hrad*, for example, is the same as Bulgarian *grad* (city). Many words, not least *pivo* (beer), are common to all. Insofar as specific slavonic spellings are concerned:

č	(Czech, Serbo-Croat, Slovak)	=	English 'ch' as in chur<u>ch</u>.
cz	(Polish)	=	English 'ch', likewise.
ć	(Serbo-Croat)	=	a rather weaker version of the above with no exact English equivalent; closest to 'tch'.
c	(Polish)	=	similar to the previous, but not confined to the end of words.
c	(Czech, Serbo-Croat, Slovak)	=	usually the English 'ts' as in ca<u>ts</u>.
j	(Czech, Polish, Serbo-Croat, Slovak)	=	English 'y' as in <u>y</u>acht when found at the beginning of words, but also, again like the English 'y', marks a diphthong after a vowel: oj = English 'oy' as in b<u>oy</u>, and aj = English 'igh' as in s<u>igh</u>t.
ł	(Polish)	=	the 'l' in English co<u>l</u>d, rather than the 'l' in English <u>l</u>amp. By an evolution similar to that in the Cockney pronunciation of cold (couwd), it can approximate to an English 'w'.
š	(Czech, Serbo-Croat, Slovak)	=	English 'sh' as in <u>sh</u>ip.
sz	(Polish)	=	English 'sh' as in <u>sh</u>ip.
szcz	(Polish)	=	a soft guttural sound with no standard English equivalent, but very close to the soft final 'ch' of the German 'I<u>ch</u>' (I).
w	(Polish)	=	English 'v' as in <u>v</u>ictor.
ž	(Czech, Polish, Serbo-Croat, Slovak)	=	English 's' as in plea<u>s</u>ure. The same sound is transliterated from the Cyrillic alphabet as 'zh', as in Zhdanov, Zhivkov, Zhukov.

Hungarian is related to no other central or eastern European language, and it has its own distinctive spelling conventions, although its pronunciation is much less problematical to the outsider than that of, say, Polish. Principal among its spelling conventions are:

cs   =   English 'ch' as in <u>ch</u>ur<u>ch</u>.

gy   =   English 'j' as in jelly. (Nagy is thus pronounced like English 'Nodge'.)

s   =   English 'sh' as in <u>sh</u>ip.

sz   =   English 's' as in <u>s</u>ing. (Stalin is thus written Sztalin.)

ö   =   the German or Swedish pronunciation of the same spelling, which has no exact equivalent in standard English but is close to the final 'er' in such words as hamm<u>er</u>.

ő   =   a more emphatic form of the foregoing, close to the standard English 'ur' as in b<u>ur</u>n.

Romanian is central and eastern Europe's only Romance (derived from Latin) language and has discernible similarities with French, Italian, Portuguese and Spanish. Its main spelling conventions are:

c   =   before 'e' or 'i' English 'ch' as in <u>ch</u>ur<u>ch</u>, otherwise English 'k' as in <u>k</u>ing.

ş   =   English 'sh' as in <u>sh</u>ip.

i   =   is mute at the end of words.

oe   =   the English 'oy' as in b<u>oy</u>.

(As an example of the three foregoing rules, the town of Ploeşti is pronounced 'Ploysht'.)

Part 1

THE BACKGROUND TO 1919

It can be argued persuasively that the First World War was a struggle for mastery between rival empires driven by economic and strategic concerns: that it was, in short, a war waiting to happen. Proponents of that view can point to the string of crises from 1900 onwards which threatened to bring Britain, France and Germany, in particular, into conflict, and the tension generated by Anglo-German naval rivalry. None of these crises, however, had actually led to war. Indeed, many of the points at issue had either been resolved or were well on the way to being resolved by the end of 1913, although the underlying animosities and suspicions certainly remained, as was witnessed by the enthusiasm with which the outbreak of war was to be received in Berlin, London and Paris. Nevertheless, the war which actually materialised was triggered by specifically Balkan rivalries and tensions.

The Balkans had been unstable for the best part of a century for several interrelated reasons, some of which were to outlive the post-war settlement of 1919 and remain live to this day. The most obvious was the progressive political decay of the Turkish Empire. The empire, which in 1683 had included Hungary and had launched the siege of Vienna – half way to London from Istanbul – had lost its dynamism during the eighteenth century, and the nineteenth century had seen successive struggles for independence by its European colonies. Serbia had been the first to rebel in 1804, and its autonomy had been internationally recognised in 1829, but Greece in 1830 had been the first to gain full independence. The Turks had been obliged progressively to recognise the autonomy of Moldavia and Wallachia, the core of the modern Romania, in 1856 and of Bulgaria in 1878. The full independence of Serbia and Romania had come in 1878 and of Bulgaria in 1908. Albania had gained independence of a kind as recently as 1912.

The national liberation movements had enjoyed little general support from the outside world, a factor which has contributed to a certain inwardness of outlook. British governments, responsible for the world's largest empire, were unsympathetic in principle and were always nervous as to the implications for Ireland. More specifically, the Turkish Empire was seen as a bulwark against Russian expansionism and it was British policy throughout the century to prop it up even at the expense of offending domestic public opinion. The Austrians, the Turks' most obvious imperial rivals in the Balkans, similarly saw the Turks as necessary for their own survival by virtue of their holding Balkan nationalist aspirations in check. They also preferred Turkish to national rule, because it provided a single framework for their plans for economic investment, notably in railways. The French were only really interested in Romania, on account of its Latin roots, and Germany's celebrated Chancellor, Bismarck, famously considered the Balkans not to be worth the bones of a single Pomeranian grenadier. Russia alone, the one power with some emotional attachment to the Balkan slavs and with its own strategic ambition of controlling Constantinople (Istanbul) and gaining access to the Mediterranean, had a clear interest in diminishing Turkish suzerainty. Russia, however, had lost the Crimean War and was not in a position to promote her own interests at the expense of those of the other powers.

In practice the Great Powers had met sporadically, most notably at the Congress of Berlin in 1878, to regulate and confirm, but not usually radically alter, what had already happened on the ground. Their real concern was to ensure that none of their own number gained sufficient advantage to disturb the wider European balance of power.

For all their ethnic and geographical differences the new states had a lot in common. They all, except Albania, belonged primarily to the Orthodox branch of Christianity organised on nationally independent (autocephalous) lines, and drew a proportion of their sense of national identity from the fight against the Turk and Islam, which were indissolubly linked. Prior to their conquest by the Turks in the fourteenth and fifteenth centuries, they had formed part of the Byzantine world (see Part 10.3). That world, however, had lost any effective central direction centuries before its final demise, and power had been exercised from a number of changing centres over expanding and contracting areas with very fluid boundaries. Virtually every one of the new national boundaries could, therefore, be contested. The new Balkan states also shared many economic and social characteristics. Production was overwhelmingly agricultural and heavy industry almost unknown, apart from mining. The Greek merchant marine which had grown apace after independence was a case apart. Railways were few and educational levels generally low. Power lay with the monarchy and a small governing class drawn from the emerging bourgeoisie. Much commerce was in Greek hands. Only Serbia was not led by a monarch drawn from the seemingly inexhaustible pool of German princes. That bond of sympathy was sometimes contradicted by the stance of the small number of intellectuals, who in Romania in particular looked towards France. It was also contradicted in the slav lands of Bulgaria and Serbia by the powerful force of pan-slavism, part intellectual, part popular, part religious, which stressed the close cultural and linguistic links of the slav peoples with each other and with their largest community, the Russians, in particular.

Not least, they shared an intense nationalism and the unstable blend of insecurity and assertiveness which is so often the legacy of colonial rule. This was a source of potential tension with the large ethnic minorities in virtually every state. When combined with the region's uncertain frontiers, conflict was predictable and the Balkan Wars of 1912 and 1913 gave the Balkans a reputation for instability which was to dog it throughout the twentieth century.

These new states adjoined the large areas of what is now Bosnia and the Former Yugoslav Republic of Macedonia, where slightly different conditions applied. Turkish influence had penetrated more deeply. The Turkish minority itself was larger, and a significant proportion of the local population in some parts had converted to Islam. To this day, the Bosnian capital, Sarajevo, has in many places the look of a Turkish city. The new fashion of nationalism also had a much less certain focus. The dialects of Bosnia could be described as Serb, but those of Macedonia were more akin to Bulgarian. There was no memory, however remote or artificial, of a predecessor state. Moreover, the rugged terrain, just as in Albania and Montenegro further to the west, and just as in the Caucasus and Afghanistan much further away, readily nourished a ready rejection of governmental authority in any form.

The area of Bosnia-Hercegovina had proved a flashpoint in 1908 when it had been annexed by the Austro-Hungarian Empire rather than the neighbouring slav states who had the most obvious claim on the grounds of ethnicity.

The Austro-Hungarian Empire was in some respects a mirror image of the Turkish. Its power was ebbing, and it had lost most of its Italian provinces during the nineteenth century. Hungarian nationalism had obliged the Habsburg monarchy in 1867 to convert the Austrian Empire into an Austro-Hungarian one under the 'Compromise' (*Ausgleich*). Such important regions as Croatia and Slovakia were technically Hungarian rather than Austrian colonies, and the Hungarians were determined to retain their dominance. It was the goal of southern slav nationalists such as the Bosnian Serb, Gavrilo Princip, who assassinated the Austro-Hungarian Crown Prince Franz Ferdinand in Sarajevo in 1914 thereby setting the First World War in motion, to liberate all the southern slavs from Austro-Hungarian as much as from Turkish rule and to unify them under Serb leadership.

The Austro-Hungarian Empire, however, was in a less advanced stage of political decay than the Turkish. It could still seize the initiative as it had in Bosnia-Hercegovina in 1908. Moreover, it was enmeshed in the system of interlocking great power alliances, which in 1914 was to escalate the localised dispute between Serbia and Austria-Hungary, following the Sarajevo assassination, into the First World War.

In the years before 1914, however, the Habsburg monarchy had probably been more preoccupied by separatism much further north in Austrian Poland. Unlike the Balkan states, which had succumbed to Turkey more than five centuries before, an independent Polish-Lithuanian Empire had been divided up between Austria, Prussia (now Germany) and Russia as recently as 1772–95. The composer, Chopin, had distilled the Polish national spirit in piano pieces played in drawing rooms across Europe and had been instrumental in persuading western public opinion, if not western governments, that Polish nationalism, like Italian, was a good cause. More violent figures culminating in Piłsudski (qv) had sought to secure an independent and united Poland by more direct means. If Austrian rule in Krakow was somewhat less arbitrary than Russian autocracy in Warsaw, it was no less minded to preserve what it regarded as its own.

The issue ultimately at stake was the proper basis for constituting a nation. In the eyes of the Austro-Hungarian monarchy, the citizen owed a personal duty of loyalty to the crown which in turn owed a duty to its citizens to treat them equally regardless of their ethnic origins. Its culture was cosmopolitan but firmly rooted in its German-speaking core. It was the world of Haydn and Mozart. For its non-German-speaking citizens, particularly the Czechs, Hungarians, Poles and Transylvanian Romanians, loyalty was increasingly felt to lie with one's ethnic group organised as a nation state. It was a western European concept transferred to the very different world of central Europe, where populations were ethnically very mixed, and cultural and religious loyalties highly diverse. It was a highly stimulating cultural impulse, at least for a time, and closely allied with the equally imported concept of liberalism. Nevertheless its inherent logic that the nation state was the particular preserve of a specific ethnic group was to cause havoc repeatedly in the twentieth century and continues to do so in the twenty-first.

It is as difficult for the historian now, however, as it was for the Imperial government then, to propose an alternative. Perhaps the Hungarian precedent could have been built upon to establish a loose central European federation still focused on Vienna. It may yet materialise nearly a century later in the wider concept of common EU membership. Habsburg rule, though, was detested by Croats, Czechs, Poles, Romanians and others alike, and their leaders had unlimited faith in the nationality principle. If they had been able to foresee the history of the twentieth century they might perhaps have felt differently.

The First World War, however, had brought all these animosities to the fore, and destroyed what limited scope there was for compromise. Austria-Hungary, Germany, and Turkey, with their Balkan ally Bulgaria, had been pitted against Russia (with its British, French and, at the end, American allies on the western front) and Italy with their Balkan allies Montenegro, Romania, Serbia and Greece. All the empires, on the eastern fronts as on the western, conscripted their citizens. Ethnic Italians from, say, Trieste had been expected to fight against the Kingdom of Italy, just as Austro-Hungarian and German Poles had been expected to fight against Russian Poles. Desertion was treason and punished as such. It had nevertheless happened, sometimes on an organised scale. A Czechoslovak Legion, for example, fought with the Italians, contributing to sympathy between the two countries for a time after 1919.

Casualties had everywhere been severe and weighed particularly heavily, perhaps, on the Balkans, which had not yet recovered from their own wars of 1912 and 1913. Serbia had lost almost a quarter of its population in six years of war, a proportion higher than that suffered by any nation state in the Second World War. The economic losses were to be longer lasting. Livestock herds were not to reach their pre-war level for another twenty years, and although economists have calculated that European productivity as a whole had returned broadly to its pre-war level as early as 1924, central and eastern European agriculture had now not only to recover but to compete with the output of the United States and Canada, and its industry with the increased productivity of western Europe and North America alike. The certainties of pre-war society were never to return.

HISTORICAL CHRONOLOGY

2.1 VERSAILLES AND THE ESTABLISHMENT OF THE NEW ORDER

The Treaty of Versailles represents the formal opening of the period covered by this book, and that is fully justified because it gave international recognition to the new Europe which the forces unleashed by the First World War had created. Indeed in retrospect, the 'creations' of the conference itself were probably negative rather than positive in their impact: the establishment of the free city of Danzig, the imposition of an unrealistic burden of reparations on Germany and reliance on a League of Nations to which nobody was willing to give serious support and which America declined ever to join.

It was, nevertheless, Versailles which endorsed the changes which had been happening on the ground since at least 1916, and in some areas even earlier. These changes had sometimes even been initiated by the combatants themselves. Germany and Austria had both promised the Poles sovereignty in 1916 in an attempt to free troops for the western front. Such promises were not necessarily honoured once victory had been secured. The secret Treaty of London of 1915 had promised Italy a large part of the Dalmatian coast then under Austro-Hungarian rule, but the treaty was disowned by America's President Wilson, who became a major player with America's entry into the war in 1917. Italy saw the coast pass to Yugoslavia. Similarly the secret Treaty of Bucharest of 1916 had promised Romania the whole of the Hungarian Banat, but it was to be divided along ethnic lines. Likewise, earlier secret agreements meant that the Czechs and the Serbs were represented at Versailles, but neither the Slovaks nor the Croats.

Governments had similarly appeared and disappeared before the conference had even been convened. The imperial governments had fallen in Russia in 1917, and in Austria-Hungary and Germany in 1918, although the Turkish Sultanate did not finally succumb until 1922. Only in Hungary, despite Béla Kun's unsuccessful revolution, was there a measure of continuity, although Admiral Horthy was not installed as regent for the absent Habsburg monarchy until March 1920. On the other hand, the Czechs, the Poles and the southern Slavs already had shadow governments with as much (or as little) practical experience as the post-imperial governments of Austria, Germany, Hungary and Russia.

Nevertheless, Versailles did not settle the peace terms between the Allies and the Austrians, the Bulgarians and the Hungarians. Those were to follow at Saint-Germain, Neuilly and Trianon. None of the treaties, however, was to settle all the frontier disputes between the central and eastern European countries, new and old. These were typically areas of mixed population, where cultural, ethnic, historic, linguistic and strategic ties pulled in different directions. Disputes rapidly flared between Italy and Yugoslavia over Fiume and Istria, between Russia and Poland over their common border, and most dramatically of all, although just outside our area, between the Turks and the Allies, notably the Greeks, over the future Turkish state. Some of the disputes were to be settled at later conferences, others were settled or revised during and after the Second World War, others remain potential flashpoints. In practice, settlement has usually meant an exchange of populations, sometimes slow and voluntary, often abrupt and brutal.

Some of the more significant events of 1917–19, which help to place the conclusions of Versailles in their historical context, are summarised below as a prologue to the ensuing chronology for the period up to 1939, which comprises Part 2.2.

1917

20 July   The Corfu Declaration determines the broad framework for establishing a unified southern slav (Yugoslav) state, when the First World War has been won.

26 November Bolshevik Russia unilaterally ends hostilities at Lenin's direction, and signs a formal armistice with Germany a month later.

1918

24 January   A Bessarabian council declares the region independent of Russia. It votes to unite with Romania in December.

3 March   Victorious Germany and defeated Russia sign the Peace of Brest Litovsk on German terms.

7 May   Victorious Germany and defeated Romania sign the Peace of Bucharest on German terms.

24 May   The Slovak National Party adopts an anti-Hungarian position.

30 June   Professor Masaryk, acting for the Czechs, signs the Pittsburgh Agreement in America, whereby he promises Slovak Americans, acting for the European Slovaks, a Slovak Diet, autonomous administration and law courts, and the use of Slovak as the official language of administration and education in the Slovak lands. The promises are never to be honoured.

29 September Bulgaria signs an armistice with the British and the French in Thessaloniki. She is the first of the Central Powers to surrender.

3–4 October Prince Maximilian of Baden, the new German Chancellor, requests President Wilson of America to arrange an immediate armistice and a start to peace negotiations on the basis of the President's Fourteen Points (see Glossary).

10

12 October	The Transylvanian Romanian National Party, meeting at Oradea Mare (Hungarian Nagyvárad), declares the right of self-determination for Romanians in Hungary.
26 October	Professor Masaryk and Gregory Žatković, a Ruthene American, sign the Philadelphia Agreement whereby Ruthenia is promised autonomy within the new Czechoslovakia. The promise is never to be honoured.
27 October	A Bukovinian National Council is established in Chernivtsi and appeals to Romania for the liberation of the province from Austria.
28 October	The Czechoslovak National Council (*Národni Výbor*) assumes the government of the Czechoslovak territories (Bohemia, Moravia, Silesia and Slovakia), previously exercised by Austria-Hungary.
29 October	The *Sabor*, the Croatian Parliament, declares the dissolution of the union with Hungary, and the establishment of a 'State of the Slovenes, Croats and Serbs'.
29 October	Slovak political leaders declare in Turčiansky Svätý Martin that there is one single Czechoslovak nation and that the land of the Slovaks shall form part of a common state.
30 October	Turkey signs the Armistice of Mudros.
31 October	Revolution breaks out in Hungary with the goal of establishing an independent republic.
3 November	Austria-Hungary signs an armistice with the Allies, excluding the Serbs, in Padova. The Serbs occupy Austrian Bosnia and Hungarian Vojvodina in the ensuing ten days.
9 November	The independence of Poland is proclaimed in Warsaw.
9 November	The declaration of a Bavarian Republic by Kurt Eisner two days earlier leads to the resignation of Prince Maximilian as German Chancellor and the abdication of Kaiser Wilhelm II as German emperor. He flees to the neutral Netherlands. The cession of the Chancellorship to Friedrich Ebert, the leader of the Social Democrats, is challenged by the soldiers' and workers' councils, the Independent Socialists and the *Spartakusbund* (Spartacus Union). The latter is to become the *Kommunistische Partei Deutschlands* (KPD) (German Communist Party) in January 1919. Ebert decides to ally himself with the Supreme Army Command against the far left.
10 November	Romania re-enters the war on the Allied side.
11 November	Germany and the Allies sign an armistice at Rethondes, France, bringing to an end fighting on the western front.
12 November	Austria is proclaimed a republic. Government is assumed by a National Assembly and interim cabinet.

11

13 November	Bolshevik Russia invites all the countries of eastern Europe to join a Union of Soviet Republics.
13 November	The Austro-Hungarian emperor, Karl, abdicates as King of Hungary.
14 November	The National Assembly in Prague formally declares Czecho-slovakia a republic, with Professor Tomáš Masaryk as its first president.
14 November	General Piłsudski, having returned to Poland, assumes supreme power, and convokes the Constituent Assembly, which confirms him in office.
16 November	An independent Hungarian People's Republic is proclaimed in Budapest. Count Mihály Karolyi is provisional president.
26 November	A Montenegrin national assembly under Serb influence deposes King Nicholas and merges Montenegro with Serbia.
28 November	A Bukovinian Congress votes for union with Romania. The union is formalised by decree on 19 December.
1 December	The Triunine Kingdom of the Serbs, Croats and Slovenes is proclaimed by the prince regent, later King Alexander. His father, Peter I of Serbia, is declared the first monarch of the new kingdom.
1 December	Representatives of the Transylvanian Romanians meeting at Alba Iulia (Hungarian Gyulafehérvar) proclaim the Union of Transylvania and Romania, and the union of all Romanians in one state.

1919

10 January	The German Army assisted by *Freikorps* (counter-revolutionary volunteers) launches the campaign against Communism by attacking the Spartacist headquarters in Spandau, a suburb of Berlin.
15 January	Karl Liebknecht and Rosa Luxembourg, the leaders of the Communist revolutionaries in Berlin, are captured and brutally murdered by the *Freikorps*. A fellow captive, Wilhelm Pieck, survives to become East Germany's first president in 1949
17 January	Ignacy Paderewski forms a Polish government of experts. He serves as his own foreign minister.
14 February	The first phase of the war between Soviet Russia and Poland over their joint border and spheres of influence opens with an unplanned confrontation at Bereza Kartuska in Belarus. Polish war aims include the independence of the non-Russian parts of the former Russian Empire. The Poles take Vilnius in April and Minsk in August.

20 March   Béla Kun becomes leader of a new Communist–Social Democrat coalition government in Hungary. Count Karolyi resigns as provisional president two days later.

1 May   The violent suppression of revolution in Bavaria by the German Army and *Freikorps* units marks the end of the immediate post-war challenge to the Ebert government from the far left.

8 May   A Ruthene National Council proclaims the union of Ruthenia with Czechoslovakia.

28 June   The Treaty of Versailles is signed in the Hall of Mirrors of the former royal palace of Versailles just outside Paris, between Germany and the victorious Allies. The Peace is imposed on the Germans who maintain that it does not respect the spirit of President Wilson's Fourteen Points (see Glossary). The principal Allied signatories, Georges Clemenceau of France, David Lloyd George of Great Britain and President Woodrow Wilson of America, have made all the key decisions, with their co-signatory, Vittorio Orlando of Italy, and the other Allied powers playing only a minor role. The treaty re-establishes an independent Poland in accordance with President Wilson's Thirteenth Point, and declares Danzig a free city. The Allies maintain that Germany carries sole moral guilt for the war and that she must pay reparations accordingly. They are to be set in 1921 at $33,000,000,000.

2.2 KEY EVENTS FROM VERSAILLES TO THE OUTBREAK OF THE SECOND WORLD WAR

COMMENTARY

The choice of the Hall of Mirrors at Versailles for the signature of the peace treaty was motivated by the overwhelming desire of the French to have their revenge for the treaty they had been forced to accept there by the victorious Germans at the conclusion of the Franco-Prussian War in 1871. Unintentionally, however, it proved to be a metaphor for the order which the treaty brought into being, not least in central and eastern Europe. It was an order based on appearances and illusions rather than on realities.

The France of Versailles appeared to be the greatest power in continental Europe and the victorious nations of central and eastern Europe relied on her protection and her training of their armies accordingly.

The comparative power of France, however, had been suffering erosion for over a century from the malign combination of a low birthrate and a shortage of many of the mineral resources needed to build up an industrial society. At the same time as the states of central and eastern Europe were looking to her for protection, she was envisaging them as future defenders of France. The years 1938–39 were to reveal her inability and reluctance to protect them and 1940 her inability (and again perhaps reluctance) to defend herself without them.

Russia was feared when she was weak in the 1920s but largely ignored in the 1930s when she was recovering her strength. No-one was to see fit to invite her to the 1938 Munich Conference which dismembered Czechoslovakia, and as late as 1939 Poland could not accept that she was the only power which could possibly protect her from Germany. Piłsudski had maintained that Poland was a great power or she was nothing. 1939 was to show that when her romantic illusions and cavalry were set against the reality of the German Stuka bomber she would be the latter before she would be the former.

The master illusionist, however, was Mussolini, who seized power in Italy in 1922. His armies were poorly equipped, his support shallow and his strategic vision defective, but none of this was to prevent him from causing apprehension everywhere. He was also to prove a master of intrigue, although that designation does not do justice to his diplomatic skills. He was to intrigue in Albania, in Austria, in Bulgaria, in Czechoslovakia, in Greece and in Yugoslavia. Moreover, he was to intrigue successfully for the best part of twenty years. Not surprisingly, he was to spawn imitators like King Carol in Romania and Dr

14

Dollfuss in Austria, and admirers like King Boris in Bulgaria, General Averescu in Romania, and King Zog in Albania. Piłsudski's march on Warsaw of 1926 was to be highly reminiscent of Mussolini's march on Rome of 1922. Mussolini's fascism and the reasons for its widespread appeal are discussed in Part 3.2.

Even Germany formed part of this pattern of appearances and illusions. The western Allies certainly had no illusions about Germany's resentment at her defeat and were to be highly alarmed in 1922 when she signed the Treaty of Rapallo with Russia. It was always implausible, though, that the two countries, with opposing philosophies and urgent internal concerns, would be jointly pro-active on the European stage. When the threat presented by Germany did become real in the mid-1930s, illusions again came to the fore. Many were to find it difficult to take Hitler with his toothbrush moustache and prominent forelock seriously: Charlie Chaplin was to try unsuccessfully in *The Great Dictator* to undermine him with ridicule. Mussolini continued to be seen by many as the real threat. When all else failed, the illusion surfaced that Hitler would be amenable to reason. The dismemberment of Czechoslovakia was to be initiated at Munich by the British and the French in the hope that it would satisfy him. Chamberlain's fond belief that Hitler's signature on a 'scrap of paper' meant 'peace in our time' proved to be the greatest illusion of all.

These illusions were to be stimulated rather than checked by the serious structural defects in the Versailles and successor settlements over and above the essential mismanagement of the whole German question. In particular no real attempt was made to balance the national ambitions and insecurities of the Europe they had created. The inconsistency in application of the ethnic nationality principle meant that whereas the Czechs and Slovaks, and the Serbs and Croats, had been placed in one state despite their uncertain enthusiasm for union, the Germans of the former Austro-Hungarian Empire were forbidden to unite with their kinsmen in Germany. They either had to become citizens of the new Austria or were incorporated in Czechoslovakia so as to give the new state an allegedly defensible frontier. Czechoslovakia was thus awarded upwards of some three million unwilling citizens. Not dissimilarly, some three of the eleven million ethnic Hungarians found themselves excluded from the new nation state, whereas the new Poland and Romania were barely 70 per cent ethnically Polish and Romanian respectively.

The victors were not necessarily any more satisfied. Italy, denied the Dalmatian coast and acquiring Istria and Fiume only after a struggle, feared the new Yugoslavia and her French ally as a threat across the Adriatic to even her modest great power ambitions. With the advent of Mussolini to power in 1922, those ambitions were to become appreciably less modest with domination of the whole Mediterranean as the ultimate goal. In the medium term, the objective was to dominate the Balkans. In practice that was to mean cultivating Albania together with Bulgaria and Hungary, which were both anxious to reverse their territorial losses to the new Yugoslavia. The Hungarians sought to recover the fertile plains of the Banat (the Vojvodina) and even entertained hopes of breaking the new Yugoslavia in two by attracting the Croats back to their Hungarian allegiance. To the south, the Bulgarians were to pursue their ancient claim to Macedonia through support for terrorism which also profited from Italian assistance. The Yugoslavs for their part had aspirations to incorporate Bulgaria in a Slav union. The containment of Yugoslavia was also to involve Italy in Austria's affairs, because she represented the only other land transit route from Italy to Hungary. For all its technical flair, however, Italy's foreign policy was strategically flawed. It had no prospect of displacing the British and the French from the Mediterranean except in alliance with Germany. Any alliance with Germany, however, would quickly underline the limitations of Italian strength. As early as 1934, the assassination by the Nazis of Dr Dollfuss in Vienna was to mark the end of Italian supremacy in Austria. Although Austro-German union (*Anschluss*) was to be deferred for three years, from then on it was Hitler rather than Mussolini who was to make the running wherever it really mattered.

Subordination to Germany, however, was not to spell the end of either Italian ambition or even its realisation. The partition of the Balkans between German and Italian spheres of influence remained plausible, and the Mediterranean was peripheral to Germany's world view. As chance would have it, Hitler appears to have been personally pro-Italian, and he and Mussolini soon mastered the art of alternately creating crises which the other would use his best offices to solve. The Munich Agreement was to be the greatest achievement of this masterly double act.

The clarity and coherence of Italian policy was to compare favourably with the vacillation of the French. Having antagonised Germany throughout most of the post-war period, she was terrified by the rise of Hitler, and was to seek agreement with Italy as a counter-balance at almost any price, undercutting her dignity and probably her self-respect in the process. She was to persuade Yugoslavia in 1934 to ignore Italian complicity in the assassination of King Alexander and the Italians themselves to encourage the Hungarians to be more conciliatory. The actual result was to prove counter-productive. Yugoslavia was to become more sympathetic to the German cause.

The British were to remain aloof until 1938, by which time the threat posed by Hitler to the established European order could no longer be ignored. Their intervention, this time in Czechoslovakia, was to prove as counter-productive as the French in Yugoslavia four years earlier. The Munich Agreement signalled to Hitler and central and eastern European governments alike that the western powers would take no serious action to deflect Hitler's ambitions. An anti-German stance was no longer a serious political option until the German invasion of Poland, by which time it was too late.

The underlying illusion generated by Versailles, however, was strategic. It partnered a resentful Germany on its eastern and south-eastern borders with a series of weak states, which could only be defended from her by genuine reconciliation, by the western Allies or by Russia. No serious attempt was made to pursue any of these options. The central and eastern European states could not even make common cause together. Although the Little Entente linked Czechoslovakia, Romania and Yugoslavia, and relations between Bulgaria and Yugoslavia greatly improved from the early 1930s onwards, Hungary and Poland remained outside, albeit for different reasons. Hungary was unreconciled, Poland had its own national agenda. Even the Little Entente was to have its illusions. It was to seem on occasion more afraid of the restoration of the Habsburg monarchy in Vienna, of which there was much talk in Austria in the mid-1930s, than of Austro-German union and subsequent German expansionism.

Such illusions were, however, as nothing compared with the self-deception to be indulged in by the Poles, which would be comic if its consequences had not been so tragic. Colonel Beck, foreign minister after 1932, persuaded himself that he could not only preserve Poland but actually enlarge it by helping the Germans to expand eastwards through Czechoslovakia and in due course defeat the Soviet Union. Poland could then remain profitably neutral if a victorious Germany turned against the western powers, which Beck assumed would be able to win. It was somewhat ironic in these circumstances that those same western powers were to go to war in 1939 to protect Polish independence as a moral commitment.

CHRONOLOGY

1919

1 August	The Hungarian Communist regime of Béla Kun collapses following the breakdown of food distribution and military mutiny. The Hungarian opposition has been aided by the Romanian Army, which occupies Budapest from August to mid-September. Béla Kun flees the country and his flight is followed by a White Terror of torture and murder.
7 August	A 'national' government is re-established in Hungary with the assistance of the Romanian Army.
10 September	The Treaty of Saint-Germain is signed at Saint-Germain-en-Laye near Paris between Austria and the victorious Allies. It recognises the independence of Czechoslovakia, Hungary, Poland and the Kingdom of the Serbs, Croats and Slovenes, later renamed Yugoslavia. Austria cedes to Poland eastern Galicia, to Romania Bukovina, and to Italy Trentino, the south Tirol, Trieste and Istria. Recognition is given to the union of Bessarabia with Romania, but this is never accepted by the Soviet Union. The Covenant of the League of Nations is an integral part of the treaty, and any union of Austria with Germany is forbidden without the express consent of the League Council. The Austro-Hungarian Navy is distributed among the Allies. Plebiscites under the treaty in due course award southern Carinthia to Austria and the town of Sopron to Hungary. Austria is placed under a duty to pay reparations, although none are ever to be paid.

17

12 September	The Italian poet, Gabriele d'Annunzio, seizes the port of Fiume, now Rijeka, the status of which was then undetermined. It had been under Hungarian administration until the collapse of the Austro-Hungarian Empire.
27 November	Paderewski resigns as Polish prime minister.
27 November	The Treaty of Neuilly is signed just outside Paris between the Allies and Bulgaria. Bulgaria is obliged to cede land and some 300,000 people to Yugoslavia and to Greece, losing in the process its outlet to the Aegean Sea. An alternative outlet is promised but the promise is never to be honoured. Bulgaria is also required to pay reparations, but they are later reduced by 75 per cent.
8 December	The Supreme Council of the Allied Powers proposes the Curzon Line as Poland's temporary eastern frontier.

1920

10 January	The Treaty of Versailles comes into force.
29 February	Czechoslovakia declares the national territory to be a single and indivisible unity. Only Carpathian Ruthenia is promised autonomy.
10 March	Soviet Russia launches a major counter-attack against the invading Poles, but with limited initial success.
4 June	The Treaty of Trianon is signed in the Trianon Palace at Versailles between Hungary and the victorious Allies. Hungary loses some two-thirds of its former population and territory: Slovakia, sub-Carpathian Ruthenia and the Bratislava region are ceded to Czechoslovakia; Croatia-Slavonia and some of the Banat (the Vojvodina) are ceded to the Kingdom of the Serbs, Croats and Slovenes; and most of the Banat and all Transylvania are ceded to Romania. Italy gains Fiume, and most of the Burgenland in western Hungary passes to Austria. The Covenant of the League of Nations is an integral part of the treaty.
4 July	The Soviet Russian Army breaks through the Polish lines on the Berezina, and sweeps into Poland in pursuit of the defeated Whites. It mistakenly expects to be welcomed as a liberator. The Conference of Allied Powers at Spa, Belgium, recommends that the Curzon Line be the armistice line between Poland and the Soviet Union.
16 July	The Treaty of Saint-Germain comes into force.
9 August	The Treaty of Neuilly comes into force.
10 August	The Soviet Russian Army crosses the Vistula west of Warsaw.
18 August	General Piłsudski and the French General Weygand devise a successful counter-attack. The Polish forces encircle the Russians and take 100,000 prisoners.

8 September   Gabriele d'Annunzio proclaims the independence of Fiume under his government which he christens the 'Reggenza del Carnaro'.

9 October   Vilnius is forcibly seized for Poland by General Zeligowski, although it is recognised as Lithuanian by the League of Nations.

12 October   Poland and Russia sign an armistice which takes effect six days later. Piłsudski is to denounce it as 'an act of cowardice'.

12 November   Italy and Yugoslavia sign the Treaty of Rapallo determining their common frontier. The Istrian peninsula, the city of Zara (now Zadar) and the four islands of Cherso, Lagosta, Lussin and Pelagosa are awarded to Italy, and Fiume is declared a Free State. The remainder of the eastern Adriatic coast as far as the Albanian border is awarded to Yugoslavia, on the understanding that Italian minorities there will be respected. (**NB:** This first Treaty of Rapallo should not be confused with the better-known Treaty of Rapallo between Germany and Russia signed on 16 April 1922.)

15 November   The Freedom of the City of Danzig is formally proclaimed. The Danzig-Polish Treaty making Danzig and Poland a single customs zone comes into force the same day. Only 6 per cent of Danzig's population is Polish.

1921

10 February   France concludes a political alliance with Poland, including a secret military convention whereby France guarantees Poland against aggression.

1 March   Montenegro joins the Kingdom of Serbs, Croats and Slovenes unreservedly on the death of the Montenegrin monarch, Nicholas.

18 March   Poland and Bolshevik Russia sign the Treaty of Riga on Polish terms. The treaty sets the Polish–Russian frontier some 150 miles east of the Curzon Line. The Polish government had rejected pleas for self-determination for the Lithuanians, White Russians and Ukrainians in the area acquired, as well as a proposed plebiscite in East Galicia. The new frontier is subsequently ratified by the Allies, although probably less than a quarter of the area's population is Polish. Poland, nevertheless, fails to secure the independence of its ally, the Ukraine.

24 April   The electorate of Fiume approves the Italian prime minister's plan for a free state of Fiume-Rijeka and for an Italo-Fiuman-'Yugoslav' consortium to run the port. The plan comes to nought with the rise of Mussolini to power in Italy.

24 October	A further Danzig-Polish Treaty provides for joint economic administration.
9 November	A declaration of the Conference of Ambassadors states that if the territorial or economic integrity or independence of Albania is threatened, Britain, France, Italy and Japan will recommend the League of Nations to intervene, with such intervention being executed by Italy.

1922

31 August	The Little Entente of Czechoslovakia, Romania and Yugoslavia is formally concluded in Mariánské Lázně. (See Part 4.1 for fuller particulars.)

1923

8–9 June	The government of Alexandŭr Stamboliyski is overthrown by a military coup in Bulgaria. Thousands die in the ensuing disorder. (See Part 3.2 for fuller particulars.)
24 July	Greece, Romania and the Kingdom of Serbs, Croats and Slovenes are co-signatories with the Allies of the Treaty of Lausanne with Turkey, which marks the final conclusion of the First World War.
17 September	Mussolini incorporates Fiume into Italy despite the protests of Yugoslavia and the Fiuman government. Mussolini had been claiming the city ever since his accession to power.

1924

25 January	France concludes a Treaty of Friendship with Czechoslovakia.

1926

12 May	Marshal Piłsudski leads a march on Warsaw by the military. The government resigns two days later.

1928

5 June	Mussolini, in a dramatic speech to the Italian Senate, urges revision of the post-war treaties, notably Trianon. His speech is greeted with wild enthusiasm in Hungary and it marks the real opening of the abyss between Italy and the Little Entente.
20 June	A Montenegrin member of the Yugoslav *Skupština* murders several Croat members during a parliamentary session, and unites the Croats against the Serbs. King Alexander offers the Croats independence, but the offer is rejected. The Croats fear Italian or Hungarian intervention and want full federalism. (See Part 3.2 for fuller particulars.)

| 1 September | Ahmed Zogu's assumption of the title 'King Zog I of the Albanians' is resented in Yugoslavia because of the implied interest in the large Albanian minority there. |

1929

| 6 January | King Alexander of Yugoslavia establishes a royal dictatorship. (See Part 3.2 for fuller particulars.) |
| 3 October | The Triunine Kingdom of the Serbs, Croats and Slovenes is renamed the Kingdom of Yugoslavia. |

1930

| 6 June | Prince Carol returns to Romania and is proclaimed King Carol two days later. He had been exiled in 1926. |

1932

| 4 October | The new Hungarian prime minister General von Gömbös, announces that his priorities will be a revision of the Treaty of Trianon and the introduction of secret ballots. |
| 16 October | Some 200,000 Slovaks demonstrate in favour of autonomy. (See Part 3.2 for fuller particulars.) |

1933

15 February	Mussolini maintains that French reports of a German–Hungarian–Italian treaty of alliance are 'a complete invention'.
17 February	Some 60,000 rifles, 200 machine guns and aircraft from Italy are intercepted by Austrian workers at Hirtenberg on the border of Austria and Hungary. Italy rebuts accusations of arms smuggling into Hungary.
16 March	Chancellor Dollfuss of Austria introduces rule by decree. (See Part 3.2 for fuller particulars.)
19 August	Italy guarantees Austrian independence at Riccione in return for the abolition of all political parties and constitutional reform on fascist lines.
21 October	Marshal Piłsudski orders a report on the state of German re-armament. Poland apparently spreads rumours that it has proposed to France a preventive war against Germany.
29 December	The Romanian prime minister, Ion G. Duca, is assassinated at Sinaia. The assassin and his two accomplices are members of the dissolved Iron Guard, but deny acting under orders.

1934

| 24 January | Marshal Piłsudski accepts Hitler's suggestion of a ten-year German–Polish non-aggression agreement, but declines later |

suggestions of a joint alliance against the Soviet Union. The agreement is signed on 26 January, and it marks the beginning of an actively aggressive policy by Poland towards Czechoslovakia.

12–18 February	Civil war breaks out in Austria between the supporters of the Chancellor, Dr Dollfuss, and the Social Democrats. Some 62 people are killed in fighting in Graz, Linz, Steyr and Vienna. The Christian Socialists (Clericals), who want an independent Austria, anticipate that by eliminating the Social Democrats they will secure Mussolini's support against Hitler. The Socialists declare a General Strike and the government martial law. The war ends after a few days with the victory of the government and the suppression of all forms of opposition. (See also Part 3.2.)
9 June	The German Nazi Party promotes a campaign of terror across Austria designed to destroy the country's tourist trade.
13 June	The Director of Security for the Austrian province of Vorarlberg seals the frontier with Germany.
21 June	The French foreign minister, Louis Barthou, advises King Carol on a vist to Romania that France will withdraw its diplomatic and financial support if he suppresses democracy and aligns Romania with the fascist states. (See Part 4.1 for fuller particulars.)
25 July	Dr Dollfuss, Austrian Chancellor and dictator, is assassinated by the Austrian Nazis during an attack on the Chancellery in Vienna. The rebellion is rapidly suppressed, but any plan of Austro-German union is deferred following Mussolini's mobilisation of troops on the Brenner Pass frontier. (See also Part 3.2.)
9 October	King Alexander of Yugoslavia is assassinated in Marseilles by *Ustaša* agents (see Glossary). The French foreign minister, Louis Barthou, is killed also.

1935

14 April	Britain, France and Italy show willingness at the Stresa Conference to discuss lifting the military constraints imposed on Bulgaria by the Treaties of Neuilly and Lausanne.
19 May	The Czechoslovak elections see the rise of a new ethnic German political party, *Die Sudetendeutsche Partei*, under the leadership of Konrad Henlein. It is the second largest political party and, although it proclaims its loyalty to democracy and the Czechoslovak republic, it increasingly promotes Nazi views.

1936

26 February Poland arrests in Katowice 75 members of the recently banned *National Sozialische Deutsche Arbeiterbewegung*, which allegedly seeks with German support to separate Upper Silesia from Poland.

2 October Austria introduces conscription for the first time since the war.

1937

1–2 April Romania and Yugoslavia refuse a Czechoslovak request that the Little Entente pledge full military aid to any member which is threatened by aggression. (See Part 4.1 for fuller particulars.)

1938

12 February The Austrian Chancellor, Dr von Schuschnigg, is pressurised by Hitler into an agreement whereby the Austrian Nazis enjoy freedom of manoeuvre. He repudiates the agreement in early March and announces that a plebiscite on union with Germany (*Anschluss*) will be held on 13 March

11 March Dr Seyss-Inquart returns from Berlin with an ultimatum demanding the postponement of the plebiscite and an end to the Chancellor's negotiations with former Social Democrats. Dr von Schuschnigg agrees to postponement but not to any other demand, whereupon a second German ultimatum is issued which the Chancellor has until 7.30pm to accept or the German Army will invade. The second ultimatum demands his immediate resignation, the appointment of Dr Seyss-Inquart as his successor, a two-thirds Nazi majority in the new cabinet, recognition of the Nazi Party throughout Austria, and the entry of the 30,000-strong Nazi 'Austrian Legion' into Vienna to keep order. At 7.30pm Dr von Schuschnigg broadcasts that the government will not shed blood, but is yielding to brute force. The Chancellor and all his cabinet except Dr Seyss-Inquart resign. Thousands of Austrian Nazis take over the public buildings in Vienna and other Austrian towns and cities. At 9.30pm Dr Seyss-Inquart telegraphs to the German government for help in preventing bloodshed, and at 10.00pm German troops enter Austria through Salzburg, Kufstein and Mittenwald. At 10.30pm the appointment by President Miklas of Dr Seyss-Inquart as Chancellor is announced on the radio.

12 March German troops continue their occupation of Austria including the cities of Graz, Linz and Innsbruck. They receive a rapturous reception from large sections of the population. Hitler arrives in Linz and in his welcome Chancellor Seyss-Inquart declares the formal annulment of Article 88 of the Treaty of

	Saint-Germain which had banned any union between Austria and Germany without the League Council's specific consent.
13 March	President Miklas resigns at the Chancellor's request. At 7.30pm, the new Austrian government dissolves the Austrian state and declares Austria to be an integral part of Germany. The union, *Anschluss*, makes Germany the largest state in Europe in area and population, apart from the Soviet Union, and larger in area than the Germany of 1914.
13 March	The Primate of Austria, Cardinal Archbishop Innitzer of Vienna, exhorts Roman Catholics 'to thank God for the bloodless course of the revolution . . . and to carry out willingly all orders of the authorities'.
10 April	A directed plebiscite approves the *Anschluss* by 99.7 per cent.
24 April	Konrad Henlein, leader of the Sudeten German Home Front demands autonomy for the Sudetenland within Czechoslovakia.
12 September	Hitler makes an uncompromising demand for the cession of the Sudeten areas of Czechoslovakia to Germany, and follows it up with an ultimatum, threatening to seize them by force on 1 October.
18 September	The Czechoslovak prime minister, Dr Hodža, rejects suggestions from abroad of either a plebiscite or any alternative means of securing the secession of the German-speaking Sudetenland from Czechoslovak territory. (See Glossary for Sudetenland.)
19 September	The British and French present a joint plan to the Czechoslovak government featuring the cession of the Sudetenland, the neutralisation of the rest of the national territory and the joint guarantee of its independence.
20 September	Hungary and Poland demand that the south Slovak and Teschen areas of Czechoslovakia inhabited by their respective minorities be ceded in the manner demanded by Germany of the Sudeten areas. (See Teschen in Glossary.)
21 September	Following strong pressure on President Beneš from Britain and France, the Czechoslovak government submits and unreservedly accepts their joint plan.
21 September	Poland denounces its 1925 treaty with Czechoslovakia over its minority in Teschen.
21 September	The Soviet foreign minister, Maxim Litvinov, reiterates that the Soviet Union will assist Czechoslovakia against German aggression, provided France does likewise.
22 September	The Czechoslovak government is ferociously attacked in the German media, which allege that it is 'completely Bolshevised'. The Sudeten German legion (*Freikorps*) increasingly attacks

Czechoslovak frontier installations and seizes some smaller towns including Cheb. Dr Hodža and his cabinet resign.

23 September   The Soviet Union warns Poland that any Polish invasion of Czechoslovak territory will lead to immediate Soviet cancellation of the 1932 Polish–Soviet Non-Aggression Pact. Poland responds that 'the measures which have been taken for the defence of the Polish State are an internal question'.

29 September   Czechoslovakia is dismembered by Britain, France, Germany and Italy at the Munich Conference, in accordance with the British–French joint plan. Chamberlain, Daladier, Hitler and Mussolini meet all together for the first and last time, but neither America nor the Soviet Union is a party to the proceedings. On his return to London, Chamberlain waves the piece of paper with Hitler's signature and declares: 'It is peace for our time.' Monsignor Tiso becomes prime minister of Slovakia in the new federal Czechoslovakia.

30 September   Poland demands that Czechoslovakia accept its demands for the evacuation of Teschen by noon on the following day, or its army will occupy the district.

1 October   Czechoslovakia cedes Teschen to Poland. (See Teschen in Glossary.)

1 October   The first German troops enter the Sudetenland.

10 October   Germany completes its occupation of the Sudetenland.

2–3 November   Czechoslovakia cedes the strip of southern Slovakia primarily inhabited by ethnic Hungarians to Hungary (see Vienna Award (First) in Glossary, Part 10.3).

20 November   The new Czechoslovak–German frontier is officially fixed.

1939

10 March   The Czechoslovak government decides to liquidate Slovak separatism, fearing a *coup d'état* on 15 March. Martial law is proclaimed in Bratislava and other large Slovak towns, and the semi-fascist Slovak 'Hlinka guard' is disarmed. Mgr Tiso, the Slovak prime minister, and all but two members of his cabinet are dismissed and the members soon arrested, as are many leaders of the Hlinka guard.

11–12 March   Violence erupts in Bratislava, and Mgr Tiso asks Hitler for German assistance. Members of the Sudeten minority in the Czech provinces riot.

13 March   Mgr Tiso meets Hitler in Berlin.

14 March   The Slovak diet in Bratislava unanimously declares Slovak independence. Mgr Tiso is appointed prime minister. Hungary demands the withdrawal of all Czechoslovak troops from

25

Ruthenia, the Czechoslovak government accepts the ultimatum, and Hungary incorporates it in its territory. President Hacha and his foreign minister leave for Berlin at the German government's invitation. German troops cross the border before the Czechs have arrived.

15 March President Hacha and Dr Chvalkovsky meet Hitler, Ribbentrop and Goering in the Chancellery just after 1am. At 3.55am, following a German threat to release 800 bombers on Prague at 4am, the Czech leaders abandon resistance and agree to place the Czech people under German protection. At 5am Dr Goebbels proclaims that Czechoslovakia has ceased to exist. At 6am German troops start to occupy the Czech provinces of Bohemia and Moravia and by 9am thay are in Prague. At 7.15pm Hitler proclaims in Prague the incorporation of Bohemia and Moravia in the Greater German Reich.

16 March Slovakia becomes a German protectorate at the request of Mgr Tiso, telegraphed to Hitler the previous day. His action may have been designed to forestall annexation by Hungary. German troops occupy Bratislava and western Slovakia. Unfettered Slovak independence has lasted two days.

23 March Germany occupies the German populated enclave of Memel (Klaipeda) in Lithuania and demands Danzig and the corridor from Poland.

31 March Britain guarantees Poland against aggression.

7 April Mussolini declares Albania an Italian protectorate with Victor Emmanuel III of Italy its king. King Zog I goes into exile.

11 April The annexation of Ruthenia by Hungary in March generates serious tension with Romania. The state of tension is heightened by German demands on Romania during trade negotiations.

13 April Britain and France assure the Romanian (and Greek) governments of all the assistance in their power in the event of any action threatening their independence.

23 August Germany and the Soviet Union sign a neutrality (non-aggression) pact. Military conversations between Britain, France and the Soviet Union earlier in the month had come to nothing in the absence of Polish cooperation.

31 August The German government broadcasts a 16-point plan for a settlement with Poland. It includes the unconditional return of Danzig.

1 September Germany invades Poland.

3 September Britain and France declare war on Germany, thus opening the Second World War. Italy declares its non-belligerence. America and the Soviet Union remain neutral.

2.3 CHRONOLOGY OF KEY EVENTS DURING THE SECOND WORLD WAR

(**NB:** This section is not a military history of the Second World War in central and eastern Europe. Interested readers are referred to the numerous specialised books available.)

1939

17 September	The Soviet Army enters eastern Poland.
21 September	Germany and the Soviet Union declare that Poland has ceased to exist.
28 September	A German–Soviet Treaty is signed in Moscow by their respective foreign ministers, Joachim von Ribbentrop and Vyacheslav Molotov, dividing Poland up between the two states. The new partition line coincides with the Curzon Line except in the north where it gives the whole province of Bialystok to the Soviet Union and in the Przemyśl region to the south where it is again more favourable to the Soviet Union.
30 September	Polish resistance to the Germans ceases, except in a small pocket north of Gdynia.
8 October	Germany formally annexes western Poland and establishes the two new provinces of West Prussia and Posen. Germany's new frontier is appreciably further to the east than that of 1914.
10 October	The Soviet Union restores Vilnius to Lithuania.
1 November	The Soviet Union formally annexes the western Ukraine, till now the larger part of eastern Poland.
2 November	The Soviet Union formally annexes western White Russia (Byelorussia), the remaining part of eastern Poland.

1940

5 March	A Soviet Politburo resolution, made public by the Russian president Boris Yeltsin in October 1992, orders the execution of some 26,000 Poles, including those to be revealed by the Nazis in the Katyn Forest in 1943.
10 June	Italy enters the Second World War on the German side.
24 June	Slovakia enters the war on the German side.

26 June	The Soviet Union demands that Romania cede Bessarabia and the northern part of Bukovina. Romania complies and the Soviet Army enters the region two days later.
1 July	The Romanian prime minister, Gheorghe Tătărescu, announces the formal renunciation of the Franco-British guarantee of April 1939 to Romania. Future Romanian policy will be aligned with 'the new orientation in Europe'.
August	The Soviet Union creates the constituent Moldavian SSR out of central Bessarabia and a strip of the Ukrainian SSR east of the River Dniestr.
16 August	Hungarian and Romanian delegations meet at the port of Turnu Severin to discuss Hungarian territorial claims on Romania. The negotiations are broken off without agreement on 24 August.
27 August	The Hungarian and Romanian prime and foreign ministers are summoned to Vienna for German and Italian mediation.
30 August	Hungary and Romania accept the 'Vienna Award' whereby the Axis powers transfer more than half of Transylvania to Hungary (see Glossary for fuller particulars).
31 August	Romania agrees under the Treaty of Craiova to cede Southern Dobruja to Bulgaria, thus restoring the 1912 frontier. The province is populated mainly by ethnic Bulgarians.
5 September	Romania declares the fascist General Antonescu 'Leader (*Conducator*) of the State'. (See Part 3.4 for fuller particulars.)
15 September	Romania is declared a 'Legionary State' with the Iron Guard as the only recognised party. (See Part 3.4 for fuller particulars.)
7 October	German troops are deployed in Romania.
20 November	Hungary signs the Axis Pact. (See Part 4.2 for fuller particulars.)
23 November	Romania and Slovakia sign the Axis Pact. (See Part 4.2 for fuller particulars.)
1 December	General Antonescu pledges to try to reunite Transylvania with Romania.

1941

1 March	Bulgaria signs the Axis Pact. German troops enter the country on 3 March and occupy Black Sea ports. (See also Part 4.2.)
25 March	Yugoslavia signs the Axis Pact. Protests erupt across the country, and the government is overthrown during the next 48 hours. (See Part 4.2 for fuller particulars.)
6 April	Germany attacks Yugoslavia with Hungarian assistance.

10 April	Germany establishes a nominally independent Croat state under Dr Ante Pavelić (qv), who enters Zagreb in triumph on 15 April. The capital, however, is to be transferred to Banja Luka in Bosnia.
11 April	Hungary invades, and in due course occupies, the Yugoslav Vojvodina which had been part of Hungary before the First World War.
16 April	King Peter leaves Yugoslavia and the High Command capitulates the next day. The Germans occupy Serbia.
28 April	Bulgarian troops occupy Yugoslav Macedonia, Greek Macedonia and eastern Thrace, and the Florina and Kastoria districts of Greece.
April–May	Albania, now an Italian protectorate, occupies the Kosovo region of Serbia.
3 May	Italy annexes the greater part of Slovenia, leaving a strip around the town of Maribor to be annexed by Germany on 1 October 1942.
21 May	Italy annexes Dalmatia, including the ports of Kotor, Šibenik and Split, and occupies Montenegro.
22 June	Germany attacks the Soviet Union without warning or declaration of war. Romania declares war on the Soviet Union.
24 June	Slovakia declares war on the Soviet Union.
27 June	Hungary declares war on the Soviet Union.
12 July	Italy declares Montenegro an Italian principality. The declaration promotes a national uprising.
19 September	Tito and Colonel Draža Mihajlović, the leader of the Četnik resistance movement, meet for the first time in the village of Struganik. Although the meeting is amicable, their aims are totally opposed. Tito seeks a new Yugoslavia created through the revolutionary struggle of the whole people. Mihajlović seeks to preserve the old Serbian order including the monarchy, the Orthodox church, the army and established society. He enjoys the support of the royal government-in-exile in London.
26 October	Tito and Colonel Mihajlović meet again in the village of Brajici, but fail to reach any firm agreement.
1 November	A major clash between the Četniks and the Partisans between Užice and Požega marks the beginning of a civil war between them which will run in parallel with the war of resistance. Faced with a major German onslaught, Tito largely withdraws from Serbia and withdraws into the Sandžak on the boundary with eastern Bosnia. Colonel Mihajlović allows Četniks to cooperate

with the forces of General Nedić the Serbian collaborationist leader, and is increasingly drawn into co-operation with the Germans.

7 December The Japanese attack on Pearl Harbor brings America into the Second World War. Germany and Italy declare war on her. Britain declares war on (Finland), Hungary and Romania in view of their refusal to stop waging war on the Soviet Union.

12 December Slovakia declares war on America and Britain, and Bulgaria and Croatia follow suit the next day.

1942

19 March A broadcast by the Romanian foreign minister, Michel Antonescu, re-opening the Transylvanian question, generates enthusiastic demonstrations of support across the country.

2 June America declares war on Bulgaria, Hungary and Romania.

16 September A 'National Front' of Albanian Communists and Nationalists is established at Peza near Elbasan to fight for Albanian liberation from the Italians.

26 November Tito opens the first meeting of the Anti-Fascist National Liberation Committee of Yugoslavia (AVNOJ) at Bihać, on the borders of Bosnia and Croatia. Dr Goebbels, the German minister of propaganda, writes in his private diary that 'the Partisans have made a football of the Croat government'.

1943

2 February The total defeat inflicted on the Germans by the Soviet Army in the Battle of Stalingrad (now Volgograd) marks the decisive turning point on the eastern front in the Second World War.

April The Germans announce the discovery of the graves in the Katyn Forest of some 14,000 Polish soldiers interned by the Soviet Union after its occupation of eastern Poland. The Polish government-in-exile in London asks the International Red Cross to investigate, whereupon the Soviet government breaks off relations with the Polish government-in-exile, maintaining that it has adopted a hostile position.

28 April The Warsaw Ghetto is finally 'liquidated' by the Germans after nine days of fierce fighting. The population of the Ghetto had already been reduced from 350,000 to 120,000 by deportation, shootings and mass slaughter in annihilation camps between July and September 1942. The 14,000 survivors are deported to eastern Poland. The Jews had been armed and assisted by non-Jewish Polish Socialists.

25 July Mussolini is overthrown and Italy effectively leaves the war.

July	Bulgaria obtains the first extension of its occupation zone in Greece, running from the Vardar to the Struma.
31 October	The Allies issue the Moscow Declaration resolving to re-establish a free and independent Austria. They agree that Austria was the first victim of Adolf Hitler and that individual Austrians could not therefore be held to account for their Nazi links.
14 November	The Americans bomb Sofia for the first time.
30 November	Under Tito's leadership, the Anti-Fascist National Liberation Committee of Yugoslavia turns itself at Jajce into a Yugoslav National Committee of Liberation with the powers of a provisional government. (See Part 3.4 for fuller particulars.)
28 November–1 December	President Roosevelt of America and the British prime minister, Winston Churchill, agree at the Tehran Conference with Marshal Stalin of the Soviet Union that the Curzon Line will delimit the new Polish–Soviet frontier.
31 December	The Polish Workers' Party under Władysław Gomulka forms the National Home Council (*Krajowa Rada Narodowa*) at Stalin's behest.

1944

29 February	It is confirmed that Bulgarian troops have some few weeks earlier replaced the Germans as the occupying forces in the Greek provinces of Edessa, Florina and Kastoria.
20 March	The Soviet Army enters Bessarabia and Bukovina.
20–21 March	Responding to the advance of the Soviet Army into Romania, the German Army moves into Hungary in force and takes control of all strategic points.
16 June	A provisional agreement is reached on the Yugoslav island of Vis between Marshal Tito and Dr Šubašić representing the royal Yugoslav government-in-exile, whereby the royal government promises to support the partisans in future and both parties agree that the question of the monarchy will be decided by the Yugoslav people after the war. Colonel Mihajlović, nominally minister of war in the royal government, is dismissed.
21 July	A Polish Committee of National Liberation (PKWN), 'the Lublin Committee', is established as an executive arm of the National Home Council formed the preceding December.
25 July	Stanislaw Mikolajczyk, prime minister of the Polish government-in-exile, informs the delegate-general of the Polish government in occupied Poland that he has full powers to order an uprising in Warsaw.

1 August   The 'Home Army' of the Polish resistance launches the Warsaw rising against the Germans. The Soviet Union is unable, or unwilling, to intervene and the uprising is finally crushed by October.

12 August   Marshal Tito meets the British prime minister, Winston Churchill, in Naples. The British government had previously brought pressure to bear on the royal government-in-exile to come to terms with Tito. Churchill acknowledges that Tito and his followers will play the preponderant role in postwar Yugoslavia.

23 August   King Michael of Romania accepts an armistice with the Allies, and hostilities against the Soviet Union formally cease at 4am the next morning. Under the terms of the armistice, the joint frontier established by the Soviet–Romanian agreement of 28 June 1940 is to be restored and the Vienna Award (see Glossary) declared invalid.

25 August   Following German attacks on her, Romania declares war on Germany.

26 August   Bulgaria withdraws from the war, and confirms that she has asked America and Britain for armistice terms. Germany is requested to remove her troops, who will otherwise be disarmed. Bulgaria declares her neutrality in the German–Soviet war.

29 August   The Soviet Union denies that it has recognised or approved Bulgarian neutrality, which it declares to be 'entirely insufficient in the circumstances of the existing situation'. It calls on Bulgaria to declare war on Germany.

31 August   The Soviet Army enters Bucharest.

5 September   The Soviet Union declares war on Bulgaria, claiming that her new neutrality is sheltering the German retreat. Bulgaria asks for an armistice.

7 September   The Soviet Army enters Bulgaria, and the capital, Sofia, two days later. Bulgaria declares war on Germany.

9 September   The Fatherland Front (*Otechestven Front*) seizes power in Bulgaria. It comprises Communist, Agrarian, Social Democrat and *Zveno* members. (See also Part 3.4 and *Zveno* in Glossary.)

21 September   Tito flies to Moscow to meet Stalin in the name of the Yugoslav National Committee of Liberation. Tito is assertive, and rather than putting his partisans under the control of the Soviet commander, Marshal Tolbukhin, as Stalin had presumed, he only allows the Soviet Army to enter Yugoslavia on the clear understanding that it will withdraw as soon as the Germans are defeated. There is no question of the partisans being placed under anyone's control but his own. Stalin does not demur but the meeting is strained.

2 October   The Polish 'Home Army' finally surrenders in Warsaw. The Germans evacuate the whole city and implement Hitler's order that it be 'razed without trace'. When the Soviet Army enters the city on 17 January 1945, 93 per cent of its buildings are destroyed or damaged beyond repair.

9–18 October   Marshal Stalin and Winston Churchill, British prime minister, come to an informal agreement at the Moscow Conference on their respective percentage degrees of influence in the Balkan states. Britain is to be 90 per cent predominant in Greece, and the Soviet Union 90 per cent predominant in Romania and 75 per cent in Bulgaria. Hungary and Yugoslavia are to be divided 50–50. In practice, neither is to exercise influence in Yugoslavia, which remains determinedly independent. Otherwise the agreement is to reflect reality until 1990.

15 October   Admiral Horthy proclaims, as head of state, that Hungary will approach the Allies for an armistice. He maintains that 'Hungary was forced into the war against the Allies through German pressure . . . We were not guided by any ambition to increase our power and had no intention of snatching a square metre of territory from anyone.' Budapest Radio announces later the same day that the Regent's proclamation does not mean that Hungarian troops have ceased, or will cease, fighting.

16 October   Budapest Radio broadcasts a new proclamation, allegedly by Admiral Horthy, withdrawing that of the day before. He resigns ten minutes later, and is accused by the German government of 'cowardly treason'. He is flown to Germany, allegedly 'for his own protection', and is replaced by a Regency Council established by Major Ferenc Szalassi, the leader of the Hungarian Nazi Arrow Cross, who declares himself prime minister.

20 October   The partisans supported by the Soviet Army enter Belgrade after a week's defence which has cost 16,000 German lives. The Soviet Army enters Debrecen, Hungary's second largest city.

28 October   The Bulgarian armistice delegation, led by Professor Stainov, foreign minister, signs an armistice agreement in Moscow with representatives of all the countries with which Bulgaria is at war.

November   Yugoslavia takes the initiative in proposing unification with Bulgaria on a federal basis, with a joint federal government, assembly and customs union.

28 November   The Albanian provisional government moves to Tiranë. The government had been formed in the October, when Colonel Enver Hoxha had ben appointed president. The Albanian forces of Colonel Hoxha are the only national forces in central and eastern Europe to have liberated their country purely by their own efforts.

23 December   A Hungarian government of liberation is established in Debrecen. General Béla Miklosz is prime minister.

1945

1 January   The Soviet Union recognises the Lublin 'Committee of National Liberation' as the provisional Polish government. The Americans and the British refuse to follow suit.

17 January   The Soviet Army enters Warsaw.

20 January   Hungary signs an armistice with the Allies. The armistice negates the two Vienna Awards, and restores the frontiers of 1 January 1938.

4–12 February   President Roosevelt of America, prime minister Winston Churchill of Britain and Marshal Stalin of the Soviet Union meet in Yalta, Crimea, Soviet Union. They come to an outline agreement on the post-war map of Europe, which includes the westward movement by some 150–200 miles of Poland's eastern and western boundaries at Germany's expense and the division of East Prussia between Poland and the Soviet Union.

13 February   The Soviet Army enters Budapest after a seven-week battle.

9 March   Stalin agrees that the new Romanian government may take over the administration of northern Transylvania (Ardeal) on the understanding that it will protect the right of all nationalities there. The administration had been suspended by Soviet Marshal Malinovsky in October 1944 because of excesses against the Hungarian population committed by the Romanian National Peasant Party militia.

27–28 March   Sixteen prominent Polish political leaders, including General Leopold Okulicki, the last commander of the Polish 'Home Army', are arrested on a visit to General Ivanov of the Soviet High Command. They include nearly all the surviving leaders of the Polish underground resistance movement. They are accused under the leadership of General Okulicki of preparing diversionary tactics in the rear of the Soviet Army and thereby causing the deaths of more than 100 officers and men.

15 April   The Soviet Army enters Vienna.

15 April   Marshal Tito makes an official claim in Moscow for the cession by Italy of Trieste and the Istrian peninsula (Venezia Giulia). Cession had been supported by the former Yugoslav royal government-in-exile in London, but is opposed by all sections of Italian opinion except the Communists.

22–24 April   Talks between American, British and Soviet representatives in Washington remain deadlocked on the question of Poland. The Americans and the British refuse to recognise the current Warsaw government and dispute the Soviet argument that the Yalta compromise agreement had given the Lublin administration the right to approve or disapprove of Polish leaders put forward by the American or British as fit to be consulted on the formation of a new Polish government.

30 April   The Soviet Army enters Berlin, and Hitler commits suicide.

1 May   The Americans and British, and the Yugoslav Partisans, arrive in the Italian city of Trieste and contest control with the danger of an armed clash. The annexation of the city had been one of Tito's war aims.

7 May   The Soviet Army enters Prague.

8 May   VE Day. Germany surrenders formally in Berlin.

2.4 CHRONOLOGY OF KEY EVENTS BETWEEN THE END OF THE SECOND WORLD WAR AND THE DEATH OF STALIN

1945

14 May   Austria, united with Germany since the *Anschluss* of 1938, is given a separate government by the occupying Allies.

16 May   The Czechoslovak government returns to Prague, following the entry of the Soviet Army into the capital. It is the only central or eastern European exile government to be permitted to return after the war.

21 May   An autonomous Ruthenian government is formed comprising Russians, Ukrainians and Jews. Ivan Turjanica is prime minister.

21 May   Marshal Tito agrees to an American–British military government in Trieste.

5 June   The Allied representatives (Eisenhower for America, Montgomery for Britain, Lattre de Tassigny for France and Zhukov for the Soviet Union) declare in Berlin that:

1. Germany, within her frontiers as they were on December 31, 1937, will for the purposes of occupation, be divided into four zones, one to be allotted to each Power as follows:
   An Eastern zone to the Union of Soviet Socialist Republics . . .
2. The area of Greater Berlin will be occupied by forces of each of the Four Powers. An inter-Allied governing authority [in Russian, *komendatura*] . . . will be established to direct jointly its administration.

9 June   Yugoslavia and the western Allies reach a provisional agreement on Trieste.

19 June   Polish troops enter Teschen, but the Czechoslovak and Polish governments remain unable to agree on its future. (See Glossary.)

21 June   American forces withdraw from Czechoslovakia, and from parts of eastern Germany in favour of Soviet forces, following delimitation of the Soviet Zone. They order many key German personnel to accompany them.

21 June	The leaders of the 'home government' of the Polish resistance are imprisoned in Warsaw for their 'anti-Soviet activities'.
28 June	A new Polish government is established in Moscow, which includes some members of the former government-in-exile in London. It is recognised by America and Britain on 5 July.
29 June	Dr Zdenek Fierlinger, the Czechoslovak prime minister, and Vyacheslav Molotov, the Soviet foreign minister, sign a treaty in Moscow in the presence of Stalin transferring Ruthenia to the Ukrainian SSR.
1 July	The British withdraw from Magdeburg and from parts of Mecklenburg, including Wismar and Schwerin, now in the Soviet Zone of Germany.
4 July	Austria, within its 1937 frontiers, is divided for the purposes of occupation into four zones. The Soviet Zone comprises the province of Lower Austria, excluding the city of Vienna, that part of the province of Upper Austria on the left bank of the Danube, and the province of Burgenland. The American Zone comprises the province of Salzburg and that part of Upper Austria on the right bank of the Danube. The French Zone comprises the provinces of Tirol and Vorarlberg and the British Zone the provinces of Carinthia and Styria. Vienna is divided into four sectors likewise.
17 July	The Big Three Summit between President Truman of America, the British prime minister, Winston Churchill (replaced by Clement Attlee following his appointment as prime minister on 26 July) and Marshal Stalin opens at the Cecilienhof, Potsdam, just outside Berlin.
19 July	Marshal Tolbukhin personally invests King Michael of Romania with the highest Soviet decoration, the Order of Victory, in Bucharest, to convey Soviet appreciation of the Romanian Army's contribution to the final defeat of Germany and Hungary.
2 August	The Potsdam Conference ends with agreement on the decartelisation, demilitarisation, denazification and democratisation of Germany. The arms industry and the monopolies are to be dismantled and an economy devoted to peaceful purposes built up. Support is pledged for the German people in establishing a unitary, democratic state and a living standard at the level of Europe excluding Great Britain and the Soviet Union. The Oder–Neisse line is accepted pending a peace settlement as Germany's boundary with Poland, and the northern part of East Prussia including Königsberg (now Kaliningrad) is to be transferred to the Soviet Union. Germans living in Poland, Czechoslovakia and Hungary are

to be transferred to Germany in an orderly manner. Germany is placed under an obligation to pay reparations, and to be treated as an economic whole.

4 September The German Red Cross estimates the overall number of German refugees coming into the Soviet Zone of Germany from the east at some 13 million, a figure in line with Allied estimates of 12–14 million. Of these perhaps 2 million are from prewar Poland, including hundreds of thousands of *Volksdeutsche* resettled there by Hitler from as far as Estonia and Romania; 3 million from the Sudetenland; 4.5 million from Silesia, now Poland; 2 million from East Prussia, now divided between Poland and the Soviet Union; and 1 million from East Pomerania, now Poland.

11 September– The London Conference of foreign ministers of the Allies,
2 October established at Potsdam to draft peace treaties with the former enemy states, collapses in disagreement.

20–25 October Constantin Brătianu and Dr Iuliu Maniu, the leaders of the Romanian National Liberal and National Peasant Parties, accuse the Romanian coalition government of dictatorship and terror. (See Part 3.6.2 for fuller particulars.)

4 November The first post-war Hungarian general election is won by the Smallholders Party with an overall majority. (See Part 3.6.2 for fuller particulars.)

8 November Serious riots occur in Bucharest on the king's birthday between some 40,000–50,000 monarchists and Communist supporters. Official reports are to say that 11 people have been killed and 85 wounded.

18 November The unofficial Bulgarian opposition, headed by Nikola Petkov, boycotts the Bulgarian general elections on the grounds that no free elections are possible while the ministries of the interior and justice are Communist-controlled. (See Part 3.6.2 for fuller particulars.)

29 November The Yugoslav constituent assembly proclaims a federative republic at a joint session of the *Skupština* and the House of Nationalities. The six republics are Bosnia, Croatia, Macedonia, Montenegro, Serbia and Slovenia.

15 December The Polish government announces the arrest of 'the underground staff in Poland of General Anders' as well as of Colonel Rzepecki, the leader of that section of the former Home Army which had refused to cooperate with the new regime and had remained underground.

24 December The Hungarian government issues a decree, pursuant to the decisions of the Potsdam Conference, expelling all Hungary's

German-speaking inhabitants, estimated at some 500,000 people. They are allowed to take with them only food and clothing.

1946

11 January	The Albanian constituent assembly proclaims Albania a republic, and forbids the former King Zog to return. He had been formally deposed on 2 January.
1 February	The National Assembly proclaims Hungary a republic.
27 February	Czechoslovakia and Hungary agree on an exchange of their Slovak and Magyar populations. The exchange is due to be completed by the middle of September 1949.
5 March	Winston Churchill, the leader of the British Opposition, maintains in a speech at Fulton, Missouri, America, that an 'iron curtain' has fallen across eastern Europe. Marshal Stalin criticises his speech on 13 March.
3 May	General Lucius Clay suspends reparations from the American Zone of Germany and charges both France and the Soviet Union with being responsible for the failure of the Allies to agree over Germany.
22 May	The British government protests sharply against the recent firing by Albanian coastal guns at the British battle cruisers, *Orion* and *Superb*, in the Corfu Channel. The Albanian government expresses regret but maintains that the nationality of the vessels had not been ascertained. This is deemed unsatisfactory by the British as the channel is an international waterway.
30 June	The Soviet authorities prevent further movement out of their zone of Germany to the three other zones.
10 June– 15 July	The prosecution at the trial of Colonel Mihajlović in Belgrade makes a number of attacks on the American and British governments.
9 August	An unarmed American transport aircraft, which had allegedly strayed across the Yugoslav frontier in a storm, is forced down by Yugoslav fighters. A second American aircraft is shot down ten days later with the loss of all on board. The exchange of angry protests is, however, followed by an expression of Yugoslav regret and an offer of compensation.
6 September	James Byrnes, American secretary of state, presages in Stuttgart a more sympathetic stance by America towards Germany. He promises that American forces will remain until a lasting peace has been achieved. His speech is strongly attacked in Poland and France.

8 September   A Bulgarian plebiscite abolishes the monarchy with 92 per cent of the electorate favouring a republic. The Republic of Bulgaria is proclaimed on 15 September.

21 October   Some thousands of East German managerial and technical staff and their families are moved with their industrial plant to the Soviet Union under Operation Ossavakim.

22 October   44 British sailors are killed when two destroyers, HMS *Saumarez* and HMS *Volage*, strike Albanian mines in the Corfu Channel. Albania protests to Britain and the United Nations on 30 October at the ships' infringement of Albanian territorial waters.

27 October   The Independent Agrarian leader, Nikola Petkov, maintains that the Bulgarian election campaign has been conducted in an atmosphere of terror. Britain considers that the elections have not been free and democratic. (See Part 3.6.2 for fuller particulars.)

4 November   The Romanian government rejects American and British charges, supported by Constantin Brătianu and Dr Maniu, that the forthcoming elections will be unfree and unfair because of manipulation of the electoral lists and persecution of the opposition.

12 November   Albania protests to Britain and the United Nations at the British minesweeping of the Corfu Channel. Britain maintains that by international usage, all ships have the right of innocent passage through the territorial waters of another state and in particular through a channel forming part of an international sea highway.

26 November   The American government declines to recognise the validity of the Romanian elections held on 19 November and won by the government bloc, the National Democratic Front. The British concur on 2 December.

5 December   The Romanian National Peasant Party boycotts the new parliament, as it regards the November elections as null and void. (See Part 3.6.2 for fuller particulars.)

10 December   The Albanian, Bulgarian and Yugoslav representatives deny Greek claims at a meeting of the UN Security Council that their governments are supporting guerrillas seeking to incorporate Greek Macedonia in the Yugoslav Federative Republic of Macedonia. The Security Council votes on 20 December to despatch a commission authorised to conduct investigations in any part of the four nation states involved.

28 December   Milovan Djilas declares at the ratification ceremony in Belgrade of the Treaty for Close Economic Cooperation between Albania and Yugoslavia, that the treaty would not mean an 'economic enslavement of Albania, as would be the case with a similar treaty between Britain and a weaker country' and that Albania would flourish, 'whether London liked it or not'.

31 December It is officially announced in Budapest that a significant number of army officers and right-wing members of the Smallholders Party have been arrested over the previous fortnight, following the discovery of an alleged conspiracy against the state. It is maintained that the conspiracy had been initiated in the autumn of 1945. (See Part 3.6.2 for fuller particulars.)

1947

by January 11.6 million German refugees from the east have arrived in the four zones of Germany, 4.3 million in the Soviet Zone, the largest proportion, where they make up a quarter of the population. The largest proportion is in Mecklenburg, where they represent 43 per cent of the population.

14 January Yugoslavia submits a memorandum to the foreign ministers' deputies, meeting in London to prepare the Austrian and German peace treaties, asking that a strip of Carinthia and a small area of Styria, with a total population of some 190,000 and including the towns of Klagenfurt and Villach, be transferred from Austria to Yugoslavia. It maintains that they are historically slav areas which had been forcibly germanised.

19 January The government bloc wins 394 of the 444 seats in the *Sejm* in the Polish general elections originally envisaged at Yalta. The four participating parties had previously agreed on the allocation of seats between them. 138 people are killed in terrorist attacks during the elections. (See Part 3.6.2 for fuller particulars.)

10 February Peace treaties are signed by the Allies in Paris with Bulgaria, Hungary and Romania (and Finland and Italy), but not with Germany. The treaty with Bulgaria restores the frontiers of 1 January 1941, and that with Italy awards Istria and Rijeka (Fiume) to Yugoslavia. The treaty with Hungary transfers the small number of communes comprising the 'Bratislava bridgehead' to Czechoslovakia. The treaty with Hungary had been preceded by an agreement with Yugoslavia that up to 40,000 Hungarians living in Yugoslavia, principally in the Vojvodina, could move to Hungary if a similar number of Yugoslavs in Hungary chose to return to Yugoslavia. The exchange would be carried out over three years

11 February Britain grants the Bulgarian government *de jure* recognition, but maintains that the methods used to consolidate the government's position and the conduct of the recent elections

	have not 'been in keeping with the spirit and intentions of the Yalta Declaration'.
22 February	The Polish *Sejm* approves a major amnesty. Some 25,000 political and other prisoners are freed, and a further 23,000 have their terms of imprisonment reduced by a third or a half. The amnesty does not, however, extend to members of German or Ukrainian terrorist organisations or to wartime collaborators.
27 February	The trial of thirteen leading members of the counter-revolutionary plot opens before the Hungarian People's Court in Budapest. Colonel-General Lajos Dalnoki-Veres, Major-General Andras and György Donat plead 'not guilty' but acknowledge a number of the charges against them. They are sentenced to death on 16 April, but the sentences on Colonel-General Dalnoki-Veres and Major-General Andras are later commuted to terms of imprisonment. The other defendants receive prison sentences ranging from one year to life. Western journalists consider the trial to have been correctly conducted. Kolomon Salata, a further leader of the conspiracy and a former Smallholders deputy, had fled.
10 March–24 April	The American, British, French and Soviet foreign ministers, meeting in Moscow, again fail to agree on a German peace treaty. Vyacheslav Molotov seeks reparations of US$10 billion at 1938 prices, recognition of the Oder–Neisse line as the German–Polish border, and a provisional all-German government based on the mass organisations as well as the political parties.
9 April	The dispute between Albania and Britain over the Corfu Channel is referred by the UN Security Council to the International Court of Justice.
23 May	The UN Inquiry Commission in Geneva adopts by majority vote an American report on the situation in Greece and her neighbours, which indicts Yugoslavia in particular, and Bulgaria and Albania to a lesser extent, for supporting the guerrilla forces against the Greek government. The Soviet Union and Poland vote against and France abstains.
7 June	The official Hungarian News Agency publishes the alleged confession of Béla Kovacs, the former Secretary-General of the Smallholders Party. It declares that the leaders of the Smallholders Party had in March 1946 planned to establish an illegal armed party organisation in western Hungary to help overthrow the government, had approved of the Party's contacts with Hungarian 'military emigrants' in the British Zone of Austria and had discussed the possibility of setting up a Hungarian counter-government-in-exile.

12 July	Albania, Bulgaria, Czechoslovakia, (Finland), Hungary, Poland, Romania and Yugoslavia do not attend the European Economic Conference in Paris on implementing the Marshall Plan. Czechoslovakia had reversed an earlier decision to keep the option open, following a visit by its prime and foreign ministers, Klement Gottwald and Jan Masaryk, to Moscow on 7 July. The plan had been designed with political conditions which it was known the Soviet Union would reject.
15 July	Leaders of the Romanian National Peasant Party, including Dr Maniu, are arrested. Dr Maniu is accused of directing a plot to overthrow the regime. (See also Part 3.6.2.)
16 August	Nikola Petkov, leader of the Bulgarian Agrarian Party, is condemned to death on charges of conspiring to overthrow the government by armed force. (See Part 3.6.2 for fuller particulars.)
28 September	Sixteen Albanians are sentenced to death in Tiranë for allegedly being in the pay of the Americans to work for the overthrow of the Hoxha government.
6 November	Austria, Hungary (and Italy) are admitted to membership of UNESCO.
11 November	Dr Iuliu Maniu, leader of the dissolved Romanian National Peasant Party, and Ion Mihalache, the Party's vice-president, are sentenced to solitary confinement for life by a military court in Bucharest. They had been found guilty of high treason, instigation to armed rebellion, seeking to flee the country, plotting with foreign governments to overthrow the regime and aiming to establish a government abroad.
27 November	Marshal Tito declares on a state visit to Bulgaria that: 'We shall establish cooperation so general and so close that the question of federation will be a mere formality.' (See also Part 4.3.)
4 December	Bulgaria is proclaimed a People's Republic.
30 December	Romania becomes a republic on the abdication of King Michael. (See also Part 3.6.2.)

1948

17 January	The Bulgarian prime minister, Georgi Dimitrov, speaks in a press interview of the possibility of an eventual federation of the eastern European nations allied to the Soviet Union. Such a federation might include Albania, Bulgaria, Czechoslovakia, Hungary, Poland, Romania, Yugoslavia and even Greece. 'If possible', it would seek trade relations with America, Britain and France 'on the principle of complete equality'. The statement is believed to have infuriated Stalin.

January	The Yugoslav leaders, Milovan Djilas and Koča Popović, are summoned to Moscow, and advised by Stalin that Yugoslavia is 'free to swallow Albania whenever she chooses'.
28 January	The Soviet newspaper *Pravda* strongly opposes the Dimitrov statement of 17 January. It maintains that: 'What [these countries] do need is the consolidation and protection of their independence and sovereignty through the mobilisation and organisation of domestic popular democratic forces, as has been correctly stated in the declaration of the Cominform.'
10 February	Delegations from Bulgaria, led by prime minister Georgi Dimitrov, and Yugoslavia, led by Edvard Kardelj, meet Stalin and Vyacheslav Molotov, the Soviet foreign minister, in the Kremlin. Stalin is scowling and surly. Molotov maintains that serious differences had arisen between Bulgaria and Yugoslavia, on the one hand, and the Soviet Union, on the other, which were 'inadmissible both from a Party and a state point of view'. What the Soviet Union now wants is the creation of three federations: Hungary and Romania; Czechoslovakia and Poland; and Bulgaria and Yugoslavia. 'The time is ripe. Bulgaria and Yugoslavia must unite immediately. Then they must annex Albania.' The Yugoslav representatives reluctantly sign a demanded agreement on mutual consultation with the Kremlin on all foreign policy issues, but agree between themselves that they must resist any immediate federation with Bulgaria, which they interpret as a Soviet manoeuvre to control Yugoslavia.
25 February	The Communists assume power in Czechoslovakia in coalition with the Social Democrats. (See Part 3.6.2 for fuller particulars.)
26 February	The Americans issue a joint statement on behalf of the American, British and French governments condemning the new Czechoslovak government as a disguised dictatorship and accusing the Communists of seizing power through 'a crisis artificially and deliberately instigated'. Many ordinary people in western Europe, perhaps for the first and last time, seriously fear the outbreak of a Third World War.
1 March	Tito summons the Yugoslav Communist Party Central Committee to his villa at Dedinje. The Committee agree that the Soviet demand for immediate federation with Bulgaria must be rejected, as they regard Bulgaria as totally subservient to the Soviet Union.
18 March	The Soviet Union withdraws its military advisers from Yugoslavia, alleging that they are 'surrounded by hostility'. Civilian advisers are withdrawn likewise almost immediately.

20 March	Tito sends a note to Molotov maintaining that he and his colleagues had been 'surprised and hurt' by the Soviet approach and asking to be 'told straight out' what the problem was.
27 March	Stalin and Molotov respond to Tito's note. They maintain that the Yugoslav Party leaders are hostile to the Soviet Union, ideologically unsound and out of touch with their own members. They are compared with Trotsky and Bukharin, and are accused of retaining an English spy in their midst.
12 April	Tito convenes a further meeting of the Yugoslav Central Committee. He claims: 'This is not a matter of theoretical discussion or ideological errors. The issue at stake is the relationship between one state and another.' The Committee agree, except for Streten Žujović, who is expelled. The Yugoslavs respond to the Soviet Union in uncompromising terms.
13 April	Romania adopts a new constitution and is declared a People's Republic.
4 May	Stalin and Molotov send a further note of 24 pages reiterating the earlier charges, and adding that the Yugoslav leaders are 'boundlessly arrogant', undemocratic and ridiculously conceited over their alleged wartime achievements.
9 May	The Yugoslav Central Committee reject the Soviet contention that the Cominform is the appropriate body to deal with the dispute as the Yugoslavs consider it to be biased against them. Streten Žujović and Andrija Hebrang, former president of the State Planning Committee, who are known to have close contacts with Moscow, are charged with high treason.
9 May	Czechoslovakia is declared a 'Democratic People's Republic'. (See also Part 3.6.2.)
19 May	The Yugoslav leaders decline to attend a meeting of the Cominform (see Part 3.6.2), convoked by the Soviet Union.
18–26 June	The *Reichsmark* (RM) is replaced in the Soviet Zone of Germany by the *Mark der deutschen Notenbank* (MDN) in response to the introduction of the *Deutsche Mark* (DM) in the western zones. The Soviet Union cites the western reform as justification for the ensuing Berlin blockade.
24 June	The Soviet Union blockades all land routes across its zone of Germany into West Berlin.
28 June	Meeting in Bucharest, the Cominform discusses developments in the absence of any Yugoslav representatives. It decides to expel Yugoslavia and denounces Tito and his colleagues, who it asserts are ideologically deviant and hostile to the Soviet Union. They are alleged to show 'boundless ambition, arrogance and conceit' and to be running a 'Turkish and

terroristic' regime. The members of the Yugoslav Party are directly invited to depose their leaders. The headquarters of the Cominform moves to Bucharest.

29 June   The Yugoslav Central Committee reject the Cominform's charges and call for a united Party.

30 June   Albania breaks off economic relations with Yugoslavia and allies itself with the Soviet Union. Albania virulently attacks the Yugoslav leaders the following day.

21 July   The Fifth Congress of the Yugoslav Communist Party gives Tito its full support.

15 August   The UN Inquiry Commission again finds that Albania, Bulgaria and Yugoslavia have been helping Greek Communist guerrilla forces.

31 December The Soviet Union and the Soviet bloc initiate a full trade embargo on Yugoslavia.

1949

25 January The Soviet Union, together with Albania, Bulgaria, Czechoslovakia, Hungary, Poland and Romania, establishes COMECON as a new commercial and economic organisation to coordinate economic development and mutual trade.

8 February Cardinal Mindszenty, Primate of Hungary, is sentenced to life imprisonment on charges of high treason, conspiracy against the state and illegal currency dealings. (See Part 3.7 for fuller particulars.)

9 April   The International Court of Justice in The Hague finds Albania responsible under international law for the damage and loss of life suffered when the two British destroyers were mined in the Corfu Channel in 1946.

12 May   The Berlin blockade is raised.

18 August   Hungary is declared a People's Republic. (See Part 3.6.2 for further particulars.)

8 September America agrees to make its first loan to Marshal Tito's Yugoslavia.

15 September The Yugoslav government describes the indictment of Laszlo Rajk in Hungary, with its charges against Yugoslavia, as 'the most shameless and baseless document in the history of the international working-class movement'. (See also Part 3.6.3.)

24 September Marshal Tito personally presents the Hungarian minister in Belgrade with a note describing the Rajk trial as a 'judicial farce whose lies and falsifications have already rebounded on their authors' and as a 'disgusting attack on the honour, independence and sovereign rights of Yugoslavia'.

28 September	The Soviet Union formally denounces the twenty-year Treaty of Friendship and Mutual Assistance it had signed with Yugoslavia on 11 April 1945. Bulgaria, Czechoslovakia, Hungary, Poland and Romania denounce their treaties with Yugoslavia similarly.
7 October	The German Democratic Republic (East Germany) is proclaimed in East Berlin, replacing the Soviet Zone. Unlike West Germany it has the power to conduct its own foreign relations. The high commissioners of the western Allies, however, argue that it is the artificial creation of a 'popular assembly' which has no mandate for the purpose. On that basis they refuse to recognise it, and other non-Communist countries follow suit.
8 October	Laszlo Rajk, formerly Hungarian foreign minister and interior minister, and member of the Politburo of the Hungarian Communist Party, is sentenced to death at the end of a 'show trial' in Budapest. (See Part 3.6.3 for fuller particulars.)
26 October	A broadcast by Moscow Radio describes Marshal Tito as a traitor, bandit, scoundrel, greedy ape, insolent dwarf and chattering parrot.
7 November	Marshal Konstantin Rokossovsky, a senior Soviet general but Polish by birth, is appointed a Marshal of Poland and commander-in-chief of the Polish Army. He assumes Polish nationality and the post of minister of national defence the following day.
14 December	Traicho Kostov, formerly deputy prime minister and secretary of the Central Committee of the Bulgarian Communist Party, is sentenced to death at the end of a 'show trial' in Sofia. (See Part 3.6.3 for fuller particulars.)
15 December	The International Court of Justice in The Hague awards Britain £843,947, the full amount claimed from Albania for the Corfu Channel incidents.

1950

1 April	Romania follows the Soviet precedent of March 1947 by banning Romanian citizens from marrying foreigners without special government approval.
May	The British and American secret services, MI6 and the CIA, start a covert training programme for Albanian émigrés which is to last until the end of 1952. The programme is abortive because the Albanian Communist government is alerted in advance by Kim Philby, the British spy in MI6 working for the Soviet Union.
23 May	The creation of the East German *Bereitschaften*, a militarised police force of some 50,000 men, is the subject of protest to

47

the Soviet Union by the western Allies. They maintain that it is contrary to the Potsdam Declaration outlawing German military organisations.

12 July Czechoslovakia and East Germany sign an agreement for mutual assistance against the Colorado beetle. Both countries had accused America of dropping large numbers of the beetle, which destroys potato crops, since 22 May. America describes the charges as 'patently absurd'.

10 August Bulgaria begins the deportation to Turkey of 250,000 Muslims of Turkish origin and advises Turkey that their allegedly voluntary repatriation is due to be completed within three months. It cites a Bulgarian–Turkish agreement of 1925 providing that 'no obstacle shall be placed in the way of voluntary emigration of Turks from Bulgaria and of Bulgarians from Turkey'. Turkey protests that the emigrants are not being allowed to take the value of their property with them.

1 October East Germany becomes a member of COMECON. (See also Part 4.3.)

21–22 October The Prague meeting of Cominform and East German foreign ministers condemns the stance on Germany of the conference of the western Allies on Germany in New York on 19 September (communiqué). In particular, it criticises the intention to terminate the state of war while retaining the Occupation Statute, the review of the agreement on prohibited and limited industries and the re-establishment of German armed forces. The meeting proposes a unified, demilitarised Germany and the creation of an All-German Constituent Council on a parity basis.

25 November The first of the Greek children taken to Yugoslavia by the Greek Communists during the Greek Civil War are repatriated.

30 November Pursuant to the Cominform meeting of 21–22 October, Otto Grotewohl, the East German prime minister, writes to Chancellor Adenauer of West Germany proposing conversations between their two governments on the establishment of an All-German Constituent Council.

1951

15 January The West German Chancellor replies indirectly to Otto Grotewohl in a statement which argues that any all-German assembly must be freely elected on the basis of freely constituted political groupings. The Chancellor also requires the prior disbandment of the *Volkspolizei* (People's Police).

21 May The Hungarian government starts the mass deportation from Budapest of what it describes as 'undesirable elements'. On

7 August, the Party newspaper, *Szabad Nep*, maintains that 4,081 members of the 'former ruling class' have been removed using a 1939 law of the Horthy regime on the banishment from the capital of those who are 'a danger to public safety and order'. Western sources put the number of deportees at more than 24,000 from a much wider social spectrum.

2–4 July   William N. Oatis, the American head of the Associated Press Office in Prague, is tried with three Czechoslovak nationals for espionage. He is sentenced to ten years' imprisonment, rather than to death, in recognition of his confession of guilt. The Americans describe the proceedings as a 'mock trial'.

13 September   The western Allies, led by America, ban Czechoslovak air flights over West Germany. The ban is interpreted as a response to the Oatis trial.

1952

10 March   The Soviet Union in the 'Stalin note' proposes a peace treaty to create a neutral, democratic and united Germany with its own defence forces. The western Allies respond cautiously on 25 March, and again on 13 May to a further note of 9 April.

21 May   The national committee of the East German National Front approves the establishment of military forces (*Streitkräfte*). Many former frontier and transport police are organised as the People's Police in Barracks (KVP). The Americans had first seriously proposed West German rearmament in September 1950.

27 May   East Germany responds to the signing of the Treaties of Bonn and Paris (restoring sovereignty to West Germany and proposing the inclusion of West German forces in a European Defence Community) by erecting a literal 'Iron Curtain' of barbed wire, minefields and watchtowers and by creating a security zone three miles deep the length of its frontier with West Germany. The security zone also extends along the Baltic coast.

27 November   Rudolf Slánský, formerly Secretary-General of the Czechoslovak Communist Party, is sentenced to death at the end of a 'show trial' in Prague. (See Part 3.6.3 for fuller particulars.)

1953

5 March   Stalin dies in Moscow.

2.5 CHRONOLOGY OF KEY EVENTS DURING THE COMMUNIST PERIOD 1953–89

1953

10 March   America maintains that two Czechoslovak fighters have attacked two American fighters over the American Zone of Germany and shot down one of them. Czechoslovakia maintains they had penetrated 25 miles inside its airspace and refused orders to land.

16–21 March   Tito pays an official visit to Great Britain, his first such foreign visit since 1948.

16 June   300 building workers on Stalinallee (now Karl-Marx-Allee) initiate a demonstration through East Berlin in favour of lower work norms. They are joined by thousands of fellow workers, but fail to be received at either official trade union or government level.

17 June   Between 300,000 and 372,000 workers, or some 5 per cent of the workforce, strike at more than 270 sites across East Germany. Some West Berliners participate in the demonstrations in East Berlin. The Soviet Army and the 'People's Police in Barracks' suppress the demonstrations, killing 21 and injuring many more. An academic assessment of 1957 was to find that more than 1,000 East Germans had subsequently been imprisoned and 7 sentenced to death. The demonstrations nevertheless succeed in their economic if not in their political objectives.

22 June   East Germany responds to the demonstrations by withdrawing the new work norms introduced in April. It also increases pensions by 15–20 per cent, restores workers' cheap fares, diverts East Mark(MDN)70 million from heavy industry to social housing, and ceases to deduct sickness leave from paid holidays.

1954

25 March   The Soviet Union recognises East Germany as a sovereign and independent state conducting its own internal and external affairs, but the former Soviet occupation forces remain in East Germany. The western Allies decline to recognise or deal with East Germany.

8 June   East Germany announces that its former Christian Democrat foreign minister, Georg Dertinger, has been sentenced to fifteen years' imprisonment with hard labour for espionage on behalf of America and Britain. He is to be released in May 1964.

5 October   An agreement is reached in London between Yugoslavia, Italy, America and Britain whereby Zone B of the Trieste Territory is transferred to Yugoslav civil administration. It had been under Yugoslav military administration since 1945.

1955

14 May   Albania, Bulgaria, Czechoslovakia, East Germany, Hungary, Poland, Romania and the Soviet Union sign the Warsaw Pact. (See Part 4.3 for fuller particulars.)

15 May   The foreign ministers of America, Britain, France, the Soviet Union and Austria sign the Austrian State Treaty in Vienna. The treaty re-establishes an independent Austria with the frontiers of 1 January 1938, but imposes an obligation of permanent neutrality.

25 May   Tito receives the Soviet leaders Nikita Khrushchev and Marshal Bulganin, in Belgrade. Khrushchev makes a lengthy apology for the Soviet Union's earlier attitude, and says: 'We sincerely regret what happened.'

The visit ends just over a week later with a Joint Declaration of Friendship and Cooperation, and emphasises that the internal and ideological affairs of each state are that state's own business.

1956

28 June   Workers in Poznan riot against the Polish government.

6 October   The reburial of Laszlo Rajk, executed in September 1949 (see Part 3.6.3), stimulates anti-government sentiment in Hungary.

19–20 October   Władysław Gomulka returns to power as First Secretary of the Polish United Workers' Party. He enjoys almost total popular support. Persecution of the Roman Catholic Church is to cease and agricultural collectivisation be abandoned. His return, together with other changes in the Politburo, provokes Nikita Khrushchev to fly to Warsaw. He rages: 'I'll show you the road to socialism . . . if you don't do what you're told, we'll wipe you out by force.' The Poles, however, stand firm, and Gomulka declares: 'Every country has the right to be independent.'

23 October   Revolution breaks out in Hungary.

1 November   The Hungarian government of Imre Nagy seeks to withdraw from the Warsaw Pact, and asks the UN for assistance. The Soviet Army enters Hungary.

3 November	János Kádár, Communist Party leader since 25 October, forms a counter-government and asks for Soviet assistance.
4 November	The Soviet Army attacks Budapest and heavy street fighting ensues with considerable loss of life and major physical damage. Thousands of refugees flee to the west through the frontier with Austria at Hegyeshalom.

1957

2 October	The 'Rapacki Plan', named after its originator, the Polish foreign minister, is submitted to the UN General Assembly. The plan envisages a nuclear armaments-free zone in central Europe including the whole of Germany.

1958

10–12 April	The foreign ministers of Czechoslovakia, East Germany and Poland denounce a West German parliamentary resolution arguing that West Germany must be equipped with the most modern weapons, in practice nuclear weapons. They repeat their support for the Rapacki Plan. It is, however, formally rejected by America on 3 May.

1961

13 August	The crisis in Berlin over the Soviet Union's intention of signing a separate peace treaty with East Germany reaches its climax. East German forces start to seal off East from West Berlin, and the Berlin Wall is erected within days.
1–6 November	President Tito hosts the first conference of the Nonaligned Movement in Belgrade. The Movement is to exercise substantial influence over the following decades.
7 November	Enver Hoxha, the First Secretary of the Albanian Party of Labour, accuses Nikita Khrushchev of abandoning Marxism–Leninism so as to open the way for 'revisionism'. Albania develops closer links with China.
15–17 November	The Central Committee of the Czechoslovak Communist Party orders the demolition of the Stalin monument in Prague. The memorial was 90 foot high and weighed 18,000 tons, and was the largest such memorial outside the Soviet Union.
3 December	The Soviet Union terminates diplomatic relations with Albania. It maintains that the position of its diplomats had been rendered 'insupportable'.
31 December	Ulbricht admits in the Soviet newspaper, *Pravda*, that the movement of East German workers to West Germany since 1949 has lost East Germany East Mark (MDN) 30 billion, equivalent to 40 per cent of national income over the same period.

1963

7 April   Yugoslavia proclaims a new constitution and changes the official name of the country to the Socialist Federal Republic of Yugoslavia (*Socijalisticka Federativna Republika Jugoslavije*).

1965

21 August   Romania changes the official name of the state from the Romanian People's Republic to the Socialist State of Romania (*Republica Socialistá România*). Article 3 of the new constitution declares that the leading political force of the whole of society is the Romanian Communist Party. The constitution is to be modified in March 1974.

1968

20 August   The armies of Bulgaria, East Germany, Hungary, Poland and the Soviet Union invade Czechoslovakia to suppress 'the Prague Spring'. About 100 people are killed during the invasion. (See Part 3.6.4 for fuller particulars.)

26 August   The enforced Moscow Agreement binds the Czechoslovak government to a policy of 'normalisation', by which is meant the revocation of most reforms, and to the stationing of Soviet troops.

12 September   Albania leaves the Warsaw Pact.

16 October   The August Moscow Agreement is confirmed by the Czechoslovak–Soviet 'Status of Forces Agreement'.

1969

1 January   Czechoslovakia is declared a federal socialist republic comprising two nations with equal rights and inalienable sovereignty.

17 January   Jan Palach, a Czechoslovak student, burns himself alive in Wenceslas Square, Prague, in a protest against repression. He dies two days later.

October   Bulgaria and Turkey sign an agreement to facilitate the emigration of Bulgarian Turks. 50,000 leave over the next ten years.

28 October   The new West German Social Democrat Chancellor, Willy Brandt, reiterates the West German position on the unity of the German people with the same right to self-determination as any other people, but reverses established policy by recognising the existence of two German states. Nevertheless, 'they are not foreign countries to each other; their relations with each other can only be of a special nature'. Recognition of East

Germany by West Germany under international law remains out of the question. He offers East Germany negotiations at government level without discrimination on either side.

1970

19 March   The East German prime minister, Willi Stoph, meets West German Chancellor Willy Brandt in Erfurt, East Germany, in the first top-level government meeting between the two states since their foundation.

21 May   Stoph and Brandt meet again in Kassel, West Germany.

12 August   The Treaty of Moscow between West Germany and the Soviet Union respects the Oder–Neisse line as the frontier between East Germany and Poland.

7 December   Chancellor Brandt of West Germany and Jozef Cyrankiewicz, the Polish prime minister, sign the Treaty of Warsaw normalising relations between the two countries and recognising the Oder–Neisse line as Poland's western frontier.
Chancellor Brandt makes a major impact on opinion throughout central and eastern Europe by falling to his knees at the Warsaw ghetto memorial in a gesture of atonement.

20 December   Władysław Gomulka is ousted as First Secretary of the Polish United Workers' Party following workers' riots in Gdánsk, Gdynia and Szczecin. He is succeeded by Edward Gierek.

1971

30 June   Amendments to the Yugoslav constitution establish a Presidency of eight members, one from each republic and autonomous province. After the death of President Tito in May 1980, its members are to take it in turns according to a fixed order of succession to become President of the Presidency of the Republic for a period of twelve months each.

23 November   Students at the University of Zagreb begin a strike in support of the leadership of the League of Communists of Croatia against the criticisms made by President Tito. Their strike is joined by students in Split and lasts till 8 December. A sense of political crisis persists.

1972

8 May   The Central Committee of the League of Communists of Croatia unanimously approve the expulsion from the League of four prominent leaders, who had resigned in December 1971, for permitting 'the infiltration of nationalist forces into the party'.

8 May	President Tito warns against the persistence in Serbia of tendencies towards 'unitarist forces [and] greater Serbian hegemony and chauvinism [which] should never be underestimated'.
26 June	A group of armed Croat émigrés enters Yugoslavia from Austria. Yugoslavia announces on 24 July that seventeen of the nineteen '*Ustaša fascists*' have been liquidated by the security forces.
16 August	Yugoslavia formally protests to Australia at the 'intensification of the anti-Yugoslav activities of terrorist *Ustašan* organisations' in Australia and demands that the Australian government curb terrorist training in Australia as well as other anti-Yugoslav acts by Croat dissidents there.
11 October	Three leaders of the Croat nationalist *Matica Hrvatska* movement, including Franjo Tudjman, are sentenced to terms of four, two and two years' imprisonment for propagating 'separatist and nationalist' ideas. A number of similar trials with similar sentences are held during 1972–73.
7–8 December	The NATO ministerial council decides to establish relations with East Germany.
15 December	Romania becomes a member of both the International Monetary Fund and the World Bank.
21 December	East Germany and West Germany sign the 'Basic Treaty' on mutual relations, whereby East Germany receives recognition from West Germany of its separate identity and equality but not of its identity as a foreign state under international law.

1973

17 March	Three members of the Croatian Revolutionary Brotherhood, all naturalised Australians, are executed in Yugoslavia for their entry from Austria in June 1972 with the intention of overthrowing the regime 'by violence, murder and terrorism'. Australia formally protests.
7 April	The Australian federal attorney-general announces on Australian television that he has evidence that Croat terrorists from Australia were planning an invasion of Yugoslavia in 1973.
26–30 June	President Ceauşescu of Romania pays an official visit to West Germany. The two sides sign a joint solemn declaration of 'the equality of rights of all states, irrespective of their size, their state of development, [and] their political, economic and social systems'.
11 December	Chancellor Willy Brandt of West Germany and Lubomir Strougal, the Czechoslovak prime minister, sign the Treaty on Bilateral Relations between West Germany and Czechoslovakia in Prague. It recognises that the provisions of the 1938

Munich Agreement which led to the transfer of the Sudetenland from Czechoslovakia to Germany were 'null and void'.

1974

5 February Pope Paul VI removes Cardinal Jozef Mindszenty from his post
as Archbishop of Esztergom and Primate of Hungary 'in view
of the pastoral problems' of the archdiocese. The Cardinal
had been allowed to leave Hungary in 1971. He declares on 7
February that he had not resigned as Primate voluntarily.

1975

10 November A final accord on the future status of Trieste is signed by the
Yugoslav and Italian governments at Osimo.

1977

7 July An editorial in the Albanian official party newspaper, *Zeri i
Popullit*, indirectly criticises the basic orientation of Chinese
policy.

18 October Sentences of imprisonment are imposed on members of
the Czechoslovak 'Charter 77' dissident group, including
Vaclav Havel.

1978

7 January It is announced in Bucharest during an official visit by Chancellor Schmidt of West Germany that over the following five
years Romania will allow some 11,000 ethnic Germans to leave
Romania annually.

7 July China advises Albania that it is to terminate all economic aid
and co-operation projects as soon as possible. China is react-
ing to Albanian anti-Chinese pronouncements over the previous twelve months.

11 September The exiled Bulgarian writer, Georgi Markov, is assassinated in
London, allegedly by a poisoned dart from an umbrella. The
Bulgarian security service is widely believed to be responsible.

16 October Cardinal Karol Wojtyla, Archbishop of Krakow, Poland, is
elected Pope. He takes the style of John Paul II.

1979

2 June Pope John Paul II makes his first Papal visit to his Polish homeland. It is also his first Papal visit to a Communist country.

1980

1 July An increase in meat prices in Poland provokes a wave of strikes
which become increasingly political.

14 August   Workers at the Lenin shipyard in Gdánsk demand an independent trade union, and workers in Gdánsk, Gdynia and Sopot elect a joint strike committee under the leadership of Lech Wałęsa.

31 August   The Polish government and Lech Wałęsa sign the 'Gdánsk Agreements' allowing the formation of free trade unions.

22 September   The Polish free trade unions form a national confederation, *Solidarność* (Solidarity). It is granted legal status on 24 October.

1981

9 February   General Wojtech Jaruzelski becomes Polish prime minister against a background of continuing unrest.

27 March   Poland remains restless and the Soviet Army conducts manoeuvres on its eastern frontier.

5 May   The ethnic Albanian leader of the League of Communists of Yugoslavia in Kosovo, Mahmut Bakali, resigns in response to serious rioting in the province since March which had led to the declaration of a full-scale state of emergency on 3 April. It is alleged by many in politics and the press that the rioting is in part attributable to the deliberate attempt of outside forces (implicitly Albanian) to destabilise Yugoslavia.

13 May   Mehmet Ali Ağca, a Turk, shoots and seriously wounds Pope John Paul II in St Peter's Square in Rome. Three Bulgarians and three other Turks, all alleged to be fellow conspirators, are later acquitted. The Pope's support for the Roman Catholic Church and for Solidarity in Poland is a possible motive.

24 May   Two bombs slightly damage the Yugoslav embassy in Tiranë on the late Marshal Tito's official birthday. The Albanian government suggests that the bombs must have been placed from inside the building.

8 October   Solidarity's first national council, opened on 4 September, closes with the adoption of a radical programme of action. Lech Wałęsa is re-elected chairman.

18 October   General Jaruzelski becomes head of the Polish Communist Party as well as prime minister.

4 November   Hungary formally applies for membership of the International Monetary Fund and the World Bank. Poland follows suit on 10 November.

13 December   The Polish government declares martial law and establishes a twenty-member Military Council of National Salvation (WRON). Solidarity is proscribed and its leaders detained. The principal motivation is to forestall a Soviet invasion.

1982

7 April   Albania and Yugoslavia agree to build a 54-mile rail link between Shkodër (Albania) and Titograd (Yugoslavia). It is due to be completed in January 1984 and will be Albania's first international rail link.

8 October   All registered Polish trade unions are legally dissolved, including Solidarity.

1983

21 July   Martial law is lifted in Poland.

1984

19 October   The kidnapping and subsequent murder of Father Jerzy Popieluszko, probably by elements in the Polish security service, renews anti-government sentiment.

1985

8–22 June   Hungary re-introduces multi-candidate elections.

1987

April   The first major Serb protest in Kosovo at alleged persecution by the Albanian majority. The reputation of Slobodan Milošević rises in Serbia as he defends protesters from being attacked by the predominantly ethnic Albanian Kosovo police.

15 November   A large anti-government demonstration involving up to 20,000 people erupts in Braşov, Romania's second city. Lesser demonstrations follow in Braile, Sibiu and Timişoara. The protests are against wage cuts, food shortages, obligatory Sunday working and further power cuts.

1988

27 June   Some 50,000 people demonstrate in Budapest against the proposed destruction of 8,000 villages in Romania, many of which are home to Romania's large Hungarian minority.

15 August   Strikes break out again in Poland.

31 August   Lech Wałęsa and the Polish minister of the interior agree to open negotiations between *Solidarność* (still formally illegal) and the Polish government.

10 November   Hungary permits the formation of alternative political parties. They are legalised on 11 January 1989.

20 November   East Germany bans the Soviet magazine *Sputnik*, alleging that it distorts history.

21 November	Five Soviet films are similarly excluded from a Soviet film festival in East Berlin.

1989

23 March	Following further conflicts between ethnic Albanians and Serbs, the Kosovo provincial Assembly endorses changes to the Serbian constitution giving the central Serbian authorities control over the internal affairs of Kosovo (and the Vojvodina). The vote sets off a wave of demonstrations across Kosovo.
5 April	The negotiations between the Polish government and *Solidarność* culminate in agreement on the formation of independent trade unions, economic reform and elections for the *Sejm*.
25 April	The Soviet Army starts to leave Hungary.
2 May	Miklós Németh, the Hungarian prime minister, orders the dismantling of the twin barbed wire fences along the frontier with Austria.
20 May	The Bulgarian government initiates a policy of suppressing the identity of its Turkish minority. Many Turks leave.
4–18 June	*Solidarność* is highly successful in the Polish elections.
7–8 July	The Bucharest Summit of Warsaw Pact members fails to agree over reform.
16 August	Imre Nagy is reburied with state honours.
24 August	Tadeusz Mazowiecki becomes Poland's first non-Communist-minded prime minister since the war.
10 September	Hungary's declaration that thousands of East Germans 'on holiday' there may cross the border into Austria initiates a wave of East German emigration to the west.
1 October	Some 10,000 East Germans are permitted to leave the West German embassies in Warsaw and Prague and travel to the west.
6–7 October	Gorbachev visits East Germany on its fortieth anniversary as a state, and criticises the government's hostility to reform. He emphasises that 'matters affecting East Germany are decided not in Moscow but in Berlin'. Demonstrations continue in favour of the democratisation of public life and 500–700 marchers are arrested in East Berlin. Almost all are released within a week.
23 October	The weekly march in Leipzig is attended by demonstrators, estimated at anything between 100,000 and 300,000 in number. They call for the removal of the Berlin Wall and for free elections.

23 October The previous People's Republic is proclaimed the Hungarian Republic.

8–10 November The East German Politburo resigns in its entirety.

9 November The border between East and West Germany, including the Berlin Wall, is opened.

17 November Miloš Jakeš resigns as General Secretary of the Czechoslovak Communist Party, as does the Politburo in its entirety, following the violent suppression of a public demonstration.

24–30 November Mass street demonstrations are organised in Prague.

17 December Nicolae Ceauşescu orders his security forces to fire on anti-government demonstrators in Timişoara.

19–20 December Chancellor Helmut Kohl and Hans Modrow, East German prime minister, agree in Dresden to conclude a 'joint treaty on cooperation and good neighbourliness' between West and East Germany by spring 1990.

22 December The Romanian Army defects to the anti-government demonstrators. Nicolae Ceauşescu and his wife flee but are captured by the military. The National Salvation Front (*Frontul Salvarii Nationale*) assumes power.

25 December Nicolae Ceauşescu and his wife, Elena, are tried and convicted by an improvised military tribunal on charges including mass murder, and are promptly shot. They are the only overthrown Communist leaders of the Soviet bloc to come to a violent end.

2.6 CHRONOLOGY OF KEY EVENTS SINCE THE FALL OF COMMUNISM

2.6.1 CENTRAL AND EASTERN EUROPE EXCLUDING YUGOSLAVIA

1990

15 January   Bulgaria terminates the formal leading role in society of the Bulgarian Communist Party.

23 January   The Soviet Union agrees to withdraw its troops from Hungary.

6 February   Chancellor Kohl declares that he is ready to negotiate with East Germany on economic and monetary union immediately.

11 February Following discussions with Chancellor Kohl, President Gorbachev states that the Soviet Union has no objection in principle to German unification. He adds, however, that unification should not disturb the present strategic balance between NATO and the Warsaw Pact and should contribute to a new European security system.

25 February The Soviet Union agrees to withdraw its troops from Czechoslovakia.

17 March   Warsaw Pact foreign ministers meet in Prague. The Soviet Union alone wants German neutrality. Czechoslovakia, Hungary and Poland want to restrain Germany from becoming a great power acting on its own.

20 March   The Romanian town of Tirgu Mures is the scene of rioting between ethnic Hungarians and Romanians which leaves three dead. Some 2,000 Romanian nationalists had attacked a peaceful demonstration by some 5,000 ethnic Hungarians, with scythes, axes and clubs.

28 March   Hungary holds its first liberal democratic general election since 1945.

12 September The Treaty on the Final Settlement with Respect to Germany (effectively the German Peace Treaty) is signed in Moscow by East and West Germany and the four wartime Allies, America, Britain, France and the Soviet Union. It gives the united Germany full sovereignty over its internal and external affairs.

3 October   East and West Germany are united as a federal state in accordance with the legal declaration of 23 August.

14 November	Germany and Poland sign a treaty pursuant to the 12 September Treaty on the Final Settlement confirming the Oder–Neisse line as their joint border and renouncing any German claims to territory lost as a result of the Second World War.
15 November	The previous People's Republic is proclaimed the Republic of Bulgaria.
11 December	The Albanian government reopens Albania to the world. It bows to popular pressure and permits the formation of opposition parties.
12 December	The respective competencies of the Czech and Slovak Republics within the Czech and Slovak Federative Republic are legally defined. Most functions are discharged by the Republics, but constitutional and foreign affairs, defence and major economic issues, and ethnic and religious affairs are devolved to the Federal Assembly.
22 December	The Albanian government orders the removal of Stalin's statue from the main square of Tiranë.

1991

25 February	The members of the Warsaw Pact dissolve their military links.
29 April	The Socialist People's Republic of Albania is renamed the Republic of Albania under a new interim constitution.
21 May	The Czechoslovak federal assembly approves legislation on the restitution of confiscated land. It excludes owners who had been 'transferred abroad' in 1945 and had not declared themselves Czechoslovak citizens (i.e. the Sudetens). (See 'Sudetenland' in Glossary for fuller particulars.)
8 December	Romania adopts a new liberal democratic constitution. Executive power is in the hands of a directly elected president who appoints a prime minister and cabinet answerable to the legislature.

1992

22 March	The Democratic Party of Sali Berisha wins a clear majority in the Albanian national elections. The former Communist Albanian Party of Labour, renamed the Socialist Party, wins about a quarter of the 140 parliamentary seats.
12 September	Albania's former president, Ramiz Alia, is placed under house arrest on charges of misusing state funds and abuse of power.
23 September	Ahmed Dogan, the leader of Bulgaria's predominantly ethnic Turkish MRF, describes the right-wing government's policies as 'blue fascism' and withdraws its parliamentary support.

8 December   Poland's interim 'small constitution' comes into force. It introduces a mixed presidential–parliamentary form of government with a directly elected president.

31 December   The voluntary dissolution of the Czechoslovak state comes into force at midnight, and the two new independent states of the Czech Republic and Slovakia succeed it.

1993

7 January   The Polish *Sejm* passes a compromise bill restricting the availability of abortion. It becomes law on 15 February.

30 July   Fatos Nano, Albanian prime minister in 1991 and leader of the Socialist, formerly Communist, Party, is arrested on charges of mishandling foreign aid. 20,000 of his supporters demonstrate in Tiranë in protest. He is sentenced to twelve years' imprisonment on 3 April 1994.

4 September   The semi-state reburial of the ashes of Admiral Miklos Horthy, Hungarian regent 1920–44, in the family vault in Kenderes, Hungary, is attended by a crowd of 30–50,000, but engenders protests from democratic and Jewish groups.

17 September The last Russian troops leave Poland on the 54th anniversary of the Soviet entry. General Władysław Sikorski, leader of the Polish government-in-exile in Paris and London 1940–43, is reburied in a state funeral in Krakow. It had been his final wish to be buried in a Poland free of foreign domination.

1994

29 April   The Czech Republic passes legislation allowing limited restitution of property to Jews dispossessed during the war.

4 May   800,000 people participate in a general strike in Bulgaria in a protest against low wages and high prices.

1 August   Georgi Atanasov, Bulgaria's Communist prime minister, 1986–90, and imprisoned for corruption in 1992, is pardoned on humanitarian grounds.

1995

5 February   Four Austrian gypsies are killed by a bomb near Oberwart in the Burgenland.

19 March   The Hungarian and Slovak prime ministers, Gyula Horn and Vladimir Mečiar, sign a Treaty of Friendship and Cooperation in Paris in the presence of the French prime minister, Edouard Balladur. 4,000 people demonstrate in Budapest against the treaty, which they maintain is a betrayal of the Hungarian minority in Slovakia.

18 October	The Czech Republic's Chamber of Deputies again votes to extend the screening or 'lustration' law which bans former secret police agents and senior Communist officials from holding public office. President Havel had sought unsuccessfully to veto the extension.
15 November	The Slovak National Council (parliament) approves a law reasserting that Slovak is the nation's only official language.
15–16 December	Albania arrests fourteen prominent members of the former Communist regime on charges of genocide and organising political deportations.

1996

28 March	Formal court proceedings open against General Wojciech Jaruzelski and eleven others in connection with the killing of 44 demonstrators by security forces when he was Polish defence minister.
29 March	President Yeltsin of Russia speculates that the accord between Russia, Belarus, Kazakhstan and Kyrgyzstan may mark the beginning of a 'new community open to other states . . . perhaps, for example, Bulgaria'. His remarks stimulate intense controversy in Bulgaria.
24 May	An Albanian court sentences three former Communist officials to death for crimes against humanity.
26 May–16 June	The Albanian general elections are won by the ruling Democratic Party among widespread charges of electoral malpractice.

1997

10 January	The governing Bulgarian Socialist Party votes against debating the opposition's 'Declaration for Bulgaria's Salvation'. The opposition initiates a parliamentary boycott and protesters break into the National Assembly. Some 200 demonstrators are injured outside during a night of demonstrations.
23 January	The Albanian People's Assembly bans pyramid schemes with a penalty of up to twenty years' imprisonment for operators. Most such schemes had, however, already collapsed. (See Glossary at 10.3.)
26 January	The Albanian president is given special powers to deal with the public disorder generated by the collapse of pyramid schemes.
5 February	A further Albanian pyramid scheme, Gjallica, based in the city of Vlorë, collapses with debts of some US$145 million.

64

Government authority in Vlorë collapses also, and is only maintained in Tiranë through recourse to violence.

10 February   Two people are killed and 25 are seriously injured when police fire on demonstrators in Vlorë. Most of the police, however, abandon the city. Mass arrests follow in the ensuing days.

1 March   The Albanian People's Assembly declares a national state of emergency in the light of armed rebellion across the south of the country. President Berisha dismisses the prime minister, Alexander Meksi.

6 March   The remaining 3,800 employees of the Gdánsk shipyard, the 1980 birthplace of *Solidarność*, demonstrate against its announced closure. It had been technically bankrupt since 1996, but is part salvaged on 20 March to become a subsidiary of Szczecin.

9 March   Following mediation by the EU and the Organisation for Security and Cooperation in Europe (OSCE), President Berisha agrees to form a broadly based Albanian government of national reconciliation.

12 March   Tiranë slides into anarchy, and more than twenty people are killed in the ensuing days. A measure of order is restored by 19 May, but some 10,000 Albanian refugees flee to Italy.

15 March   President Berisha pardons Fatos Nano, Albanian prime minister in 1991, for the offences of which he had been found guilty in 1994.

29 March   The UN Security Council votes in favour of an OSCE proposal that individual states be permitted to assist the Albanian government in restoring order.

8 April   The Slovak government issues a statement accusing President Havel of the Czech Republic of 'insults and lack of esteem' for the Slovak prime minister, Vladimir Mečiar, and demands an apology. President Havel had talked of the prime minister's 'customary paranoia'.

11 April   Advance units of the Italian-led Multinational Protection Force for Albania secure Tiranë Airport.

13 April   The exiled Albanian pretender, Leka Zogu, returns to Tiranë and calls for a referendum on the restoration of the monarchy.

25–27 April   President Arpád Goncz pays the first-ever visit to Romania by a Hungarian head of state. Some 1,000 people demonstrate in protest in the Romanian city of Cluj, the capital of Transylvania.

27 April   President Havel describes the relations between the Czech Republic and Slovakia as 'polite but very cold'.

65

4 June	Pope John Paul II on an eleven-day visit to Poland declares in Kalisz that Poland should outlaw abortion and that any nation which permits it deserves to be described as a barbarian civilisation.
18 July	The Albanian Socialist Party, the reformed Communist Party, returns to power with the formal announcement of the results of the tumultuous general election held in June–July. It has won 101 of the 155 seats in the People's Assembly. The state of emergency is lifted on 24 July.
11 August	The last members of the Multinational Protection Force leave Albania, and the operation ends formally on 14 August. Much of Albania nevertheless remains lawless.
14 October	Albania drops the charges of genocide against Ramiz Alia, its last Communist president.
17 December	The Polish *Sejm* votes to accept a ruling by the Constitutional Tribunal to rescind the legislation of 1996 legalising abortion on social or economic grounds. The SLD announces that it will oppose the decision, which effectively restores the restrictive legislation of 1993.

1998

5 February	Polish and Jewish leaders sign an agreement on the development and preservation of the former Auschwitz (Oswiecim) and Birkenau concentration camps. The agreement provides for the re-siting of all Christian symbols, including the 1979 Cross marking the visit of Pope John Paul II, several hundred yards away from the Auschwitz camp together with a relocated Carmelite convent. (See also Part 3.3.)
22 March	Cardinal Jozef Glemp, Roman Catholic Primate of Poland, announces that the Roman Catholic Church will not allow the removal of the Cross marking the Pope's 1979 visit to Oswiecim.
22 August	Six leading members of the opposition Democratic Party of Albania are arrested and charged with crimes against humanity during the previous year's civil disorder.
12 September	Azem Hajdari, a prominent member of the opposition Democratic Party of Albania, is assassinated in Tiranë. The ensuing rioting in the capital threatens to reduce the country to chaos.
14 September	Supporters of the Albanian opposition mount an unsuccessful coup.
3 October	The Pope overrides the objections of Jewish groups and beatifies Cardinal Stepinać, wartime Roman Catholic Primate

of Croatia. He had been found guilty in 1946 of collaboration with the Germans, the Italians and the *Ustaša*.

8 October   The opposition maintains its boycott of the Albanian assembly.

21 October   Bulgaria closes its criminal enquiry into the 1978 assassination of Markov in London. The assassination had been widely alleged to be at the behest of the Bulgarian secret service.

1999

4 January   A coal miners' strike in the Jiu Valley leads to Romania's worst civil disorder since 1991.

11 January   The Czech government announces that it will veto the erection of a fence in the town of Usti nad Labem, deemed to be an attempt to create a gypsy ghetto. The Romany Rainbow organisation agrees, however, to such a fence on 15 April.

22 January   President Constantinescu threatens to introduce a state of emergency if the coal miners' dispute is not resolved.

5 February   Leka Zogu, the son of the late ex-King Zog of Albania, is arrested in South Africa for the illegal possession of munitions. They had allegedly been assembled in 1979 for a proposed attack on the Communist government and might have been kept for the abortive 1997 royalist coup.

15 February   The Romanian miners' leader, Miron Cosma, is sentenced to eighteen years' imprisonment by the Supreme Court for 'undermining state authority' in the September 1991 riots. He leads a protest march of 4,000 Jiu Valley miners the next day but is arrested on 17 February. The protest is directed at IMF-supported plans for the restructuring of the mining industry.

5 March   The chairman of the Slovak National Party, Jan Slota, calls at a rally in Kysucke Nove Mesto for Budapest to be flattened if Hungarian language and culture make any further progress in Slovakia.

early June   President Constantinescu of Romania immediately rejects a call by a group of Romanian and ethnic Hungarian intellectuals for autonomy and self-government for Transylvania and the Banat region. He maintains that he will never accept proposals compromising the 'sovereignty, unity, or indivisibility of Romanian territory'.

28 August   The mausoleum in Sofia, which until 1990 had contained the embalmed body of Bulgaria's first Communist leader, Georgi Dimitrov, is demolished. The Bulgarian Socialist Party (the reformed Communist Party) maintains that the decision is political.

2000

3 February   The former Romanian prime minister, Radu Vasile, establishes the new far-right Romanian People's Party. Its manifesto claims that the party is based on 'the central role of the nation and the church, authoritarianism and rejection of multiculturalism' and it continues that 'suspicion of foreigners should be thought of as a natural instinct'.

4 February   The far-right Freedom Party (*Freiheit Partei Österreichs*) becomes a member of Austria's new federal government coalition. Its charismatic leader, Jörg Haider, had earlier expressed sympathy for Hitler, and was a highly controversial figure inside the country. The EU suspends bilateral political relations with Austria.

6 March   Vaclav Havel, the Czech president, urges Madeleine Albright, the US Secretary of State, to stand for the Czech presidency when he stands down in 2003. Madeleine Albright is Czech by birth and fluent in the language, but only lived in the former Czechoslovakia as a small child.

6 November   The resignation of a third minister from the Austrian far-right populist Freedom Party of Jörg Haider puts in question the future of the ruling Austrian federal government, the future of the Party and the future of Jörg Haider himself.

2001

4 January   Poland expresses its concern at the confirmed stationing of Russian tactical nuclear missiles in the Kaliningrad enclave since mid-2000.

17 June   The National Movement Simeon II, established by the former king two months previously, wins some 45 per cent of the vote in the Bulgarian national elections.

24 July   Simeon Saxe-Coburg-Gotha, the former King Simeon II, is sworn in as Bulgaria's prime minister.

16 October   The trial opens of General Wojciech Jaruzelski, the former Polish president.

2.6.2 THE DISINTEGRATION OF YUGOSLAVIA AND ITS AFTERMATH

1989

28 June   Slobodan Milošević addresses a million Serbs at a nationalist rally at the Kosovo Polje battlefield on the 600th anniversary of the final defeat of medieval Serbia by the Turks. He is to be elected president of Serbia in Serbia's first multi-party election since before the Second World War.

1990

2 July   The Slovene Assembly adopts a 'declaration of sovereignty'.

2 July   114 of the 130 ethnic-Albanian members of the Kosovo provincial Assembly vote for full republican status for Kosovo. The Serbian National Assembly declares the vote invalid and unanimously votes to dissolve the Kosovo Assembly. Direct Serbian rule is imposed.

23 December   Slovenia holds a referendum on independence and 88.5 per cent of the votes cast are in favour.

1991

25 June   Slovenia declares its independence from Yugoslavia. A brief outbreak of fighting with the Yugoslav National Army is concluded by a ceasefire in the July.

25 June   Croatia declares its independence from Yugoslavia. The Yugoslav National Army enters the republic and heavy fighting breaks out between Croats and ethnic Serbs.

8 September   Macedonia proclaims its sovereignty.

25 September   The UN Security Council imposes a mandatory arms embargo on the whole of Yugoslavia.

8 October   Croatian and Slovenian independence becomes effective.

15 October   The National Assembly of Bosnia–Hercegovina adopts a Memorandum on Sovereignty. The Serb deputies abstain.

8 November   Trade sanctions are applied on Yugoslavia, but are confined to Serbia after two weeks.

19 December   Rebel Serbs declare independence in the Krajina and Slavonia regions of Croatia.

1992

15 January   The EU recognises Croatia and Slovenia as independent states, on German insistence.

29 February–1 March	Bosnia–Hercegovina holds a referendum on independence. 99.78 per cent of the votes cast are in favour, but the Serbs have largely boycotted the referendum.
27 March	Bosnia's Serbs proclaim a separate republic of their own, *Republika Srpska*, within Bosnia–Hercegovina.
5 April	Bosnia–Hercegovina proclaims its independence from Yugoslavia.
7 April	The EU and America recognise the independence of Bosnia–Hercegovina. War breaks out between its government and the Serb minority, which forms more than 30 per cent of the new state's population. The capital, Sarajevo, is besieged by local Serbs.
27 April	The two remaining republics (Montenegro and Serbia) of the former Socialist Federal Republic of Yugoslavia proclaim the Federal Republic of Yugoslavia with a new constitution.
24 May	Ibrahim Rugova is pronounced president of the 'Republic of Kosovo' proclaimed by the Serbian province's ethnic Albanians. It achieves recognition from Albania alone, which declares that it will be forced to intervene if the Serbs resort to 'ethnic cleansing'.
30 May	Comprehensive United Nations sanctions and an EU trade embargo are imposed on Yugoslavia for its role in the continuing civil war in Bosnia–Hercegovina.
29 June	The UN Security Council unanimously votes for the deployment of UN forces in Bosnia–Hercegovina to secure the functioning of Sarajevo airport and to protect humanitarian aid missions.
3 July	Bosnian Croat nationalists proclaim the Croatian Community of Herceg–Bosna.
2 August	The nationalist HDZ wins independent Croatia's first general election.
6 August	Russia, followed by Albania, Bulgaria and Turkey, recognises Macedonian independence. Greece, which is trying to hinder Europe's recognition of Macedonia, protests.
13 August	The UN Security Council authorises the use of force if necessary to ensure the delivery of humanitarian aid to civilians under siege in Bosnia–Hercegovina.
20 August	Macedonia requires all former Yugoslav citizens who have lived there for less than twenty years to leave the country.
5 October	President Tudjman of Croatia and President Dobrica Ćosić of Yugoslavia agree to an 'orderly' transfer of populations if Bosnia should be partitioned into ethnic sectors.
20 November	Macedonia declares its independence from Yugoslavia.

1993

14 January   Attempts in Geneva to achieve peace in Bosnia fail, and war breaks out between the Muslims and the local Croats, who had previously been allied against the Serbs.

22 January   The Croatian Army opens an offensive to reclaim part of the Serbian Krajina.

7 April   Macedonia is admitted to the UN under the name of Former Yugoslav Republic of Macedonia.

1994

5 February   At least 68 people are killed by an unidentified mortar bomb in the marketplace of Sarajevo. The Bosnian Serbs deny any responsibility.

10 February   NATO imposes a twenty-kilometre heavy-weapons exclusion zone around Sarajevo and threatens air strikes on any such weapons remaining after 20 February. NATO attacks Bosnian Serb forces at Gorazde.

16 February   Greece imposes a trade ban on Macedonia, reflecting its anger at the use of the name Macedonia for a nation outside Greece.

23 February   A ceasefire is declared between the Bosnian Croats and Bosnian government forces.

28 February   NATO shoots down four Serb bombers for attacking a Bosnian government munitions factory at Novi Travnik in defiance of the no-fly zone imposed over Bosnia–Hercegovina.

18 March   The Washington agreement reached between the Bosnian government and the Croats envisages a Federation of Bosnian Muslims and Croats, associated in a long-term confederation with Croatia. The Serbs veto participation in the confederation.

22 April   Bosnian Serb forces capture the eastern enclave of Gorazde, a UN-protected 'safe area', after a massive assault. Civilian losses are heavy.

26 April   A Contact Group is formed of diplomats from America, Britain, France, Germany and Russia, to work for a ceasefire in Bosnia–Hercegovina.

30 May   Croatia introduces a new currency, the *kuna*, which also circulates in the Croat areas of Bosnia–Hercegovina. Wartime Croatia under Dr Pavelić and the *Ustaša* (see Glossary) used a currency of the same name and Gypsies, Jews and Serbs protest.

9 June   A ceasefire agreement is signed in Bosnia–Hercegovina between the Croats, the Muslims and the Serbs, but it unravels within days.

6 July	The Contact Group puts forward peace proposals with a map allocating the Bosnian government 51 per cent of Bosnia–Hercegovina and the Bosnian Serbs 49 per cent. The government accepts the map but the Bosnian Serbs reject it.
5 August	Yugoslavia imposes an economic blockade on the Bosnian Serbs for rejecting the peace proposals put forward by the Contact Group.
21 August	Bosnian government troops capture the northwestern enclave of Bihać, a UN-declared 'safe area', and expel the rebel Muslim leader, Fikret Abdić.
11 November	America announces that its forces will no longer enforce the international arms embargo against Bosnia–Hercegovina.
18 November	Bosnian Serb aircraft bomb Bihać with napalm.
21 November	NATO attacks Croatian territory for the first time by bombing the Udbina airfield in the Krajina, with the objective of discouraging Serb aircraft from bombing Bihać.
31 December	A four-month Bosnian ceasefire, negotiatied by former President Carter of America, is signed and comes into force the next day. It is to be ignored, however, both by the Croatian Serbs and the rebel Muslim forces of Fikret Abdić.

1995

12 January	The Croatian president, Franjo Tudjman, gives formal notice that the mandate of the 14,000 UN peacekeepers in UNPROFOR would be terminated on 31 March. He maintains that the 'present situation in the [Serb-]occupied territories [of Croatia] is wholly unacceptable'. The self-declared 'Republic of Serbian Krajina' declared in December 1991 is predominantly ethnic Serb, but represents 30 per cent of Croatia's territory.
15 February	An ethnic Albanian university, deemed illegal by the Macedonian government in December 1994, is formally established in a ceremony in the village of Mala Recica near Tetovo. Riots ensue two days later in which one rioter is killed and fifteen injured.
12 March	President Tudjman withdraws his termination of the UNPROFOR mandate in Croatia but its continuation is to be on much revised terms.
1–2 May	The Croatian Army captures Western Slavonia from the ethnic Serb rebels who had held it since December 1991.
7 May	Fighting flares up again in Sarajevo between Bosnian Serbs and Muslims.

8 May   In the presence of President Milošević of Serbia, President Tudjman of Croatia sketches out on the back of a menu, at a VE-Day banquet in London's Guildhall, a division of Bosnia between the two countries, which is how he envisages the region as looking ten years from then. The sketch is for the benefit of Paddy Ashdown, the leader of the British Liberal Democrats.

12 July   Thousands of Bosnian Serb troops enter the UN 'safe haven' of Srebrenica, which is defended by 150 lightly armed Dutch peace-keepers. The Muslim population is rounded up and the men and the boys are separated from the women. At least 2,500, and probably more than 5,000, of the males are subsequently shot.

4 August   The Croatian Army invades the Krajina and captures the whole region by 9 August. Some 150,000 Serbs flee or are forcibly expelled, some are killed as they flee, and many villages are burned. The Bosnian Serbs and the Serb opposition criticise President Milošević of Serbia for not responding militarily. The capture of Slavonia and of the Krajina creates some 300,000 Serb refugees in all. The Americans and the Germans broadly support the invasion, but Britain, France and Russia condemn it. America denies allegations that it had trained the Croatian Army, but admits that commercial consultants are advising the army under American licence.

30 August   NATO initiates a bombing campaign against Bosnian Serb forces and positions.

3 October   President Gligorov of Macedonia is seriously injured in an assassination attempt in Skopje which kills two.

12 October   A negotiated Bosnian ceasefire comes into force.

15 October   Greek and Macedonian representatives put their names to an accord on mutual relations, in Skopje. Macedonia had adopted a less sensitive symbol for its national flag, and Greece had qualified its objections to the use of the name 'Macedonia'. Greece lifts its trade embargo.

21 November   The prime ministers of Bosnia–Hercegovina, Croatia and Serbia initial the Dayton Peace Accords at Dayton, Ohio. America and Germany ask the United Nations to lift sanctions on Yugoslavia.

14 December   'The Peace Agreement on Bosnia–Hercegovina' is signed at the Elysée Palace in Paris by President Izetbegović of Bosnia–Hercegovina, President Tudjman of Croatia and President Milošević of Serbia. President Clinton of America, John Major, British prime minister, President Chirac of France,

73

Chancellor Kohl of Germany, Viktor Chernomyrdin, Russian prime minister, and Felipe Gonzalez for the EU sign as sponsors.

The Agreement provides for a central government responsible for foreign affairs and commerce, together with a Muslim-Croat Federation with 51 per cent of the national territory and a Serb Republic with 49 per cent, both being responsible for their internal affairs. Parallel relations between Croatia and Serbia and those entities are limited by a provision that they shall respect the sovereignty and territorial integrity of Bosnia.

20 December A NATO force of 63,000 men (IFOR) is deployed for twelve months to enforce the Paris Peace Agreement and to maintain a separation zone between the two Croat-Muslim and Serb entities.

1996

14 August President Izetbegović of Bosnia–Hercegovina and President Tudjman of Croatia agree in Geneva to dissolve the Croatian Community of Herceg–Bosna.

November The Serbian opposition parties accuse Slobodan Milošević of electoral fraud and their supporters march on Belgrade. Milošević had refused to recognise the opposition's gains in the local polls.

20 December A new NATO stabilisation force of 30,000 men (SFOR) is deployed in Bosnia–Hercegovina on the expiry of IFOR's mandate. Czech, Polish and Russian troops also are attached to SFOR.

1997

2 January The Serbian Orthodox Church offers its support to the Serbian opposition.

4 February President Milošević backs down after 88 days by recognising the victories of the *Zajedno* opposition coalition in the Serbian municipal elections of November 1996.

10 February Bosnian Croats fire on some 200 Muslims trying to travel between the Muslim and Croat areas of the city of Mostar. At least one Muslim is killed and 30 injured. The city's joint police force collapses.

28 February President Zoran Lilić of Yugoslavia and Momčilo Krajisnik for the Bosnian Serb Republic sign an accord on 'special ties' to increase trade and cooperation.

22 May The Macedonian Constitutional Court rules that the Albanian flag may not be flown in Macedonia. The ruling provokes demonstrations by ethnic Albanians on the following day, and the flag continues to be flown.

1998

12 January	Some 15,000 supporters of the outgoing Montenegrin president, Momir Bulatović, try to storm government buildings in Podgorica on the eve of his successor's inauguration.
15 January	All demonstrations are banned throughout Montenegro.
15 January	Croatia formally resumes control of eastern Slavonia, the last Serb enclave in Croatia, captured by Croatian Serbs in 1991.
21 January	The Yugoslav prime minister, Radoje Kontić, negotiates an agreement whereby demonstrations in Montenegro are called off in return for elections in May.
31 January	The People's Assembly of the *Republika Srpska* moves the seat of government from Pale to Banja Luka.
11 February	The former Montenegrin president, Momir Bulatović, is accused under the criminal law pursuant to the January riots of attacking the constitutional order.
28 February	The newly formed, separatist Kosovo Liberation Army (UCK) kills four Serb policemen in the village of Likosane in central Kosovo. The Serb police kill 24 ethnic Albanians in the area in retaliation, claiming that they are UCK members, which the villagers deny.
2 March	50,000 ethnic Albanians demonstrate in protest in Pristina, the capital of Kosovo. America condemns Serbia's use of force, and threatens to re-impose full sanctions on Yugoslavia. Its senior envoy to the Balkans, Robert Gelbard, had, however, earlier described the UCK as a 'terrorist organisation', a description which the ethnic Albanian leaders claimed had encouraged the Serb retaliation.
5 March	President Milošević of Yugoslavia insists on the normalisation of relations between the EU and Yugoslavia before the EU can be allowed to open a monitoring mission in Kosovo.
5–6 March	Serb security forces kill 53 ethnic Albanians around the village of Lausa, 40 kilometres west of Pristina. They include women and children, but all are alleged to be UCK members.
9 March	The Contact Group on the former Yugoslavia, comprising the foreign ministers of America, Britain, France, Germany and Italy, and a Russian deputy foreign minister, meeting in London, threatens to freeze Serbia's foreign assets and to impose a range of sanctions on Yugoslavia if Serbian security

75

forces are not withdrawn by 19 March and talks opened on the future status of Kosovo. The Russians, however, express considerable reserve over the use of sanctions.

13 March   50,000 ethnic Albanian students and trade unionists demonstrate without interference in Pristina.

19 March   Rival Serb and ethnic Albanian demonstrators clash in Pristina.

10 June   Tens of thousands of ethnic Albanians demonstrate in Skopje, the Macedonian capital, in support of the Kosovo Liberation Army (UCK).

24 June   The Kosovo Liberation Army (UCK) seizes the Belacevac opencast coal mine. It is a significant blow to the Serbian economy. The mine is recaptured by Serbian forces, who kill ten UCK members, on 29 June.

3 September   The Yugoslav army shells a number of villages near Prizren in its fight against the UCK. There is speculation that Yugoslavia is seeking to crush the UCK before the pressure from NATO becomes unacceptable.

23 September   The UN Security Council adopts Resolution 1199 which demands an immediate ceasefire in Kosovo and condemns 'all acts of violence by any party'. It also expresses grave concern 'at the recent intense fighting in Kosovo and in particular the excessive and indiscriminate use of force by Serbian security forces'.

24 September   NATO approves an 'activation warning' authorising the Supreme Allied Commander, General Wesley Clark, to ask member states for the forces necessary to execute military intervention on Kosovo.

28 September   Mirko Marjanović, the Serbian prime minister, declares to the Serb National Assembly that 'peace reigns in Kosovo . . . as of today all anti-terrorist activities have ended'. He also undertakes that special police units will return to barracks as demanded by both American and EU diplomats.

30 September   The British foreign secretary, Robin Cook, calls for an emergency meeting of the UN Security Council to condemn three massacres in Kosovo in which Serb forces had reportedly killed 35 people. He says they are 'not an act of war [but] plain cold murder'.

5 October   The American envoy, Richard Holbrook, outlines a deal to avoid air attacks. NATO gives Slobodan Milošević four days in which to cease his offensive against the ethnic Albanians in Kosovo.

6 October   Russia warns that it will veto any new UN resolution authorising military action over Kosovo.

12 October	President Milošević pledges himself to comply with UN demands and to accept a 2,000-strong international observer force in Kosovo under OSCE command.
17 October	The UCK breaks its ceasefire, announced on 8 October, by killing three policemen at Orlate.
24 October	General Wesley Clark warns President Milošević that Yugoslavia faces air strikes unless it removes its forces from Kosovo by 27 October.
27 October	NATO suspends its threat in the light of Yugoslav military withdrawals from Kosovo.
6 November	The fragile ceasefire in Kosovo is broken when five ethnic-Albanians are killed in exchanges with Serb police. Two police are murdered in a revenge attack on 9 November.
14 December	31 UCK guerrillas are killed by Yugoslav troops near Prizren as they try to smuggle guns into Kosovo from Albania. Perhaps 30 people are killed during the month in further fighting.

1999

2 February	NATO threatens to bomb Yugoslavia if Serbia does not attend the proposed Rambouillet peace talks on the future of Kosovo.
6 February	Peace talks open at Rambouillet, France, on a Contact Group peace plan for Kosovo. The plan would disband all military groups, including the Kosovo Liberation Army (UCK), reduce the Serb police force to 2,500 men and the Yugoslav Army presence to 1,500, and introduce a NATO peace-keeping force of some 35,000 men. It would effectively terminate Serbian jurisdiction over its Kosovo province.
14 February	The American secretary of state, Madeleine Albright, attends the Rambouillet talks. She repeats that NATO will bomb Serbia if the Contact Group peace plan is not accepted.
23 February	The ethnic Albanian and Serb delegations at Rambouillet agree 'in principle' to autonomy for Kosovo, but no agreement is signed.
1 March	Hasim Thaci, head of the political directorate of the ethnic Albanian Kosovo Liberation Army (UCK), is appointed head of the 'provisional government in Kosovo'.
2 March	Adem Demaci, a hardliner who had blocked the signature by the ethnic Albanian side of the Rambouillet peace plan in the February, resigns as a negotiator.
10 March	President Milošević of Yugoslavia refuses to accept the stationing of a 28,000-strong NATO peace-keeping force in Kosovo, as envisaged in the Rambouillet plan.

19 March	The British and the French terminate the further talks in Paris on the Rambouillet plan when the talks fail to achieve agreement with the Serbian delegation led by President Milutinović. An agreement had been signed by the Albanian delegation.
	The collapse of the talks leads to a drive by Serbian security forces to clear ethnic Albanians from strategically significant areas of northern Kosovo adjacent to Serbia proper.
20 March	The NATO Supreme Allied Commander in Europe maintains that more than 60,000 ethnic Albanians have been displaced in Kosovo since December 1998.
23 March	In the face of continuing failure to persuade President Milošević to accept the Rambouillet plan, NATO announces that it is to launch air attacks on Serbia. Yugoslavia mobilises its army.
24 March	NATO opens its bombing campaign against Serbia. Yugoslavia responds by declaring a state of war and embarking on a systematic campaign to clear northern and western Kosovo of ethnic Albanians. The NATO action is allegedly to avert a humanitarian disaster in Kosovo. The British all-party House of Commons Defence Committee is to conclude on 24 October 2000, however, that 'all the evidence suggests that plans to initiate the air campaign hastened the disaster'.
2 April	Albania and Macedonia appeal for urgent aid to cope with the flood of ethnic Albanian refugees from Kosovo. By the end of the month there are some 300,000 in Albania and 160,000 in Macedonia.
12 April	The Yugoslav parliament votes to apply to join a pan-slav union with Russia and Belarus. The vote has little practical significance.
12 April	Ten train passengers are killed and sixteen injured when a NATO air-launched missile hits a railway bridge. The pilot had allegedly not seen the approaching train.
23 April	NATO launches a missile attack on State Television in the centre of Belgrade. At least ten people are killed including make-up girls, tea boys and technicians.
29 April	Yugoslavia brings proceedings against several NATO members, including Britain, before the International Court of Justice in The Hague, arguing that the NATO intervention is illegal. Britain successfully resists the Court's jurisdiction on a legal technicality.
1 May	At least 23 passengers are killed when a NATO missile directed at the Luzane bridge north of Pristina hits a civilian bus.

7 May	American NATO bombers attack the Chinese Embassy in Belgrade, killing four Chinese and injuring twenty. The Americans claim that they were intending to attack the Yugoslav Federal Directorate of Supply and Procurement, but were misled by an out-of-date map. It is a claim the Chinese decline to accept. It is disclosed later that the embassy was a centre for Chinese intelligence gathering in Europe.
27 May	NATO drops cluster bombs by mistake on the centre of Niš, rather than on a military building near the airport. At least 33 civilians are killed and scores of others seriously injured. In response to suggestions that cluster bombs are banned under the Geneva Convention, a NATO spokesman claims that their use is allowed 'in open countryside against ground troops'.
27 May	President Milošević is indicted for war crimes by the UN International Tribunal for the Former Yugoslavia. It is the first time that a sitting head of state has been so indicted. The Tribunal had been established by the UN Security Council in 1993. Its prosecution receives about a third of the UN's annual sponsorship of the court, and its members and judges enjoy the same status as diplomats. The defence does not enjoy the same official status or resources.
late May/ early June	British prime minister Tony Blair persuades a reluctant American President Clinton to accept the possibility of a ground invasion of Kosovo.
3 June	President Milošević accepts a Kosovo peace plan tabled jointly by President Ahtisaari of Finland on behalf of the EU and Viktor Chernomyrdin on behalf of Russia. All Serb forces are to be withdrawn from Kosovo, an international security presence with a substantial NATO component is to be deployed there under UN auspices, and refugees are to be allowed to return in safety. Kosovo will, however, remain formally part of Serbia, and the terms of the joint plan are more favourable to Serbia than those offered at Rambouillet, insofar as NATO forces are to be restricted to Kosovo and there is no requirement for a referendum on the future status of the province.
6 June	The cost to NATO members of the bombing campaign on Yugoslavia is estimated at US$7 billion. The cost of the damage inflicted by NATO on Serbian infrastructure is however to be put at some US$50–150 billion. Some 1,250 civilians have been killed.
9 June	NATO and Yugoslav delegations meeting at Kumanovo sign a Military Technical Agreement to implement the agreed plan.
10 June	The UN Security Council adopts Resolution 1244 approving the international peace plan for Kosovo.

11–13 June	International (KFOR) troops enter Kosovo.
20 June	Yugoslav forces complete their withdrawal from Kosovo. Many ethnic Serbs flee with them, as ethnic Albanian refugees return. The damage inflicted on the military appears to have been appreciably less than NATO had supposed.
24 June	According to a report published in the authoritative British newspaper, *The Times*, the Serbs claim to have lost only 13 tanks during the NATO air attacks. NATO had claimed more than 120.
2 November	Montenegro further distances itself from Serbia within the Yugoslav Federation by adopting the German Mark (DM) as its national currency.

2000

20 January	The funeral in Belgrade of the assassinated Serbian warlord, Arkan (Zeljko Raznatović), attracts the largest crowds since Tito's in 1980. Many have come from the Bosnian Serb Republic and from Montenegro, his family's native republic.
8 February	Pavle Bulatović, the Yugoslav defence minister, is assassinated in Belgrade. The motive is unknown. He was a senior member of the Socialist People's Party, the Montenegrin opposition party.
July	The Yugoslav government changes the federal constitution so as to make the presidency and membership of the upper house directly elected.
24 September	The first round of the Yugoslav presidential election results in the effective defeat of Slobodan Milošević by Vojislav Koštunica.
30 September	The Yugoslav Federal Electoral Commission demands a rerun of the presidential poll.
2 October	Tens of thousands of protesters stage a nationwide day of protest across Yugoslavia in an attempt to force Slobodan Milošević to accept defeat. His support in the media begins to crumble, but he still behaves as if the second round of presidential voting will go ahead on 8 October. Vojislav Koštunica expresses disappointment at both American and Russian attempts to reduce tension in Serbia, and maintains that the Serbs must resolve the crisis on their own.
3 October	The Serbian government begins to arrest the ringleaders of the growing campaign of civil disobedience which paralyses the country for a second day. The opposition plans to bring hundreds of thousands of Serbs into Belgrade to bolster the capital's own protests.

4 October	The Yugoslav supreme court annuls the 24 September election result on the grounds that there had been irregularities in the 'voting process, counting and confirmation'. The significance of the court's ruling is unclear, and the opposition sets a deadline of 6 October for Milošević to concede defeat. Tens of thousands of protesters demonstrate in Belgrade and 30,000 more disperse 800 riot police at the Kolubara mines.
5 October	Slobodan Milošević resigns when the Yugoslav army and police side with the protesters. Vast crowds of demonstrators had earlier set fire to the federal parliament and Radio Television Serbia as symbols of the Milošević regime.
8 October	Vojislav Koštunica is sworn in as president of the Federal Republic of Yugoslavia.
9 October	Activists storm a number of factories, banks, universities and civil service offices across Yugoslavia to expel their former chiefs. Fearing possible anarchy, the leaders of the Democratic Opposition of Serbia distance themselves from direct action.
9–10 October	The EU lifts its oil embargo and flight ban on Serbia following the swearing in of Vojislav Koštunica as president of the Federal Republic of Yugoslavia. America follows suit. The EU proposes that Yugoslavia participate in the stabilisation and association process for South-Eastern Europe, launched at the European Council in June 1999.
15 October	Chris Patten, EU external affairs commissioner, admits that more than £350,000 of EU money had been channelled covertly into Serbia's independent media prior to the September election to counter pro-Milošević propaganda in the state-controlled media.
15 October	Crown Prince Alexander of Yugoslavia meets President Koštunica in Belgrade to assess the prospects of restoring the monarchy. The president had been a self-proclaimed monarchist.
24 October	President Koštunica acknowledges that Yugoslavia's army and police had murdered many ethnic Albanians in Kosovo during 1999.
1 November	Britain expresses its concern to America at suggestions by American diplomats that Kosovo could become a fully independent state even under UN Resolution 1244, which guarantees the integrity of Yugoslavia and substantial autonomy for Kosovo. Britain does not wish to see the creation of any more mini-states in the region.
22 November	Ethnic Albanian separatists of the Liberation Army of Presevo, Bujanovac and Medvedjam (UCPMB), a splinter group of the

81

officially dissolved Kosovo Liberation Army, attack Serb targets in the Presevo Valley area of Serbia, adjacent to Kosovo. The attacks and the deaths are to continue despite UN and NATO attempts to restrain them.

25 November   Slobodan Milošević is re-elected leader of the Yugoslav Socialist Party.

2001

9 January   Biljana Plavsić, a former president of the *Republika Srpska* within Bosnia, gives herself up to the International Criminal Tribunal for the Former Yugoslavia in The Hague.
She is charged on 11 January with genocide and ethnic cleansing between July 1991 and December 1992.

3 February   The American secretary of state, Colin Powell, declines to meet President Djukanović of Montenegro, who has travelled to Washington for the purpose, because he does not wish to 'encourage the further changing of borders in the region'.

26 February   Dario Kordić, the former vice-president of the Bosnian Croat Republic, is sentenced in The Hague to 25 years' imprisonment for planning and instigating the ethnic cleansing of Muslims from Bosnia in 1992–93.

14 March   Fighting between rebel ethnic Albanians and the Macedonian Army spreads for the first time from remote rural areas to the outskirts of Tetovo, Macedonia's second city.

25 March   A fifth Balkan war appears possible as the Macedonian Army launches a full offensive against an ethnic Albanian rebel stronghold near Tetovo. Albanian rebels had been attacking Macedonian troops sporadically for a month, and could rely on supplies from Kosovo across the border which NATO, despite protestations to the contrary, had been unable to close.

28 March   The Macedonian Army continues its assaults on suspected positions of the Albanian National Liberation Army (NLA). The army enjoys the strong support of the country's slav majority, which fears partition to create a Greater Albania, but the condemnation of the Albanian minority which represents about a third of the population. The attacks appear to prove successful in their immediate objective. The Macedonian government maintains that it will open a dialogue to address ethnic Albanian demands for more constitutional rights and greater representation in the civil service, education and the state-run media. The likelihood of an agreed settlement is however questionable.

1 April   Slobodan Milošević is arrested in his villa in Belgrade by Yugoslav federal police following a three-day stand-off. Four police officers had been injured in an attempt to storm the villa the day before. He is accused before a Yugoslav court of corruption and of breaking the law so as to retain power, as well as of inciting his bodyguards to shoot at the officers who tried to arrest him.

2 April   Slobodan Milošević denies embezzlement, but admits that he covertly funded the Bosnian and Croat Serb Armies.

3 April   President Koštunica reiterates that federal Yugoslavia has no intention of handing Slobodan Milošević over to the Tribunal in The Hague. Both the president and his prime minister had expressed scepticism as to the impartiality of the Tribunal.

4 April   The British foreign secretary, Robin Cook, advises the federal Yugoslav president, Vojislav Koštunica, that the west will help Yugoslavia to rebuild its economy provided it in due course hands Slobodan Milošević over to the Tribunal in The Hague. The Tribunal, with the support of many in America, wants him handed over immediately.

5 April   The Serbian justice minister, Vladan Batić, declines to accept a warrant from the Tribunal in The Hague for the arrest of Slobodan Milošević. The court's registrar is referred to Momčilo Grubać, the Yugoslav federal justice minister.

Vladan Batić does, however, urge the Tribunal to prosecute Hashim Thaci, the former commander of the Kosovo Liberation Army (UCK) and other Kosovar Albanian leaders for the murder of Serb civilians.

8 April   The campaign by Croat nationalists to form a Bosnian Croat state spreads to Croatia. War veterans announce that they will blockade NATO bases on the Dalmatian coast supplying peacekeeping forces in Bosnia.

Their action is interpreted as retaliation for the seizure by UN officials, supported by Sfor soldiers, of the *Hercegovacke Banka* in Mostar. The bank was believed to have been financing the proposed Bosnian Croat state, and its closure prompts rioting by thousands of Bosnian Croats.

18 April   Colonel Dragan Obrenović, a Bosnian Serb, is accused at the Tribunal in The Hague of orchestrating the slaughter of more than 5,000 Muslim civilians near Srebrenica in 1995.

22 April   The pro-independence 'Victory for Montenegro' coalition, led by President Djukanović, wins 36 of the 77 seats in the Montenegrin parliamentary elections. The rival 'Together for

Yugoslavia' coalition wins 33 seats and only some 5,000 fewer votes.

25 April President Djukanović of Montenegro insists that his country will press ahead with independence, but that he will negotiate with Serbia rather than act unilaterally.

3 May The use of helicopter gunships and tanks by the Macedonian Army against ethnic Albanian rebels renews fears that Macedonia is slipping into civil war.

3 May Slobodan Milošević declines to accept an arrest warrant for war crimes issued by the Tribunal in The Hague. The warrant is left in the bars of his cell.

7 May Bosnian Serb rioters trap western diplomats in a building in Banja Luka in protest at ceremonies marking the start of the reconstruction of the city's sixteenth-century Ferhadija mosque, destroyed by Bosnian Serbs in May 1993.

7 May The Macedonian government steps back from plans to announce a state of war. Pressure from the EU and NATO had probably contributed to the decision.

24 May Some 4–5,000 Serb troops and paramilitary police complete the Serb return to the Presevo valley, the buffer zone in southern Serbia established by NATO as part of the 1999 peace agreement. The ethnic Albanian separatists of the Liberation Army of Presevo, Bujanovac and Medvedjam (UCPMB) raise little resistance.

24 May A political crisis erupts in Skopje when it is revealed that the ethnic Albanian party leaders, who had agreed twelve days earlier to join a new national coalition government, have made a peace deal with the rebels, and that the deal has been part-brokered by an American envoy of the Organisation for Security and Cooperation in Europe. The deal is condemned by the American Embassy in Skopje and by the British Secretary-General of NATO, who maintains that the rebels have no place in negotiations on Macedonia's future.

6 June Shots are fired at the office of the Macedonian president in Skopje, raising fears of a campaign of terror in the capital. The prime minister, Ljubco Georgievski, renews his call for the country to declare 'a state of war' on ethnic Albanian rebels: a measure which needs a two-thirds majority in parliament and would probably bring down his ruling coalition which includes two ethnic Albanian parties.

14 June America's President Bush, EU leaders and NATO broadly endorse the Macedonian president's proposals for a ceasefire, a partial amnesty for the ethnic Albanian rebels, and enhanced political representation for the ethnic Albanian minority. The rebels are seeking direct NATO military intervention.

17 June President Putin of Russia on a trip to Kosovo rules out any redrawing of Balkan borders as 'extremely dangerous and destructive'. Both he and President Koštunica had also attacked the UN plan for self-government in Kosovo unveiled by Hans Haekkerup, the UN's Kosovo governor in May, and President Putin maintains that: 'Too many concessions have been made to radicals . . . The legal framework of future self-government is raised almost to the standard of a constitution.' Local elections are scheduled for 17 November.

20 June Peace talks break down between the Macedonian government and ethnic Albanian rebels.

25 June Thousands of Macedonian nationalist demonstrators storm the presidential palace in Skopje in protest at a government ceasefire agreement with ethnic Albanian rebels in the village of Aracinovo. Their rallying cry is: 'Gas chambers for the Albanians!' The Macedonian Paramilitary 2000 group orders Albanian businesses in Skopje to close or face fire-bombing. The ceasefire agreement had been brokered by Javier Solana, the EU's security and foreign policy chief, and permitted ethnic Albanian rebels to retreat with their weapons under the escort of American KFOR troops. The deeply unpopular EU insists on a political settlement as a precondition of further aid.

25 June The Yugoslav government formally requests the Belgrade court to extradite former President Milošević to the Tribunal in The Hague, in accordance with a government decree.

27 June America announces that it will participate in a conference in Brussels on rebuilding Yugoslavia on 29 June, co-chaired by the European Commission and the World Bank, and give substantial financial aid, provided the Yugoslav government cooperates fully with the Tribunal in The Hague. It is envisaged that the conference will raise some $1.3 billion overall for reconstruction.

28 June The Yugoslav government hands former President Milošević over to the Tribunal in The Hague. The handover follows a ruling by Yugoslavia's Constitutional Court that the government's extradition request of 25 June breaches a constitutional ban on extraditing Yugoslav citizens. The Yugoslav prime minister calls the Court decision invalid. It appears that President Koštunica, who is a critic of the Tribunal, was not informed of the government's decision in advance.

6 July   The Serbian prime minister, Zoran Djindjić, admits that his decision to extradite Slobodan Milošević to The Hague may prompt the break-up of the Yugoslav federation. The federal prime minister, Zoran Zizić, had resigned in protest earlier in the week.

8 July   Four Croat cabinet ministers, all members of the Social Liberal Party, resign in protest at the government's decision to hand two generals over to the Tribunal in The Hague. The two generals are understood to be Rahim Ademi, a Kosovar Albanian who fought for Croatia, and Ante Gotovina, commander of the Croatian forces, 1991–95. Both are widely seen as national heroes in Croatia.

Mirko Condić, the Croatian veterans' leader, says that they will prevent any extradition, but General Ademi surrenders to the Tribunal voluntarily on 25 July.

23 July   Fighting breaks out again between the Macedonian Army and ethnic Albanian rebels in Tetovo.

10–12 August   Ten ethnic Albanians are killed and 22 houses and ancillary buildings burnt by security forces in the Macedonian village of Ljuboten, four miles north of Skopje. The government claims all the casualties were terrorists, but critics allege that it was a revenge raid for the earlier deaths of eighteen Macedonian soldiers in the vicinity.

13 August   Ethnic Albanian and slav politicians sign a framework agreement to bring the fighting in Macedonia to an end. The agreement increases the rights of the ethnic Albanian community, but many rebels, including a number from Kosovo, are likely to continue to strive for the union of all ethnic Albanians.

14 August   Ali Ahmeti, the leader of the ethnic Albanian National Liberation Army in Macedonia, signs an agreement with NATO on decommissioning and deployment. There are fears, however, that the agreement will not be observed by the radical Albanian National Army. Ali Ahmeti had been regarded by the west as a terrorist and still was by slav Macedonians. The Macedonian interior minister, Ljube Boskovski, is to maintain on state television on 20 August: 'He is nothing but a criminal responsible for crimes against humanity, committed against his people. Ali Ahmeti must be brought to the Macedonian independent courts and judged for crimes against humanity.'

15 August   NATO approves a first-phase deployment of 3,500 troops to Macedonia to prepare for the collection of up to 3,000 weapons to be surrendered by the ethnic Albanian National Liberation Army (NLA). The disarming is supposed to last for only 30 days. The troops will be lightly armed as they are intended neither to partition the country nor to enforce the weapons' handover.

16 August The leader of Macedonia's ethnic Albanians, Ali Ahmeti, declares that he will not hand over any weapons until the peace agreement has been ratified by the Macedonian parliament.

21 August It is alleged by western defence sources that the Macedonian Army is rapidly increasing its stockpile of weapons with semi-secret deliveries from Russia and the Ukraine. It is estimated, however, that there are some 600,000 weapons available to the rebels on the Albanian black market which had been stolen during the disorder of 1997. A bomb partly destroys a fourteenth-century Orthodox monastery near Tetovo, but it is unclear who is responsible.

23 August NATO launches its operation to collect 'one weapon' from each member of the ethnic Albanian National Liberation Army in Macedonia. The army has some 2,500–6,000 men.

30 August Slobodan Milošević makes his second appearance before the Tribunal in The Hague. The Tribunal's chief prosecutor, Carla del Ponte, declares that she is to submit indictments for genocide in Bosnia, and perhaps Croatia, on 1 October and that the trial is likely to start in autumn 2002. Slobodan Milošević is currently charged with mass murder, deportation and persecution of ethnic Albanians in Kosovo in 1999. He maintains, however, that the charges are false, the Tribunal illegal and his imprisonment unlawful. Some 45 other alleged war criminals of all the former Yugoslavia's ethnic and religious groups are held in Scheveningen with him.

9 September EU foreign ministers agree on sending a 'small but robust' force of probably more than a thousand men to Macedonia to defend the unarmed international observers from the EU and the Organisation for Security and Cooperation in Europe. The observers are intended to help prevent renewed violence between the Macedonian Army and ethnic Albanian rebels. NATO troops are not wanted by Macedonia's own Security Council.

12 September British military sources report that about one-third of the weapons so far handed over to the British contingent of NATO troops in Macedonia are defective or unused.

16 September It is accepted that at least 350 NATO troops will remain in Macedonia after the end of their weapons collection mission on 26 September.

28 September The ethnic-Albanian National Liberation Army in Macedonia is formally disbanded.

9 October Former President Milošević is indicted by the Tribunal in The Hague for the expulsion of 170,000 non-Serbs from the predominantly ethnic-Serb regions of the Croatian Krajina and Slavonia in 1991–92.

11 November Three Macedonian policemen are killed by ethnic Albanian rebels near the village of Trebos. Some argue that the presence of the police had been a deliberate provocation inspired by Ljube Boskovski, the hard-line interior minister. The Macedonian parliament is yet to ratify the August peace accord.

16 November The Macedonian *Sobranje* approves the constitutional reforms giving increased rights to the ethnic Albanian community.

GOVERNMENT AND POLITICS

3.1 THE CONCEPT AND HISTORY OF NATIONALISM IN EASTERN EUROPE

It was noted in Part 1 that nationalism was essentially a western European concept transferred to the very different conditions of central and eastern Europe. It was also noted that it contrasted markedly with the dynastic principle. That is not to suggest that central and eastern European nationalism had no local roots. On the contrary, it was often rooted in a strong sense of cultural and often religious identity, which the ruling imperial powers had normally tolerated. Ironically, perhaps, the Muslim Turks had often been more tolerant than the Christian Austrians and Russians. The Austrians had forcibly suppressed Czech protestantism and national rights, and Austrians, Germans and Russians alike had sought to suppress the Polish sense of identity after the partitions at the end of the eighteenth century.

What did distinguish central (including German and Italian) and eastern European nationalism from the nationalism of England, Denmark, France, Spain or Sweden was that in the western cases the creation of the nation state had predated any strong popular sense of cultural or national identity. The states were above all the creations of powerful individual monarchs who stimulated the creation of the cultures which sustained them. The great power of the monarch had in its turn provoked counter claims of individual liberty and, in France, the truly revolutionary concept that the foundation of the state was a social contract between freely consenting citizens.

The pattern of development in central and eastern Europe was the reverse. There (as in Ireland and Norway), the sense of cultural identity had come first and it demanded a nation state for its expression. The nation was a cultural and ethnic community rather than a political one. By definition it looked back into the past. This historicising trend, operating after centuries of foreign rule, often associated with heavy destruction at the time of invasion, frequently gave nationalist sentiment a very introverted, romanticised quality. Comparatively brief periods of national prominence were disproportionately glorified, and much was imagined and indeed invented. This is easy to mock from a western European perspective, but the visitor to, say, Hungary cannot but be struck by the virtual absence of any extant monuments dating from before 1700.

This romanticism, which extended to Germany, was associated with a conspicuous vein of exclusivity. Having finally achieved recognition of their national identity, the peoples concerned reacted by both overlooking the ethnic intermingling which had been proceeding for centuries and persuading themselves that they were intrinsically superior to their neighbours. Hitler's concepts of Aryan purity and superiority were only particularly extreme forms of views widely held across central and eastern Europe.

It was also a nationalism which percolated downwards from the artists, the intellectuals, the military and even the Church and, if there was one, the aristocracy, rather than upwards from the people at large. It was a nationalism that was taught, and sometimes taught without sophistication because the teachers themselves were in places men of limited learning.

It also has to be said that the very concept of nationalism had a darker side to it than its proponents, many of them humanitarian and liberal men like Czechoslovakia's Professor Masaryk and America's President Wilson, appreciated. The stress on the unity of one people implied its lack of unity with any other people and it was a very short step from inclusiveness to exclusiveness, from nationalism to racism, from tolerance to intolerance. This had been less obvious in the case of the great nineteenth-century models of German and Italian unification which had been focused primarily on joining together petty statelets and sweeping away semi-feudal administrations, although the outlook of the German educated classes had been transferred from a liberal to a nationalist stance after 1871. In central and eastern Europe, though, there were not the same homogeneous culturally defined populations, and where there were, they could contradict the ethnic principle. Areas like Macedonia and Transylvania had a measure of regional consciousness, but a German, a Hungarian or a Romanian could equally claim to be a good Transylvanian.

The proponents of the national ideal also failed to realise the ease with which the goal of unity could be translated into the suspicion of, and then suppression of, dissent. They and their nineteenth-century predecessors had linked the ideal of nationalism with the ideals of liberalism and parliamentarianism, but nationalism was related at least as closely to corporatism (see Part 3.2), and in times of stress, like those introduced by the end of the First World War, the simplicities of nationalist corporatism were progressively to overwhelm the sophisticated complexities of parliamentarianism. Moreover, cultural and ethnic nationalism was emotional and bound up with the land and the spirit of the people it had brought forth. It readily opposed itself to, and despised, the intellectual concepts, popularised by the French revolution, of the rights of man. Democracy and individual rights were increasingly seen as alien western values, particularly once the west had become an economic competitor.

Romantic, exclusive and introspective nationalism, therefore, grew ever stronger in the inter-war years, rather than weaker as might have been expected as the experience of independence matured. Similarly it became ever more dominant in the universities, not least in Germany. It was rendered even more compulsive by the very need to overcome the reality of cultural, ethnic, political and religious fragmentation. The vicious circle was further poisoned by the stresses induced by the continuous economic crisis. Whether more favourable economic conditions would in due course have directed central and eastern European nationalisms into more constructive channels cannot now be known, but many in the ruling classes gained substantial private benefit from nationalistic economic policies. Corruption and profiteering were widespread, though certainly not universal.

The victims of this virulent form of nationalism were the minorities, and above all the Jews. Anti-Semitism flared in the universities, especially in Poland where the Jews were particularly unpopular for reasons suggested in Part 3.3 following. The scale of Hitler's 'Final Solution' has tended to deflect attention from the fierce anti-Semitism prevalent in many of Germany's neighbours as it has from the role of their citizens in the concentration camps, in national SS units and the like.

Special mention must also be made of the nationalist cross-currents within the new states of Czechoslovakia and Yugoslavia. There was always a measure of optimism in the belief that ethnic and linguistic similarity and, perhaps, military common interest would be sufficient to weld the new states together, and at no stage had union enjoyed unanimous support. Divisions, however, readily opened over the presumption of the Czechs and Serbs that, as they had played the leading role in defeating imperial rule, they should also play the leading role in running the new state. Piedmont and Prussia had made similar presumptions on Italian and German unification some fifty years earlier. Moreover, the Czechs could point to their financial support for Slovakia, and the Serbs to their military and other wartime losses in the interests of the southern slavs as a whole. This did not stop the presumption from being resented, or the perceived lack of appreciation which it provoked from being resented in its turn. Moreover, both the Czechs and the Serbs felt the insecurity engendered by being minorities in the states they aspired to lead. A not dissimilar pattern of tension has been discernible between western and eastern Germany since unification in 1990. In the nineteenth century Germany and Italy had succeeded in resolving such problems, but against a favourable economic background. The economic background in the inter-war years was unfavourable, and such resentments festered. They festered all the more because the then guardians of both Croat and Slovak nationalisms were men of narrow vision whose final rise to power under Nazi auspices only increased their paranoia. The genocide of Serbs and other minorities in Croatia under Dr Pavelić, which on occasion provoked even the Germans to intervene, was to leave scars which became all too apparent when Yugoslavia fractured in the 1990s.

The vicious circle of ever-more introverted nationalism was broken by the defeat of Germany and the victory of the Soviet Union, followed by the progressive assumption of power by Communist regimes. The problem of minorities had in some cases been eased by the conduct of the war itself. Some 13 million Germans were forcibly ejected, or fled, from across central and eastern Europe in Europe's largest population movement in over a thousand years. It was 'ethnic cleansing', to employ a later term, on a scale to dwarf anything which would happen subsequently in the Balkans, and it was approved by all the Allies at Potsdam. In association with the westward movement of her frontiers, it meant that Poland was now ethnically Polish in a way she had never been before. Not least, perhaps 6 million Jews had been annihilated across Nazi Europe, and the goal of many of the survivors was to emigrate to what was to become Israel, as quickly as possible.

Communist education and propaganda now glorified proletarian internationalism rather than the nation state. It is easy to be cynical about the endless talk of fraternal friendship, and it concealed much that was far from fraternal, but it is harder not to feel that some such corrective was needed. Eastern Europeans were now obliged to master one another's languages and to learn about each other's customs. Their very isolation from the west threw them back on their own resources. This did not mean that nationalism disappeared. It quickly surfaced, or rather was not suppressed, in Yugoslavia and Albania. It was part of the particular genius of Tito that he was able to harness the Yugoslav ideal of 1918 to a new forward-looking nationalism which would for several decades supersede and transcend the traditional nationalisms of Croatia and Serbia. Nationalism resurfaced successively in East Germany, Poland, Hungary and Romania, although the experience of the war made nationalism a sensitive subject in East and West Germany alike. Successive Romanian Communist governments, on the other hand, self-consciously exploited nationalist sentiment to the end to enhance their popularity. Moreover, the Communist regimes sought to insulate their peoples from each other. It could be as difficult to travel from one Soviet bloc state to another as to cross the Iron Curtain itself. Nevertheless, the whole philosophy of communism was internationalist, and economic and military necessity drove contact and cooperation. COMECON and the Warsaw Pact were as unlike the national chauvinism of the pre-war years in the east as the EEC and NATO were in the west. Again, as in the west, the new forces of tourism and television helped to break down national barriers.

The collapse of communism in 1990 tilted the balance back in favour of nationalism. The Soviet Union dissolved into its constituent republics and, although the Russian Federation itself has held, Estonia, Latvia, Lithuania, Belarus, Ukraine, Moldova, Armenia and Georgia have been added to the number of European states, all but the first three loosely grouped under the umbrella of the Commonwealth of Independent States. Yugoslavia fractured more slowly but much more painfully into its constituent republics of Bosnia–Hercegovina, Croatia, Macedonia and Slovenia, leaving only Serbia and Montenegro as the 'Yugoslav Federation'. Neither the Soviet Union nor Yugoslavia, however, fully dissolved into truly national units. The boundaries, and indeed sometimes the very existence, of the constituent republics had been determined by the need to accommodate or balance ethnic and religious groupings within the wider federation, not to form the nucleus of a nation state. Neither Bosnia, nor Macedonia nor Moldova was in any sense a nation in waiting. This may or may not prove fatal. Belgium has thrived, at least comparatively, since 1830 from similarly inauspicious beginnings.

The process of dissolution also involved Czechoslovakia, which split by agreement into its constituent Czech and Slovak parts in 1992/93. Only Germany had gone against the trend with the unification of East and West in 1990.

The future is open to differing interpretations. On the one hand, the process of dissolution may continue. As the Marxist historian E. J. Hobsbawm has caustically observed: 'The eggs of Brest-Litovsk are still hatching.' Kosovo and Montenegro are the most immediately plausible candidates for independence, but it is not difficult to imagine others. This may or may not matter. If the EU or the CIS provides an environment within which small independent nations can thrive, then all may be well. The pressures for autonomy and independence are, after all, equally marked in western Europe, with the diminutive Faroe Islands being just the latest applicant for independence. Even under the most favourable scenario, however, Poland alone of the central and eastern European states outside the CIS now has the area and population to exercise any meaningful influence at EU level. If enhanced cooperation focused on France and Germany materialises, as anticipated, their influence is likely to be even less. That is an essentially unstable scenario. Moreover, the level of public support for EU entry in the candidate countries of central and eastern Europe is far from overwhelming and could fall appreciably, while there is evidence of a return to the virulent nationalism of the 1930s. The extreme nationalist, Corneliu Vadim Tudor, leader of the Greater Romania Party, came second in the Romanian presidential election of December 2000. President Havel of the Czech Republic feared in the November that any moves to postpone EU enlargement would play into the hands of 'xenophobes, chauvinists and nationalists' – a less than optimistic analysis of his political environment. Wider travel, particularly by the young, the trend towards urbanism and service industries, and greater cultural sophistication, may or may not help to keep such extremism in check.

On the other hand, there could ultimately be some form of consolidation, particularly if public opinion turns against the prospect of EU membership. Belarus and Russia have set a precedent with a measure of reunification. Even 'liberal' western opinion is coming to question the viability of some of the mooted nation states. Consolidation would probably be most beneficial in the Balkans, but the NATO attacks on Serbia of 1999 have probably set the prospects for comprehensive regional cooperation back by at least a decade.

Uncertainty also hangs over the long-term impact on the local nationalisms of the NATO and UN presence in Bosnia, Kosovo and Macedonia, and the practical espousal of the Albanian over the slav cause by the latter-day Great Powers. Much of the area has effectively returned to the autonomous semi-colonial status it enjoyed under the Turkish Empire in the nineteenth century. That again is an essentially unstable scenario.

3.2 AUTHORITARIANISM, FASCISM AND THE PROBLEM OF NATIONAL MINORITIES FROM 1919 TO 1939

COMMENTARY

By 1921, virtually all the states of central and eastern Europe had adopted liberal democratic constitutions. By 1939, authoritarianism was to have triumphed everywhere except Czechoslovakia. Such a universal trend, which also extended to the Baltic States, Finland and Greece, was not coincidental and, although the precise circumstances varied from country to country, common factors were at work everywhere. They can be broadly classified as political, economic and social.

At the political level, the pluralism on which liberal democracy depends was widely the subject of suspicion. This was not always unjustified. Parliamentary democracy can only really work when there is broad agreement on the purposes of the state, and in many countries even a minimal sense of common purpose was lacking. Moreover, many of the liberal democratic leaders were necessarily inexperienced. These political difficulties could perhaps have been overcome had it not been for the economic problems. The new countries were going to face daunting challenges in the most favourable circumstances, as were those countries like Austria and Hungary with drastically revised frontiers, because economically integrated regions had been split and cities separated from their hinterland. The all-important railways had often been built to serve imperial rather than national objectives. These economic challenges became almost insurmountable with the global financial crises of the interwar years, ultimately attributable to the destabilising impact of the totally unrealistic burden of reparations imposed on Germany at Versailles. The social unrest resulting from the collapse of markets and from unemployment exacerbated the existing political difficulties to make many countries virtually ungovernable. Ever more authoritarian rule was the almost inevitable outcome.

The authoritarian trend was strongly reinforced by social factors, although they operated in a more subtle manner. Central and eastern Europe, other than the Czech parts of Czechoslovakia and pockets of Poland and Hungary, was overwhelmingly agricultural. Power was exercised by the crown and aristocracy, where they existed, and by a small bourgeoisie of sometimes aristocratic but more usually rich peasant, and only rarely commercial, origin. The power of the crown lay in its control of the army and its skill in the art of divide and rule. In Romania, a large part of the nation's industry was the king's personal property. In Hungary, one-third of the national territory was held by the large estate owners and just 63 families owned 1½ million acres between them. They had been terrified by Béla Kun's brief communist revolution of 1919 and anything was a lesser evil than communist expropriation. As the inter-war years advanced and the power of Germany and the Soviet Union grew, the governing classes of the countries in between increasingly opted for the former, however reluctantly, because their self-interest dictated it.

It also has to be said that, again with the general exceptions of Austria before 1932 and Czechoslovakia before 1939, the liberal democracy of the constitutions frequently bore little resemblance to the reality on the ground from the very beginning. Ballots were often rigged, candidates drawn from a restricted pool, and voting conducted in public. In Bulgaria, at the extreme, formal parliamentarianism went hand in hand with state terror after the military coup of 1923. The violent right-wing Inner Macedonian Revolutionary Organisation (IMRO) was regularly used by the government to assassinate radical peasant leaders, and its leaders, Commander Alexandrov and General Protogerov, were assassinated in their turn when they plotted to establish an independent Macedonia. Bulgarian elections were simply suspended between 1931 and 1938, and when they were restored candidates were not allowed to represent political parties.

Authoritarianism, as distinct from the royal autocracy of the nineteenth century, first appeared in twentieth-century Europe in Italy in the guise of fascism. The word 'fascism' is derived from the *fasces* or bundle of rods bound up with a projecting axe which the magistrates of Ancient Rome carried as their symbol of authority and which Mussolini adopted as the badge of his Italian political movement, but the more instructive description is 'corporatism' derived from the Latin word for the body. Corporatism saw the state as an organism like the human body in which each part had an allotted function and which was under the leadership of the head. Parallels were readily drawn with the traditional family in which the husband and wife had distinct and separate roles, and in which there was an accepted generational and functional hierarchy. It was as disastrous for the state to harbour elements unwilling to play their allotted role as it was for the body to harbour malignant organisms. It was a concept which contrasted markedly with the individualism, pluralism and compromise inherent in liberal democracy, and even more with the Communist perception that loyalty was owed to social class rather than nation.

It was not in itself an unworthy concept. It valued family loyalty, patriotism, responsibility and self-sacrifice. The practice, though not the theory, differed little from the dominance of the aristocracy and the gentry virtually everywhere in rural Europe in earlier centuries. That very fact, however, pointed to some of the inherent weaknesses of the corporate concept of society. It was backward-looking, it was intolerant of diversity and innovation, and it was out of tune with the real needs of industrial society. Those very features, however, were for many the source of corporatism's attraction. It provided a sense of belonging, a sense of continuity and tradition, and a sense of personal worth. Those virtues were particularly attractive in the insecure world which was

97

the aftermath of the Great War of 1914–18. Equally attractive to some was the legitimacy given to the frustration, resentment and blind hatred engendered by that insecurity. Not surprisingly, corporatism appealed to princes of church and state, whose world was one of hierarchy and authority. The power of the Roman Catholic church in Hungary, in fields ranging from education to public appointments, increased dramatically after 1919 as it became a pillar of the new corporatist order. It also appealed to business, which preferred the security of the cartel to the uncertain prospects of unfettered competition. The high water mark of corporatist thinking was to be represented by the Papal encyclical *Quadragesimo Anno*, promulgated by Pope Pius XI in 1931.

The imagery of corporatism and its sense of a body ruled by the head was readily associated with the concept of the superman which had originated with Nietzsche and gained increasing currency as the nineteenth century advanced. It had attracted D. H. Lawrence and Shaw in Britain, and numerous other philosophers and writers across Europe. Like corporatism, it was not of itself an ignoble concept. The artist as man of action and the very notion of the 'hero' had ancient roots. Who, though, was to distinguish between 'man' and 'superman'? The only very plausible answer was the majority, inspired by an individual's acts of courage and daring, charisma, contempt for constraint and power of leadership. Some plausible candidates could be put forward – Garibaldi, perhaps, in Italy, Napoleon in France – but their claims could only be considered in retrospect. The aspiring superman had to seize power first and justify it later. This was an open invitation to the bully and the braggart, and the first of the heads of the inter-war corporate states, the Italian Benito Mussolini, had both traits in abundance. Nevertheless the concept had its positive side. Mussolini was a great admirer of, and was himself admired by, Gabriele d'Annunzio, who was both Italy's greatest late nineteenth/early twentieth-century poet and a daring man of action, having flown an audacious propaganda flight to Vienna in 1917 and seized Fiume for Italy in 1919. For good measure, he had also conducted a passionate and publicised affair with Italy's most famous actress, Eleonora Duse. The 'masterly inactivity' of Stanley Baldwin, who was to become British prime minister in 1924, could hardly have stood in greater contrast, except perhaps for Herbert Hoover, American president from 1929, who was alleged by wags at the time to be living proof that there was life after death.

Mussolini was also successful. He gave Italy confidence and direction, and he understood well before most other politicians the positive economic impact of government spending on public works in times of recession. Like Hitler later, he saw himself as a great moderniser. He also appreciated the power of propaganda and show: he was a media man long before his time with his flags, his mass meetings, his salutes and his uniforms. Of course the show was hollow, but the totality impressed governments, including the British, and public alike.

The impact on central and eastern Europe was direct. Marshal Piłsudski's march on Warsaw of 1926 echoed Mussolini's march on Rome of four years earlier, and similarly marked the end of parliamentarianism. Chancellor Dollfuss was to abolish the Austrian parliament likewise in 1932 and to seek to establish a corporate state under Mussolini's guarantee. King Zog in Albania was to be increasingly an acolyte of Mussolini and King Carol II in Romania directly imitated him, as did the Hungarian prime minister, General Gyula (von) Gömbös. Both the Romanian Iron Guard and the Hungarian Party of National Unity were modelled on Italian fascism. Tsar Boris III of Bulgaria and General Averescu in Romania were both Italian in sympathy.

This is not to say that the corporatist ideal was identical everywhere. It could not be by definition, because the nation state was at its core and every nation was different. Dr Dollfuss was to state explicitly that he did not want to imitate Italian fascism. There was the further problem of establishing what fascism actually stood for. The very concept of the 'will to power' was supported by the philosophical belief that blind action would cause new institutions and structures to grow organically. Moreover, to meet its claims of being a party for the whole nation, fascism tended to seek to appeal to all interests, however contradictory, at one and the same time. Many industrial workers were initially to support Mussolini and Piłsudski, as they later did Major Szalassi in Hungary, because of their earlier socialist backgrounds. Business interests on the other hand were to support them as a defence against trade unionism and communism. Fabri, the Italian revolutionary anarchist, described the fascism of the early 1920s as inspiring 'preventive counter-revolutions'. This dichotomy was exacerbated by Mussolini's tendency constantly to change his mind on any subject, not infrequently several times on the same day. In practice, though, the logic of anti-communism and of the central role allocated to the nation was to push fascism ever further to the right. Piłsudski was mobilising aristocratic support almost as soon as he had seized power.

Despite their admiration for Mussolini, the presidential and royal dictators of central and eastern Europe did not run truly fascist regimes. Their power, which in the case of the monarchs dated back to the nineteenth century, was rooted in their control of the army, the bureaucracy and of certain key elites, but not in a mass fascist party on Italian lines. Indeed they were often to see their national fascist parties as threats to their own position. Their preferred response was to control all political parties as much as possible, if not to ban them outright, but in practice fascist sentiment was too strong and their own power too weak. Those that survived, particularly after the rise of Adolf Hitler to power in Germany in 1933, were to seek to harness fascism and increasingly to try to outflank it by promoting programmes which were more fascist than those of the fascists themselves. It was a maelstrom of accelerating viciousness, and the positive desire, or the perceived need, to cultivate Germany was to accelerate it yet further. Churchill was to say in 1941 that the attitude of the Yugoslav regent, Paul, 'looks like that of an unfortunate man in a cage with a tiger, hoping not to provoke him while steadily dinner time approaches'. None of the western powers had developed enough economic or political influence in the region to provide an effective counter-force. Specifically Nazi groups were to grow at the expense of those of a more traditionally autocratic, fascist orientation.

The strongest link in central and eastern Europe between these groups, apart from their common authoritarianism, was their anti-Semitism, which had been peripheral to Mussolini's fascism. It had, though, been rife in the Austro-Hungarian and Russian Empires and had blossomed after 1919. Nazi Germany was to export its own anti-Semitism eastwards as a means of gaining friends and influence and was to support national anti-Semitic movements, like the Romanian Iron Guard, financially. It was to gain its reward in the pro-German orientation of many of the ambitious young, who considered the Jews to be occupying jobs in business and industry which were rightfully theirs. The subject of anti-Semitism is discussed more fully in Part 3.3 following.

Hitler was to give to German corporatism the heady fusion of cunning, surgical precision in political action and utter ruthlessness in the pursuit of absolute power which continues to fascinate and appal seventy years later. He was also to underline the essential weakness of corporatism: if the head is rotten, the whole nation is corrupted. Mussolini had been implicated in a political murder, Hitler directed mass murder as a matter of course. His allies in central and eastern Europe, some of them men of the same unstable, charismatic stamp, others only intolerant and of narrow outlook, were to be similarly corrupted with equally negative effect.

CHRONOLOGY

1919

26 January Poland holds elections for a constitutional assembly, and Piłsudski hands power over to the newly elected *Sejm* on 20 February.

16 November The counter-revolutionary army of Admiral Horthy arrives in Budapest and brings the Hungarian White Terror to the capital. Between two and four times as many people are killed as during Béla Kun's Red Terror. Famous writers and musicians who had served in the Hungarian Soviet Republic, including Bartók (qv) and Kodály (qv in Biographies) are 'disciplined', and many left-wing individuals are imprisoned or interned. Some thousands of intellectuals emigrate.

28 December A general strike is declared in Bulgaria. The Stamboliyski government responds by proclaiming martial law. The strike is abandoned on 5 January 1920.

1920

25–26 January Hungary holds national elections under theoretical universal suffrage as granted in December 1918. In practice, the White

Terror is still in progress, the elections are boycotted by the Socialists and the Communist Party is illegal.

29 February Czechoslovakia adopts a liberal constitution but declares the national territory to be a single and indivisible unity. Only Carpathian Ruthenia is promised autonomy.

1 March The Hungarian Parliament, having opted for the restoration of the monarchy, elects Admiral Horthy regent of Hungary. The monarchy is formally proclaimed on 23 March.

19 March Jozef Piłsudski is made marshal of Poland.

1921

17 March Poland adopts a liberal constitution.

28 June The 'Yugoslav' constitutional assembly approves the centralist 'Vidovdan Constitution' which is designed to promote the unification of the country. The Croat Peasant Party, however, refuses to recognise, and boycotts, the assembly. Article 126 of the constitution stipulates a 60 per cent majority for any future amendment. King Alexander survives an assassination attempt as he prepares to swear to uphold the new constitution.

The Hungarian government enacts a law banning all Communist activities and authorising the banning of the distribution of newspapers and books without prior legal proceeding.

1922

2 March Hungary abolishes the universal franchise with a new system which disenfranchises about 25 per cent of the electorate and imposes educational and residence qualifications for the vote. Ballots are secret in urban areas but public in rural ones. The opposition is not allowed to organise in the villages. The prime minister, Count Bethlen, maintains that a secret ballot is 'irreconcilable with the open character of the Hungarian people'.

14 December Gabriel Narutowicz assumes office as president of Poland in succession to his friend, Piłsudski, but is assassinated two days later. He is succeeded by Stanisław Wojciechowski, another member of Piłsudski's circle.

1923

29 May Marshal Piłsudski resigns as chief of the Polish general staff and goes into retirement.

8–9 June A *coup d'état* led by General Peter Midilev, Colonel Kimon Georgiev and Colonel Damian Velchev overthrows the

101

Bulgarian government. The prime minister, Alexandŭr Stamboliyski, is killed and his Agrarian Party ministers arrested. The coup is backed by officer and professional interests. Thousands die in the ensuing disorder.

23 September An armed attack by the Communists on the new Bulgarian government is part-thwarted by advance intelligence. It only receives substantial support in the Plovdiv, Vratsa and Stara Zágora areas, and is suppressed by 28 September.

6 November Strikes engulf Poland and the workers in Krakow rebel, clashing with police. 32 people are killed and many are wounded. Similar events occur in Łódz and Dabrowa.

1924

24 December Ahmed Zogu summons an Albanian constitutional assembly on a restricted franchise. It abolishes the regents in favour of a republic of which Zog becomes president.

1925

16 April A bomb explodes in Sofia cathedral killing over a hundred people. Two Communists are found guilty, who appear to have acted on their own initiative. More than 300 people are sentenced to death and hundreds more murdered unofficially. The Communist Party is again declared illegal.

18 July An 'R-R Coalition' agreement is signed between the Serb Radicals of Nikola Pašić and the Croat supporters of Stjepan Radić. It allows for a modest degree of Croat autonomy.

November President Wojciechowski of Poland warns General Sikorski, one of the country's most powerful army leaders, not to instigate a military coup. Sikorski, together with Roman Dmowski, had formed the secret *Pogotowie Patriotów Polskich* (Polish Patriots' Readiness) to plan the overthrow of democracy and to introduce a dictatorship.

1926

12 May Marshal Piłsudski, disillusioned with parliamentary democracy, leads a march by military units on Warsaw. President Wojciechowski and his government resign two days later, after a battle for the inner city which has cost the lives of 300 people.

19 May Polish workers announce a general strike in support of Piłsudski, who they mistakenly think will introduce a socialist programme.

15 September	Piłsudski's most trusted aide, Colonel Walery Slavek, secretly meets prominent aristocrats at Dzikow in a three-day meeting, to establish a conservative power base for autocratic rule.
4 December	Roman Dmowski founds the Camp for a Great Poland (*Obóz Wielkiej Polski*). It regards itself as a movement not a party, and is focused on the cult of the leader. It is autocratic, militantly nationalist and anti-Semitic, and it agitates for dictatorship.
10 December	The death of Pašić leads to the collapse of the 1925 compromise agreement. Stjepan Radić, the leader of the Croat Peasant Party, returns to an oppositional role.

1928

1 January	Vojtech Tuka, editor of *Slovak*, the newspaper of Father Andrej Hlinka's Slovak People's Party, maintains that the October 1918 Turčiansky Svätý Martin declaration of a single Czechoslovak nation included a secret clause limiting the union to ten years. If the promised Slovak autonomy had not materialised by that October, the Slovaks would be free to make new decisions. He is accused of conspiring with Hungary to undermine the republic and sentenced to fifteen years imprisonment.
20 June	A Montenegrin member of the 'Yugoslav' *Skupština* murders four Croat members during a parliamentary session, including Stjepan Radić, the Croat leader. His assassination unites the Croats against the Serbs, and the other Croat members withdraw from the *Skupština*. Dr Vlako Maček succeeds Radić as party leader.

1929

6 January	Having failed to negotiate a viable settlement, King Alexander of 'Yugoslavia' dissolves the *Skupština*, quashes the 1921 constitution, bans all the existing political parties and establishes a royal dictatorship. He also divides the country into new administrative provinces (*banats*).
18 August	Two thousand Austrian *Heimwehr* (extreme nationalist) stormtroopers attack a Social Democratic Party celebration in St Lorenz. Three people are killed and two hundred wounded. A similarly fatal attack is made at Vösendorf, near Vienna, two days later.
3 October	In his continuing attempt to unify his country, King Alexander formally changes its name from the Triunine Kingdom of Serbs, Croats and Slovenes to Yugoslavia. He also bans all political parties rooted in ethnic, religious or regional loyalties,

103

and standardises the legal and educational framework. In addition, he seeks to ease the lot of the peasantry.

1930

9 September Following the comparatively poor showing of Piłsudski's *Bezpartyjny Blok* (Non-party Block) in Poland's March 1928 national elections, he has nineteen opposition members and senators arrested, who are soon followed by a further sixty together with several thousand members of the public. Later national elections are a formality to endorse Piłsudski's power, which is rooted in his control of the army.

28 October Mussolini overtly abandons his earlier thesis that fascism is not for export.

1931

3 September King Alexander introduces a new constitution which makes Yugoslavia an authoritarian, though technically parliamentary, state. No candidate may stand for the *Skupština* unless his name is included on a 'national list', and all such lists must include a representative nominated from each national electoral division. The *Skupština* will be elected by direct universal suffrage, but half the members of the Senate will be appointed by the king.

14 September Yugoslavia enacts a new electoral law pursuant to the new constitution. Its tenor is undemocratic, as the ballot is not secret. Moreover, the party with most votes is automatically to be awarded 204 of the 305 parliamentary seats and, if it obtains an overall majority, it is to be awarded all 305 seats. The opposition parties boycott the forthcoming elections in protest. The new *Skupština* sees the formation of a single Yugoslav Party under the effective control of the crown. That basic framework is to remain in place until 1937.

1932

23 March Czechoslovakia bans the wearing of the swastika emblem. It had been a more common sight in the Sudetenland (see Glossary) in the immediate post-war years than in Germany itself.

19 May Dr Dollfuss, a Christian Socialist, becomes Austrian Chancellor. He leads a cabinet of Christian Social, *Heimwehr* (extreme nationalist) and Agrarian members.

25 May Czechoslovakia dissolves all illegal groups of the fascist youth movement.

26 September The Bulgarian Labour Party, the legal front for the banned Communist Party, wins 22 of the 35 seats on the Sofia

Municipal Council. The result represents a doubling of the 'Communist' vote and a halving of the government vote in comparison with the national election of 1931. It provokes a wave of terror, and anticipation that the result will prompt the government to ban the Labour Party.

October	The Hungarian prime minister, General Gyula (von) Gömbös, renews fascism in Hungary. The established ruling party is reorganised on the leadership principle as the Party of National Unity with its own vanguard fighters. Its corporatism is based on the Italian model.
16 October	Some 200,000 people demonstrate at Altfohl in favour of Slovak autonomy. Autonomy had been conceded under the Treaty of Bratislava signed by President Masaryk, but had not materialised.

1933

14 January	A new Romanian government is formed under Dr Vaida Voevod, leader of the semi-fascist Romanian Front.
23 January	A fascist coup is foiled near Brno, Czechoslovakia. The fascist leader, retired General Rodola Gajda, the hero of the Czechoslovak Legion, is arrested, but claims to have had no knowledge of the planned coup.
30 January	Adolf Hitler is appointed as Chancellor of Germany.
3 February	Martial law is proclaimed in Bucharest and the oil-producing regions of Romania, following rioting.
21 February	The Romanian government introduces a parliamentary bill aimed at strengthening public order and state security. It prohibits terrorist organisations, inflammatory pamphlets and provocative cartoons, unauthorised public demonstrations, uniforms and emblems, and unauthorised official reports on the state of the country.
16 March	The Austrian Christian Socialists (Clericals) resolve to rule by decree without parliament. The Christian Socialist government has a parliamentary majority of one.
24 March	The 'enabling law' makes Adolf Hitler not only Chancellor but dictator of Germany.
12 April	The Labour members of the Bulgarian *Sobranje* are excluded by decree.
30 April	A new Austrian constitution is enacted abolishing parliamentarianism and making the Chancellor, Dr Dollfuss, effectively a dictator.
14 May	40,000 members of the *Heimwehr* (extreme nationalists) celebrate in Vienna the liberation of the city from the Turkish

	siege of 1683. Dr Dollfuss takes the salute accompanied by the *Heimwehr* commander-in-chief, Prince Rudiger von Starhemberg, whose ancestor had been Austrian commander at the time. Dr Dollfuss declares that neither parliament nor parliamentary government will ever return to Austria in its previous guise.
14 May	The Austrian Social Democratic Party formally deletes from its programme its demand for union with Germany, for as long as Germany remains a Nazi dictatorship.
19 May	Austria bans the flying of flags other than Austria's own national, provincial and municipal ones.
13 June	Austria arrests Theo Habicht, a German national, Reichstag deputy-inspector of the Austrian Nazi Party and press attaché to the German legation in Vienna, in Linz. All Nazi meetings are banned and 170 'Brown Houses' are closed.
25–26 June	Sofia is placed under martial law for 24 hours during which time citizens are confined to their homes. Some 1,200 people are arrested, including 1,100 Macedonian revolutionaries and 100 Communists.
9 September	Dr Dollfuss announces to the Austrian Catholic Congress in the presence of the Papal Legate that he proposes to rebuild the state in the Christian German spirit. The new Austrian constitution will be on the corporatist lines of the Papal encyclical *Quadragesimo Anno*. He adds at a further session three days later that his goal is a Catholic Peasant Commonwealth rather than a Fascist State on the Italian model. Warm relations are nevertheless to be cultivated with Italy.
10 September	Theo Habicht broadcasts against the Austrian government. He announces that the Austrian Nazis will only be willing to come to terms with the Dollfuss government on the following conditions:

  • that the Nazis be completely rehabilitated as a political party, and that all steps taken against them be rescinded
  • that they be admitted to an interim cabinet in proportion to their numerical strength, pending early elections which should produce a government constituted in proportion to the results

11 September	Dr Dollfuss explains the aims of the new organisation, *Vaterländische Front* (Fatherland Front), founded by him to realise his new corporatist state.
21 September	Dr Dollfuss reconstructs his cabinet on an authoritarian, non-party basis.
5 October	Czechoslovakia bans the German Nazi Party and the German Nationalist Party within its territory.

6 November   Following a ban by the Hungarian prime minister, General von Gömbös, on the wearing of the swastika, the Hungarian National Socialists adopt the 'Arrow Cross', a cross combined from four arrows, as their emblem. The swastika had been banned as a foreign official symbol on 10 September.

11 December   The Romanian government dissolves the 'Iron Guard' as a terrorist organisation aiming to establish its own 'storm troops'. (See Glossary for fuller particulars.)

14 December   The Polish government parties announce a programme of constitutional reform. The lower house (*Sejm*) is to become advisory and the Senate nominated, one third by the president and two thirds by legionaries and others with military decorations. The president is to have the sole right to appoint and discharge ministers, to determine the agenda of the *Sejm* and to enact legislation. The president is to be elected by direct suffrage, but only two candidates will be permitted, of which one will be nominated by the retiring head of state.

22 December   The Austrian bishops' conference issues a pastoral letter supporting Chancellor Dollfuss's attempt to establish a 'great Catholic state' and denouncing Hitler and the Nazis. It singles out for condemnation 'Nazi racial madness', 'aggressive anti-Semitism' and 'extreme State nationalism'.

29 December   The Romanian prime minister, Ion G. Duca, is assassinated by a member of the dissolved 'Iron Guard'. He and his accomplices deny acting under orders.

30 December   Martial law is proclaimed throughout Romania in response to the Duca assassination. Press censorship is universal and the most prominent members of the dissolved Iron Guard are arrested.

1934

12 January   Alfred Frauenfeld, the leader of the Austrian Nazi Party, is arrested by Austria for continuing to work for the party.

26 January   The new Polish constitution is approved by the *Sejm*.

8 February   Major Emil Fey, Austrian vice-Chancellor and *Heimwehr* chief in Vienna, orders the searching and ransacking of the headquarters of the Social Democratic Party and the arrest of its leaders and the commanders of the *Schutzbund* (defence force). Similar action is taken in Linz on 12 February.

12 February   Civil war breaks out in Austria between the Social Democrats and the Clericals in government. Dr Dollfuss resolves to dissolve parliament and the Socialist Party in its entirety. Troops occupy Vienna's City Hall (*Rathaus*) and arrest the

Burgomaster. The flag of the *Heimwehr* (qv) flies over the build-ing, a Socialist stronghold since 1920. (See also Part 2.2.)

18 February   The government is victorious in the Austrian civil war. All trade unions are declared illegal and 36 Socialist organisations are dissolved. The *Heimwehr*, which played a leading role in the fighting, strengthens its position in government. The war has claimed the lives of 132 government troops and 137 civilians.

19 February   Theo Habicht offers an eight-day truce to the Dollfuss govern-ment in a broadcast from Munich. If no satisfactory answer is received, the struggle will resume on 28 February.

3 March   Austria publishes the draft of the new National Syndicate of Austrian Workers and Salary Receivers, which is to replace the former trade unions and is a significant step in the reorder-ing of Austria as a corporate state.

15 March   Corneliu Codreanu, leader of the Romanian Iron Guard until its dissolution, is arrested. He had disappeared follow-ing the assassination of Ion G. Duca, the prime minister, in December 1933.

19 May   A *coup d'état* installs Colonel Kimon Georgiev as Bulgarian prime minister. King Boris was allegedly unaware of the planned coup.
The new government, which is led by the leaders of the 1923 coup, announces that the *Sobranje* will be reduced in size from 270 to 100 members, of which 75 will be nominated by the government and 25 by the corporations into which Bul-garia is to be divided. All political parties are to be abolished. Unofficially, Germany welcomes the coup as 'a new blow at parliamentarianism'.

28 May   Danzig bans the Communist Party and its subsidiaries, al-legedly in the interests of public security.

15 June   The Polish minister of the interior, Colonel Bronisław Pieracki, is assassinated by Ukrainian separatists.

18 June   Colonel Georgiev, the Bulgarian prime minister, announces that he proposes to govern by decree for one year in accord-ance with Article 47 of the Constitution. The Article provides that in crisis conditions and when the *Sobranje* cannot be re-assembled, the king, advised by and on the responsibility of his ministers, may rule by Royal Decree for one year, fol-lowing which the *Sobranje* must ratify all the decrees passed.

25 July   Dr Dollfuss is assassinated by the Austrian Nazis. (See Part 2.2 for fuller particulars.)

9 October   King Alexander of Yugoslavia is assassinated in Marseilles. (See Part 2.2 for fuller particulars.)

5 November	250 leading Croats, including the Archbishop of Zagreb, submit a petition to the Yugoslav Regent, Prince Paul. They ask, first, that the Court for the protection of the Realm be abolished and that the arrest and imprisonment of political opponents be discontinued; second, that a general amnesty be declared for political prisoners and for Dr Maček, the leader of the opposition, in particular, and that nationalist organisations be dissolved forthwith; and third that new elections be held on the basis of a free and secret ballot.

1935

22 January	Colonel Georgiev resigns as Bulgarian prime minister under royal pressure, and Tsar Boris III effectively becomes Bulgarian dictator.
19 April	The Bulgarian government of General Zlatev resigns following the arrest of two former prime ministers: Professor Aleksandŭr Tsankov, leader of the Bulgarian National Socialists (fascists), and Colonel Georgiev. The arrests are attributed to fear of a putsch organised by Professor Tsankov.
5 May	The Yugoslav general election results in victory for the government of Bogolyub Jevtić. Only four political groups had been allowed to participate in the election. The Social Democrats and the Yugoslav Popular Party had been excluded for failure to comply with legal requirements and the Slovene Popular Party had boycotted it.
20 June	The Yugoslav government of Bogolyub Jevtić falls on the resignation of all its Croat members. The opposition declares that its members will not attend parliament in view of the 'terrorist methods practised at the election'.
7 July	Bulgaria bans political parties and their newspapers by decree. Contravention is punishable with three years' imprisonment and heavy fines.
22 July	The Yugoslav parliament, the *Skupština*, authorises the government to widen the franchise, and re-establish freedom of assembly and of the press. Prime Minister Stojadinović nevertheless emphasises that the new law will not allow any party organised on a religious, regional or tribal basis.
22 July	The Bulgarian government legalises the two fascist organisations dissolved in 1934 as the nucleus of a new state party.
20 August	A new Yugoslav governmental party is established comprising three of the parties banned on the proclamation of a dictatorship by the late King Alexander. They are the Radical Party of prime minister Stojadinović, and the Slovene Clerical and Bosnian Muslim Parties. The new party supports the

109

monarchy and the ruling dynasty, a united nation and a single citizenship.

2 October   The Bulgarian government declares martial law in response to an alleged revolutionary conspiracy by the republican Svevo group and the Radical Peasant group.

24 November Boris III of Bulgaria asserts his power with the installation of his favourite, Dr Georgi Kiosseivanov, as prime minister.

1936

5 January   The Bulgarian government again dissolves two of the leading fascist organisations: the National Legion, with 40,000 members organised on Nazi storm trooper lines, and the smaller Home Defence (*Rodna Zachtita*), inspired by the Austrian *Heimwehr*.

3 March   Bulgaria dissolves the Military League and bans officers from participating in politics.

10 October   Dr Kurt von Schuschnigg, the Austrian Chancellor, dissolves the *Heimwehr* and excludes Prince Starhemberg from national political activity. Major Fey, who had led a second faction of the *Heimwehr*, pledges the Chancellor his support.

1937

15 July   Hungary passes a law whereby the Regent (Admiral Horthy) is no longer responsible to parliament.

15 September An 'opposition front' of Croats and dissatisfied Serb political groups is announced, with the intention of forcing the replacement of the 1931 Constitution.

October   Major Ferenc Szálassi announces at a mass rally the foundation of the Hungarian Arrow Cross Party (*Nyilaskeresztes-part*) through the fusion of earlier Nazi and fascist groups. The new party is both demagogic and mystical in tone and appeals in particular to young workers and the lower middle class.

25 October   The Polish government arrests 80 leaders of the *Falanga* faction of the Nazi-inspired National Radical Camp, named after General Franco's Falange Party in Spain. The Camp had been established in 1934 and the *Falanga* was involved in preparations for a coup.

28 December Octavian Goga of the National Christian Party forms a new Romanian government. The National Christians are less extreme than the 'All-for-the-Fatherland' Party of Corneliu Codreanu, but they still believe in close cooperation with the fascist countries, adherence to the anti-Comintern pact, and radical anti-Semitism. The party's co-leader, the poet laureate Professor Cuza, had been one of the founders of organised anti-Semitism in Romania and had adopted the swastika long before Hitler.

1938

12 February A new Romanian 'Government of National Concentration' is formed under the Romanian Orthodox Patriarch, Dr Miron Cristes. The new government excludes the National Peasant Party, whose leader Dr Maniu, a former prime minister, refuses to participate on the grounds that the new regime is undemocratic, the All-for-the-Fatherland Party and the National Christian Party of Professor Cuza and Octavian Goga.

21 February King Carol publishes a new constitution establishing a corporatist dictatorship. No citizen is to be allowed either in speech or in writing to argue for a change in the structure of government or the distribution of property rights, for exemption from taxation, or for class warfare. Corneliu Codreanu voluntarily dissolves his All-for-the-Fatherland Party. An oral plebiscite held three days later delivers 4,297,581 votes in favour, and 5,483 votes against the new constitution.

10 March Rioting breaks out in Vienna, Graz, Linz and Innsbruck between supporters of the Nazis and of the *Vaterländische Front* (Fatherland Front). Dr Seyss-Inquart, Austrian Nazi minister of the interior and public security, flies to Berlin for consultations with the German government.

11 March The Austrian Chancellor, Dr Kurt von Schuschnigg, resigns under German pressure, and the Austrian Nazis take over the public buildings in Vienna and other Austrian towns and cities. The swastika flies from St Stephen's cathedral in Vienna. Dr Seyss-Inquart, the Austrian Nazi leader, becomes Chancellor. (See Part 2.2 for fuller particulars.)

13 March Austria's new Nazi government dissolves the Austrian state and declares Austria an integral part of Germany (*Anschluss*). The Fatherland Front is dissolved likewise. (See Part 2.2 for fuller particulars.)

21 March The five Austrian Roman Catholic bishops, led by Cardinal Innitzer of Vienna, declare:

> From our deepest conviction and free will we joyfully recognise that the National Socialist movement has achieved and is achieving outstanding results for the *völkische* and economic reconstruction and the social policy of the German Reich and people, particularly for the poorer classes. We are also convinced that the National Socialist movement has banned the danger of all-destroying godless Bolshevism. The bishops give their blessing to

these activities and will exhort the faithful in the same sense. On the day of the plebiscite it is a natural national duty for us bishops to declare ourselves as Germans for the German Reich and we expect from all faithful Christians that they know what they owe their people.

[*Source*: Keesing's Contemporary Archives 1937–40, p.3014]

The declaration arouses the concern of the Vatican, and certain provisos are incorporated in a further statement published by the Cardinal on 6 April.

12 April   Germany abolishes the Austrian law which had enabled extraordinary measures to be taken against those involved in the assassination of Dr Dollfuss, and his assassin, Otto Pianetta, is officially rehabilitated. Many streets are to be named after him.

17 April   Corneliu Codreanu, leader of the former Romanian All-for-the-Fatherland Party and of the Iron Guard, is arrested for allegedly planning a *coup d'état*. He is sentenced to six months' imprisonment two days later for writing an insulting letter.

11 May   The Central Committee of the Ukrainian National Democratic Organisation resolves to abandon as unsuccessful its three-year-old policy of cooperation with the Polish government. It maintains that promised minority rights have not materialised and it demands autonomy for eastern Galicia, home to 4–5 million Ukrainians.

27 May   Corneliu Codreanu is sentenced by a Romanian military court in Bucharest to ten years' imprisonment for treason.

15 August   The Croats and the Serb democratic opposition unite to demand the resignation of the Stojadinović government and the reintroduction of a democratic constitution.

6 October   Mgr Jozef Tiso is appointed prime minister of autonomous Slovakia in the newly federated Czechoslovakia.

9 October   A mob with many apparent Nazi members storms the palace of Cardinal Archbishop Innitzer of Vienna, causing serious damage and some injuries. The Cardinal had opposed the abolition of compulsory religious education in schools and the voluntary secularisation of marriage. The Cardinal had been fiercely attacked in the Nazi newspaper, *Völkischer Beobachter*, as a 'political epileptic', but the Nazis blame the rioting on Czechs and Czech Jews.

10 October   The Yugoslav government dissolves the *Skupština* with immediate effect, pending elections on 11 December.

29 November   King Carol and his interior minister agree on severe measures against the former Iron Guard following a renewal of terrorism and the attempted assassination of Professor Goanga, the rector of the University of Cluj.

29–30 November 'The Night of the Vampires.' Corneliu Zelea Codreanu and thirteen other leading members of the Iron Guard are shot by their guards, allegedly for seeking to escape. Those killed include the assassins of Ion Duca.

4 December Three members of the Iron Guard, arrested in connection with the attempted assassination of the rector of the University of Cluj, are shot dead by their police escort, allegedly for trying to escape. General Antonescu and Prince Cantacuzeno are both arrested as prominent members of the Guard.

15 December The new Romanian *Frontul Renaşterii Naţionale* (Front of National Rebirth) is proclaimed by royal decree. It incorporates the Liberal Party, the National Peasants' Party, the National Christian Party, the Romanian Front and all Crown Councillors, who are the king's own nominees. The king is party leader. All other political parties and activities are banned.

1939

4 January The statute is promulgated of the Romanian Front of National Rebirth. The party motto is 'King and Nation, Work and Faith'. The fascist salute is adopted with the greeting *Sanitate* (Good Health).

5 February Dragiša Cvetković succeeds Milan Stojadinović as Yugoslav prime minister. He holds talks with the Croat leader, Dr Maček, over the following three months. Although Dr Maček maintains that the Croat question is being discussed along the right lines for the first time in twenty years, no solution is reached. It is understood that the most difficult task is to define the boundary between Serbia and Croatia, particularly in Bosnia where the populations are mixed.

26 February The Hungarian 'Arrow Cross' Party is temporarily banned in Hungary on the day that parliament is due to debate the country's second anti-Jewish law. It is part of the Horthy regime's attempt to limit the influence of the far right by moving ever further to the right itself.

11 April The Bulgarian government dissolves the Bulgarian National Socialist Party, the *Ratnizi*. The party was already technically illegal, but had been allowed to continue on the grounds of its patriotism.

2 May The German government disestablishes the Roman Catholic Church in Austria, and ten days later deprives the Supreme Council of the Protestant Churches of Austria of its official status.

29 May The 'Arrow Cross' wins 20 per cent of the vote in the Hungarian national elections. It obtains nearly 42 per cent in

113

the industrial 'red suburbs' of Budapest where it displaces the previously dominant Social Democrats.

7 June   King Carol opens the new Romanian corporatist parliament. All members are required to wear the uniform of the Front of National Rebirth, and the small number who refuse, including the former prime minister, Dr Maniu, are not allowed to take their seats.

26 August   Dragiša Cvetković and Dr Maček finally conclude the *Sporazum* (Agreement) on future national relations within Yugoslavia.

3.3 ANTI-SEMITISM

The wider causes of anti-Semitism are probably to be found in the historic Christian antipathy to Judaism, Jewish particularism and the Jewish involvement in finance, common to Europe as a whole, and cannot be discussed in a book of this compass. The particular strength of anti-Semitism in late nineteenth- and twentieth-century central and eastern Europe, however, calls for additional explanation rooted in the particular circumstances of place and time and, although the phenomenon escapes final explanation, the following factors must have made a significant contribution.

The nationalist movements in the ascendant across central and eastern Europe were echoed among the Jews, and Jewish national councils were established everywhere except Hungary under nationalist Jewish leadership. They sought traditional minority rights including the right to education in their own language, territorial autonomy and sometimes even statehood. Such councils operated in parallel with the more familiar and ultimately more successful Zionist movements for the establishment of a Jewish homeland in Palestine, and sought at Versailles, for example, to secure a constitutional guarantee of Jewish national autonomy in Poland. There were similarly powerful pressures in Lithuania and Ruthenia. Although national councils enjoyed much less support among assimilated Jews, it is not difficult to understand how they could be perceived as a threat in new insecure nations. The same must be said of the Jewish political parties and alliances formed in Czechoslovakia, Lithuania and Romania.

The Chief Rabbi of Great Britain, Dr Jonathan Sacks, argued in his Reith lectures broadcast in 1990 that Jews had to be bilingual: their second language was of identity, their first was of shared citizenship. Much suffering might have been averted if the Jews of up to a century earlier had placed more emphasis on that ideal of shared citizenship.

The Jews were also often literally alien. Eighty per cent of Polish Jews spoke Yiddish as their mother tongue and a further 8 per cent Hebrew, and in the first Lithuanian census 98 per cent of all 'Jews by religion' claimed also to be 'Jews by nationality'. Only 3 per cent of Latvian Jewish primary school children attended Latvian-speaking schools. This was a recipe for disaster in the circumstances of the time and it is surely not coincidental that the pogroms which broke out in Lviv (Lvov) in November 1918 and in Pinsk, Lida and Vilnius in April 1919 were in regions of contested national identity. Later attempts at assimilation, however sincere, were a classic case of too little, too late. Another difficulty was that Jews were often disproportionately represented in the wealthier professions and the universities on the one hand and in the impoverished industrial working class, as well as in the populations of whole cities and districts, on the other. Although Hungary was only 5 per cent

Jewish, the percentage rose to 25 in the capital, Budapest, where 66 per cent of its shopkeepers and nearly 50 per cent of its doctors and journalists were Jewish. Hitler wanted to turn Prague into a museum of Jewish life.

There could also be specifically national problems. Educated young Hungarians had traditionally entered the military or civil services of the empire and left commerce to others, in practice to the Jews. When their former career paths disappeared after 1918, they perceived themselves as excluded from jobs which were properly theirs.

More generally, anti-Semitism had a wider economic dimension. The Jewish community was both rooted in the family and deeply cosmopolitan, and it was natural and comparatively easy for aid to flow across frontiers in times of financial difficulty. Natural mutual help was easily seen by outsiders as unfair advantage. At a deeper level, the nation states of central and eastern Europe were acutely aware of the tensions between the interests of international capital, over which Jews had, and have, power quite disproportionate to their numbers, and the interests of nation states seeking to promote autarkic economic policies. It was all too easy to see those tensions in terms of the international Jewish conspiracy of which Dr Goebbels, as Nazi Germany's minister of propaganda, was to speak with such fear and loathing.

It is also possible, perhaps, to be misled by the scale of Hitler's 'Final Solution' into making the nature of central and eastern European anti-Semitism more complex than it really was. In decades of national self-assertion and economic difficulty, they simply did not 'fit'. Some, like Béla Kun, were Communists, many more were socialists, a few were nationalists, again like Béla Kun. Hardly any, however, could be described as being in communion with their native soil, unless, of course, that was construed as Palestine. They were, in a very real sense, rootless.

The Allied victory in 1945 obviously brought Nazi and fascist persecution to a close, although only after its elimination of perhaps six million Jews, but it did not mark the end of anti-Semitism. Polish anti-Semitism in particular was rekindled by the ongoing struggle between the Roman Catholic Church and the Communist Party, many of whose leaders were Jewish. It has also outlasted communism, with ugly disputes over 'moral ownership' of the victims of the Oswiecim (Auschwitz) concentration camp repeatedly coming to the surface during the 1990s.

The following chronological entries are not presented as a comprehensive review of anti-Semitism after 1919, which is a major subject in its own right, but rather as an indication of its character, scale and scope across the region.

1920

Hungary introduces the *numerus clausus,* a law restricting the numbers of Jews admitted to universities to the same proportion as their representation in the population as a whole. In consequence the proportion of Jewish students is to fall from 34 per cent in 1917–18 to 8 per cent in 1935–36. It is the beginning of the new wave of European anti-Semitic legislation.

1931

3 November   Anti-Semitic agitation recurs at the University of Warsaw. 60 people are wounded.

12 November   The anti-Semitic disturbances spread to Lwow, where nationalist students prevent Jewish students from entering the university. 20 people are wounded.

13 November   The disturbances extend to all Polish universities except Poznan and the Roman Catholic university at Lublin.

1933

9 May   Fighting between Nazi, and Jewish and Socialist, students temporarily closes the Anatomical Institute in Vienna. Some 30 students are injured.

21 November   Nationalist students in Hungary adopt a memorandum against Jewish students. It demands strict observance of all provisions relating to them, as well as the cancellation of all work permits for foreigners and stricter immigration control.

1934

2 April   A substantial number of Jewish and 'non-religious' doctors in Vienna, appointed under the city's socialist regime, are dismissed.

1937

13 September   Poland's anti-Semitic, fascist parties declare an 'anti-Jewish month'. Its observation causes substantial economic distress to its Jewish victims.

1938

May   Hungary passes the first general anti-Semitic legislation to be introduced outside Germany.

1946

5 July   A pogrom erupts in the Polish town of Kielce and 45 Jews are killed and a further 40 wounded. The Jewish population had numbered 850, as against 15,000 pre-war. A western newspaper report says that a crowd of at least 5,000 people participated, that few Jews were saved by the intervention of Polish civilians and that the resident priest in Kielce had declined to intervene. Nine of the ringleaders are tried before a military court and executed by 16 July. The pogrom nevertheless stimulates the exodus of a further 100,000 Jews from Poland.

8 July   The Polish prime minister, Eduard Osubka-Morawski, accuses the Polish Roman Catholic Church and members of the Polish

Peasant Party for part-responsibility for the pogrom. He notes that Cardinal Sepicha, Prince-Archbishop of Krakow, had earlier refused to sign an anti-Semitic appeal, and that the Bishop of Kielce had refused to sign a denunciation of the progrom.

12 July   Cardinal Hlond, Archbishop of Gniezno and Poznan, declares in a statement: 'The fact that the condition [of the Polish Jews] is deteriorating is to a great degree due to the Jews who today occupy leading positions in Poland's government and endeavour to introduce a governmental structure which the majority of the people do not desire.'

1951

5 July   Israeli sources maintain that the Hungarian deportations commenced in May (see Part 2.4) have extended beyond the capital and include a large number of Jews. The entire Jewish community in Debrecen is said to have been deported.

1952

23 March   It is announced in Prague that Mordecai Oren, an Israeli political leader, has been arrested for espionage. The arrest is believed to be associated with that of Rudolf Slánský and other Czechoslovak Jewish Communists, accused of working for 'western imperialism', 'world Zionism' and 'Jewish cosmopolitanism'.

27 November   Eleven of the fourteen officials, including Slánský himself, found guilty at the Slánský trial of high treason against the Czechoslovak state, are Jewish.

1954

March   Three of the chief leaders of the Romanian Jewish community, Dr M. Benvenisti, Jean Cohen and A. L. Zissu, are sentenced to life imprisonment on charges of espionage, anti-state activity and 'Zionist crimes'. A number of parallel trials are conducted between the autumn of 1953 and the spring of 1954 involving some 150 people.

1968

A Polish government campaign persuades 25,000 Jews to emigrate. It forms part of a wider anti-Zionist campaign.

1998

19 August   The Polish government takes legal action to terminate the erection by radical Catholics of Christian crosses outside the former Oswiecim (Auschwitz) concentration camp. The Israeli government had officially asked on 5 August for the crosses to be removed.

1999

28 May   Polish police, supported by the army, remove 300 crosses erected by radical Roman Catholics from outside the former Oswiecim camp. The cross erected to commemorate the visit of Pope Paul John II in 1979 is left untouched.

2000

30 October   Israeli historians claim that the Slovak bishop, Jan Vojtassak, whom the Pope planned to beatify, had been present at the meeting of the Slovak National Council in March 1942 when plans were outlined to deport 58,000 Jews, most of whom died in the concentration camps. Bishop Vojtassak had been sentenced to 24 years' imprisonment in 1950, but released under an amnesty in 1963. He had died in 1965 but his conviction had not been quashed until 1990.

2001

10 July   President Kwasniewski of Poland formally apologises for the massacre of 1,600 Jews by Poles in the village of Jedwabne on 10 July 1941. The massacre had previously been blamed on the German Nazis.

3.4 THE SECOND WORLD WAR

3.4.1 WARTIME ADMINISTRATION, COLLABORATION, GOVERNMENT AND RESISTANCE

1939

17 September   Bulgaria confirms her continuing neutrality.

21 September   The Romanian prime minister, Armand Calinescu, is assassinated by the Iron Guard near Bucharest. The assassins are publicly executed that night and 292 members of the outlawed Guard are soon shot likewise. Romania declares that its policy of strict neutrality will continue. Germany alleges that the assassins were acting on British initiative, an allegation the British descibe as 'pure invention'.

30 September   Professor Ignacy Móscicki resigns as Polish president and a new 'government in exile' is formed in France. The new president, Władysław Raczkiewicz, appoints a 'Cabinet of National Unity' with General Władysław Sikorski, commander-in-chief of the Polish Army in France, as prime minister. The new government, which has its seat in Angers, is immediately recognised by Britain and France.

17 November   A Czechoslovak National Committee is formed in Paris under Dr Beneš. It maintains that the agreement to the protectorate of Bohemia and Moravia signed by President Hacha is juridically null and void. The Committee is recognised by France the same day and by Britain on 20 December.

1940

14 January   A new Yugoslav law enables the establishment of a Croat Diet. The enabling law is signed by Prince Paul on his first official visit to Croatia since his appointment as regent in 1934. Direct and secret ballots are approved for both the new Diet and the *Skupština*.

28 January   Bulgaria holds national elections on a non-party basis. Candidates are only allowed to be pro- or anti-government. The government wins 140 of the 160 seats in the *Sobranje*.

21 June   Romania establishes a new 'National Party' with King Carol as supreme leader. The new party, unlike the Front of National Rebirth which it replaces, includes members of both the National Peasants' Party and the Iron Guard. All Romanians, except Jews, are eligible for membership. All former members of the Iron Guard are amnestied.

23 July   The British government recognises the Czechoslovak National Committee in London as the provisional Czechoslovak government.

3 September   King Carol asks General Ion Antonescu to form a new Romanian government.

5 September   A Romanian decree abolishes the authoritarian royal constitution of 1938 and restricts the royal prerogative. It also dissolves parliament and makes General Antonescu 'Leader of the State'.

6 September   Following consultations with General Antonescu, King Carol abdicates in favour of his son, Michael, who becomes king, formally, for the second time. General Antonescu expresses loyalty to the 'Vienna Award' (see Glossary) to the German and Italian governments, and arrests many of his leading opponents including Georghe Tatărescu and Constantin Argetoianu, both former prime ministers.

8 September   The Antonescu government announces a programme of social reforms and of investigation into governmental and ministerial corruption since 1930. King Carol's accounts are blocked. Dr Maniu and Constantin Brătianu, leaders of the National Peasant and Liberal Parties respectively, support General Antonescu provided he reintroduces some form of constitutional government.

11 September   Horea Sima, leader of the Iron Guard, maintains that the new Romanian government is neither willing nor able to 'cooperate intimately with the Axis' powers and is only a 'pace-maker' for the Iron Guard.

15 September   A royal decree makes Romania a 'Legionary State' with the Iron Guard as the only recognised party. General Antonescu is 'Leader of the State' (*Conducator*), prime minister and head of the 'legionary regime'. Horea Sima is deputy prime minister and commander of the legionaries.

30 September   The Hungarian 'Arrow Cross' and National-Socialist Parties merge under Major Szálassi. They are joined on 6 October by the Christian National Socialists. Major Szálassi had been amnestied from a long term of imprisonment on 19 September, and the ban on the Arrow Cross and similar parties had been repealed on 29 September.

5 November   Dr Beneš in exile inaugurates a Czechoslovak Council of State of some 40 members to work as a consultative and controlling body with the provisional government. He transfers legislative powers to the presidency.

27 November   The Romanian Iron Guard carries out mass assassinations of those alleged to have been involved in the Codreanu assassination. Victims include General Argescanu and Professor Iorga, both former prime ministers, and number perhaps 2,000.

1941

21 January   The faction of the Iron Guard opposing total Romanian subservience to Axis interests rebels against the Antonescu government. Heavy street fighting and rioting ensues across the country, and some 6,000 people are killed.

25 January   General Antonescu re-establishes control with German assistance. An arrest warrant for the Guard's leader, Horea Sima, 'dead or alive', is issued the next day.

29 January   General Antonescu confirms that Romania will 'march without hesitation on the side of the great Führer and Duce'.

20 February   The decree of 15 September 1940 making Romania a 'Legionary State' based on the Iron Guard is abrogated.

26–27 March   The pro-German Yugoslav government is overthrown in a coup led by General Dušan Simović, chief of the Yugoslav Air Force. The prime and foreign ministers are arrested and King Peter II assumes the throne, six months under age.

10 April   Germany establishes a nominally independent Croat state under Dr Ante Pavelić (qv), with widely drawn boundaries. Its minister of religion, Dr Budak, is to announce of the Serbs who comprise one-third of the population: 'We shall kill some of the Serbs . . . we shall drive out others and the remainder will be forced to embrace the Roman Catholic faith.'

16 April   King Peter leaves Yugoslavia and a royal government-in-exile is established in London.

4 May   The Yugoslav government of Dušan Simović, in exile in Jerusalem, reiterates that the *Sporazum* is one of the political foundations of the state.

14 May   Dr Pavelić proclaims the establishment of a Croat monarchy and the intended accession of an Italian nominee, the Duke of Spoleto of the House of Savoy, as King Almone. The Duke, however, stays in Italy.

4 July   Yugoslav Communist partisans under the direction of Josip Broz (Tito), General Secretary of the Yugoslav Communist Party since January 1939, organise the extension of their guerrilla campaign against the Axis powers. Their aim is both to drive out the enemy and to create a Communist Yugoslavia. The Germans put a price of Reichsmark 100,000 on his head, dead or alive.

11 July	A Montenegrin National Assembly petitions the Italian High Commissioner for autonomy under a monarch within the Italian Empire. The grandson of the former King Nicholas nevertheless declines the crown.
23 August	Tito signals to the Soviet government that: 'Partisan operations in Serbia are assuming to an ever greater extent the character of a national uprising. The Germans are only holding the larger towns while the villages are in the hands of the Partisans.'
14 September	Martial law is imposed throughout Bulgaria.
1 November	A civil war opens between the Yugoslav Četniks and the Partisans which will run in parallel with the war of resistance. (See Part 2.3 for fuller particulars.)

1942

14 January	Britain disowns any attempt by ex-King Carol to create a Free Romanian Movement. America adopts a similar line on 13 February. The former monarch was then in Mexico.
19 February	Admiral Horthy's son, István, is elected Deputy Regent of Hungary in the light of his father's desire to retire. He is, however, killed in action in Russia in the August.
26 May	Reinhard Heydrich, Deputy Protector of Bohemia and Moravia and deputy head of the German Gestapo, is fatally wounded in the suburbs of Prague by two Czechs. He dies on 3 June. 207 Czechs are executed as a reprisal.
9 June	The Czech village of Lidice is 'liquidated' by the Germans as part of the reprisals for the assassination of Reinhard Heydrich. Although the total population is only about 450, the thoroughness of the destruction is to make Lidice a byword for the brutality of Nazi occupation.
16 September	An Albanian 'National Front' is established to fight for Albanian liberation from the Italians.
26 November	Tito opens the first meeting of the Anti-Fascist National Liberation Committee of Yugoslavia (AVNOJ) at Bihać on the borders of Bosnia and Croatia.

1943

22 January	A Polish Note to the Allies reports that the Germans have established at least 24 concentration camps on Polish territory, including Majdanek, Oswiecim (German Auschwitz), Sobibor, and Treblinka. The most notorious is Oswiecim. Large numbers of Poles are to be found in about 80 camps across Germany and Poland.
26 June	The new royal Yugoslav government-in-exile decides to prepare to transfer its seat from London to Cairo.

7 August	The Croat and Serb ministers of the royal Yugoslav government-in-exile in London fail to agree on the structure of the post-war Yugoslav state, and the cabinet resigns.
9 September	The Bulgarian *Sobranje* unanimously approves a Regency Council comprising Prince Kiril, the boy king's uncle, Professor Bogdan Filov, the prime minister, and General Mikhov, the minister for war.
14 September	The new Bulgarian government of Dr Bojilov, consequent upon the appointment of Professor Filov to the Regency Council, is considered more moderate in tendency than its predecessor.
30 November	Under Tito's leadership, the Anti-Fascist National Liberation Committee of Yugoslavia turns itself at Jajce into a National Committee of Liberation with the powers of a provisional government, designed to supersede the monarchy and exiled government. Tito is granted the title 'Marshal of Yugoslavia' and is made prime minister and minister of defence.
6 December	The Bulgarian minister, Kristov, announces that the government has been forced to take resolute action against 'Communist partisans' of whom over 1,000 had been killed or arrested. He is to threaten them with 'severe methods of liquidation', but is to admit that many of his own appointees as mayors had 'proved to be Communists'.

1944

23 March	A new Hungarian government is formed under Major-General Doeme Sztojay. The German and Hungarian governments agree 'to mobilise all the resources of Hungary for the final victory of the common cause'. The previous prime minister, Kallay, takes refuge in the Turkish Legation in Budapest on 26 March.
13 May	The Allies warn all Axis satellite countries of the consequences of their continued cooperation with Germany.
21 July	The Soviet Union establishes a Polish Communist-dominated 'Committee of National Liberation' in Lublin, and recognises it as the provisional Polish government in January 1945. (See also Part 2.3.)
24 August	A new all-party Romanian government is formed under General Constantin Sanatescu. It comprises members of the National Peasant, National Liberal, Social Democratic and Communist Parties. General Antonescu is arrested.
29 August	Major-General Sztojay resigns as Hungarian prime minister on health grounds and his death is reported erroneously two days later.

4 September A royal decree re-establishes the Romanian liberal constitution abrogated in 1938. It implies the revocation of the anti-Jewish legislation enacted in the interim.

9 September The pro-German Bulgarian Regency Council is dismissed and a new council appointed comprising Professor Venelin Ganev (Radical Democrat), Zvetko Boboshevsky (Conservative) and Todor Pavlov (Communist). The Council of Ministers decides to arrest all cabinet ministers who had held office in January 1941 and all members of the *Sobranje* who had supported the war policy.

18 September It is announced that the Soviet Command in Romania has arrested Marshal Ion Antonescu, dictator (*conducator*) since 1941, and leading members of his regime, as probable war criminals.

5 October The Romanian cabinet decides to purge all those responsible for the pro-fascist orientation of national policy between 1938 and 1944, and to place them before courts martial.

16 October Major Ferenc Szálassi, leader of the Hungarian Nazi Arrow Cross, establishes a Regency Council to replace Admiral Horthy and declares himself prime minister. (See Part 2.3 for fuller particulars.)

October Differences arise between the four parties comprising the Romanian National Democratic bloc (the National Liberal, National Peasant, Social Democrat and Communist Parties). The Social Democrats and Communists and two smaller left-wing groups form the National Democratic Front which seeks a larger share in government and accuses Brătianu and Maniu of opposing essential reforms and not joining fully in the alliance with the Soviet Union.

5 November Following representations by the Allied Control Commission that the Romanian government of General Sanatescu is slow in fulfilling the armistice terms, King Michael increases the representation in the government of the National Democratic Front.

12 November Romanian decrees provide for the arrest of all former members of the Iron Guard, the abrogation of all fascist racial legislation and the post-war expulsion of over 300,000 Romanian-born Germans.

28 November The Albanian provisional government moves to Tiranë. (See Part 2.3 for fuller particulars.)

30 November The Hungarian government of Major-General Szálassi moves to Sopron near the Austrian border.

20 December A People's Court in Sofia opens its hearings into war crimes charges. It sentences to death the three former regents, Prince

Kiril, Professor Filov and General Mikhov, and 98 others, comprising two former prime ministers, Dr Dobri Bojilov and Ivan Bagrianov, 20 other ministers, 68 deputies, and 8 personal advisers of the late King Boris. The last premier, Konstantin Muraviev, a further minister, 23 deputies and another two royal advisers are sentenced to life imprisonment with hard labour. The regents are executed on 1 February 1945.

24 December   A provisional Hungarian national assembly meets in Debrecen and constitutes a provisional national government comprising all the main parties.

1945

11 February   The Romanian prime minister, General Radescu, denies in a broadcast allegations by the National Democratic Front (*Frontul National Democratic*) (*FND*) that the armistice is being sabotaged by 'reactionary' ministers and 'pro-fascist' officials.

22 February   Moscow Radio broadcasts a *Pravda* article attacking what it alleges is 'the undecided and very often anti-democratic policy' of the Radescu government in Romania.

24 February   Romania experiences widespread public disorder, and a mass political demonstration is forcibly suppressed in Bucharest. General Radescu maintains that FND elements, including its Hungarian secretary-general and Ana Pauker, are 'trying to gain power by terror and criminal acts committed under the mask of democracy'. He denies that the army has provoked incidents. He resigns three days later.

1–12 March   The first Congress of the Bulgarian *Otechestven* (Fatherland) *Front* adopts a Communist resolution in favour of early free parliamentary elections.

6 March   Dr Petre Groz(e)a, previously vice-premier, and leader of the far-left Ploughmen's Front, foms a new, mainly FND, Romanian government. It fails to secure recognition from the Americans or the British.

8 March   Attacks on General Radescu continue in the Romanian press and in Soviet broadcasts, accusing him of plotting a 'dictatorship of reactionary militarists' and seeking to provoke civil war. He takes refuge in the headquarters of the British representative in Bucharest.

22 March   King Michael signs a major decree on land reform. It aims to enlarge existing holdings to 5 hectares, and to create new ones by expropriating land belonging to Germans, collaborators, war criminals and absentee landlords. In addition, all individiual estates of more than 50 hectares are expropriated, except for those belonging to the churches, cultural and scientific institutions or the crown.

3 April   Dr Beneš and the Czechoslovak government in exile return to Košice, Slovakia, as the Czechoslovak provisional capital.

7 April   The composition of the Czechoslovak provisional government, negotiated in Moscow, is announced. Dr Zdenek Fierlinger is non-party prime minister but is a left-wing socialist by conviction and a believer in close political relations with the Soviet Union.

end April   Consequent on the government's pledge of Slovak autonomy, the Slovak National Council (*Slovenska Narodni Rada*) elects a new Executive Committee comprising four Communists and four Democrats.

3.4.2 RETRIBUTION AND REVENGE

1945

10 May   Konrad Henlein, the former leader of the Czechoslovak Sudeten German Party, commits suicide in an Allied prisoner-of-war cage.

22 June   The Czechoslovak government decrees the expropriation of all land held by Germans and Hungarians, as well as by traitors and collaborators. Some 270,000 farms are involved covering 6,240,000 acres.

8 August   Bulgaria announces that 10,907 people had been indicted for treason and collaboration between the end of 1944 and the end of March 1945 and that 2,680 of them have been condemned to death.

18 October   The Czechoslovak government orders the permanent closure of the German University in Prague.

25 October   The city president of Wroclaw, formerly Breslau, announces that the 250,000 Germans still in Wroclaw will be evicted to Germany at the rate of 4,000 a week and that within six months it will be the second city in Poland.

28 October   The newly elected Czechoslovak Provisional National Assembly meets in Prague, and confirms Dr Beneš as president of Czechoslovakia. President Beneš declares that the only possible solution to the German problem is the total expulsion of all Czech Germans. 'They must go. In the interest of the peoples and the peace of Europe, there can be no other solution.' The Hungarian problem also had to be solved but rather on the basis of an exchange of populations.

4 November	A special Hungarian High Court finds Laszlo de Bardossy, a former prime minister, guilty of high treason for involving the country in the war against the will of the Hungarian people. He is hanged on 10 January 1946.
23 November	The same court finds Dr Béla de Imredy, a former prime minister and foreign minister, similarly guilty of high treason. He is hanged on 28 February 1946.

1946

6 February	General Milan Nedić, the collaborationist wartime prime minister of Serbia, commits suicide before being tried as a war criminal.
1 March	The Hungarian High Court finds Ferenc Szálassi, the leader of the Hungarian Nazi Arrow Cross and a former prime minister, guilty of high treason. He is hanged on 12 March. Nine members of his cabinet, including Dr Sandor Csia of the Regency Council, are also hanged between March and May.
22 March	The same court finds Major-General Doeme Sztojay, a former prime minister and ambassador to Berlin, guilty of high treason. He is shot by a firing squad on 24 August.
29 April– 31 July	Five leading ministers in the wartime government of the Protectorate of Bohemia and Moravia, including Professor Jaroslav Krejci, its prime minister, are tried in Prague as collaborators. Four are found guilty and sentenced to imprisonment, with Krejci receiving a term of 25 years.
22 May	Karl Hermann Frank, a Sudeten German and wartime Reichs-Protector of Bohemia and Moravia, is publicly hanged as a war criminal in the courtyard of the Pancrac Prison in Prague in front of 5,000 people. They include the survivors of Lidice who had been specifically invited to be present, as Frank had been found guilty of responsibility for ordering the massacre.
1 June	General Ion Antonescu, former *conducator* of Romania, is executed near Jihlava as a war criminal.
17 July	Colonel Draža Mihajlović is executed in Belgrade for high treason, collaboration with the enemy and war crimes. He had admitted that certain of his subordinates had reached accommodation with the enemy, but denied all charges of terrorism. In the words of his final speech: 'I wanted much . . . I began much, but the gale of the world carried me and my work away.'
29 July	Dr Bela Tuka, former prime minister of Slovakia, is put on trial for high treason, collaboration, the suppression of freedom and crimes against humanity. He is found guilty, and hanged on 20 August.

30 September The trial opens in Zagreb of Cardinal Stepinać, Archbishop of Zagreb and the head of the Roman Catholic Church in Croatia. He is to be sentenced to sixteen years' hard labour for collaboration with the Germans, the Italians and the *Ustaša*, complicity in their crimes, and resistance to the new Communist government of Yugoslavia.

16 October Dr Arthur Seyss-Inquart, the Austrian Nazi leader, is hanged at Nuremberg with nine other leading Nazis.

28 November Dr Ludwig Fischer, the wartime governor of Warsaw, Josef Meissinger, the SS chief in Warsaw, and Max Daume, the German chief of police, are put on trial in Warsaw on charges of ordering the massacre of some 500,000 Jews in the destruction of the Warsaw Ghetto, the execution of thousands of Polish patriots and the systematic destruction of Polish culture. They are found guilty, and hanged in Warsaw on 7 March 1947.

2 December Mgr Jozef Tiso, former president of Slovakia, is put on trial for high treason, collaboration, the suppression of freedom and crimes against humanity. He is found guilty, and hanged in Bratislava on 18 April 1947.

1947

30 January–
21 April Rudolf Beran, Czechoslovak prime minister after Munich, and General Jan Sirovy, interim prime minister who demobilised the army after the decision to cede the Sudetenland, are tried in Prague for collaboration and sharing responsibility for the destruction of the pre-war Czechoslovak Republic. They are found guilty and each sentenced to twenty years' imprisonment.

11 March Rudolf Hoess, commandant of the Oswiecim (Auschwitz) concentration camp, is put on trial before a Polish tribunal in Warsaw on charges of responsibility for the murder of four million Jews from all parts of German-occupied Europe, of another 300,000 inmates and of 12,000 Soviet prisoners of war. Hoess accepts full responsibility and maintains that he would have burned or gassed his own children if ordered to do so. He is hanged on his own gallows in Oswiecim on 15 April. A further 23 members of the staff at Oswiecim are sentenced to death in Krakow on 22 December 1947.

1995

8 March The Czech Constitutional Court upholds the Beneš decrees of 1945 which had evicted the Sudeten Germans and deprived them of their property.

3.5 THE LIBERAL TRADITION

It was noted in Part 3.2 that liberal constitutions had been adopted virtually everywhere by 1921 but had disappeared everywhere by 1939, and an attempt was made to explain the appeal of authoritarianism and corporatism, of fascism and Nazism. It was also noted that the practice of democracy had often fallen widely short of the theory.

Liberal democracy was, though, not without roots. The Austro-Hungarian Empire had been an imperial autocracy, but it had had a parliament in which the nationalities had been represented and in which views could be freely expressed even if its powers were very circumscribed. The obstructionism of its national, particularly Czech, members, extending on occasion to the throwing of inkwells, had nevertheless reduced its value as a school for the potential new democracies. Moreover Austrian, though not Russian, Poland had had a consultative assembly.

Bulgaria, Romania and Serbia prior to 1914 were perhaps better described as constitutional monarchies than as democracies in any true sense. Power was shared and elections were held for functioning parliaments, but the political class represented the interests of only very small parts of the population. The peasantry which formed its overwhelming bulk was effectively disenfranchised. It had risen in rebellion in Romania in 1907 and the suppression of the revolt had cost some 10,000 lives. It was the conventional wisdom that Romanian elections were held merely to confirm what had already been decided elsewhere. The power of the crown remained considerable everywhere, although Peter I of Serbia had been a strong but probably unique advocate of the merits of constitutionalism.

These weaknesses were exacerbated by the First World War settlement. Romania and Serbia had to extend their own fragile constitutional structures out to the 'new territories' of Bessarabia, Bukovina and Transylvania, and of Croatia, Bosnia and Macedonia respectively. They did not, and probably could not, succeed because the inherited administrative, legal and political structures were just too diverse, and the core nations did not have the maturity and sophistication to cope with such demanding challenges as autonomy. The newly independent African and Asian states of the former European Empires were to wrestle with very similar problems in the second half of the twentieth century. The newly created states of Czechoslovakia and Poland were in the same situation. The disaffection of the large Sudeten German minority hindered the establishment of a viable Czechoslovak liberal democracy, and in Poland Marshal Piłsudski simply lost patience with the efforts of the parliamentarians to build the new state. His impatience was widely shared and found expression in the view of observers of central and eastern Europe that every politician had a different view on every subject, but that none of them would take responsibility for anything. Their level of mutual respect was also often minimal.

A further common problem was their rather narrow interpretation of democracy. It was often seen in legalistic terms, which had little regard to the real world and in particular to the interests of the peasantry which everywhere formed the bulk of the population. The masses were electoral currency and the passive objects of policy, not its instigators. As in so many other fields, the politics of the central and eastern European states after 1919 had a great deal in common under their national dress. The Radicals in Yugoslavia, the Agrarians in Czechoslovakia and the Liberals in Romania were all increasingly bourgeois parties which could offer patronage through their long spells in power. Although they often relied on peasant votes, they primarily represented businessmen, tradesmen and public officials, and tended to be narrowly self-interested. Nominally Liberal parties, like the Romanian, were better understood as progressive conservatives than as liberals in the western sense, although their sympathies lay with France. Many, if not most, politicians of all parties were opportunists. Social democracy was normally weak, partly because it was associated with things German but more because the number of industrial workers was small. In addition, the post-war split in the socialist movement had normally produced a larger Communist than Social-Democrat grouping. Although the Communists attracted considerable support in early post-war elections (see following Part 3.6) they were progressively declared illegal, except in Czechoslovakia, and estimates of their level of support thereafter must be highly conjectural. There is, though, good reason to believe that by 1939 liberal democracy had lost much of its credibility in Yugoslavia, and that the educated young in particular were seeing the future as lying with communism.

Liberal democracy in central and eastern Europe between the wars was deeply flawed, but it would be unjust to depict it in overly negative terms. It was faced from the very beginning with enormously challenging problems of government in circumstances which were not only difficult to start with but which worsened as time went on. Its politicians received little positive help from outside, and were sometimes thwarted and ultimately even betrayed by their supposed allies. They were exposed to the hostility and in due course the vituperative abuse of the fascist and Nazi powers. Moreover, it was a personally dangerous calling, with assassination a commonplace. The persistence of men like Dr Maniu in Romania in trying to work within some sort of constitutional framework remains remarkable.

Not least it must be remembered that liberal democracy was under great strain in western Europe as well, and did not always acquit itself with any very great distinction. Universal suffrage, even for men, did not come to Britain until 1918. Moreover, the matching of the façade to the reality of democracy is in all countries a challenge which is always only imperfectly met. The ballot box is never enough. It must be backed up by a framework of trust in chosen representatives, in a representative assembly, in authority and in the rule of law. It cannot evolve until such trust has been nurtured by a culture of contract and obligation, extending beyond family, clan and socio-economic group.

3.6 MARXISM–LENINISM

3.6.1 COMMUNISM BETWEEN THE WARS

The story of communism between the wars is a story of anticlimax. Its leaders, from Marx and Engels, who had written the Communist Manifesto as long before as 1848, up to and including Lenin, had presumed that the coming revolution would break out in Germany, as Europe's most socialist-minded state. The successful Russian Revolution of 1917 was seen as an almost irrelevant precursor in a backward agricultural country to the real revolution, which would erupt in Germany and spread to the rest of western Europe. It did not happen. German social democracy split at the end of the war between the Communist revolutionaries in Berlin and Munich and the liberal Social Democrats who had come to power in the political vacuum caused by the flight of the Kaiser. The liberal Social Democrats allied themselves with the army establishment bloodily to suppress revolution, leaving scars between the two wings of the socialist movement which contributed significantly to the rise of Hitler. Lenin's strategy of exporting revolution westwards through Poland had lost its point. Communist revolution in Hungary temporarily enjoyed more success, partly because it was associated with Hungarian national resistance to the territorial changes sought by the Allies, notably the loss of Slovakia. Nevertheless by August 1919 it had been overcome by a combination of internal and external pressures.

In the longer term, the much more important development was the continued splitting in the socialist movement between its revolutionary Communist and liberal Social Democrat wings. The most successful, and the only continuously legal, Communist Party was the Czechoslovak, *Komunisticka Strana Ceskoslovenska*, founded in 1921, which by 1939 had attracted some one million supporters. In central and eastern Europe, except for Austria, the Communist wing enjoyed much more electoral support than the Social Democratic wing on the limited number of occasions when their rivalry could be put to the test, and it was a gap which appeared to be widening. In the successive Bulgarian elections of 1919 and 1920, for example, the Communists, who had been the 'Narrows' prior to May 1919, increased their share of the vote by more than half, whereas the Social Democrats lost one third of theirs. By 1923 the Communist vote was nearly ten times that of the Social Democrats.

In practice, though, the fear of revolution caused governments progressively to introduce measures of repression. The Hungarian White Terror of 1920 suppressed communism as did the Polish victory over Soviet Russia of the same year. In some countries the Communists may have weakened their position by boycotting elections, or refusing to enter into governing coalitions when they did enjoy electoral success, as in Bulgaria in August 1919, when they were the second largest political party. In any event, the Bulgarian Communist Party was made illegal on 1 April 1924, although it did resurface as the Bulgarian Labour Party. Romanian and Yugoslav communism were similarly declared illegal in 1924 and 1920 respectively.

Such considerations make estimates of Communist support in most countries between the wars little better than guesswork. Czechoslovakia is the exception, although the Bulgarian Labour Party was sufficiently successful for its members to be suspended from the *Sobranje* in 1933. There was obviously always a vast difference between the numbers of members of outlawed Communist Parties and the numbers of sympathisers and potential voters.

Another difficulty is represented by the changing role of the Soviet Union. The revolutionary expectations of 1919, which led to the establishment of the Third or Communist International (the Comintern) in Moscow to direct the anticipated national revolutions, were replaced within a few years by the perceived need to harness national revolutionary fervour to the interests of the Soviet Union as the world's pioneering Communist state. This meant on the one hand that many post-war Communist leaders, including Dimitrov, Tito and Ulbricht, spent years in Moscow, but on the other that Communist Parties were expected to enter into 'popular fronts' with their rivals, or could even, like the Polish Communist Party in 1938, be disbanded at Stalin's behest. The wheel turned full circle when Stalin dissolved the Comintern itself on 15 May 1943 so as to improve his relations with the western Allies.

3.6.2 THE POST-WAR CONSOLIDATION OF COMMUNIST POWER

Commentary

Much has been written about the progressive assumption of power by Communist regimes across central and eastern Europe from 1944 onwards, and the subject is likely to remain intensely controversial. Nevertheless, it can probably be said that many fewer analysts than was once the case now believe that the Communists came to power in accordance with a master plan devised in, and administered from, the Kremlin. It now seems at least as likely that the Soviet Union, like the western Allies, responded to unpredictable events as they unfolded and tried to turn them to its advantage, not always successfully. In particular, it seems implausible that the Soviet Union after its appalling economic and human wartime losses was ever minded to pursue a war policy.

On the other hand, the Communists were determined revolutionaries, hardened by persecution before and during the war, and all too conscious of the extent to which the failed German and Hungarian revolutions of 1919 had led, immediately in the latter case and within fourteen years in the former case, to right-wing dictatorship. They were no less conscious of the ruthlessness with which the infant bourgeois French Republic had suppressed the Paris Commune in 1870 and of how the rivalry between communism and social democracy in Germany had let in Hitler.

Communists who had led the liberation of their countries and experienced great personal danger like Hoxha in Albania and Tito in Yugoslavia, Communists who had been active in the resistance like Gomulka in Poland and Husák in Czechoslovakia, Communists who had spent the war in concentration camps like Honecker in Germany, and Communists who had spent the war in the strictly comparative safety of Moscow like Ulbricht, also in Germany, were all united in their determination to build a quite different type of society. They could rely on some solid pillars of support. The economic and political failures of the liberal capitalism and liberal democracy of the 1920s and 30s had widely discredited them and boosted the attraction of Marxism as a viable alternative. The Left throughout Europe, including Britain, was determined to nationalise and place under governmental control key industries and financial institutions. Not least, it was the Communist Soviet Union which had driven the Germans out of central and eastern Europe, and power always commands respect. It was also the Communists who had spearheaded the resistance, most obviously the Albanian and Yugoslav Partisans, but also the Slovaks of the 1944 Uprising.

Needless to say, the Communist programme and Soviet power meant very different things to different peoples and places. To the Czechs, who had been abandoned by the western powers at Munich and had a large established Communist Party, the Soviet Union was a true liberator who had initiated the highly popular expulsion of the Sudeten Germans for good measure. In Albania and Yugoslavia, the Communists had overcome both internal and external opposition to become the national party, and both initially assumed that the Soviet Union was their natural ally. In Bulgaria the Communists were aided by the people's close bonds of sympathy with the Russians and might well have won free and open elections. In Hungary, on the other hand, which had been Germany's most consistent ally, as in the Soviet Zone of Germany itself, the Communists, although they had deep traditional roots, could only exercise influence under the umbrella of their nation's recent enemy.

In both Poland and Romania, attitudes were more ambiguous. The Romanians had allied themselves with the Germans but had then had to surrender as much territory to Hungary as to the Soviet Union. Specifically Communist support was very low, but the promise of land reform was attractive to a disadvantaged peasantry. Poland was torn. Inclined to see the Germans and the Russians as equal enemies, she still had to recognise that the Soviet Union had accepted an independent Poland as an integral part of the post-war settlement, albeit one with radically changed boundaries, whereas Nazi Germany had sought to starve it out of existence. The Polish Communists were at least Poles. Suspicions were none the less strong that the Soviet Union had deliberately withheld support from the Warwaw Uprising to enable the Germans to eliminate many of Poland's non-Communist leaders.

True or false, it is necessary to repeat that the Communists everywhere were determined revolutionaries aiming to exercise power, who saw the Soviet victory over Nazi Germany as evidence that their hour had come. The churches, the establishment and the middle classes, which had indeed all too often temporised with the fascists and the Nazis, were to be swept aside and the interests of the masses made paramount. The objective of democracy was to mobilise the masses not to marginalise them through the fragmentation of parliamentary systems which served only the interests of a narrow political class. It was a conviction which lacked humility but could be burningly sincere. Its single-mindedness, though, and its sheer radicalism meant that ends were frequently seen as justifying means. The interests of the party as the vanguard of the revolution were above the law and, if need be, above common humanity. Recourse to terror was never very far away even if it was actually unnecessary. Neither were deceit and guile, particularly perhaps in the Balkans where they were a traditional means of accommodating superior force. Neither was opportunism. The Czech Communists, for example, were to promise that entry into party membership would be taken as payment in full for collaboration with the Nazis. East Germany was to establish a specific political party under the umbrella of the SED to represent the interests of former nominal Nazis and medium- and higher-ranking military personnel. It should, perhaps, be added that the western Allies were no less opportunistic and that denazification was to be much more thorough in what became the Soviet bloc.

The establishment of Communist power was, however, complicated from the beginning by the interaction of three major factors. The first was the Soviet Union's perception of its own interests. The Soviet Union had been forced since the early 1920s to pursue a policy of 'socialism in one country' and the ideal of exporting revolution associated with Lenin and Trotsky had been inverted under Stalin to the ideal of preserving the Soviet Union as the world's pioneering Communist state. The perceived interests of the Soviet state were to be promoted much as those of any other state. The 1939 non-aggression pact with Germany and the subsequent alliance with the west had had no regard to ideological considerations and Communists elsewhere had been required to switch their loyalties with bewildering rapidity. Similarly, the Soviet Union had backed cooperation with non-Communist elements in national resistance movements throughout the war whenever it had believed that a more broadly based group would be more effective. It had repeatedly denied supplies to Tito, for example, urging him to make common cause with other groups, and his constant refusal to do so was to contribute to the rupture of 1948.

The second factor was the tension between the different strands in the Communist movement itself. The popular image of a monolithic Communist movement is increasingly seen as a myth which owed more to western fears and Communist propaganda than to reality. The repeated charges of national deviationism and Titoism levelled against different Communist leaders were often false in their detail, but they reflected the widespread reality of differing national and personal approaches. Władysław Gomułka, secretary-general of the Polish Communist Party until 1948, as just one prominent example, disagreed with the expulsion of Yugoslavia from the Cominform, opposed the collectivisation of Polish agriculture and opposed the then Soviet promotion of a united Germany in view of the potential threat to Poland. He even foreshadowed the later reforms of the Prague Spring and western Eurocommunism by dispensing with the Leninist concept of the dictatorship of the proletariat. The sheer virulence of the charges against Tito and any possible sympathisers was as much an admission of actual weakness as a proof of the urge to dominate, insofar as the two were not opposite sides of the same coin. It may have been further aided by the curious fact that the Russian ability at the personal level to live in relative harmony with different races and cultures, first in the Russian Empire and then in the Soviet Union, has never appeared to be exportable. The Russians were never to seem able to make themselves much liked either in their own bloc or outside it. In any event, Communist leaders across central and eastern Europe were regularly to take initiatives of which the Soviet Union disapproved. The January 1948 Dimitrov proposal of an eastern European federation was to be perhaps the most blatant example during the period of consolidation, but many more were to follow in later decades.

The third and probably the most important, and certainly the most contentious, of the complicating factors was the need for the Communists to work through coalitions with other parties. It is a historical fact that by 1952 and in many cases appreciably earlier the Communists had everywhere absorbed, eliminated or marginalised all their coalition partners. Some argue that this was intended from the very beginning. Others are much more doubtful, noting the sheer untidiness of the process and its inherent contradictions. Hungary, for example, as a defeated Axis power, could have been given a Soviet military government in 1945 rather than allowed to elect freely a parliament dominated by a Smallholders Party with influential right-wing and even far right-wing elements. The Soviet Union may at that time simply have put more importance on maintaining a collaborative relationship with the western Allies than on achieving a Communist Hungary. It never even tried to draw Finland into its orbit. There is evidence, particularly perhaps from Romania, that it was the national Communist Parties who were making the running on their own initiative. It was not necessarily only Tito and Hoxha whom Stalin found difficult to control.

This is not to suggest that the Soviet Union did not exercise powerful influence. It forcefully encouraged the fusion of Communist and Social Democratic Parties starting with the East German in 1946, although it was a pattern which also enjoyed support from a large number of Social Democratic Party members. Both Otto Grotewohl and Jozef Cyrankiewicz, the long-serving prime ministers of East Germany and Poland, came from the Social Democratic wing of their respective united parties. The Soviet Union also enjoyed prestige as the home of successful Communist revolution and as the conqueror of Germany alike.

The concept of the single list of candidates, with the prearrangement by the parties of their respective numbers of representatives, has similarly been seen as a ruse to achieve Communist domination 'by the back door'. Such interpretations, however, have tended to reflect American and British traditions and their suspicion of coalitions and referenda as such. Government by party machine is much more the norm in mainland Europe and indeed the four leading Swiss parties at the federal level have been sharing power on an agreed, virtually permanent, formula basis ever since 1959.

There seems little room for doubt that calculations were drastically altered by the breakdown in relations between the western Allies and the Soviet Union over the future of Germany, which can perhaps be pinpointed to the abortive foreign ministers' meeting of March–April 1947 in Moscow. The Soviet Union no longer had anything to gain by being conciliatory to the west, and the central and eastern European Communist Parties were its natural allies until the dramatic shock of Tito's independent line in the spring of 1948. The accretion of Communist power was now to be as unstoppable as the insistence on orthodoxy. Any possibility of compromise disappeared. (See also following sections.) The pace of revolution accelerated, and the level of opposition rose likewise.

Revolutions, like wars, are an angry and ugly process in which injustice and suffering are endemic, whether one ultimately identifies with their objectives or not. Communist revolutions were no exception, but they underlined the nature of Lenin's legacy. The concept of the primacy of a tightly organised party made the Communists effective and successful in a way which had eluded the liberal revolutionaries of 1848 and 1919, but at the price of the subjection of the law and of human rights to the interests of the party. It was a baleful legacy which they would never be able to discard.

Chronology

1945

22 August	Having failed to persuade the Groz(e)a government to resign, King Michael of Romania appeals to the American, British and Soviet governments for help in establishing a government which they will recognise and which will permit the signature of peace treaties and admission to the United Nations.
23 August	King Michael breaks off all relations with the Groz(e)a government and refuses to sign any of its decrees. He does, however, continue to maintain friendly relations with the Soviet representatives in Romania.
20 October	Constantin Brătianu, the leader of the Romanian National Liberals, maintains of the Groz(e)a government that 'this government, which bears all the stigmata of dictatorship, constitutes a real danger both to internal order and to the foreign position of Romania'. He maintains that 'it is certain that the government has no credit in any of the country's social categories'.
25 October	Dr Iuliu Maniu, the leader of the Romanian National Peasant Party, maintains that:

The Groz(e)a government is the most hateful Romania has ever possessed . . . It holds its power solely thanks to its armed guards, censorship and a regime of terror such as Romania has never known. It has set up concentration camps for its political opponents and all prisons are now full of members of the National Peasant and National Liberal Parties, while newly recruited police agents are maltreating and torturing political prisoners. Anarchy rules in Romania. Those Romanians who became notorious under the dictatorship, by transferring their allegiance to the Communist Party, escaped punishment as war criminals and now exercise a new dictatorship through their ministerial positions in this so-called democratic regime.

[*Source*: Keesing's Contemporary Archives p.7664]

4 November   The first post-war Hungarian general election is held fairly and freely. The Smallholders Party wins with 245 seats, followed by the Communists with 70, the Socialists with 69, the National Peasants with 23 and the Democrats with 2.

11 November   The Yugoslav general elections are won by Marshal Tito's 'People's Front' with 90 per cent of the vote. There had been a single list of 510 candidates of which 470 were Communists and the balance Communist-sponsored.

18 November   The Bulgarian general elections are won by the government with 86 per cent of the vote, as against 12 per cent for the unofficial opposition comprising a single list of candidates headed by Nikola Petkov, the leader of the Agrarians. The elections had been postponed so as to enable the four opposition groups to become legal political parties, but they had boycotted the elections on the grounds that no free elections were possible while the ministries of the interior and justice were Communist-controlled.

Colonel Georgiev forms a second 'Fatherland Front' government comprising 5 Communists, 5 *Zveno* members, 4 Agrarians, 1 Social Democrat and 1 Radical.

2 December   The Democratic Front wins 93.18 per cent of the votes in the Albanian national elections, which are described by western correspondents as being held in a free and orderly atmosphere.

1946

4 January   Following negotiations with the Allies, the Romanian opposition parties agree to appoint representatives to join the government. The government, however, rejects the nominations of Constantin Brătianu and Ion Michalache the following day on the grounds that they are 'reactionaries'. Alternative nominations are accepted on 7 January.

25 February	Negotiations between the Polish National Peasant Party (PSL) and other parties for an electoral bloc with a single list of candidates for the forthcoming elections break down.
11 March	The Romanian Social Democratic Party resolves by a large majority to put forward election candidates on joint lists with the Communists and other left-wing groups of the National Democratic Front. The party leader, Titel Petrescu, opposes the decision and announces his decision to re-found the party.
12 March	Following a security police raid on PSL headquarters, the Polish government alleges that documents have been found showing that the PSL had been in touch with 'imprisoned terrorists'.
21–22 April	The German Communist and Social Democratic Parties in the Soviet Zone merge at a Unification Congress in Berlin to form the Socialist Unity Party of Germany (*Sozialistische Einheitspartei Deutschlands – SED*).
28 April	The National Peasant Party leaves the Polish government and goes into opposition.
26 May	The Czechoslovak general elections are won by the Communists with 38 per cent of the vote and the support of some other left-wing groups. A Communist-led coalition government is formed.
29 May	Dr G. M. Dimitrov, the former leader of the Bulgarian Agrarian Party, is sentenced to life imprisonment for 'undermining the morale of the Bulgarian Army during the 1944 campaign against Germany'.
28 June	Kristu Pastukhov, the veteran Bulgarian Social Democrat leader, is sentenced to five years' imprisonment for criticising a speech to the Bulgarian Army by the prime minister, Georgi Dimitrov.
30 June	Poland holds a referendum on three questions designed to assess 'whether the policy of [successively] the National Council, the Polish Committee of National Liberation and the provisional Government of National Unity is in harmony with the will of the people'. The three questions are: Are you for the abolition of the Senate; Are you for making permanent through the future constitution the economic system instituted by land reform and nationalisation of basic industries, with maintenance of the rights of private initiative; and, Are you for the Polish western frontiers as fixed on the Baltic and on the Oder and Neisse? The final results announced on 12 July are all in the affirmative. Stanisław Mikolajczyk, leader of the National Peasant

139

Party, had protested on 1 July, however, that there had been irregularities in the vote.

14 July   The new Romanian electoral law extends the vote to women for the first time.

22 September   Poland adopts an electoral law providing for free, private ballots. Economic and other collaborators are disenfranchised. Stanisław Mikolajczyk opposes the law, alleging that it would prevent his party from obtaining fair representation.

27 October   The Bulgarian general elections are won by the Communists with 277 seats in the *Sobranje* as against 69 for the Agrarians, 9 for the Social Democrats, 8 for *Zveno* and 1 for the Radicals. Turnout is 96 per cent and the elections are conducted in a quiet and orderly manner. The Independent Agrarian leader, Nikola Petkov, maintains, however, that the election campaign has been conducted in an atmosphere of terror.

The principal issue in the elections had been the proposed new constitution which would proclaim a People's Republic. The opposition wishes to retain the 1879 constitution, but with the monarch replaced by a president.

19 November   The Romanian general elections are won by the government bloc, the National Democratic Front, with 70 per cent of the vote. The National Democratic Front comprises the Liberals of Gheorghe Tatărescu, the foreign minister, with 75 seats, the Social Democrats, also with 75, the Communists with 73, the Ploughmen's Front (*Frontul Plugarilor*) with 70, the National People's Party with 26, dissident National Peasants with 20 and others with 9.

The opposition comprises the National Peasant Party with 32 seats, the National Liberals with 3, the Democratic Peasant Party with 2 and the Hungarian People's Union with 29. Constantin Brătianu and Titel Petrescu are both defeated.

22 November   Georgi Dimitrov, the Bulgarian Communist leader, forms a third 'Fatherland Front' government. It comprises 9 Communists, 5 Agrarians, 2 Social Democrats, 2 *Zveno* members and an independent Communist. The former prime minister, Colonel Kimon Georgiev (*Zveno*) becomes foreign minister.

5 December   Dr Maniu informs the president of the Romanian National Assembly that the National Peasant Party regards the elections as null and void, and will boycott the new parliament accordingly.

10 December   Dr Maniu maintains that the National Peasant Party alone had actually won 70 per cent of the vote in the Romanian elections and that the National Democratic Front had won not more than 16 per cent.

| 31 December | It is announced in Budapest that a significant number of army officers and right-wing members of the Smallholders Party have been arrested following the discovery of an alleged conspiracy against the state. (See also Part 2.4.) |

1947

| 19 January | The government bloc wins 394 of the 444 seats in the *Sejm* in the Polish general elections. The government bloc comprises the Polish Workers (Communist) Party (PPL), the Polish Socialist Party (PPS), the Democratic Party (SP) and a dissenting portion of the Peasant Party (PS). The four parties had previously agreed on the allocation of seats between them. |

| 23 January | Stanislaw Mikołajczyk declares that he will appeal to the Supreme Court for the elections to be declared null and void. |

| 28 January | Ferenc Nagy, the Hungarian prime minister and Smallholders Party leader, declares at a meeting of the Party's Parliamentary Club that the party will expel those of its members whose actions had 'obscured its progressive and parliamentary character'. |

| 31 January | The Hungarian Communist Party executive accuses the Smallholders Party of 'delaying tactics' which are favouring the 'rallying of reactionary forces'. The attacks by the Communists and the Socialists are focused on Béla Kovacs, the party's Secretary-General. |

| 4 February | The political committee of the Smallholders Party expels a further five deputies from the party and suspends another three, as well as Béla Kovacs, pending further investigation. These reduce the party's strength in the National Assembly to 203, as against 245 after the elections of November 1945 and 222 after expulsions in 1946. The party remains the strongest in the Assembly, but loses its overall majority. |

| 7 February | The new Polish government comprises 8 Socialists, including the prime minister, 5 Communists, 5 members of the dissenting portion of the Peasants Party, 3 Democrats, 2 Catholic Labour and 1 non-party member. |

| 7 February | Laszlo Rajk, the Hungarian Communist minister of the interior, asks the National Assembly to withdraw the parliamentary immunity enjoyed by Béla Kovacs, Secretary-General of the Smallholders Party, so as to permit his arrest. It is alleged that he had known of an 'underground organisation' and of the plan to form a counter-revolutionary government. The Smallholders reject the charges, while admitting that some party members had aimed to overthrow the regime. |

20 February	Béla Kovacs voluntarily resigns his party offices, asserting that he had had no involvement in the conspiracy but accepted a measure of political responsibility.
25 February	Béla Kovacs is arrested by the Soviet military authorities and charged with 'organising secret armed anti-Soviet terrorist groups'. The Americans protest to the Soviet government and the Soviet chairman of the Allied Control Commission at what they describe as 'unjustified Russian interference in Hungarian internal affairs'.
12 March	Following Communist and Socialist pressure, Ferenc Nagy, the Hungarian prime minister, forms a new coalition government with three fewer Smallholder ministers. A further five deputies are expelled. The new coalition's programme includes the abolition of compulsory religious education in schools and the regulation of the relations between church and state.
5 May	The Romanian ministry of the interior announces that a number of people have been arrested on charges of conspiring to overthrow the regime, subversion and sabotage.
31 May	Ferenc Nagy resigns as Hungarian prime minister following Soviet assertions that Béla Kovacs had implicated him in the counter-revolutionary plot. The new prime minister, Lajos Dinnyes, also of the Smallholders Party, accuses his predecessors of having been surrounded by a 'clique who desired the restoration of reactionary rule in Hungary'. Ferenc Nagy is expelled from the party on 4 June.
6 June	Nikola Petkov, leader of the Bulgarian Agrarian Party, a bastion of anti-Communist sentiment, and leader of the Opposition in the *Sobranje*, is arrested as he leaves the *Sobranje* building. He is accused of conspiring to overthrow the government by armed force. The American and British representatives in Sofia protest at the banning of *Narodno Zemedelsko Zname* and *Svoboden Narod*, the organs of the Agrarian and Social Democrat Parties respectively.
10 June	The Hungarian minister of justice, István Riesz, announces that under the new electoral law about 500,000 people, or some 10 per cent of the previous electorate, will lose the vote, including all those sentenced for 'crimes against democracy', 'collaborationists', and those who had returned from western Europe since 1 January.
12 June	The *Sobranje* resolves by a large majority to unseat 23 Agrarian Party deputies because they had earlier written 'unconstitutional letters of loyalty' to Nikola Petkov. The deputies are to be replaced by an equal number from the party's electoral list.

15 July	Dr Maniu, Ion Michalache and other leaders of the Romanian National Peasant Party are arrested, and the party newspaper, *Dreptatea*, banned. Dr Maniu is accused of directing a plot to overthrow the regime. He is to be found guilty on 11 November and sentenced to life imprisonment. (See also Part 2.4.)
29 July	The Romanian government officially dissolves the National Peasant Party of Dr Iuliu Maniu. Its representatives continue to sit in parliament as independents.
5–16 August	The trial of Nikola Petkov in Sofia ends with his condemnation to death. His four co-defendants, who unlike him had pleaded guilty, receive prison sentences of from five to fifteen years. He is hanged on 23 September. The proceedings are denounced by the American and British governments.
26 August	The *Sobranje* approves legislation dissolving the Bulgarian Agrarian Party, alleging that it had become 'a centre for fascist forces seeking revenge' and was responsible for 'terrorist sabotage and diversionist acts aimed at provoking the foreign occupation of Bulgaria'.
5 October	The Communist Parties of nine European countries, the Soviet Union, Bulgaria, Czechoslovakia, Hungary, Poland, Romania and Yugoslavia (together with France and Italy) decide in Warsaw to establish a Communist Information Bureau based in Belgrade to 'organise the exchange of experiences' and 'where necessary to coordinate the activities of the Communist parties on the basis of mutual agreement'. The text bitterly attacks 'American imperialism' and the western Social Democrat and Labour Parties, particularly in Britain and France. The new 'Cominform' is seen in the west as a renewal of the Communist International (Comintern) which had been closed down in 1943.
26 October	Stanisław Mikolajczyk, the leader of the Polish National Peasant Party, flees Poland.
22 November	The Bulgarian Communist Party introduces a law in the *Sobranje* whereby the 'Fatherland Front' will be turned into a single 'people's organisation' and the government be authorised to nationalise all remaining private industries.
4 December	The *Sobranje* adopts the proposed new constitution and proclaims Bulgaria a 'People's Republic'.
11 December	Georgi Dimitrov forms a fourth 'Fatherland Front' government following the enactment of the new Bulgarian constitution. The new government comprises 14 Communists, 5 Agrarians, 2 Social Democrats and 2 *Zveno* members.
30 December	King Michael abdicates and Romania becomes officially the Romanian People's Republic.

1948

13 January The small Bulgarian opposition opposes the government's budget in the *Sobranje*. The prime minister, Georgi Dimitrov, reminds them that the executed Agrarian Party leader, Nikola Petkov, is 'under the ground' and tells them: 'If you have not been wise in the past and do not try to gain wisdom you will receive a lesson that you will remember until you meet St Peter.' He continues that if the Americans and the British 'had not intervened . . . the death sentence [on Nikola Petkov] could have been commuted to other punishment'.

17 February Underlying tensions come to a head at a cabinet meeting of the Czechoslovak 'National Front' coalition government. The Communist ministers insist on immediate and extensive measures of nationalisation, and the non-Communists protest at the appointment of Communists to important security service posts in contravention of agreed cabinet policy.

18 February The Czechoslovak Communist Party accuses the non-Communist parties in the coalition government of provoking a crisis in the cabinet, of delaying the government's programme by 'dilatory' tactics and of working to overthrow the coalition before the May general elections.

21 February The Czech National Socialist Party of President Beneš, the People's Party and the Slovak Democratic Party decide to withdraw from the cabinet in view of the minister of the interior's refusal to rescind his security service appointments. The Czechoslovak Communist Party urges President Beneš to accept the ministers' resignations and expresses the belief that the Social Democratic Party would 'find it necessary to remain in the government at the side of the Communist Party for the sake of the realisation of the Government's programme'. The President, however, declines to allow ministers of any party to resign before general elections.

22 February The Czechoslovak Communist Party leader, Klement Gottwald, addresses a mass party demonstration in Wenceslas Square, Prague, and calls for the establishment throughout the country of 'Action Committees' to form the basis of a 'new National Front'.

25 February President Beneš reluctantly accepts the resignations of the twelve ministers and the formation of a new coalition government, in which Communist ministers hold half the cabinet posts and most of the major ones. He also releases the text of a letter to the Praesidium of the Communist Party the previous day in which he had written: 'It is clear to me that Socialism is the way of life desired by an overwhelming part of our nation. At the same time I believe that with Socialism a certain measure of freedom and unity is possible, and that these are the vital principles of our national life.' The Communists, with 144 seats, have a working majority in coalition with the Social Democrats, who have 39, in the 300-seat National Assembly.

2 March Dr Cepicka, the Czechoslovak minister of justice, issues the first official order on the role of the 'Action Committees'. They are to be recognised as the 'supreme organs on cultural and political matters', and their chief task is to 'cleanse' the Czech National Socialist, People's and Slovak Democratic Parties. A Central Action Committee is to be formed in Prague to create at all levels 'organisations of reliable persons' whose duty it would be to 'remove everyone whose loyalty is doubtful', and that until that process was complete, the parties to be 'cleansed' were not to be allowed to form new party associations. Only the Central Action Committee and the political committees to 'cleanse' the parties are envisaged as permanent.

11 March The Czechoslovak prime minister swears in a new Slovak Board of Commissioners. It is predominantly Communist and led by Dr Gustav Husák.

9 April All parties in the Czechoslovak 'National Front' government agree to present a single list of candidates for the forthcoming elections 'to confirm the results of the events of February in a democratic, constitutional and parliamentary fashion'.

10 April The executive committee of the Czechoslovak Social Democratic Party votes unanimously to merge with the Czechoslovak Communist Party.

9 May Czechoslovakia adopts a new constitution, declaring it a 'Democratic People's Republic'.

30 May The Czechoslovak general elections produce 6,431,963 votes for the governing 'National Front', as against 772,293 blank votes, the only legally permitted alternative. 78.3 per cent of the seats in the new Assembly are held by the Communists and Social Democrats.

7 June President Beneš refuses to sign Czechoslovakia's new constitution and resigns.

8 December The political committee of the Hungarian Smallholders Party declares that the party must be purged of its 'bourgeois' elements.

15–21 December The Polish Workers' (Communist) and Socialist Parties merge at a congress in Warsaw as the Polish United Workers' Party.

1949

19 February   The Bulgarian *Zveno* Party of Colonel Kimon Georgiev, following the example of the Radical Party, resolves to discontinue its existence as an independent party and to merge into the 'Fatherland Front'. Its members should 'support the establishment of socialism in Bulgaria'. The 'Fatherland Front' henceforth consists of only the Communist and Social Democratic Parties.

2 April   The American and British governments protest to the Romanian government at its violation of the peace treaty by allegedly curtailing in a systematic manner the fundamental freedoms of expression, press and publication, of political opinion and of religious worship.

15 May   The People's Independence Front, comprising five parties under the direction of the United Workers Party, on a single list wins 95.6 per cent of the vote in the Hungarian general elections. The new parliament comprises: United Workers Party 270 seats, Smallholders 62, National Peasants 30, Independent Democrats 12 and Radicals 4.

18 August   The National Assembly approves a new Hungarian constitution modelled on the Soviet constitution of 1936 and paralleled in the other 'people's democracies'. It declares the Hungarian People's Republic a state of the workers and working peasants which 'organises all forces of society for the struggle for socialism'. Natural resources, banking, transport, public utilities and the chief industries are declared to be the property of the state. The national flag is revised to feature a five-pointed red star rather than the former coat of arms.

early October   10–50,000 people are arrested in Czechoslovakia in a purge of 'unreliable', predominantly middle-class elements.

12 October   The first East German government is announced under Otto Grotewohl of the SED, which has a clear majority in the government of ten to eight.

18 December   The single list of candidates presented by the 'Fatherland Front' wins 98.89 per cent of the vote in the Bulgarian general elections. The proportion of party strengths within the list was pre-arranged. The new *Sobranje* comprises 156 Communists, 48 Agrarians, and 35 Independents, and the new cabinet 22 Communists, 3 Agrarians and 1 Independent.

1950

31 May   The trial opens in Prague of thirteen leading figures, including prominent members of the Czech National Socialist, Social Democratic and Catholic People's Parties, on charges of high treason and espionage. All plead guilty. All are found guilty on 8 June and Jan Buchal, Milana Horakova, Professor Zavis Kalandra and Dr Oldrich Pecl are sentenced to death.

1951

3 March The new Politburo of the Hungarian United Workers Party contains only one former Socialist – Sandor Ronai, the national president.

1952

30 May The dismissal of Dr Jan Sevcik as vice-prime minister and minister for physical culture marks the removal of the last non-Communist Czechoslovak vice-prime minister.

9 July Walter Ulbricht announces that the Central Committee of the SED has decided that 'the planned construction of socialism should begin' in East Germany. He adds, in accordance with Stalinist orthodoxy, that 'the intensification of the class struggle is inevitable'.

22 July Poland adopts a new constitution, modelled on the Soviet constitution of 1936, whereby the country becomes officially the Polish People's Republic (*Polska Rzeczpospolita Ludowa*).

24 September Romania adopts a new constitution modelled on the Soviet constitution of 1936. The new constitution emphasises more strongly than that of 1948 Romania's links with the Soviet Union.

30 November Romania holds elections for a new Grand National Assembly. There is only one candidate, representing the People's Democratic Front, in each constituency.

3.6.3 THE PURGES AND THE SHOW TRIALS

Commentary

The Communist Party purges of 1948–53 had several different strands of inspiration. On the one hand they were reminiscent of the purges of the Soviet Party in the 1930s which, as well as being a means of eliminating political rivals, were also almost an institutionalised means of stimulating ever greater commitment and effort by party members. It was a rather literal case of the survival of the fittest and the exclusion of dead wood, or, to adapt Voltaire, of shooting one to encourage the rest. It was also a way of meeting the permanent Russian challenge of imposing the will of the centre on what is essentially a continent.

They also had the purpose, shared by the purges of central and eastern Europe, of imposing strict party discipline. The execution of the Communist revolutionary programme demanded party cadres able and willing to cajole and persuade and, if necessary, to overcome hostility and opposition, but also to administer in an approved manner myriad new organisations spawned by the revolution. With the outbreak of the Cold War and Tito's declaration of independence, it also became more necessary than ever to ensure that party members were loyal. As is so often the case in communities under stress, loyalty was interpreted as orthodoxy. Although often hijacked for strictly personal motives, the purges were in essence the simple exclusion of dissent for reasons akin to those of the religious persecutions of earlier centuries.

On the other hand, the purges were also driven by the need to reduce the proportion of party members attracted by purely mercenary motives. Once the Communists were in power, many people joined the party to be in the swing of things or even, as the English would say, 'to keep up with the Joneses'. Unchecked, it could have proved as harmful to the party's effectiveness as heresy; in the longer term probably more so.

The show trials of the period are in contrast among the most difficult phenomena to understand fully in the whole period since 1919. Communist leaders of many years' standing were accused by colleagues of offences of which they were almost always totally innocent and of which their accusers knew they were innocent. The 1938 Soviet show trials were clearly a precedent, and many accusers no doubt felt that Stalin's paranoia had been so fed by the Cold War and Tito's independent line that 'traitors' would have to be identified and sacrificed. It was clearly preferable to be an accuser than to be accused, and charges could mask a naked struggle for power akin to that of a medieval monarchy. It was also, no doubt, an opportunity for the unscrupulous to settle some old scores. The results could be arbitrary. The losing faction in Romania of Georgescu, Vasile Luca and Ana Pauker was believed to be specifically pro-Soviet. Anti-Semitism played a role, particularly after Israel had allied herself with America, but again with inconsistent effect. In Hungary, the Jewish Rakosi triumphed over the non-Jewish Rajk; in Czechoslovakia it was the Jewish Slánský who succumbed.

Other factors, though, must have been at work. As clandestine revolutionaries pursuing intrigue for decades, many no doubt saw themselves as victims of intrigue in their turn. There was distrust, not confined to Stalin, between those Communists who had spent the war in Moscow and those involved in the national resistance movements or held in prison. The western intelligence services certainly sought to promote such distrust for their own ends. Some, like Gomulka in Poland who was lucky to escape with imprisonment and Gheorghe Gheorghiu-Dej in Romania, were basically orthodox but nationally minded Communists. Others had perhaps been exposed to, and then themselves perpetrated, so much terror that it had lost its meaning. Revolutions often consume those which make them, with the French Revolution as the classic example, and Rajk and Slánský can be seen as a latter-day Danton and Robespierre.

148

Perhaps the strangest aspect, though, of the trials was an apparent readiness of at least some of the defendants to accept their guilt in a manner which could not be totally ascribed to 'brainwashing' or torture. Slánský's last words were: 'I got what I deserved.' Perhaps faith in the scientific truth of communism, in the role of the party, and in the future of the Soviet Union as the world's pioneering Communist state was so deep that the defendants felt that none of them could err. If that is so, it would reflect the strand of Byzantine tradition absorbed by Leninism, whereby the emperor was absolute at one and the same time in both the secular and spiritual fields. In the west, it would perhaps be most reminiscent of Tudor England where the king's rule became similarly absolute in spiritual and temporal matters alike.

It is also worthy of note that the phenomenon of the show trial was not universal across the Communist world, and that its national incidence was unpredictable, apart from the obvious exception of Yugoslavia whose Titoism was part of the motivation. No true show trials, for example, were held in East Germany or Poland, although there were certainly purges of the party membership.

Chronology

1948

5 September The Polish president, Boleslaw Bierut, resumes an openly party political role and himself replaces Władysław Gomułka as Secretary-General of the Polish Communist Party. The party executive's eight-point programme includes: the 'purification' of the party by the removal of all those suspected of 'questionable loyalty' or of 'rightist and nationalist deviation'; stricter party discipline; continued opposition to American imperialism and its agents; the removal of 'bureaucracy' from within the party; and more 'self-criticism' by party members.

7 September Władysław Gomułka declares to a party meeting in Warsaw that he had been guilty of 'rightist and nationalist deviation' and had been wrong on the subject of Yugoslavia.

20–23 September The Polish Socialist Party meets in conference in Warsaw to 'eliminate faults and deviations' within the party. It dismisses fifteen members of its central committee for 'nationalism', 'deviationism' and allegedly opposing the proposed merger with the Communists. Among those dismissed is Eduard Osubka-Morawski, prime minister from the liberation until January 1947.

10 December It is reported that the Albanian government has conducted a widespread purge of officials deemed sympathetic to Titoism. They include Lt-Gen. Kochi Dodze, formerly vice-prime minister, minister of the interior and secretary of the Albanian Communist Party.

149

1949

26–27 March The Central Committee of the Bulgarian Communist Party remove Traicho Kostov, vice-prime minister since the establishment of the 'Fatherland Front' government and formerly Secretary-General of the Communist Party, from the Politburo and from his government posts. He had allegedly pursued an 'insincere and unfriendly policy towards the Soviet Union' in the course of trade negotiations, shown a 'nationalist deviation' and 'ignored the party leadership'. He is later made director of the National Library. He is, though, to be expelled from the Communist Party on 14 June and from the *Sobranje* on 17 June.

19 June Twenty people, including Laszlo Rajk, are arrested in Hungary on charges of spying for a foreign power.

16 September Laszlo Rajk, formerly Hungarian foreign minister and interior minister and member of the Politburo of the Hungarian Communist Party, is accused in Budapest with seven other leading figures of conspiring with Yugoslavia to overthrow the government, with plotting to assassinate Mátyás Rákosi, the Communist Party leader, and with conducting espionage on behalf of Yugoslavia and the west. He pleads, and is found, guilty and is hanged with two others of the accused on 15 October.

29 September Traicho Kostov, together with ten others, is charged in Sofia with high treason, espionage and conspiracy to overthrow the regime. The eleven are tried on 7–14 December and found guilty. Traicho Kostov is sentenced to death and executed on 16 December; the other accused are sentenced to varying terms of imprisonment.

1950

5 May Dr Gustav Husák is dismissed as chairman of the Slovak Board of Commissioners. He is later accused of promoting 'Slovak separatism'.

1951

22 February Josef Frank, a member of the Czechoslovak Communist Party praesidium, announces to the Central Committee that 169,544 members had been expelled from the Czechoslovak Party in the previous six months following extensive 'screenings' which would remain a feature of party discipline. The attitude to the party and to the Soviet Union would be paramount. As a result, party membership stood at 1,677,433, as against more than 2 million twelve months earlier.

22 February   President Gottwald claims in a speech to the Central Committee of the Czechoslovak Communist Party that Dr Vladimir Clementis, foreign minister until March 1950, Otto Sling, Communist Party Secretary in Brno until November 1950 and allegedly a British agent, and Marie Svermova, Assistant Secretary-General of the Communist Party and the widow of a wartime resistance leader, are the leaders of a plot to dominate the Communist Party, overthrow the regime and seize power. It is announced five days later that Dr Clementis had been arrested during an extensive party purge and was to be charged with espionage, treachery and working for the establishment of a separate Slovak republic.

14 March   General Reicin, deputy Czechoslovak defence minister, and Colonel Kopold, a member of the General Staff and son-in-law of Marie Svermova, are arrested for complicity in the Clementis plot.

24 April   Rudolf Slánský, Secretary-General of the Czechoslovak Communist Party, declares that the party has been 'too lenient' to those who joined it for 'opportunist' motives, and that the purge would continue 'without mercy' until all 'anti-Bolshevik ideas and deviations from Marxism–Leninism' had been eliminated.

7 September   The Central Committee of the Czechoslovak Communist Party abolishes the post of Secretary-General, previously held by Rudolf Slánský, but makes him a member of the new party praesidium. He is appointed a vice-prime minister two days later.

23 November   Rudolf Slánský is arrested and charged with treason.

1952

27 November   Rudolf Slánský, and ten other party officials, are sentenced to death at the end of a 'show trial' in Prague on charges of high treason, espionage and sabotage against the state. A further three officials are sentenced to life imprisonment. It is alleged that Slánský had wanted Czechoslovakia to follow the Yugoslav path and was the real leader of the Clementis plot. He had pleaded guilty and is executed on 3 December.

1954

14 April   Lucretiu Patrascanu, a former Romanian minister of justice, is sentenced to death by a military court in Bucharest on charges of treason.

14 July   East Germany announces that Dr Karl Hamann, formerly Liberal minister of supply, has been sentenced to ten years' imprisonment for having 'sabotaged the nation's food supply'.

He had been dismissed and arrested in December 1952. He is to be pardoned in October 1956.

10 October   It is announced that Vasile Luca, a former Romanian deputy prime minister and minister of finance, has been sentenced by a military court in Bucharest to hard labour for life. He had been charged with forming an anti-state organisation to disrupt the economy and hinder the construction of socialism.

3.6.4 ORTHODOXY AND REFORM 1953–90

1956

25 February   Khrushchev's address to the Twentieth Congress of the Soviet Communist Party denounces Stalin, and enunciates the doctrine of different roads to socialism.

18 April   The Cominform is abolished.

28 June   The Poznan riots provoke Khrushchev to send a secret circular to all the Communist Parties in the Soviet bloc, warning of the Yugoslav example and reasserting that the Soviet is the 'directing Party' and the only valid model for other Communist movements.

1 November   The Hungarian government of the independent Communist, Imre Nagy, seeks neutrality and reform. Nagy had written on the preceding regime of Mátyás Rákosi (qv):

> cowardice, hypocrisy, servility, falsehood and opportunism are praised as virtues. The degeneration and corruption of public life lead to the corruption of hearts and the degradation of character. The debasement of the soul to be observed in society is one of the gravest manifestations of the ethical and moral crisis taking place at this moment . . . humanism, which should be the characteristic trait of socialism, is repressed and its opposite, a cold inhumanity, reigns in public relations.
>
> (Source: *Political Memoirs*, p.115)

(See also Part 2.5.)

1968

5 January   The Central Committee of the Czechoslovak Communist Party replaces Antonin Novotny as First Secretary with Alexander Dubček.

5 April   The Central Committee of the Czechoslovak Communist Party approves an action programme which commits the party to economic liberalisation, the restoration of the freedom of the press, assembly and travel, more power and independence for the parliament and the non-Communist political parties, and more internal party democracy.

The programme maintains that the party's monopoly on power has arisen 'from the erroneous thesis that the Party is an instrument of the dictatorship of the proletariat'. It nevertheless rejects multi-party democracy.

8 May 'The Group of Five', comprising Bulgaria, East Germany, Hungary, Poland and the Soviet Union, holds discussions in Moscow on Dubček's liberalisation in Czechoslovakia, 'the Prague Spring'.

14–15 July The 'Group' meets in Warsaw to prepare a joint letter to the Czechoslovak Communist Party. The letter, criticising the liberal reforms, is signed on 17 July. A reliable Czechoslovak public opinion poll, conducted during the month, finds that only 5 per cent of respondents want a return to capitalism and 89 per cent want to continue on the road to 'socialism with a human face'.

29 July–
2 August The Soviet and Czechoslovak leaderships meet in Cierna, Slovakia. The outcome of the discussions fails to satisfy the Soviet Union, which is particularly apprehensive of the impact of reformism on the adjacent Ukraine.

3 August The 'Group' meets the Czechoslovak leadership in Bratislava.

12 August Walter Ulbricht follows up the letter by meeting Dubček in Karlovy Vary. He receives a cool reception from the Czech crowds.

20 August The armies of the 'Group of Five' invade Czechoslovakia.

26 September The Soviet Communist Party newspaper, *Pravda*, publishes the 'Brezhnev Doctrine', as enunciated by Leonid Brezhnev, First Secretary of the Soviet Communist Party. It maintains that 'every Communist Party is responsible not only to its own people but also to all the socialist countries, and to the entire Communist movement. Whoever forgets this by placing sole emphasis on the autonomy and independence of Communist Parties lapses into one-sidedness, shirking his internationalist obligations'.

1969

17 April Alexander Dubček is demoted to the symbolic post of Chairman of the Czechoslovak National Assembly and is replaced as First Secretary of the Czechoslovak Communist Party by Dr Gustav Husák.

1980

8 October Erich Honecker claims in an East German television interview that Poland 'belongs inseparably to the world of socialism, and no one can turn back the wheel of history . . . Together with our friends in the socialist camp, we will see to that.'

1981

6 April   With regard to Poland, President Husák advises the 16th Congress of the Czechoslovak Communist Party that:

> History has taught us what it means to have a good neighbour, a reliable ally. We belong to the same political, economic and defensive alliance. We have common objectives, common friends and enemies. We are linked by a thousand and one ties; we have the longest common frontier. That is why we are profoundly anxious to see that the Polish People's Republic should develop as a firm, orderly and socialist state.

1988

20–22 May   A special Conference of the Hungarian Socialist Workers' Party replaces János Kádár as party leader and embraces a radical programme of reform.

20 July   Three leading Bulgarian Communist Party reformers (Chudomir Aleksandrov, Stanko Todorov and Stoyan Mikhailov) are dismissed from their posts. The dismissals are interpreted as a conservative backlash orchestrated by Zhivkov as party leader.

1989

7–9 October   The Hungarian Socialist Workers' Party dissolves itself at its fourteenth Party Congress at the instigation of Imre Pozsgay and is reconstituted as the Hungarian Socialist Party.

18 October   Erich Honecker resigns as First Secretary of the East German SED in favour of Egon Krenz.

10 November   Todor Zhivkov is ousted as Bulgaria's Communist Party leader in favour of Petar Mladenov, a reformer.

3.6.5 MEMBERSHIP STATISTICS AND PARLIAMENTARY REPRESENTATION

Communist Party membership

(It should be noted that, except in Czechoslovakia, Communist Parties were illegal everywhere for most of the inter-war period. Estimates of their strength in 1939 should therefore be treated with care. Figures by 1950 relate to the combined Communist, Socialist and other parties formed after the war which were not always formally Communist Parties, although they usually behaved as such and were always described as such in the west. The East German figures relate to the SED throughout.)

Albania

1939	1 000 **
1950	70 000 **

Bulgaria

1939	8 000 **
1945	300 000
1947	500 000 *
1950	460 000 **
1981	825 876

Czechoslovakia

1939	85 000 *
1947	1 250 000 *
1950	2 300 000 **
1951 (February)	1 677 433 †
1981	1 550 000

East Germany

1946	1 298 412
1950	1 750 000
1987	2 328 331

Hungary

1939	30 000 **
1950	950 000 **

Poland

1939	20 000 *
1947	800 000 *
1948 (December)	1 200 000 full and 300 000 candidates †
1950	1 360 000 **

Romania

1944	1 000 *
1947	700 000 *
1950	1 000 000 **

Yugoslavia

1940	7 000 and 17 200 in the Young Communist League
1947	400 000 *

Sources: * Soviet journal *Party Life* (November 1947)
   ** Soviet journal *Bolshevik* (April 1950)
   † Official Party statistics

Early Communist parliamentary representation

Bulgarian *Sobranje*

Election of 28 March 1920: 49 seats out of a total of 227 (25 per cent of the vote)
Election of 18 November 1923: 99 seats out of a total of 362

Yugoslav *Skupština*

Election of 1921: 54 seats

3.7 THE STRUGGLE BETWEEN CHURCH AND STATE

1946

30 September   The trial opens in Zagreb of Cardinal Stepinać, Archbishop of Zagreb and Roman Catholic Primate of Croatia, on charges of wartime collaboration and of resistance to the new Communist government. He is to be sentenced to sixteen years' hard labour. (See Part 3.4.2 for fuller particulars.)

1948

9 August   Romania forbids the organisation of any political party on a confessional basis, requires all clergy to take an oath of loyalty to the state, bans foreigners from serving as clergy, lays down that all religious bodies should be maintained from their own national resources, and forbids any contacts between Roman Catholics, Protestants, Jews and Muslims with their co-religionists abroad except of a religious nature.

1949

5 February   Cardinal Josef Mindszenty, Archbishop of Esztergom and Roman Catholic Primate of Hungary, together with six others, is found guilty in Budapest on charges of high treason, conspiracy against the state and illegal currency dealings. In the 'Yellow Book' containing his alleged confession, he was said to have aimed for a new federated Central European monarchy under the Habsburgs. He is sentenced to life imprisonment on 8 February.

12 February   The Vatican excommunicates all those in any way concerned in the trial of and the 'iniquitous sentence' imposed on Cardinal Mindszenty.

24 February   A new Bulgarian law lays down that the leadership of each church has a responsibility to the state and that ministers of churches maintaining 'canonical relations with churches abroad' cannot take up office without official sanction.

25 February   Fifteen pastors of the United Evangelical Churches in Bulgaria are put on trial in Sofia on charges of espionage and high treason. The accused include the respective heads of the Baptist, Congregational, Methodist and Pentecostal Churches.

All plead guilty and the leaders are sentenced to life imprisonment. The Bulgarian Protestant community comprises some 14,000 people only, but is disproportionately represented in education and welfare.

13 July   The Apostolic *Acta* of Pope Pius XII condemns all those who support communism.

6 September   A Hungarian decree makes religious instruction no longer compulsory in schools.

1950

20 March   Poland nationalises without compensation all church estates of more than 100 hectares in the provinces of Poznan, Pomerania and Silesia, and of more than 50 hectares elsewhere, together with their livestock, buildings and associated businesses. Farms owned by parish priests are exempted.

5 April   Ten leading members of the Czechoslovak religious orders are sentenced in Prague to long terms of imprisonment for treason and espionage.

18 April   The Czechoslovak government takes over most of the country's monasteries and amalgamates the remainder to 'bring the orders back to their original Christian mission'.

1 June   Jozsef Revai, Hungarian minister of education, launches an attack on the Roman Catholic Church in Hungary. He criticises the bishops for refusing to take the oath of allegiance to the state, although they had done so under Admiral Horthy, and for reactionary attitudes. He announces that the government will exercise the right of the Habsburg emperors to approve all appointments to the episcopate.

9 June   The Hungarian government initiates the closure of many monasteries and convents and the requisitioning of their premises, sometimes for use as schools and nurseries.

30 August   Archbishop Grosz of Kalocsa and Jozsef Darvas, Hungarian minister of education and religious affairs, sign a church–state agreement. The government recognises freedom of religion and agrees to the retention of some monastic orders and church schools. The church agrees to work with the government, to respect the constitution, not to oppose the agricultural producers' cooperative movement, and to oppose nuclear weapons. The Vatican maintains on 12 September that the agreement has been reached 'in an atmosphere of intimidation and terror prepared with assiduous care'.

7 September   The Hungarian government dissolves 59 of Hungary's 63 religious orders, leaving only the Benedictines, Franciscans, Piarists and a teaching order of nuns. The 63 different orders had owned 636 major buildings, and the church estimates that 10,000 monks and nuns will have to return to secular life.

27 September The People's Assembly of the Yugoslav constituent republic of Bosnia–Hercegovina bans the wearing of the veil by Muslim women.

1951

10 March Mgr Josef Beran, Archbishop of Prague and Roman Catholic Primate of Czechoslovakia, who had been confined incommunicado in his palace in Prague since June 1949, is banished from Prague and fined, for his 'negative attitude' to the government's church laws.

18 March The Vatican excommunicates all those involved 'either physically or morally' in the persecution of the Roman Catholic Church in Czechoslovakia. Offences under the excommunication decree include bringing bishops before lay judges.

25 June Archbishop Joszef Grosz of Kalocsa, acting head of the Roman Catholic Church in Hungary, together with eight other Roman Catholic priests and laymen, is found guilty by a Budapest court of conspiracy to overthrow the government and of illegal currency dealings. He had pleaded guilty and is sentenced to fifteen years' imprisonment on 28 June.

29 June The Vatican excommunicates all those who have taken a major part in the trial, arrest and conviction of Archbishop Grosz.

21 July The Hungarian Roman Catholic Bench of Bishops takes an oath of loyalty to the People's Republic in Budapest.

14 September Ten Romanian Roman Catholic priests and laymen, including the Bishop of Timişoara, are found guilty by a military court in Bucharest on charges of espionage and anti-state activities. Four are sentenced to hard labour for life and the Bishop (aged 81) to eighteen years' solitary confinement.

18 September The Vatican excommunicates all Romanians who have persecuted, or helped persecute, servants of the Roman Catholic Church.

1952

19 July East Germany enforces its requirement that the churches sever connections with the west by refusing clergymen visas to attend congresses in West Germany.

3.8 TITOISM

Titoism is an informal, but inescapable, name for the interrelated initiatives taken by Yugoslavia under Tito's leadership after the break with Stalin in 1948. It is no discredit to those initiatives to emphasise that they were responses to unforeseen circumstances. Prior to the break, Tito's Yugoslavia was among the most rigorously orthodox of all the Communist states.

Although it was Tito's nationalist approach to foreign policy which prompted the rupture with the Soviet Union, his final response of constructive non-alignment was the last of his initiatives to coalesce. Ideologically unsympathetic to western capitalism but mindful also of the fragility of the 1955 reconciliation with Khrushchev's Soviet Union, he pursued negotiations with Egypt's Colonel Nasser and India's prime minister Jawaharlal Nehru in June 1956 with a view to developing links between those states which were not directly involved in the confrontation between east and west. It was a daring tactic at the time because Nasser was being depicted by Britain and France as a dangerous dictator for his role in the Suez Canal dispute. Nevertheless, Tito's initiative culminated in the first meeting of representatives of the non-aligned states in Belgrade in 1961.

The movement increased the confidence and standing of its members and greatly enlarged Yugoslavia's international profile and own self-image. Its focus on 'active non-alignment' was a welcome and perhaps necessary relief from the sterility of east–west ideological confrontation. Nevertheless, its level of achievement in generating alternatives to, or adaptations of, capitalism and communism was much more questionable, and the attempt largely ceased with the demise of European communism in 1990. The historical evidence since, however, suggests that such endeavours are as necessary as ever, but the disintegration of Yugoslavia has effectively ruled out the chances of its contributing to the debate.

Tito's earlier and more radical initiative was his dismantling of the framework of central planning and nationalisation, which had extended to the whole economy except for small handicraft enterprises, in favour of worker control. Legislation introduced in 1950 transferred ownership to the workers in each enterprise and enabled them to appoint their own management boards, subject only to the constraints of centrally determined overall plans. It was a daring initiative which liberated Yugoslav communism from the rigidity of the Soviet model, and it achieved a remarkable degree of success. That is not to conclude that it was perfect. There was always potential tension between the perceptions of worker owners and their chosen managers, and between the interests of individual enterprises and of the determined plan. Nevertheless all economic systems have their internal tensions, and the system might have surmounted the enormous challenges presented to economies everywhere by the great increase in the price of oil imposed by OPEC in the 1970s had it not been for inherent political weaknesses related to the third element in Titoism, the personality of Tito himself.

Tito was by common consent a remarkable man who imposed his will and sense of purpose on a grouping of people of uncommon determination and pride but with little else in common except for language and southern slav ethnicity. The substantial minorities did not even share that. Neither his predecessors nor his successors could make the Yugoslav concept work, and some did not even really want to. His political 'system', for the lack of a better word, rested on a balance of power between the nationalities and traditions, including the Albanian minority in Kosovo and the Hungarian minority in the Vojvodina, all of whom enjoyed considerable autonomy, with the unifying element being provided by the Communist Party (the Yugoslav League of Communists) and ultimately himself as both party and national president. The real problems arose as the traditional prescriptions of the Yugoslav League of Communists increasingly lost credibility during the 1960s, leaving Tito as the sole vital unifying force – and Tito needless to say was mortal. Perhaps he could have countered Croat–Serb rivalry by moving the federal capital from Belgrade to a new neutral site (as was done with Washington and Canberra), or even to Sarajevo. Perhaps he was wrong to resist party decentralisation, when faced with the logical consequence of worker self-management. Democratic centralism was probably outmoded. Rather than allowing growing autonomy in other fields, but denying party decentralisation, he should perhaps have done the reverse and retained the loyalty of liberal sentiment in Croatia and permitted a climate in republics like Slovenia in which political pluralism could evolve. Nevertheless it is perhaps clearer now that it was then that even residual communism provided an essential common framework for the whole of society, without which the most basic relationships would falter. The tragedy is that the fundamentals of his system offered far more hope to the peoples of Yugoslavia than the alternatives, but that a combination of greed, selfishness and short-termism allowed it and the whole nation to be destroyed. His own people and the wider world are the losers.

3.9 THE REFORMED COMMUNIST PARTIES SINCE 1990

COMMENTARY

It was almost a truism of the period 1989–90 that communism was discredited for at least a generation, and that the Communist successor parties, however reformed or renamed, could only look forward to a marginal existence. Like some of the other presumptions of the time, however, it proved to be a half truth at best. By the autumn of 1993, parties rooted in the Communist past had returned to power in Poland of all places in free and open elections. The reformed Hungarian Party, now the Socialist Party, soon similarly returned to government. These democratic renewals were to be paralleled by the ability of the renamed Albanian, Bulgarian and Romanian Parties to retain much of their earlier influence and to alternate in government through somewhat less open means.

There were various reasons for this unexpected development. Perhaps the most important was the bureaucratic nature of established Communist systems. Their cadres were administrators as much as politicians and perhaps more so. The penetration of the Communist Party through national life had as its corollary the absence of alternative expertise in running a country. Experienced meant Communist.

Another factor was the widespread failure of right-wing groups to coalesce as a coherent moderate grouping along the lines of German or Italian Christian Democracy in the immediate post-war years. Right-wing too often meant particularist.

The reformed Communists to be returned to power were, however, no longer Marxists, let alone Leninists. Whether by choice or necessity, they were managerial pragmatists supporting such previously unthinkable policies as free markets, privatisation and entry into the EU and NATO. They were not infrequently to find themselves 'to the right' of more protectionist, nationally minded parties. The change in outlook may actually have occurred much earlier. Aleksandr Kwasniewski, now president of Poland and a junior member of Poland's last Communist government, maintained in 1995: 'From an ideological point of view I was never a Communist. In Poland I've seen very few Communists, especially since the 1970s. I met a lot of technocrats, opportunists, reformers, liberals.' (Source: Higley *et al.*, quoted by Bastian.) The Hungarian Communist Party, or United Workers' Party to give it its proper title, initiated pluralistic reform at its Party Congress in May 1988 where it became to all intents and purposes a mainstream Social Democratic Party.

The real exception is Germany's Party of Democratic Socialism (*Partei des Demokratischen Sozialismus*) which draws virtually all its support from what was East Germany. Unlike its fellow parties it remains Marxist in its analysis and to some extent in its prescriptions, but it also enjoys substantial and seemingly growing electoral support.

CHRONOLOGY

1990

January   The Polish United Workers' Party (PZPR) is dissolved and its replacement is the SdRP. The SdRP, however, is only to stand at elections as part of the Polish Democratic Left Alliance (SLD).

1993

19 September   The Polish Democratic Left Alliance (SLD) and the Polish Peasant Party (PSL), both rooted in the former Communist Polish United Workers' Party (PZPR), are the principal victors in Poland's general elections. They obtain 20.4 per cent and 15.4 per cent of the vote respectively.

1994

29 May   The Hungarian Socialist Party (*Magyar Szocialista Part – MSzP*), the reformed former Hungarian Socialist Workers' Party, wins an overall majority of seats in the National Assembly (*Orszaggyules*) in Hungary's general elections. Its leader, Gyula Horn, becomes prime minister on 15 July.

18 December   The Bulgarian Socialist Party (BSP), the reformed former Bulgarian Communist Party, wins, in alliance with two minor parties, an overall majority of seats in the National Assembly in Bulgaria's general elections. Zhan Videnov becomes prime minister on 25/26 January 1995.

1995

1 March   The Polish Democratic Left Alliance, the reformed former Communist Party, achieves power as the leading force in a new coalition government.

19 November   Aleksandr Kwasniewski, a former Communist and a member of the last Polish Communist government, defeats Lech Wałęsa in the Polish presidential elections.

1998

2 November   The Party of Democratic Socialism (PDS), the reformed East German Socialist Unity Party, enters into coalition with the

163

Social Democrats to govern the eastern German *Land* (province) of Mecklenburg–Vorpommern (West Pomerania).

1999

29 May   Slovakia, after more than a year's delay, succeeds in electing a new president. Rudolf Schuster is a former high-ranking Communist official.

2000

8 October   The Polish president, Aleksandr Kwasniewski, a former Communist, wins a second five-year term with 55 per cent of the vote. None of the eleven other contestants, including Lech Wałęsa, wins even a third as many votes.

3.10 OFFICE HOLDERS

3.10.1 HEADS OF STATE

Albania

1919–24	Council of Regents drawn from the Baktashi Muslim, Sunni Muslim, Catholic and Orthodox religious communities
1925–28	Ahmed Bey Zogu (*President*)
1928–39(46)	[above as] Zog I (*King*)
1946–53	Dr Omer Nichani (*Head of State*)
1953–82	Haxhi Lleshi (*Head of State*)
	(*Presidents*)
1982–92	Ramiz Alia
1992–97	Sali Berisha
1997–	Rexhep Meidani

Austria

	(*Presidents*)
1920–28	Dr Michael Hainisch
1928–38	Wilhelm Miklas
1946–51	Dr Karl Renner
1951–57	Dr Theodor Körner
1957–65	Dr Adolf Schärf
1965–74	Franz Jonas
1974–86	Dr Rudolf Kirschschläger
1986–92	Kurt Waldheim
1992–	Dr Thomas Klestil

Bosnia–Hercegovina

	(*Presidents*)
1992–95	Alija Izetbegović
	(*A three-member rotating presidency functioned 1995–2000*)
1995–98	Alija Izetbegović
1998–99	Zivko Radisić
1999–2000	Ante Jelavić
	(*Presidents*)
2000	Alija Izetbegović
2000–	Jozo Krizanović

Bosnian Serb Republic (*Republika Srpska*)

	(*Presidents*)
1992–96	Dr Radovan Karadzić
1996–98	Biljana Plavsić
1998–99	Nikola Poplasen
2000–	Mirko Sarović

Bulgaria

1918–43	Boris III (*King*)
1943–46	Simeon II (*King*)
1943–44	Prince Kiril, Professor Filov and General Mikhov (*Regency Council*)
1944–46	Professor Venelin Ganev, Zvetko Boboshevsky and Todor Pavlov (*Regency Council*)
1946–47	Vassil Kolarov (*Acting president*)
1947–50	Dr Mincho Nechev (*President of the Presidium of the Republic*)
1950–58	Lt-Gen. Georgi Damianov (*President of the Presidium of the Republic*)
1958–64	Dimiter Ganev (*Head of State*)
1964–71	Georgi Traikov (*Head of State*)
1971–November 89	Todor Zhivkov (*Chairman of the Council of State*)
November 89–July 1990	Petar Mladenov (*President*)
August 1990–97	Zhelyu Zhelev (*President*)
1997–2001	Petar Stoyanov (*President*)
2001–	Georgi Parvanov (*President*)

Croatia

	(*Presidents*)
1941–45	Dr Ante Pavelić (*Head of State*)
1991–99	Franjo Tudjman
2000–	Stipe Mesić

Czechoslovakia

	(*Presidents*)
1918–35	Professor Tomáš Masaryk
1935–5 October 1938	Dr Edvard Beneš
5 October 1938– 30 November 1938	General Sirovy (*interim head of state*)
30 November 1938– 15 March 1939	Dr Emil Hacha*

1945–48	Dr Edvard Beneš
1948–53	Klemens Gottwald
1953–57	Antonin Zápotocký
1957–68	Antonin Novotný
1968–75	General Ludvik Svoboda
1975–89	Dr Gustav Husák
1989–92	Václav Havel
1992	Jan Strasky (*acting*)

* Remained formally in office during the ensuing Protectorate of Bohemia and Moravia

Czech Republic

(*Presidents*)

1993–	Václav Havel

East Germany

1949–60	Wilhelm Pieck (*President*)
1960–73	Walter Ulbricht (*Chairman of the Council of State*)
1973–76	Willi Stoph (*Chairman of the Council of State*)
1976–89	Erich Honecker (*Chairman of the Council of State*)
1989	Egon Krenz (*Chairman of the Council of State*)
1989–90	Manfred Gerlach (*Chairman of the Council of State*)
1990	Sabine Bergmann-Pohl (*President*)

Hungary

16 November 1918– 22 March 1919	Count Mihály Karolyi (*provisional President*)
1 March 1920– 16 October 1944	Admiral Miklós Horthy (*Regent*)
16 October 1944–45	Colonel-General Karoly Beregfay, Dr Ferenc Rajniss and Dr Sandor Csia (*Regency Council*)
1946–48	Rev. Zoltan Tildy (*President*)
1948–50	Arpád Szakasits (*President until 1949, thereafter Chairman of the Presidium of the Republic*)
1950–52	Sandor Ronai (*Chairman of the Presidium of the Republic*)
1952–67	István Dobi (*Chairman of the Presidium of the Republic*)
1967–87	Pál Losonczi (*Chairman of the Presidium of the Republic*)

1987–88	Karoly Németh (*Chairman of the Presidium of the Republic*)
1988–89	Bruno Ferenc Straub (*Chairman of the Presidium of the Republic*)
1990–2000	Arpád Göncz (*President*)
2000–	Ferenc Madl (*President*)

Macedonia (FYROM)

	(*Presidents*)
1992–99	Kiro Gligorov
1999–	Boris Trajkovski

Montenegro (*Crna Gora*)

	(*Presidents*)
1991–98	Momir Bulatović
1998–	Milo Djukanović

Poland

	(*Presidents*)
1918–December 1922	Jozef Piłsudski
14–16 December 1922	Gabriel Narutowicz
20 December 1922– 14 May 1926	Stanisław Wojciechowski
1926–30 September 1939	Professor Ignacy Móscicki
30 September 1939–45	Władysław Raczkiewicz (*in exile*)
1945–52	Boleslaw Bierut (*provisional 1945–47*)
1952–90	(15-person Council of State)
November 1985–90	General Wojciech Jaruzelski (*Chairman of the Council of State and President from July 1989*)
22 December 1990–95	Lech Wałęsa (*President*)
1995–	Aleksandr Kwasniewski (*President*)

Romania

(1914)–27	Ferdinand I (*King*)
1927–30 (supplanted)	Michael (*Prince under a Council of Regency*)
1930–40 (abdicated)	Carol II (*King*)
1940–47 (abdicated)	Michael (*King*)
1948–52	Professor Constantin Parhon (*President of the Presidium of the Republic*)
1952–58	Dr Petru Groz(e)a (*President of the Presidium of the Republic*)

1958–61	Ion Gheorge Maurer (*President of the Presidium of the Republic*)
1961–65	Gheorghe Gheorghiu-Dej (*President of the Presidium of the Republic*)
1965–67	Chivu Stoica (*President of the Presidium of the Republic*)
1967–74	Nicolae Ceauşescu (*President of the Presidium of the Republic*)
1974–89	Nicolae Ceauşescu (*President*)
1990–96	Ion Iliescu (*President*)
1996–2000	Emil Constantinescu (*President*)
2000–	Ion Iliescu (*President*)

Serbia

	(*Presidents*)
1989–97	Slobodan Milošević
1998–	Milan Milutinović

Slovakia

	(*Presidents*)
28 October 1939–45	Mgr Jozef Tiso
1991–2 March 1998	Michal Kovac
29 May 1999–	Rudolf Schuster

Slovenia

1991–	Milan Kucan

Yugoslavia

1918–21	Peter I (*King, previously only of Serbia*)
1921–34	Alexander (*King*)
1934–45	Peter II (*King*)
1934–41	Paul (*Regent*)
1945–53	Dr Ivan Ribar (*President*)
1953–80	Marshal Tito (*President*)
	(*Presidents of the Presidency of the Republic*)
4–15 May 1980	Lazar Kolisevski (*Macedonia*)
1980–81	Cvijetin Mijatović (*Bosnia–Hercegovina*)
1981–82	Sergej Kraigher (*Slovenia*)
1982–83	Petar Stambolić (*Serbia*)
1983–84	Mika Spiljac (*Croatia*)
1984–85	Veselin Djuranović (*Montenegro*)
1985–86	Radovan Vlajković (*Vojvodina*)

1986–87	Sinan Hasani (*Kosovo*)
1987–88	Lazar Mojsov (*Macedonia*)
1988–89	Raif Dizlarević (*Bosnia-Hercegovina*)
1989–90	Janez Drnovsek (*Slovenia*)
1990–91	Borisav Jović (*Serbia*)
1991	Stipe Mesić (*Croatia*)
	(*Presidents*)
1992–93	Dobrica Cosić
1993–97	Zoran Lilić
1997–2000	Slobodan Milošević
2000–	Vojislav Koštunica

3.10.2 HEADS OF GOVERNMENT (PRIME MINISTERS/PREMIERS, UNLESS OTHERWISE INDICATED)

Students are reminded that except in the Communist period, and for some of the time even then, almost all central and eastern European governments are, and have been, broad coalitions, and that descriptions such as 'liberal' and 'socialist' can have wide and even contradictory meanings. Their use below is only to provide the most general of guides.

Albania

December 1921–22	Hassan Prishtina
1922	Djaffer Ypi
December 1922–June 1923	Ahmed Bey Zogu
1923–24	Mgr Fan Noli
December 1924–36	Ahmed Bey Zogu (*Presidential and then royal regime*)
1936–39	Constantine Kotta
1942	Shevket Vrlaci (*Collaborationist*)
3 December 1942– 19 January 1943	Mustafa Merlika Kruja (*Collaborationist*)
19 January–13 February1943	Ekrem Libohova (*Collaborationist*)
13 February–12 May 1943	Malik Bushati (*Collaborationist*)
12 May 1943–44	Ekrem Libohova (*Collaborationist*)
1944–54	Colonel-General Enver Hoxha (*Communist*)
1954–81	Colonel-General Mehmet Shehu (*Communist*)
1982–91	Adil Çarçani (*Communist*)
1991	Fatos Nano (*Socialist*)
December 1991–March 1992	Vilson Ahmeti
1992–97	Aleksander Meksi
March–July 1997	Bashkim Fino (*Socialist*)
1997–98	Fatos Nano (*Socialist*)

| 1998–99 | Pandeli Majko (*Socialist*) |
| 1999– | Ilir Meta (*Socialist*) |

Austria

	(*Chancellors*)
November 1918–June 1920	Dr Karl Renner (*Social Democrat*)
1921–22	Dr Johann Schober (*non-party*)
1922–29	Mgr Dr Ignaz Seipel (*Christian Socialist*)
1929–30	Dr Johann Schober (*non-party*)
1930–32	Dr Otto Ender (*Christian Socialist*)
1932	Dr Karl Buresch (*Christian Socialist*)
1932–34	Dr Engelbert Dollfuss (*Christian Socialist – Fascist*)
1934–11 March 1938	Dr Kurt von Schuschnigg (*Christian Socialist*)
11–13 March 1938 (The *Anschluss*)	Dr Arthur Seyss-Inquart (*Nazi*)
April–December 1945	Dr Karl Renner (*Social Democrat*)
1946–53	Dr Leopold Figl (*People's Party (Conservative)*)
1953–59	Dr Julius Raab (*People's Party (Conservative)*)
1959–64	Alfons Gorbach (*People's Party (Conservative)*)
1964–70	Dr Josef Klaus (*People's Party (Conservative)*)
1970–83	Dr Bruno Kreisky (*Social Democrat*)
1983–86	Fred Sinowatz (*Social Democrat*)
1986–97	Franz Vranitzky (*Social Democrat*)
1997–2000	Viktor Klima (*Social Democrat*)
2000–	Wolfgang Schüssel (*People's Party (Conservative)*)

Bohemia–Moravia (Protectorate of)

| 1939–19 January 1945 | Professor Jaroslav Krejci |
| 19 January–14 May 1945 | Rudolf Bienert |

Bosnia–Hercegovina

June–November 1992	Jure Pelivan
November 1992–October 1993	Mile Akmadzić
October 1993–January 1996	Haris Silajdzić
1996	Hasan Muratović (*interim*)
1996–98	Haris Silajdzić ⎫ (*Co-prime ministers*)
1996–98	Boro Bosić ⎭
1999–2000	Haris Silajdzić ⎫ (*Co-prime ministers*)
1999–2000	Svetozar Mihajlović ⎭
2000	Spasoje Tusevljak

2001	Bozidar Matić
July 2001–	Zlatko Lagumdzija

Bosnian Serb Republic (*Republika Srpska*)

1996	Rajko Kasagić (*non-party experts*)
1996–98	Gojko Klicković
18 January 1998–2000	Milorad Dodik (*non-party experts*)
2001–	Mladen Ivanić

Bulgaria

1919–23	Aleksandŭr Stamboliyski (*Radical Agrarian*)
1923–25	Professor Aleksandŭr Tsankov (*Fascist*)
1926–31	André Liapchev
1931–33	Nicholas Mushanov
1934–35	Colonel Kimon Georgiev (*Militarist*)
January–April 1935	General Peter Zlatev
April–November 1935	Andreas Toshev
November 1935– 15 February 1940	Dr Georgi Kiossevanov
16 February 1940– 9 September 1943	Professor Bogdan Filov (*Fascist*)
14 September 1943– 21 May 1944	Dr Dobri Bojilov (*Fascist*)
1 June–1 September 1944	Ivan Bagrianov
2–8 September 1944	Konstantin Muraviev (*Agrarian-led coalition*)
9 September 1944–46	Colonel Kimon Georgiev (*Zveno*)
1946–49	Georgi Dimitrov (*Communist*)
July 1949–January 1950	Vassil Kolarov (*Communist*)
February 1950–54	Vulko Chervenkov (*Communist*)
1954–62	Anton Yugov (*Communist*)
1962–71	Todor Zhivkov (*Communist*)
1972–81	Stanko Todorov (*Communist*)
1981–86	Grisha Filipov (*Communist*)
1986–90	Georgi Atanasov (*Communist*)
February–November 1990	Andrei Lukanov (*Communist*)
1990–91	Dimitur Popov (*Independent*)
1991–92	Filip Dimitrov (*Right-wing-led coalition*)
1992–94	Professor Lyuben Berov (*non-party experts*)
1994	Reneta Indzhova (*non-party experts*)
January 1995–96	Zhan Videnov (*Socialist-led coalition*)
February–May 1997	Stefan Sofiyanski (*interim*)
1997–June 2000	Ivan Kostov (*Centre-right coalition*)
24 July 2001–	Simeon Saxe-Coburg-Gotha (*National Movement Simeon II*)

Croatia

1941–45	Dr Nikola Mandić
1991–93	Hrvoje Sarinić
1993–95	Nikica Valentić
1995–2000	Zlatko Matesa
2000–	Ivica Racan (*Social Democrat*)

Czechoslovakia

1918–19	Dr Karel Kramář (*National Democrat*)
1919–20	V. Tusar (*Social Democrat*)
1920–21	Dr Jan Černy (*non-party*)
1921–22	Dr Edvard Beneš
1922–25	Antonin Švehla (*Agrarian*)
1925–26	Dr Jan Černy (*non-party*)
1926–29	Antonin Švehla (*Agrarian*)
1929–32	František Udržál (*Agrarian-Socialist coalition*)
1932–35	M. J. Malypetr (*Agrarian*)
1935–September 1938	Dr Milan Hodža (*Agrarian*)
September–November 1938	General Jan Sirový
December 1938–March 1939	Rudolf Beran
1945–46	Dr Zdenek Fierlinger (*non-party provisional*)
1946–48	Klement Gottwald (*Communist-led coalition*)
20 February–13 June 1948	Klement Gottwald (*Communist*)
14 June 1948–53	Antonin Zapotocký (*Communist*)
1953–64	Viliam Široký (*Communist*)
1964–68	Jozef Lenart (*Communist*)
1968–69	Oldřich Černik (*Communist*)
1969–88	Lubomir Strougal (*Communist*)
1988–89	Ladislav Adamec (*Communist*)
December 1989–92	Marián Calfa
1992	Jan Strasky

Czech Republic

1993–November 1997	Václav Klaus (*Conservative*)
December 1997–July 1998	Josef Tosovsky (*caretaker administration*)
July 1998–	Milos Zeman (*Social-Democrat minority administration*)

East Germany

1949–64	Otto Grotewohl (*SED*)
1964–73	Willi Stoph (*SED*)
1973–76	Horst Sindermann (*SED*)
1976–7 November 1989	Willi Stoph (*SED*)

13 November 1989– 18 March 1990	Hans Modrow (*SED*)
18 March 1990– 3 October 1990	Lothar de Maizière (*Christian Democrat*)

Hungary

2 November 1918– 22 March 1919	Count (*Grof*) Mihály Károlyi (*Radical*)
20 March 1919–1 August 1919	Béla Kun (*Communist*)
August 1919	Peidl (*Socialist*)
August–November 1919	István Friedrich (*Royalist*)
November 1919–January 1920	Károly Huszár (*Clerical*)
March–July 1920	Sandor Simonyi-Semadam
1920–21	Count (*Grof*) Pal Teleki (*Conservative nationalist*)
1921–31	Count (*Grof*) István Bethlen (*Conservative nationalist*)
22 August 1931– 21 September 1932	Count (*Grof*) Gyula Károlyi
4 October 1932–1936	General Gyula (von) Gömbös (*Fascist*)
1936–38	Dr Kaloman de Darányi
1938–39	Dr Béla de Imrédy (*pro-Nazi economist*)
15 February 1939–3 April 1941	Count (*Grof*) Pal Teleki (*Conservative nationalist*)
3 April 1941–9 March 1942	Laszlo de Bardossy (*Fascist*)
9 March–22 March 1943	Nicolas de Kallay
23 March–29 August 1944	Major-General Doeme Sztojai (*Nazi*)
31 August–15 October 1944	Colonel-General Lakatos
16 October 1944–45	Major Ferenc Szálassi (*Nazi Arrow Cross*)
23 December 1944–45	General Béla Miklosz (*the Debrecen government*)
15 November 1945– 3 February 1946	Rev. Zoltan Tildy (*Smallholders*)
4 February 1946–47	Ferenc Nagy (*Smallholders*)
1947–48	Lajos Dinnyés (*Smallholders*)
1948–52	István Dobi (*Smallholders*)
1952–53	Mátyás Rákosi (*Communist*)
1953–55	Imre Nagy (*Communist*)
1955–56	Andras Hegedus (*Communist*)
1956	Imre Nagy (*independent Communist*)
1956–58	János Kádár (*Communist*)
1959–61	Ferenc Münnich (*Communist*)
1961–65	János Kádár (*Communist*)
1965–76	Jenö Fock (*Communist*)
1976–87	György Lazár (*Communist*)

1987–88	Károly Grósz (*Communist*)
1988–89	Miklós Németh
1990–93	Jozsef Antall (*Hungarian Democratic Forum*)
1993–94	Peter Boross (*Hungarian Democratic Forum*)
1994–98	Gyula Horn (*Socialist*)
1998–	Viktor Orban (*Centre-right*)

Macedonia

1992–98	Branko Crvenkovski (*Socialist*)
1998–	Ljubko Georgievski (*Macedonian Nationalist Party and Democratic Party of Albanians coalition*)

Montenegro (*Crna Gora*)

1991–98	Milo Djukanović
1998–	Filip Vujanović (*Democratic Socialist*)

Poland

November 1918–January 1919	Jędrzej Moraczewski
January–December 1919	Ignacy Paderewski
December 1919–June 1920	Leopold Skulski
June–July 1920	Władysław Grabski
July 1920–September 1921	Wincenty Witos
September 1921–June 1922	Antoni Ponikowski
June–July 1922	Artur Śliwlński
July–December 1922	Julian Nowak
16 December 1922–May 1923	General Władysław Sikorski
May–December 1923	Wincenty Witos
December 1923–November 1925	Władysław Grabski
November 1925–May 1926	Aleksander Skrzyński
10–15 May 1926	Wincenty Witos
May–September 1926	Professor Kazimierz Bartel
October 1926–June 1928	Marshal Józef Piłsudski
June 1928–April 1929	Professor Kazimierz Bartel
April–December 1929	Kazimierz Świtalski
December 1929–March 1930	Professor Kazimierz Bartel
March–August 1930	Colonel Walery Slawek
August–December 1930	Marshal Józef Piłsudski
December 1930–May 1931	Colonel Walery Slawek
1931–33	Aleksandr Prystor
1933–34	Janusz Jedrzejewicz

May 1934–March 1935	Leon Kozlowski
March–October 1935	Colonel Walery Slawek
October 1935–May 1936	Marjan Zyndram Kosciałkowski
May 1936–39	Felician Sławoj Skladkowski
30 September 1939–43	General Władysław Sikorski (*in exile*)
1943–44	Stanisław Mikolajczyk (*in exile*)
1944–45	Tomas Arciszewski (*in exile*)
1944–47	Eduard Osubka Morawski (*Socialist*)
1947–74	Jozef Cyrankiewicz (*Socialist/Communist*)
1974–80	Piotr Jaroszewicz (*Communist*)
February–August 1980	Edward Babiuch
1980–81	Jozef Pinkowski
February 1981–85	General Wojciech Jaruzelski
1985–88	Zbigniew Messner
1988–August 1989	Mieczslaw Rakowski
2–14 August 1989	Czeslaw Kiszczak
24 August 1989– December 1990	Tadeusz Mazowiecki
January–December 1991	Jan Bielecki
December 1991–June 1992	Jan Olszewski
July 1992–May 1993	Hanna Suchocka
September 1993– February 1995	Waldemar Pawlak (*Polish Peasant Party – PSL*)
1 March 1995–January 1996	Jozef Oleksy (*Socialist – SLD*)
February 1996–October 1997	Wlodsimierz Cimoszewicz (*Socialist – SLD*)
October 1997–2001	Jerzy Buzek
2001–	Leszek Miller

Romania

1918–19	Ionel Brătianu (*Liberal*)
1919–20	Dr Alexandru Vaida-Voevod (*Liberal*)
1920–22	General Averescu
1922–26	Ionel Brătianu (*Liberal*)
1926–27	General Averescu
June 1927	Ionel Brătianu (*Liberal*)
1927–30	Dr Iuliu Maniu (*National Peasant*)
1930–31	Mironescu (*National Peasant*)
1931–32	Professor Nicholas Iorga (*National Peasant*)
1932	Dr Alexandru Vaida-Voevod (*Liberal*)
1932	Dr Iuliu Maniu (*National Peasant*)
January–November 1933	Dr Alexandru Vaida-Voevod (*Liberal*)
November–December 1933	Ion G. Duca (*Liberal*)
1933–28 December 1937	Gheorghe Tatărescu (*Monarchist*)
28 December 1937– 11 February 1938	Octavian Goga (*National Christian*)

12 February 1938– 6 March 1939	Patriarch Dr Miron Cristes
6 March 1939– 21 September 1939	Armand Calinescu
21 September 1939– 28 September 1939	General Argescanu
28 September 1939– 23 November 1939	Constantin Argetoianu
24 November 1939– 4 July 1940	Gheorghe Tatărescu (*Monarchist*)
4 July 1940–3 September 1940	Ion Gigurtu (*pro-German*)
3 September 1940–44	General Ion Antonescu (*Fascist*)
August–December 1944	General Sanatescu
2 December 1944– 27 February 1945	General Nicola Radescu
6 March 1945–52	Dr Petru Groz(e)a (*Ploughmen's Front*)
1952–55	Gheorghe Gheorghiu-Dej (*Communist*)
1955–61	Chivu Stoica (*Communist*)
1961–74	Ion Gheorghe Maurer (*Communist*)
1974–79	Manca Manescu (*Communist*)
1979–82	Ilie Verdeţ (*Communist*)
1982–89	Constantin Dascalescu (*Communist*)
1989–92	Petre Roman
1992–96	Nicolae Vacaroiu
1996–30 March 98	Victor Ciorbea (*Centre-right*)
31 March–14 April 1998	Gavril Dejeu (*caretaker administration*)
15 April 1998– 13 December 1999	Radu Vasile (*Centre-right*)
December 1999	Alexandru Athanesiu (*interim*)
December 1999–2000	Mugur Isarescu (*interim*)
December 2000–	Adrian Nastase

Serbia

1941–44	General Milan Nedić (*Collaborationist*)
1991–93	Dragutin Zelenović (*Socialist*)
1993–94	Nikola Sainović (*Socialist*)
1994–2001	Mirko Marjanović (*Socialist*)
2001–	Zoran Djindjić

Slovakia

(29 September 1938) 14 March–27 October 1939	Mgr Jozef Tiso
28 October 1939–45	Dr Bela Tuka
1993–94	Vladimir Mečiar (*Nationalist*)

March–December 1994	Jozef Moravcik
December 1994–98	Vladimir Mečiar (*Nationalist*)
1998–	Mikulas Dzurinda (*Left-right coalition*)

Slovenia

1991–2000	Janez Drnovsek (*Liberal*)
2000–	Andrej Bajuk

Yugoslavia (Federation restricted to Serbia and Montenegro from 1992)

1919–20	Stojan Protić
1921–24	Nikola Pašić (*Radical*)
July–October 1924	Ljubomir Davidović
1924–26	Nikola Pašić (*Radical*)
1927	Nikola Uzunović
1928	Velje Vukicević
1929–4 April 1932	General Petar (Pera) Živković
4 April–29 June 1932	Dr Vojislav Marinković
2 July 1932–23 January 1934	Dr Milan Serškić
27 January–18 December 1934	Nikola Uzunović
21 December 1934– 20 June 1935	Bogoljub Jevtić
24 June 1935–February 1939	Dr Milan Stojadinović (*Yugoslav Radical Union (Fascist)*)
February 1939–March 1941	Dragiša Cvetković (*Fascist*)
March–April 1941	General Dušan Simović (*latterly in exile*)
11 January 1942–26 June 1943	Professor Slobodan Jovanović (*Royal government-in-exile*)
27 June–6 August 1943	Milos Trifunović (*Royal government-in-exile*)
7 August 1943–31 May 1944	Dr Bozidar Purić (*Royal government-in-exile*)
1 June 1944–45	Dr Ivan Subasić (*Royal government-in-exile*)
1943–53	Marshal Tito
1969–70	Mika Špiljak
1970–72	Mitja Ribičić
1972–77	Djemal Bijedić
1977–80	Veselin Djuranović
1982–86	Miika Planinć
1986–89	Branko Mikulić
1989–91	Ante Marković
1991–December 1992	Milan Panić
December 1992– February 1993	Nikola Sainović
February 1993–May 1998	Radoje Kontić
May 1998–2000	Momir Bulatović

November 2000–July 2001	Zoran Zizić
July 2001–	Dragiša Pesić

3.10.3 HEADS OF THE COMMUNIST PARTY POLITBURO

Albania (Albanian Party of Labour)

1944–85	Enver Hoxha
1985–90	Ramiz Alia

Bulgaria

1945–49	Georgi Dimitrov
1950–56	Vulko Chervenkov
1956–89	Todor Zhivkov
November 1989– February 1990	Petar Mladenov

Czechoslovakia

1946–53	Klement Gottwald
1953–68	Antonin Novotný
1968–69	Alexander Dubček
1969–87	Dr Gustav Husák
1987–89	Miloš Jakeš

East Germany (Socialist Unity Party – *Sozialistiche Einheitspartei Deutschlands* – *SED* from 1946)

1950–71	Walter Ulbricht
1971–89	Erich Honecker
October–November 1989	Egon Krenz

Hungary (Hungarian Socialist Workers' Party from 1948)

1944–56	Mátyás Rákosi
1956	Ernö Gerő
1956–88	János Kádár
1988–89	Károly Grósz

Poland (Polish United Workers' Party from 1948)

1945–48	Władysław Gomulka
1948–March 1956	Boleslaw Bierut
April–October 1956	Edward Ochab

179

1956–70	Władysław Gomulka
1970–5 September 1980	Edward Gierek
5 September 1980– 18 October 1981	Stanisław Kania
1981–89	General Wojciech Jaruzelski

Romania

| 1952–65 | Gheorghe Gheorghiu-Dej |
| 1965–89 | Nicolae Ceaușescu |

Yugoslavia

| (1939)–80 | Marshal Tito |

FOREIGN POLICY

4.1 REGIONAL AGREEMENTS AND ALLIANCES 1919–39

1920

14 August   Dr Edvard Beneš of Czechoslovakia signs a Convention of Alliance with Yugoslavia, and soon afterwards comes to a preliminary agreement with Romania. It is the beginning of the future 'Little Entente'.

1921

10 February   France concludes a political alliance with Poland, including a secret military convention, whereby France guarantees Poland against aggression.

23 April   Czechoslovakia and Romania sign a Convention of Alliance in Bucharest.

7 June   Romania and Yugoslavia sign a Convention of Defensive Alliance in Belgrade.

December   Dr Johann Schober, the Austrian Chancellor, seeks to establish friendly relations with the successor states of the Austro-Hungarian Empire by signing the Treaty of Lány with Czechoslovakia.

1922

31 August   The Treaty of Alliance signed by Czechoslovakia and Yugoslavia at Mariánské Lázně completes the Little Entente. The entente claims not to be anti-Hungarian, but the two attempts by the former Austro-Hungarian Kaiser Karl to return to Hungary the previous year had raised apprehension.

1923

March   The signature of the Treaty of Niš by Bulgaria and Yugoslavia testifies to improved relations between the two countries. They agree to cooperate in the containment of, in practice Macedonian, terrorism.

1924

25 January   France concludes a Treaty of Friendship with Czechoslovakia.

27 January   Mussolini, Nikola Pašić the Yugoslav prime minister, and Momčilo Nينčić, the Yugoslav foreign minister, sign the Pact of Rome whereby Yugoslavia recognises the incorporation of Fiume in Italy, although the suburb of Susak becomes Yugoslav. They also sign an agreement not to intervene in Albania's internal affairs.

5 July   Italy concludes a Treaty of Friendship with Czechoslovakia.

1925

21 July   Italy and Yugoslavia sign the Nettuno Conventions governing mutual economic and social relations. The Croat deputies in the *Skupština* refuse to ratify them claiming that they put the Italians in Dalmatia in a favoured position.

16 October   Germany signs the Treaty of Locarno with her former enemies. The treaty guarantees western but not eastern European frontiers.

1926

10 June   France concludes a Treaty of Friendship with Romania.

17 September   Italy concludes a Treaty of Friendship with Romania.

27 November   An Italian–Albanian Treaty of Friendship and Security is signed in Tiranë. It records the interest of both countries in the preservation of the Albanian status quo and commits them to 'mutual support and cordial collaboration'. Neither is to enter into any political or military agreement with a third party at the expense of the other.
The treaty is deeply resented in Yugoslavia, not least because it had received firm British government backing.

1927

4 April   Italy concludes a Treaty of Friendship with Hungary, having failed to woo either Czechoslovakia or Romania from the Little Entente.

11 November   A Franco-Yugoslav Treaty of Friendship is signed in response to the Italian–Albanian Pact of the previous year. It is a modest document with no military content, but it enrages Italy.

22 November   Albania and Italy sign a formal twenty-year defensive military alliance in Tiranë to counter the Franco-Yugoslav Treaty.

1928

5 June   Mussolini, in a dramatic speech to the Italian Senate, urges revision of the post-war treaties, notably Trianon. His speech is greeted with wild enthusiasm in Hungary and it marks the real opening of the abyss between Italy and the Little Entente.

1932

25 January Poland signs a non-aggression pact with the Soviet Union.

23 November The Soviet government breaks off negotiations for a non-aggression pact with Romania because Romania will not allow the question of Bessarabia (their common frontier) to be discussed. Both France and Poland had urged Romania to conclude such a pact.

1933

15 February Alarmed by the rise of Hitler, the foreign ministers of the Little Entente (Beneš for Czechoslovakia, Titulescu for Romania and Jevtić for Yugoslavia) sign a new accord in Geneva. It confirms their determination to resist any attempt to destroy existing treaties and commits them to not signing any treaty with a third party without consulting the other two member states. The entente also establishes a permanent secretariat in Geneva.

15 February Mussolini maintains that French reports of a German–Hungarian–Italian treaty of alliance are 'a complete invention'.

16 February The Little Entente of Czechoslovakia, Romania and Yugoslavia is reinforced by the creation of a permanent council which is to meet at least three times annually. The ambition of Eduard Beneš, the Czechoslovak foreign minister, to make the entente the starting point for close cooperation between all the Danubian nations founders, however, on the failure to reconcile Hungary, which can continue to rely on the protection of at least one of the major powers.

18 March Mussolini formally proposes a Four-Power Pact of Britain, France, Germany and Italy, and indicates informally that they should determine European affairs, including frontier revisions, between them. Following intense opposition from the Little Entente and Poland, France insists on such amendments to the pact, which is initialled on 7 June, that the final version has little practical significance.

1934

26 January Poland signs a ten-year non-aggression pact with Germany.

9 February Romania and Yugoslavia, together with Greece and Turkey, sign the treaty establishing the Balkan Entente (Pact). The entente is a response to common fears of Italian expansionism and hostility to Bulgarian terrorism. Although neither Albania nor Bulgaria is invited, the treaty leaves open the possibility of accession by other Balkan countries. Although not a party to the treaty, Czechoslovakia gives it strong support as the basis for a diplomatic front against external interference for all the Balkan states. The treaty contains a 'secret clause', of which the British, French and Italians are advised, that if a signatory should be attacked by a non-Balkan power, and the latter be joined by a Balkan power, then the other signatories would declare war on the Balkan power. In practice, however, the entente never becomes more than an alliance against Bulgaria.

February Marshal Piłsudski sends Colonel Beck, Polish foreign minister, to Moscow, where the existing Soviet–Polish non-aggression pact is extended to 31 December 1945.

17 March The Rome Protocols are signed allowing for regular consultations on policy between Austria, Hungary and Italy.

19 May The Bulgarian military coup raises fears in Greece that the new government will try to revise the Treaty of Neuilly, but hopes in Yugoslavia that it will help to suppress terrorism in Macedonia. In practice, the new government is to adopt a more conciliatory attitude towards its Balkan neighbours.

9 June Czechoslovakia, Romania and the Permanent Council of the Little Entente jointly recognise the Soviet Union.

21 June The French foreign minister, Louis Barthou, advises King Carol on a vist to Romania that France will withdraw its diplomatic and financial support if he suppresses democracy and aligns Romania with the fascist states. The security of her frontiers would then be at risk. Nevertheless, Louis Barthou is made an honorary Romanian citizen and declares: 'Your frontiers have been, are, and will be, always yours. Know that if a square centimetre of your territory is attacked, France will be at your side.'

30 September The kings of Bulgaria and Yugoslavia and their foreign ministers conclude a pact establishing closer economic and cultural relations between the two countries.

1935

16 May Dr Beneš for Czechoslovakia signs a treaty of mutual assistance with the Soviet Union in Prague.

1936

14 September Romania and Yugoslavia sign a defence pact whereby all Yugoslav air force and naval liquid fuels will be supplied by Romania in return for Yugoslav raw materials for the Romanian arms industry. Romania will also supply common aircraft fuel and oil for Czechoslovakia and Yugoslavia in the interests of standardisation among the armies of the Little Entente.

1 December The parliaments of the states comprising the Little Entente, Czechoslovakia, Romania and Yugoslavia, hold their first joint sitting, in Bucharest. They proclaim a parliamentary union to complement their existing military cooperation, and emphasise their total opposition to any revision of the peace treaties.

1937

24 January The prime ministers of Bulgaria and Yugoslavia, Dr Kiosseivanov and Dr Stojadinović, sign a non-aggression pact between their two countries in Belgrade. It is the culmination of a process of reconciliation initiated by the exchange of royal visits three years previously, prior to which the two countries had been almost in a state of war. Yugoslavia hopes that Bulgaria will in due course become a member of the Balkan Entente.

26 March Count Ciano, the Italian foreign minister, and Dr Stojadinović, the Yugoslav prime minister, sign an Italian–Yugoslav political treaty and a new trade treaty.

1–2 April Romania and Yugoslavia refuse a Czechoslovak request that the Little Entente pledge full military aid to any member which is threatened by aggression. It marks the end of the entente's political importance.

7 May The Little Entente Parliamentary Union holds its first formal meeting, in Belgrade.

1938

31 July A non-aggression agreement is signed in Thessaloniki, Greece, between General Metaxas, as president of the council of the Balkan Entente, comprising Greece, Romania, Turkey and Yugoslavia, and Dr Kiosseivanov, the Bulgarian prime minister. The participants renounce any recourse to force in their mutual relations, but also cancel the limitations in the Treaties of Neuilly and Lausanne on Bulgaria's right to re-arm and to deploy troops in the frontier zone with Greece and Turkey.

23 August The Bled Conference, between representatives of the Little Entente and of Hungary, recognises Hungary's right to re-arm, but the participants renounce any recourse to force in their mutual relations.

1939

24 February Hungary signs the Anti-Comintern Pact.

18 March Germany and Slovakia sign a treaty of collaboration.

4.2 WARTIME ALLEGIANCES

COMMENTARY

The basic facts on the changing allegiances of the states of central and eastern Europe up to and during the war are set out in Parts 2.2 and 2.3 and may be readily summarised. Virtually all their governments sought accommodation with the Germans either because it was a means of redressing national grievances, as with Bulgaria and Hungary, or a means of pursuing national ambitions, as with Poland, or, more generally, because of a sense that Germany was in the ascendant and resistance was pointless. That sense was strongly reinforced by the Munich Agreement, which appeared to establish that the western European nations would not risk war to protect those of eastern Europe. When the British and the French had taken the initiative in dismembering Czechoslovakia to placate Hitler, accommodation was hardly an unreasonable policy for the other governments to follow.

Although by 1940 government was everywhere in the hands of men of a dictatorial or fascist temper (except in Albania, Czechoslovakia and Poland, which had all effectively ceased to exist), it was not totally subservient to German interests, partly because of its own intense nationalism, partly because of an element of reserve over the nature of Hitler's Nazism, and partly because of a sense of self-preservation. Boris III in Bulgaria always knew that the pro-Russian sentiment of his people would not allow him to declare war on the Soviet Union, although he could on America and Britain. Yugoslavia's regent, Paul, was deposed as soon as he tried to override public opinion and ally his country with Germany.

Public opinion in most countries, though, was extremely divided. Righting perceived injustices to the nation was always popular, as was anti-Semitism, and Hitler's calls for a campaign against Bolshevism met with a ready response in the middle and upper classes. The newly empowered nationalisms of Croatia and Slovakia were dependent on German support for survival. On the other hand, many nationalists, particularly the aristocracy even in Germany, found Hitler's Nazism distasteful. The disenfranchised peasantry, which everywhere formed the majority of the population, followed rather than led, but bore the brunt of the war losses and soon questioned the value of the cause for which it was fighting. Regardless of earlier alignments and interests, however, virtually nobody wanted to be on the losing side once the tide of war had turned. Italy again acted as a model for central and eastern Europe, although for the last time, when it changed sides and declared war on Germany on 13 October 1943.

The resistance movements which arose were similarly divided, and reflected the internal conflicts of the 1920s and 1930s. Some devoted as much attention to fighting each other as to fighting the external enemy. The Communists, though, proved to be the most determined and effective of the competing groups as well as the best organised. The war, also, imposed its own remorseless logic. One was either for or against the Germans and, in the circumstances of central and eastern Europe, that also meant was either for or against the Soviet Union. The latter was no more willing to let Bulgaria sit on the fence than Germany was Hungary. That same logic, once the Soviet Union had seized the military advantage, meant that foreign policy could only be pro- or anti-Soviet. Neutrality was not on the agenda.

Moreover, the Soviet Union was to repeat at Yalta, with American and British agreement, that the future governments of central and eastern Europe would have to be governments 'friendly' to the Soviet Union so as to create what it saw as a cordon sanitaire to protect it from any further attack from Germany. The Soviet Union's definition of 'friendly' did not extend to cabinet ministers who had come to any form of accommodation with fascism, whether they had a popular mandate or not. That was hardly surprising when Hitler had enjoyed just such a popular mandate. *Pravda* declared on 9 April 1945 that 'there can be no question of politicians, styling themselves democrats but actually supporting reaction, being included. Mikolajczyk, for instance . . . actually still supports the fascist 1935 constitution . . .'. The declaration concerned strategically vital Poland, but it was of general relevance.

The creation of 'friendly' governments was to happen naturally in Albania, Czechoslovakia and Yugoslavia, but it was more problematic elsewhere. It was to be eased in Bulgaria by traditional pro-Russian sympathy, but both Hungary and Romania (like Finland) were to enjoy a greater measure of discretion than might have been expected by recently pro-Axis nations. Free national elections were to be held in Hungary as early as November 1945, nearly four years before West Germany, and government entrusted to a broadly based Smallholders Party. The situation in Romania was to remain confused partly because, like Poland, it was suffering from the widespread breakdown of law and order. It seems probable though that the autocracy of the Groz(e)a government was to be attributable to domestic factors rather than to intrigue by the Soviet Union, which was to remain willing for several years to work with and through King Michael.

CHRONOLOGY

1940

20 November The Hungarian prime and foreign ministers, Count Teleki and Count Csaky, sign the Tripartite (Axis) Pact in Vienna in the presence of Hitler. Consideration of major policy issues is, however, confined under the pact to the original signatories: Germany, Italy and Japan.

23 November The Romanian and Slovak prime ministers, General Antonescu and Dr Tuka, sign the Tripartite (Axis) Pact in Berlin.

12 December The Hungarian and Yugoslav foreign ministers sign in Belgrade a 'pact of lasting peace and eternal friendship'.

1941

1 March The Bulgarian prime minister, Professor Bogdan Filov, signs the Tripartite (Axis) Pact in Vienna.

25 March The Yugoslav prime minister, Dragiša Cvetković, and his foreign minister sign the Tripartite (Axis) Pact in Vienna in the presence of Hitler. Major protests erupt in Belgrade and across the country.

3 April The Hungarian prime minister, Count Teleki, commits suicide by shooting himself in the head at dawn. He had been unable to reconcile the pact, signed with Yugoslavia under his auspices in the December, with German demands for active cooperation in the invasion of that country.

18 July The Czechoslovak government-in-exile and the Soviet Union sign an agreement in London on joint action in the war against Germany.

25 November Bulgaria signs the Anti-Comintern Pact.

1942

28 March The Bulgarian prime minister, Professor Filov, maintains in a speech to the *Sobranje* that: 'The prosperity of our country could not exist outside the new European order. The first condition for the establishment of this order is the destruction of Bolshevism . . . The Bulgarian people should know clearly that though we are not fighting we are in a state of war.'

1943

9 December Shishmanov, the Bulgarian foreign minister, pays a glowing tribute to Germany before the *Sobranje* and maintains that Bulgarian foreign policy has for the last 25 years been an organic whole, aiming 'at the undoing of the Treaty of Neuilly and Bulgaria's right to exist'.

12 December Dr Beneš for Czechoslovakia signs a Treaty of Friendship, Mutual Assistance and Post-war Collaboration with the Soviet Union, in Moscow in the presence of President Kalinin and Marshal Stalin. The protocol to the treaty envisages the possibility of a tripartite treaty with Poland in due course. The treaty is welcomed by the Americans and the British.

1944

22 August Draganov, the Bulgarian foreign minister, in a debate in the *Sobranje*, stresses Bulgaria's friendly relations with the Soviet

Union, and announces that Bulgarian forces will be withdrawn from Yugoslavia and that Bulgaria will try to make peace with America and Britain. He maintains that the declaration of war on them had been a 'mistake', but that Britain was responsible because she had not 'honoured her promises of 1919'. Moreover, Bulgaria had not wanted to fight Greece but Thrace and Macedonia were 'hers by right'. Professor Tsankov, an influential former prime minister, severely criticises the new approach.

5 September   Bulgaria denounces the Tripartite (Axis) and Anti-Comintern Pacts.

1945

7 April   The foreign policy of the provisional Czechoslovak government includes the closest alliance with the Soviet Union on the basis of the 1943 treaty and on practical cooperation in the military, political, economic and cultural fields. An alliance is promised with a new democratic Poland, friendly relations with Bulgaria and Yugoslavia 'in the spirit of Slav friendship', a rapprochement with Austria and Hungary after the rectification of injustice, and consolidated relations with Britain.

11 April   Marshal Tito and Vyacheslav Molotov, the Soviet foreign minister, sign a Treaty of Friendship, Mutual Assistance and Postwar Collaboration in Moscow.

21 April   Boleslaw Bierut, president of the National Council of Poland, Eduard Osubka-Morawski, prime minister of the provisional Polish government, and Marshal Stalin sign a Treaty of Friendship, Mutual Assistance and Post-war Collaboration in Moscow.

4.3 THE COMMUNIST PERIOD

1945

end May Marshal Tito declares: 'We do not want to get involved in any policy of spheres of influence . . . Never again will we be dependent on any one.' The Soviet Union protests officially a week later.

10 November The American, British and Soviet governments announce their intention of recognising the provisional Albanian government established by Colonel Enver Hoxha. American and British recognition is, however, dependent on the holding of free elections. The Allied decision is bitterly resented in Greece, where all parties other than the Communists are demanding the annexation of northern Epirus as a predominantly Greek inhabited area.

1946

16 March Poland and Yugoslavia sign a Treaty of Friendship and Mutual Aid in Warsaw. Marshal Tito emphasises that the initiative for the strictly bilateral treaty had come from him and that he disapproves of the formation of any blocs. The treaty and the parallel treaties that follow across the Soviet bloc are formally directed against future aggression by Germany or any state in alliance with her.

4 April Britain breaks off diplomatic relations with Albania in view of her allegedly unfriendly and uncooperative attitude.

9 May Dr Zdenek Fierlinger, the Czechoslovak prime minister, and Marshal Tito sign a twenty-year Treaty of Friendship, Mutual Assistance and Cooperation in Belgrade.

10 July Colonel Enver Hoxha, the Albanian prime minister, and Stanoje Simić, the Yugoslav foreign minister, sign a twenty-year Treaty of Friendship and Mutual Assistance in Tiranë.

29 August The United Nations rejects Albania's application for membership. It is favoured by the Soviet Union, Poland and France but opposed by America and Britain.

8 November America breaks off diplomatic relations with Albania.

27 November The Albanian and Yugoslav governments sign an agreement coordinating the economic plans of both countries, abolishing Customs frontiers and duties, and establishing a currency union by providing for monetary equality between their two currencies.

1947

10 March Czechoslovakia and Poland sign a twenty-year Treaty of Friendship and Mutual Aid. A rider to the treaty states that all territorial questions outstanding will be settled by mutual agreement within two years and that Czechs and Slovaks in Poland, and the Polish minority in the Teschen area of Czechoslovakia, will enjoy a legal right to national, political, cultural and economic development, with their own schools, associations and cooperative organisations.

18–21 August The United Nations Security Council rejects applications for UN membership from Albania, Bulgaria, Hungary and Romania. The Soviet Union vetoes the applications of Austria and Italy.

27 November Georgi Dimitrov, the Bulgarian prime minister, and Marshal Tito sign a twenty-year Treaty of Friendship, Collaboration and Mutual Aid in Varna, Bulgaria. Marshal Tito's official visit is the occasion for large-scale celebrations, and he declares in Sofia that: 'We shall establish cooperation so general and so close that the question of federation will be a mere formality.'

8 December Lajos Dinnyés, the Hungarian prime minister, and Marshal Tito sign a Hungarian–Yugoslav Treaty of Friendship and Mutual Assistance in Budapest.

16 December Colonel-General Enver Hoxha, the Albanian prime minister, signs a similar Albanian–Bulgarian treaty in Plovdiv, Bulgaria. The associated communiqué declares that neither nation will 'give any assistance whatever' to the Balkans Commission established by the UN to investigate the situation in northern Greece. Both regard the Commission as a 'violation of the UN Charter and against the sovereignty of the Balkan nations'. (See also Part 2.4.)

19 December Ana Pauker, the Romanian foreign minister, and Marshal Tito sign a parallel Romanian–Yugoslav treaty in Bucharest.

1948

14 January Georgi Dimitrov, the Bulgarian prime minister, signs a twenty-year Treaty of Friendship, Cooperation and Mutual Assistance with Romania, in Bucharest.

4 February Petru Groz(e)a, the Romanian prime minister, and Vyacheslav Molotov, the Soviet foreign minister, sign a twenty-year Treaty of Alliance and Mutual Aid, in Moscow.

18 February	Lajos Dinnyés, the Hungarian prime minister, and Vyacheslav Molotov sign a parallel treaty in Moscow.
23 April	Georgi Dimitrov, the Bulgarian prime minister, and Klement Gottwald, the Czechoslovak prime minister, sign a twenty-year Treaty of Friendship and Mutual Aid.
30 May	Georgi Dimitrov, the Bulgarian prime minister, signs a twenty-year Treaty of Friendship, Cooperation and Mutual Aid with Poland, in Warsaw.
19 July	Bulgaria and Hungary sign a twenty-year Treaty of Friendship and Mutual Aid in Budapest.
21 July	Czechoslovakia and Romania sign a twenty-year Treaty of Friendship and Mutual Aid in Bucharest.

1949

16 April	The Czechoslovak and Hungarian prime ministers, Antonin Zapotocký and István Dobi, sign a twenty-year Treaty of Friendship and Mutual Assistance in Budapest.
28 September	The Soviet government formally denounces the twenty-year Treaty of Friendship and Mutual Assistance it had signed with Yugoslavia on 11 April 1945. The rest of the Soviet bloc follows suit: Hungary and Poland on 30 September, Romania on 1 October, Bulgaria on 3 October and Czechoslovakia on 4 October.
8–21 October	Yugoslavia protests to Hungary, Bulgaria, Romania and Poland in turn for denouncing their Treaties of Friendship and Mutual Assistance with her.

1950

20 February	America breaks off diplomatic relations with Bulgaria when the latter refuses to withdraw its charges that the American minister in Sofia has intervened in Bulgaria's internal affairs. A week later America bans its nationals from travelling to Bulgaria.
6 March	Albania follows the other Cominform countries in withdrawing from the World Health Organisation (WHO).
30 May	Yugoslavia closes its legation in Albania in view of 'discriminatory measures . . . against Yugoslav diplomats'.
23 June	Antonin Zapotocký, Czechoslovak prime minister, and Walter Ulbricht, East German deputy prime minister, declare that their countries have no territorial claims on each other and that the resettlement of Germans from Czechoslovakia has been settled in an unalterable, just and permanent manner.
24 June	Walter Ulbricht, the East German deputy prime minister, and István Dobi, the Hungarian prime minister, make a formal

declaration of friendship, in which they assure each other of their permanent loyalty to the great Soviet Union, to which they both owe their liberation.

6 July East Germany and Poland sign a treaty in Görlitz recognising the Oder–Neisse line as their joint frontier.

1 October East Germany becomes a member of COMECON.

1951

19 January Yugoslavia terminates its state of war with Austria. The declaration is a technicality, as neither state had been formally at war with the other, but is welcomed by Austria as a sign of Yugoslav goodwill.

6 December Czechoslovakia is agreeable to a requested revision of the Italian Peace Treaty, provided the treaties with Bulgaria, Hungary and Romania are revised likewise. It is similarly agreeable to Italian membership of the UN, provided the three other countries are admitted.

1952

16 February Albania is only agreeable to the requested revision of the Italian Peace Treaty if Italy leaves NATO.

1953

28 February The foreign ministers of Greece, Turkey and Yugoslavia sign a Tripartite Treaty of Friendship and Cooperation in Ankara, Turkey. It is the first international agreement of its kind which Yugoslavia has entered into since the rupture with the Cominform. Edvard Kardelj, a Yugoslav vice-prime minister, states that adherence to the treaty is open to Italy, and appeals in any event for Italo-Yugoslav cooperation.

1954

19 June Romania and Yugoslavia restore normal diplomatic relations. They also agree on 14 August to restore the direct rail connections between them, terminated in 1950.

7 November Yugoslavia restores normal diplomatic relations with Bulgaria and Hungary.

23 December Albania and Yugoslavia restore the diplomatic relations broken off in 1950.

1955

11–13 May Albania, Bulgaria, Czechoslovakia, Hungary, Poland, Romania and the Soviet Union sign twenty-year Treaties of Friendship,

Cooperation and Mutual Assistance with East Germany in Warsaw. A unified military command is created for all of the signatories bar East Germany, whose participation is to be examined later. It follows on 27–28 January 1956.

14 May Albania, Bulgaria, Czechoslovakia, East Germany, Hungary, Poland, Romania and the Soviet Union sign the Warsaw Treaty of Friendship, Cooperation and Mutual Assistance (the Warsaw Pact).

15 May The Austrian State Treaty (the peace treaty) is signed in Vienna. (See Part 2.5 for fuller particulars.)

2 June The week-long visit of reconciliation paid by the Soviet leadership to Yugoslavia culminates in a Joint Declaration of Friendship and Cooperation. (See Part 2.5 for fuller particulars.)

1956

1 November Hungary, under the leadership of Imre Nagy, seeks to withdraw from the Warsaw Pact. (See Part 2.5 for fuller particulars.)

1957

1–2 August President Tito and Nikita Khrushchev, First Secretary of the Soviet Communist Party, meet again in Romania. The Soviet invasion of Hungary had again strained Soviet–Yugoslav relations.

2 October The 'Rapacki Plan', envisaging a nuclear armaments-free zone in central Europe, is submitted to the UN General Assembly. (See Part 2.5 for fuller particulars.)

15 October East Germany and Yugoslavia agree to establish diplomatic relations. West Germany breaks off relations with Yugoslavia in protest on 19 October.

1961

1–6 November President Tito of Yugoslavia hosts the first conference of the Nonaligned movement in Belgrade. (See also Part 2.5.)

19 December East Germany announces that it has decided to recall its ambassador from Tiranë as Albania is making normal diplomatic activity impossible. Albania is in the course of breaking with the Soviet Union and developing close links with China.

1964

12 June East Germany and the Soviet Union sign a twenty-year Treaty of Friendship, Cooperation and Mutual Assistance in Moscow. An accompanying statement declares that the two countries, with the other members of the Warsaw Pact, will ensure their own security if West Germany acquires nuclear weapons within the framework of NATO.

1965

27 January　It is announced in East Berlin that Walter Ulbricht, First Secretary of the East German SED, is to make an official visit to Egypt at the end of February at the invitation of President Nasser. Nasser maintains that secret West German arms supplies to Israel are a source of concern to the whole Arab world.

1966

31 March　East Germany applies to join the United Nations. It is rejected by America, Britain and France.

7 April　Nicolae Ceauşescu declares that Romania is an independent state within the Soviet bloc.

1967

31 January　Romania and West Germany agree to establish diplomatic relations. Romania thereby becomes the first Communist state other than the Soviet Union to have diplomatic relations with West Germany. *Neues Deutschland*, the East German party newspaper, describes the Romanian decision as deplorable.

8–10 February　The venue of the conference of foreign ministers of the Warsaw Pact is moved from East Berlin to Warsaw in the light of Romanian anger at the East German attitude.

15 March　Walter Ulbricht, First Secretary of the East German SED, signs a twenty-year Treaty of Friendship, Cooperation and Mutual Assistance with Poland in Warsaw.

17 March　Ulbricht signs a parallel treaty with Czechoslovakia in Prague. It declares in addition that the 1938 Munich Agreement was invalid from the very beginning.

10–13 May　Bulgaria signs a second twenty-year Treaty of Friendship, Cooperation and Mutual Assistance with the Soviet Union.

17–18 May　Ulbricht signs a parallel treaty with Hungary in Budapest.

7 September　Ulbricht signs a parallel treaty with Todor Zhivkov of Bulgaria in Sofia, and Hungary renews its 1948 treaty with the Soviet Union for a further twenty years.

1968

8 May　The 'Group of Five' launch the diplomatic pressure on Czechoslovakia which is to culminate in invasion to crush 'the Prague spring'. (See Part 3.6.4 for fuller particulars.)

12 September　Albania leaves the Warsaw Pact.

26 September	The Soviet newspaper, *Pravda*, publishes the 'Brezhnev Doctrine' on the conditional sovereignty of Communist states. (See Part 3.6.4 for fuller particulars.)

1969

30 April	Iraq is the first Arab country to decide to give full diplomatic recognition to East Germany. West Germany describes the decision as 'an unfriendly act' on 1 May.
2–3 August	The visit by President Nixon of America to Romania during his European tour disturbs the Soviet Union.

1970

19 March	The East German prime minister, Willi Stoph, meets West German Chancellor Willy Brandt in Erfurt, East Germany, in the first top-level government meeting between the two states since their foundation.
May	Czechoslovakia signs a twenty-year Treaty of Friendship, Cooperation and Mutual Assistance with the Soviet Union.
10 July	Todor Zhivkov and János Kádár, First Secretary of the Hungarian Socialist Workers' Party, and Jenő Fock, the Hungarian prime minister, sign in Sofia a twenty-year Treaty of Friendship, Cooperation and Mutual Assistance.
7 December	Chancellor Brandt of West Germany and Jozef Cyrankiewicz, the Polish prime minister, sign the Treaty of Warsaw. (See Part 2.5 for fuller particulars.)

1972

21 November	East Germany becomes a member of UNESCO.
13 December	East Germany becomes a member of the UN Economic Commission for Europe.
21 December	Under the terms of the 'Basic Treaty' signed between them, East Germany receives recognition from West Germany of its separate identity, but not of its identity as a foreign state under international law.

1973

9 February	Britain and France announce that they have both established diplomatic relations with East Germany.
18 September	Both East and West Germany are admitted to the United Nations.
11 December	Chancellor Brandt of West Germany and Lubomir Strougal, the Czechoslovak prime minister, sign the Treaty of Prague. (See Part 2.5 for fuller pariculars.)

1975

7 October   Erich Honecker, First Secretary of the East German SED, and Leonid Brezhnev, First Secretary of the Soviet Communist Party, sign a twenty-five-year Treaty of Friendship, Cooperation and Mutual Assistance.

1978

7 July   China's suspension of all aid to Albania marks Albania's final isolation from the rest of the Communist world. (See Part 2.5 for fuller particulars.)

1979

19 February   Erich Honecker, General Secretary of the East German SED, signs a twenty-year Treaty of Friendship and Cooperation with President Agostinho Neto of Angola. It is East Germany's first such treaty with an African country.

1980

1 June   East Germany and Cuba sign a twenty-five-year Treaty of Friendship and Cooperation, but it makes no reference to military cooperation.

1981

13 September President Husák of Czechoslovakia signs a twenty-year Treaty of Friendship and Cooperation with Ethiopia and South Yemen.

21 October   Czechoslovakia and Mozambique sign a Friendship Agreement establishing a framework for closer economic and political collaboration.

2–5 November President Losonczi of Hungary signs a twenty-year Treaty of Friendship and Cooperation with President Mohammed of South Yemen, in Budapest.

11 November   President Zhivkov of Bulgaria signs a twenty-year Treaty of Friendship and Cooperation with President Mohammed of South Yemen, in Sofia.

1982

19–23 May   East Germany and President Karmal of Afghanistan sign a twenty-year Treaty of Friendship and Cooperation in East Berlin.

1984

22–23 August Erich Honecker is the only party leader from the Soviet bloc to attend the 40th anniversary celebration of the Romanian Revolution in Bucharest.

1985

25–26 April   The signatories of the Warsaw Pact, other than Albania, renew the Warsaw Treaty for twenty years.

1986

21 October   A joint paper produced by the West German Social Democratic Party and the East German SED, and endorsed also by the Czechoslovak Communist Party, proposes the establishment over three years of a 300-kilometre-wide nuclear-weapons-free corridor along the West German border with East Germany and Czechoslovakia.

1987

7–11 September   Erich Honecker pays an official visit to West Germany. It is the first official visit to be made there by an East German head of state.

4.4 REGIONAL RELATIONS AND RELATIONS WITH THE EU AND NATO AFTER 1990

1991

5–6 October   Czechoslovakia, Hungary and Poland (the Visegrad Three) sign a treaty of cooperation.

1992

23 January   Representatives of Hungary, Poland, Romania, Slovakia and the Ukraine found the Carpathia–Tisza Economic Working Community at Nyiregyhaza, Hungary.

3 February   Albania, Armenia, Azerbaijan, Bulgaria, Georgia, Greece, Moldova, Romania and Turkey found the Black Sea Economic Cooperation Project on the initiative of the Turkish government. It aims to establish a new trading zone and to encourage regional economic cooperation.

2 November   The Visegrad Three (Czechoslovakia, Hungary and Poland) agree in Budapest to establish a free trade zone with effect from 1 January 1993.

1 December   The economic and trade cooperation agreement between Albania and the EU comes into force.

December   Albania applies to become a member of NATO, but receives an ambiguous response.

21 December   The foreign ministers of the Czech Republic, Hungary, Poland and Slovakia sign the Central European Free Trade Agreement (CEFTA) in Krakow. It aims to eliminate mutual trade barriers by the end of the century and to ensure compatibility with European Union and European Economic Area regulations.

1993

1 February   The EU signs an association agreement with Romania.

8 March   The EU signs an association agreement with Bulgaria.

21–22 June   The EU's Copenhagen European Council agrees that the associated countries in central and eastern Europe that so desire shall become members of the European Union. Accession will take place as soon as an associated country is able to assume the obligations of membership by satisfying the economic and political conditions required. Membership requires that the candidate country has achieved stability of institutions guaranteeing democracy, the rule of law, human rights and respect for and protection of minorities, the existence of a functioning market economy as well as the capacity to cope with competitive pressure and market forces within the Union. Membership presupposes the candidate's ability to take on the obligations of membership including adherence to the aims of political, economic and monetary union. The EU proposes that the associated countries enter into a structured relationship with the Institutions of the Union within the framework of a reinforced and extended multilateral dialogue and concertation on matters of common interest.

4 October The EU signs association agreements with the Czech Republic and Slovakia.

1994

1 February The Hungarian and Polish association agreements (Europe Agreements) with the EU come into force.

1 April Hungary applies to become a member of the European Union.

5 April Poland applies to become a member of the European Union.

12 June Austria in a referendum approves EU membership by a large majority. It accedes to the EU on 1 January 1995.

9–10 December The EU's Essen European Council declares that with effect from 1 January 1995 the EU will embark on its programme to prepare for the accession of all the European countries with which it has concluded Europe Agreements. The necessary strategy is being politically implemented by the creation between the associated states and the Institutions of the EU of structured relations.

1995

1 February The Bulgarian, Czech, Romanian and Slovak association agreements with the EU come into effect.

19 March The Hungarian and Slovak prime ministers, Gyula Horn and Vladimir Mečiar, sign a Treaty of Friendship and Cooperation in Paris. (See Part 2.6 for fuller particulars.)

22 June Romania applies to become a member of the EU.

1996

23 January The Czech Republic applies to become a member of the EU.

1997

17 February   Bulgaria announces its intention of applying for full NATO membership.

23–24 May   A controversial referendum is held in Slovakia on NATO membership and direct presidential elections. It is declared invalid after a turn-out of only 9.6 per cent.

8 July   Javier Solana, NATO secretary-general, formally invites the Czech Republic, Hungary and Poland to become members of NATO. He declares that the door will be kept open for future members and specifically mentions Romania, Slovenia and the three Baltic states.

July   The EU Commission document *Agenda 2000* deems it unlikely that the candidate countries will be able to join the 'euro' area immediately on accession. The document proposes that the existing 'structured dialogue' be replaced by the new instrument of the accession partnership. The granting of EU assistance under the partnership will be conditional on achieving priority objectives and on progress generally.

1998

1 January   The imposition of new visa regulations on Poland's eastern frontier at EU insistence leads to strains between Belarus and Poland. The tighter regulations, which also have the effect of restricting the black market, are unpopular with many in Poland.

4 February   The European Commission decides detailed plans and goals known as 'accession partnerships' which the central and eastern European applicants for EU membership will need to meet by the end of 1998.

3 March   The Austrian government rules out NATO membership and proposes to remain neutral for at least another 5–10 years.

30 March   EU accession talks are formally opened in London with the Czech Republic, Estonia, Hungary, Poland, Slovenia, Bulgaria, Latvia, Lithuania, Romania and Slovakia. More detailed talks open on the following day with the first five, which are considered to have made the necessary economic and political reforms for the opening of full negotiations. No accessions are anticipated, however, before 2004.

15 April   The Czech Chamber of Deputies approves NATO membership. The Senate follows suit on 30 April.

1999

1 February	Slovenia's association agreement with the EU, signed in 1996, comes into force.
9 February	The Hungarian National Assembly votes in favour of NATO membership and the treaty is signed by the Hungarian president the following day.
17 February	The *Sejm* and the Senate ratify Poland's accession to NATO.
12 March	The Czech Republic, Hungary and Poland are formally admitted to NATO at a ceremony in Independence, Missouri, America. Russia deplores the development and some leading British military figures maintain that it will not contribute to peace and security.
13 October	An EU Commission paper considers it possible to conclude negotiations with the most advanced candidate countries in 2002.

2000

3 February	The new Austrian government includes representatives of the far-right Freedom Party (FPÖ) of Jörg Haider. Portugal, which holds the EU presidency, states that ministerial relations between Austria and other EU member states will be downgraded to the lowest possible level.
4 February	The EU suspends bilateral political relations with Austria following the inclusion of the far-right Freedom Party in the new federal government coalition. (See Part 2.6 for fuller particulars.)
27 June	EU governments agree a face-saving formula to lift the sanctions imposed on Austria following the entry of Jörg Haider's Freedom Party into the federal coalition. An assessment will be made of Austria's commitment to European values.
9–11 December	EU heads of government agree the Treaty of Nice which reforms the Union's decision-making machinery to help it to cope with a significant number of new members, mainly from central and eastern Europe. It is envisaged that the first new members may join in 2004. The treaty has to be ratified by all fifteen existing member states by the end of 2002.

2001

June	The Hungarian parliament passes the Status Law, due to come into force in January 2002, whereby the 3.5 million ethnic Hungarians living in the neighbouring states will enjoy childcare, education, employment and healthcare rights funded by Hungary. Romania and Slovakia strongly object to

the law, which they maintain is discriminatory, and allege that it would be contrary to EU law once they had acceded to the EU. The law does not apply to the 70,000 ethnic Hungarians in Austria, for related reasons.

8 June   The timing of future EU enlargement into eastern Europe is put in doubt by the refusal of the Irish electorate in a referendum to approve the Treaty of Nice.

Part 5

THE ECONOMY

5.1 THE ECONOMY 1919–39

The economic history of central and eastern Europe between the wars closely mirrored its political history: indeed trends in the one reinforced trends in the other and vice versa. Again also, there were deep underlying similarities across the region despite the obvious national differences.

The immediate challenge was to turn the new states into viable economic units. This was far from straightforward. The distribution of natural resources bore no relationship to the distribution of ethnic communities and economic development had proceeded within imperial frontiers and, if it had had any political purpose, with imperial objectives in mind. Austria–Hungary had built a major railway from Vienna to its important naval base at Fiume (Rijeka), but the new Poland had no port at all, and once it had constructed one at Gdynia, there was no rail connection to it. The new Czechoslovakia inherited a network of railways running north–south, whereas its own needs were for railways running east–west. The one line it did have linking Bohemia and Slovakia ran through what was now Poland.

More generally, economically integrated regions such as Silesia were divided into two or even three parts. This could disadvantage the new victorious nation as much as or more than the defeated one. The Slovak regions of Czechoslovakia, for example, had their own iron ore and textile industries developed under Hungarian auspices, but after 1919 they were in the impossible position of being cut off from their Hungarian markets on the one hand, but of being too remote from the new Czechoslovakia's industrial heartland in Bohemia on the other. The Slovak peasantry were in no better position. Those in the mountain areas had traditionally found agricultural employment on the Hungarian plain but after 1919 were no longer able to do so.

The creation of viable economic units also involved the equally problematic task of creating new stable currencies. This meant not only issuing the new but also withdrawing the old; a complex undertaking in countries like Poland where Austro-Hungarian, German and Russian currencies were all in circulation. Yugoslavia and, to a lesser extent, Romania were in the same position. These problems were compounded everywhere by the inflation engendered by the destruction and dislocation arising from the First World War. The Bulgarian *lev*, which was not even a newly introduced currency, had fallen to one-seventh of its 1919 value by the middle of 1923. Such inflation was destabilising not just on its own account but because its impact on society was so uneven. The Bulgarian cost of living, as just one example, had increased twelve-fold since 1914 but the wages of the urban worker over the same period by only half as much. The corollary was the unemployment and social discontent which were such a feature of the inter-war years.

National and international policies alike worked to make these problems harder rather than easier to resolve. The disastrous concept of reparations was extended to all the defeated Central Powers, with Bulgaria being expected under the Treaty of Neuilly to pay 2.25 billion gold francs over a thirty-seven-year period. Although these demands were progressively scaled down and then totally abandoned at the 1932 Lausanne Conference, they had a serious effect on confidence. Of nowhere was this truer than Austria where, although no reparations were actually ever paid, it was common ground between the political parties that the country was unviable.

The only real answer to such problems, pending the long-term restructuring of business and industry, was a degree of regional cooperation which would have gone some way to restoring the earlier economic structures. This was sensed at the time by some leaders, like Czechoslovakia's Dr Beneš who acknowledged that the former Austro-Hungarian monarchy had been a sound economic construction, but national and international politics alike pulled in the opposite direction. For the individual states, economic independence, beneficial and realistic or not, was almost as important as political independence. At the international level, any moves towards regional cooperation went against the perceived interests of at least one of the states concerned and of one of the western powers always in the background. Czechoslovakia and Yugoslavia both feared Hungary, as did Romania, but Hungary was an Italian sphere of interest. Czechoslovakia also feared Austria, but Austria also was an Italian sphere of influence as well as a German one. Bulgaria and Yugoslavia were almost belligerents throughout the 1920s and economic warfare was the norm everywhere. Telephone and water communications were regularly cut off, and Czechoslovakia tried to starve Austria and Hungary of coal. The only real exception to this negative pattern was Albania, where a National Bank was established with 53 per cent Italian capital in 1925. The following year the bank launched a Society for the Development of the Economic Resources of Albania. The price of such economic development, though, was a progressive loss of independence. Albania had to undertake, in return for the loans, that for a forty-year period it would take no action which might reduce income without prior consultation with Italy. In the same year oil was discovered off Vlorë and the concession again went to Italy.

Developments, though, were not purely negative. Europe slowly recovered from the dislocation of war although on terms which did not favour central and eastern Europe. The Dawes Plan of 1924 brought some order to the repayment of German reparations. There was a perception that the worst was over and that conditions would continue to improve. The perception was misplaced. For the first time since Versailles, it was to be America rather than western Europe which had the decisive impact on central and eastern Europe. On 29 October 1929 the American stock market crashed, introducing the Great Depression which was to show no sign of easing until the autumn of 1932. The effect on Europe was immediate. In Poland, as just one example, production fell to just 46 per cent of the 1913 level between 1931 and 1933. Tariffs were increased everywhere in an attempt to protect vulnerable national producers, and national quotas and cartels together with export subsidies reduced international trade even further. Such measures had the further negative effect of enriching some sectors of the population while impoverishing others, notably the smallholders.

Rather than joining together to stimulate trade, the central and eastern European states compounded the problem by opposing any such moves. In 1930 Czechoslovakia denounced a trade treaty with Hungary, but worse was to come. The collapse of Vienna's *Kreditanstalt* Bank confronted Austria with national bankruptcy, but the vociferous opposition of the Little Entente supported by France led to the abandonment of her logical response of concluding a Customs union with Germany. Obstructionism was mutual. When France convened the Stresa Conference in an effort to alleviate the problems faced by the Danubian countries, it failed in its attempts to create a Danubian Customs union in the face of opposition from Germany and Italy, seconded by Austria and Hungary, who wanted to see neither any threat to their own national interests nor any possibility of political consolidation which might reduce their scope for intrigue.

Such successes as were in due course achieved continued to reflect the shared interests of a small group of nations rather than any wider regional interest. Italy in October 1933, for example, advocated a revised framework for the economic activities of the Balkan nations. The 1934 Rome Protocols (see Part 2.2) followed this up by envisaging the development of Italian markets for Austrian industry and for Hungarian agriculture, and the promotion of the largely redundant port of Trieste as an outlet for Austrian and Hungarian exports.

Behind this pattern of national assertion in a dislocated world, however, there loomed a common challenge which long predated the war: that of a disaffected peasantry clamouring for land reform. Although the challenge was old, the youth of the population and its new military experience gave it a much sharper edge. Only in Romania, though, was there a serious approach to it, but even there some ½ million families remained landless as the Second World War approached. Moreover, holdings were too small and yields too low. Agricultural underemployment was rife.

Such structural imbalances, though, almost receded into the background as the impact of the Great Depression mounted. Prices plummeted and the value of the exports of raw materials and food, on which central and eastern Europe was particularly dependent, fell with them. The solution to this disastrous scenario was provided by Germany. The Nazis reversed the previous policy of higher tariffs on imported agricultural produce, and undertook to buy first Hungarian grain and meat, and then Romanian oil and Yugoslav produce, on initially advantageous terms. In itself this was constructive, but the true price soon had to be paid. Germany, as the increasingly dominant and exclusive customer, could, and did, dictate the terms of trade to the universally weak central and eastern European nations. By 1938, Germany alone was taking 42 per cent of Hungary's exports. Some historians have even gone so far as to claim that by 1939 Hitler had already won the first phase of the Second World

211

War – the struggle for German economic supremacy across the eastern part of the continent.

That supremacy was to prove short-lived, but one other developement at the national level was to help the establishment of the much longer-lived period of Communist rule. Even pre-war governments took the initiative in establishing industries in an attempt to meet the difficulties experienced by their own small firms in attracting capital. State-run did not equate with Communist to the extent that later generations would tend to assume.

5.2 THE IMPACT OF THE SECOND WORLD WAR

The Second World War intensified and extended the pre-war pattern of German economic domination across central and eastern Europe, but it also introduced new divisions. Austria, Bohemia and Moravia and those parts of the Baltic nations actually incorporated in the German state benefited from enormous German investment and the widespread development of strategic industries and infrastructure. The conquered territories on the other hand, notably Poland and the Ukraine, were seen merely as sources of plunder. Their populations were to be kept at starvation level pending their displacement to provide *Lebensraum* (settlement space) for the Germans. Two million Poles were transported to provide forced labour in addition to that of her 700,000 prisoners of war. A quarter of Poland's forests were felled for timber.

In some respects, though, particularly as the war advanced, the economic distinction between Germany's allies and conquered peoples meant little. Some 75–80 per cent of the trade of the allied nations was with Germany, but deliveries were increasingly not paid for. Mark 1 billion was owing to Slovakia, Mark 1.2 billion to Bulgaria, Mark 2.5 billion to Hungary and Mark 4.6 billion to Bohemia and Moravia.

The final consequences were even worse than those of the First World War, and the suffering was most acute in those countries like Germany, Poland and Yugoslavia where ground fighting had been particularly severe. Warsaw had almost ceased to exist and a quarter of Budapest had been destroyed or heavily damaged. Berlin was thought by some to be beyond reconstruction. The overall level of destruction exceeded 350 per cent of Poland's 1938 gross domestic product (GDP) and 370 per cent of Yugoslavia's. Hungary had lost twice its annual GDP, Czechoslovakia more than its annual GDP and Bulgaria and Romania about a third of theirs. Hungary, Poland and Yugoslavia had all lost one-half of their railway potential and between one-half and three-quarters of their animal stock. In the worst affected areas, which were often extremely large, communications had returned to the level of 80 years before, and agricultural output and industrial capacity to those of 50 years before. Anything removable or useful was likely to have been removed by the retreating German or advancing Soviet Armies. When it is remembered that some 17 million refugees and displaced persons (see Part 7.4) were moving over these same areas, it still seems a miracle that central and eastern Europe did not descend into the final anarchy of disease and starvation. It was an achievement of those in power which has not always received due credit and recognition.

5.3 POST-WAR RECONSTRUCTION UNDER COMMUNIST RULE

The problems engendered by the level of death and destruction were not, however, the only economic problems facing governments. Just as after the First World War, inflation was rife and both Hungary and Romania had in addition been placed under an obligation to pay reparations. The practical consequence of all these problems was an early economic dependence on the Soviet Union not so much for ideological reasons as through sheer necessity, as the only source of essential raw materials, as the only market for the little there was to export, and as the only supplier of transportation. Not least, only the Soviet Union had the potential to fill the economic vacuum created by the defeat of Germany. Joint companies were a logical development.

Like Britain in western Germany, the Soviet Union was also soon obliged to ship large quantities of badly needed food to Bulgaria, to the Soviet Zone of Germany and to Romania, to stave off starvation.

Furthermore, the devastation caused by the war was so great across Europe as a whole, that governments everywhere had no option but to pursue policies of direction, planning and rationing which had a Communist flavour. That was particularly the case in central and eastern Europe whose pre-war capitalist systems, outside Czechoslovakia, had been rudimentary. The entrepreneurial middle class had been small, often largely Jewish and again often German in the north of the region and Greek in the south. Much of it had now simply disappeared, and Czechoslovakia deliberately expelled all its Germans despite their entrepreneurial traditions. Land reform similarly, which had a particularly dramatic effect in the Soviet Zone of Germany, Hungary and Poland, demanded a high level of governmental organisation. In short, circumstances bred a climate of egalitarianism and government intervention without either Communist doctrine or Soviet political influence needing to make itself felt.

Nationalisation of major enterprises was a common policy. Czechoslovakia led in October 1945 by nationalising its mines, natural resources, large iron and steel enterprises, some larger food and drinks businesses, the banks and the insurance companies. Non-Communist Hungary nationalised its mines in 1946 and its large banks in 1947.

The growing political influence of the Communists naturally accelerated this trend. Hungary followed up its earlier nationalisations by placing heavy industry, power generation, food processing and all companies employing more than 100 people under state control. By the end of 1947, 95 per cent of Bulgaria's admittedly very small industrial sector was nationalised, and by 1948 60 per cent of East Germany's was. The Czechoslovak government crisis of spring 1948 was part triggered in the February by Communist pressure for more extensive nationalisation. Yugoslavia nationalised all businesses other than small handicrafts. Poland nationalised all businesses employing more than 50 people. By the end of 1949 Romania had nationalised 85 per cent of its industry, assisted by general public hostility to foreign ownership.

Whether promoted specifically by Communists or not, nationalisation was a broadly popular policy echoed in western Europe in the early post-war years. It was only in Czechoslovakia after 1948, where there remained a significant middle class, that the comprehensive nationalisation of commerce and industry met significant opposition. These trends, which would have been powerful in any event, were further reinforced by the unwillingness of the western Allies after the rejection of the Marshall Plan to consider alternative forms of aid or to increase the low level of mutual trade. The Soviet Union willingly filled the gap and provided credit.

The popularity of state planning owed more to Soviet influence, but again it was reflected in western Europe, although more weakly except in France. Again, also, it was often seen, at least initially, as a necessity. The initial plans were modest in both duration and scope. The first East German plan was for only six months, the Bulgarian for two years and the Hungarian for three. Most failed to meet their targets, but were nevertheless positive in their impact.

From 1947 onwards, however, state planning acquired a different flavour. It grew more ambitious and much more directed along Soviet lines at the development of heavy industry at the expense of all other considerations. The motivation was mixed. Marxism–Leninism saw industrialisation and the industrial working class as the future. Even agriculture would be 'industrialised' as much to stamp out (sometimes very real) rural obscurantism as to increase production. Heavy industry, particularly iron and steel, spelt independence for backward countries, and not just in the Soviet bloc. It also meant a capacity to produce munitions and military hardware: a capacity which had hitherto been largely confined to the Czechoslovak Škoda complex in Plzeň. That capacity grew rapidly in importance as the Cold War matured. Not least, the Soviet model enjoyed enormous prestige because on the one hand it had defeated Nazi Germany, and on the other hand it was simply the only model of industrialisation available in a backward country. The development of India and other Third World countries all lay in the future.

The impact of the introduction of this Stalinist style of state planning, focused on the development of heavy industry, was huge in every sense of the word. The plants themselves were enormous, modelled as they were on Soviet prototypes more in scale with the seemingly unlimited spaces of Russia herself. They were sometimes deliberately placed in sensitive locations to underline the break with the past. The advantages, at least potentially, were also enormous. Output was high on the basis of making maximum possible use of limited managerial and technical resources, and the plants dealt directly with the scourge of virtually all the central and eastern European countries: the great pool of unemployed or underemployed labour in the countryside. They also formed a basis for providing modern education and health care. The disadvantages were similarly enormous. Overly ambitious and lopsided plans led to high production, but also to waste, inflexibility and distortion. Otherwise promising sectors, such as precision tools and electrical goods in Hungary, were needlessly neglected. The impact on the environment was very bad, although it was not an issue which concerned either east or west at the time.

The more obvious victims were the workers in whose name industrial progress was being pursued. Contrary to promises, production norms rose while real wages fell. The standard of living of the Hungarian working population declined by some 18 per cent between 1949 and 1952. As had been the case in the Soviet Union, the peasantry effectively subsidised industrialisation by supplying forced deliveries at low prices. It had become a system which could only be maintained by a discipline so rigorous that it was coercion at best and terror at worst.

It was to meet its end in East Berlin, where the unpopularity of the Soviet Union as the late enemy, and perhaps some encouragement from the west, provided the additional impetus needed for revolt. The new Soviet leadership accepted the need for a move away from the preoccupation with heavy industry and for a greater focus on consumer goods. The political climate progressively relaxed and by 1956 Gomulka had returned to power in Poland and was reversing the collectivisation of agriculture as being contrary to Polish needs. It seems clear in retrospect that, although the Hungarian revolt of 1956 was infinitely more dramatic than the Berlin riots of 1953, it was less of an actual turning point.

It is, though, a reminder that there was to be constant tension for the next 35 years between party orthodoxy and economic experimentation. Sometimes the pressure for experimentation came from below, sometimes it came from the leadership. Sometimes it was foiled by a reluctant membership, sometimes by a reluctant leadership. At other times it succeeded. Yugoslavia apart, which broke completely new ground, economic experimentation was pioneered by Hungary. Under the New Economic Mechanism of 1968, economic management was decentralised and farm and plant managers given greater direct responsibility for their enterprises. The profit motive was recognised if not totally reintroduced. The results were spectacular. Hungary became very visibly the most economically buoyant of the Communist states. Whereas it had seemed backward compared with its neighbour Czechoslovakia, it was now Czechoslovakia which seemed to be beating time. Hungary was also to be comparatively open to the west. Budapest had its Hilton Hotel: an unimaginable development in, say, East Berlin. Bulgaria trod a similar path in March 1979 by approving the reforms known as the New Economic Model (NEM), operative from the beginning of 1982.

Other countries were less fortunate. A combination of orthodoxy and Soviet pressure for mutual trade had foiled Erich Apel's comparable 'New Economic System' of 1963 in East Germany.

The East German experience underlined the problems which underlay the Communist experiment across central and eastern Europe. The Soviet Union was by far the largest and most powerful party, and for strategic reasons she wished to bind the economies of the Warsaw Pact countries together through the machinery of COMECON. Her own scientific and technological resources, however, were limited and disproportionately geared to military purposes. She and her Warsaw Pact partners needed trade and exchange with the west but were inhibited by geopolitical considerations from achieving it to the degree required. All too often, mutual trade within COMECON meant dumping, by mutual barter, substandard or otherwise unwanted manufacturers and produce. The problem of motivation was also always present. In the absence of profit, or the fear and terror of the revolutionary 1940s and early 1950s, workplace morale was dependent on pride in work, self-discipline, social solidarity and status: a difficult though far from impossible climate to achieve. The problems could also be assets. The bond with the Soviet Union which denied western stimulus also meant access to the Soviet Union's enormous natural resources, not least cheap natural gas at low prices. Specialisation within COMECON also brought its advantages, even if there was the risk of losing national economic independence. Romania's nationalistic unwillingness to cooperate has many echoes in more recent western fears as to the powers of the European Union.

Ultimately though the COMECON countries failed economically, even if the failure was essentially comparative. Living standards had after all soared compared with the 1950s. Apparent advantages such as low energy and materials costs stimulated waste rather than output. Czechoslovakia, for example, used twice as much energy and steel as America or Britain for the same value of output. Technical sophistication, not least automation and computerisation, lagged well behind western levels. Pollution was excessive and tending to destroy crucial environmental assets (see Part 6). They had also perhaps been unlucky. The dramatic increase in the international oil price imposed by OPEC in the 1970s had a highly destabilising impact on all European economies, but it hit countries such as Poland, Romania and Yugoslavia particularly hard because they were exceptionally vulnerable at that time in view of their high levels of borrowing for development. What had appeared a challenging economic strategy became a doomsday scenario. It also needs to be said that even if its factories were generally old-fashioned and its economies uncompetitive, the bloc had its centres of high competence and even excellence. Most important of all perhaps it could bequeath a trained and educated labour force almost unimaginable in 1945.

5.4 THE IMPACT OF 1990

The economic impact of the collapse of the Communist system was in many ways comparable to the impact on the countries of central and eastern Europe of the two successive world wars. Trading patterns were dislocated, markets collapsed, inflation was a permanent threat and unemployment rose. Not least, the balance of economic power within many of the countries concerned profoundly changed. Again, as was the case after the First World War at least, these consequences came irregularly and were spread over a considerable period of time. They may be far from over. The Czech economy was again contracting between 1997 and 1999, and Bulgarian inflation soared in January 1997.

The dislocation of trading patterns was associated primarily with the virtual dissolution of COMECON and the internal economic difficulties of the Soviet Union's successor states. Whereas the Soviet Union had been responsible for most of the region's imports, Russia, Belarus and the Ukraine were in no position to import comparably. The former Communist states also saw western links, and the EU's single market in particular, as the key to their economic future. This transition was a great deal simpler for the Visegrad and Baltic states than for those in the Balkans.

Inflation threatened as countries grappled with introducing western banking systems, new concepts of company law, the privatisation of former state enterprises, and market prices. It touched an annual rate of 600 per cent in Poland in 1990, 334 per cent in Bulgaria in 1991, and 250 per cent in Romania in 1993. It was still 43 per cent in Poland and 100 per cent in Bulgaria in 1992. Restructuring added further strains.

Not surprisingly, the implications for national economies were severe. By 1995, the GDP of even Poland was still below the 1989 level, although in 1992 the Polish economy had been the first to start growing again. In the Czech Republic, Hungary, Romania and Slovakia, it was 14 per cent below the 1989 level and in Albania and Bulgaria it was some 25 per cent below.

Such economic problems were distressing to an already confused public which had been led to believe that the adoption of western systems would bring western wealth. The International Monetary Fund (IMF) was now imposing disciplines different from but no more welcome than the Soviet Union's. Worse in its impact was the collapse in the framework of the Communist social order, which introduced crime on a major scale ranging from petty swindling to corruption throughout the whole governmental system. In 1990 some unwary East Berliners were suddenly faced with landlords out of a black farce, who first charged the room rent then followed it up with separate bills for the doors and other fittings. At the other extreme, in 1997 Albania virtually descended into gun law. 'Crony capitalism', whereby the elite benefited disproportionately from privatisation, was widespread.

Such extremes have been overcome or at least controlled, but corruption remains a major problem throughout the Balkan region. In war-torn Bosnia and Serbia, it has been gravely exacerbated by the profits to be made from sanctions-breaking and the continuing absence of any real relationship between power and responsibility. The ultimate consequences of the US$50–150 billion cost of damage to Serbian infrastructure caused by the NATO air attacks of 1999 can only be guessed at.

Such challenges aside, the Czech Republic, Hungary, Poland, Slovakia and Slovenia, which not coincidentally are likely to be in the first wave of new EU members, appear to have stabilised their economies on the western model. The price, though, has been heavy. Some citizens have become very much richer, a rather larger number have become appreciably poorer, with uncertain long-term social effects. Wealth is increasing, sometimes rapidly. Average GDP in the Warsaw region grew from 55 per cent of the EU average in 1995 to 65 per cent in 1996. Such progress, though, which is far from the norm, must always be set against the long fall from the 1989 level and the progress which would have been achieved in most places in any event under the previous system.

5.5 COMPARATIVE GDP

Comparative GDP per head in the richest and poorest regions in each country of central and eastern Europe (excluding Austria and the former Yugoslavia) in 1996.

Regional GDP as a percentage
of EU average

Bulgaria

| Richest | Burgas | 34 |
| Poorest | Sofia region | 24 |

Czech Republic

| Richest | Prague | 120 |
| Poorest | Středočesky | 49 |

Hungary

| Richest | Budapest city | 88 |
| Poorest | Nógrád | 27 |

Poland

| Richest | Warsaw | 65 |
| Poorest | Suwalskie | 23 |

Romania

| Richest | Bucharest | 44 |
| Poorest | Vaslui | 20 |

Slovakia

| Richest | Bratislava | 97 |
| Poorest | Trenčiansky | 37 |

Part 6

THE ENVIRONMENT

6.1 THE COMMUNIST LEGACY

It has to be said at the very beginning that environmental awareness in the modern sense does not predate the 1960s anywhere. Industrial development had advanced throughout the nineteenth and the greater part of the twentieth centuries in western Europe and America with little regard for resource consumption or environmental impact, although outbreaks of cholera and typhoid had stimulated significant public health legislation. Social concern had similarly stimulated radical improvements in public housing and space provision. Major rivers, however, such as the Rhine, were highly polluted, urban air quality, particularly in the more heavily industrialised areas, left much to be desired, and land contamination was widespread. The Soviet Union had followed a very similar path, although at a much more frenetic pace.

The industrial development pursued as a political priority across central and eastern Europe after 1945 was no different, and it had a similar environmental impact. The Elbe and the Danube grew dirty, air quality around the new industrial centres like Sztalinvaros in Hungary was visibly bad, and land disappeared under spoil and chemical wastes. Although Communist development was not qualitatively different, however, it was quantitatively different. Preference was given to extremely large interlinked plants forming industrial concentrations of remarkable size. Agriculture, similarly, was not only collectivised in most countries but managed along industrial lines. The corollary was that environmental impact was concentrated likewise.

Energy was a particular problem. Supplies of hard coal were limited and some traditional western sources were now cut off. Industrialisation meant increasing reliance on sub-surface brown coal or lignite, particularly in East Germany where supplies were plentiful. The environmental impact, however, was severe. At the immediate level, huge tracts of countryside disappeared under mining excavators creating a lunar landscape. The greater impact, though, was much wider. Lignite and other forms of soft coal are highly sulphurous and their burning results in the production of very large quantities of sulphur dioxide (SO_2). The sulphur dioxide emitted into the atmosphere combines with water in the air to form dilute sulphuric acid, which returns to earth as 'acid rain'. It causes widespread damage, and in particular it kills trees and eats into building stone. Alarm was rapidly generated when West Germans observed from the mid-1960s onwards that their forests, particularly those close to the frontiers with Czechoslovakia and East Germany, were literally dying from such transboundary airborne pollution. Environmental impact apart, many of the central and eastern European countries under Communist rule remained seriously short of fuel. The dim street lighting of East Berlin and Dresden in the late 1960s was visible evidence of the extent to which power was an East German luxury.

The answer, as in some western countries, notably France, was the widespread use of nuclear power. Environmentalists remain deeply suspicious of civil nuclear power because of the risks of accident and the problem of radioactive waste disposal, but its advantages in the non-generation of environmentally damaging emissions are equally real. Nuclear power was promoted in east and west alike, however, for geopolitical and strategic rather than environmental reasons. The links with the development of military nuclear power are obvious. Countries such as Bulgaria and the Baltic States became dependent on nuclear power for the greater part of their energy needs. It is a matter of history that the major explosion at the Soviet reactor at Chernobyl in the Ukraine turned public opinion against nuclear power to a dramatic degree, in many countries seemingly lastingly. There is nevertheless still room for argument as to whether the explosion should be attributed primarily to management error, to inadequate safety provisions in the design, or to the risks inherent in the nuclear option. In any event, it can be accepted that later generations of Soviet-designed reactors were already appreciably safer than the early Chernobyl design.

The overall effect of these trends was somewhat contradictory. Agricultural and industrial concentration meant that environmental degradation was similarly concentrated, although its impact travelled far and wide. Neverthe-less there was a very marked contrast between the almost unimaginable grime of, say, East Germany's Bitterfeld chemicals complex and the great tracts of untouched countryside, even in East Germany but much more so almost everywhere else. Wolves and bears still roamed in Poland and Slovenia.

This contrast must always be borne in mind when assessing environmental data on central and eastern Europe, but this is not to make light of the problems which the Communist style of industrialisation bequeathed. Major industrial complexes were frequently adjacent to large cities which suffered pollution directly. It was increasingly realised in east and west alike that the high chim-ney stacks which ringed industrial cities like Plzeň did not disperse pollutants harmlessly but merely spread them over a much larger area. The urban fabric was visibly suffering from their attack on brick, stone and stucco. The security of Budapest's water supply was threatened by the level of pollution of the Danube, which was also leaching into the water table and contaminating sources many miles away.

The political climate was unhelpful. The primacy of the industrial proletariat in Marxist–Leninist philosophy discouraged any questioning of industrialisa-tion as a process. It represented evolutionary progress. The general absence of individual property rights stunted objection on the grounds of personal interest. More perhaps than anything else, the cold war imposed a psychology of production at any cost, inspired by a Soviet Union whose resources and ability to absorb pollution both appeared to be limitless. East Germany's uranium was too valuable militarily and economically for its extraction to be restrained by any consideration and, no doubt for this reason among others, environmental data were state secrets. It must also be said that the influence of a west which, well into the 1970s, was still minded to see environmental protection as an environmental burden, and as a generator of unemployment, could be unhelpful. The West German city of Hamburg, for example, paid East Germany welcome hard currency to dispose of its domestic waste, which was tipped, adding to East Germany's already substantial problems.

Nevertheless, it must again be repeated that the balance was not all negative. Environmental awareness was growing in the east as it had in the west fifteen to twenty years earlier. In East Germany it could escape government control by organising itself under the shelter of the Protestant churches. Governments too, though, were becoming more aware, and increasingly formed links with each other. Czechoslovakia and East Germany initiated cooperation on cleaning up the Elbe and joined with Poland in addressing the problems caused by the burning of lignite. The West German government soon recognised that it would be cheaper to invest in pollution prevention measures at source in Czechoslovakia, East Germany and Poland than to undertake expensive clean-up operations at home. East Germany established a state environmental inspectorate in 1985, one year before West Germany established its own ministry.

The east had its own strengths. Town planning had been taken seriously and problems like urban sprawl and random development were much less serious than in some western countries. Town centres had not been sacrificed to the car and Czechoslovakia had declared many of its smaller towns like Telč, urban reservations, whose care could be immaculate. Public transport was sophisticated and rail played a leading role in the movement of both goods and people, limiting the emissions of greenhouse gases which are such a disadvantage of road transport.

Not least, there were numerous nature protection zones and national parks, covering some of Europe's most remote countryside outside the Pyrenees.

6.2 THE IMPACT OF 1990

The collapse of the Communist system in 1990 eased some problems but generated others. The economic slowdown and the widespread closure of factories perceived to be uneconomic drastically reduced the emission of many pollutants, notably sulphur dioxide. In the Czech Republic between 1989 and 1994, as just one example, emissions of sulphur dioxide fell by 36 per cent, of nitrous oxides by 60 per cent, and of particulates by 49 per cent. Western investment was sometimes available for cleaning up and modernising polluting plant deemed to have an economic future. Other developments, though, were less benign. Much more emphasis was placed on the flexibility of road transport, and as the number of lorries and cars increased so did the output of carbon dioxide, the key greenhouse gas. Road building was similarly stimulated and brought its own environmental impact.

One undeniable advance was the impetus given to environmental legislation and policies. Czechoslovakia and Slovenia passed environmental protection acts in 1992 and 1993 respectively, and Poland and Slovakia adopted national environmental policies and strategies in 1991 and 1993 respectively. The EU's new European Environment Agency brought a new understanding of the reality of the eastern, central and western European environments alike with its Dobřiš Assessment of 1995, the first ever comparable review of the continent's environment. The countries of the Visegrad group led in applying for EU membership, which entailed ultimate compliance with EU environmental policy. This was a daunting commitment because the cost of bringing air quality, drinking water, and sewage disposal and similar standards up to EU levels was ' put by the EU Commission at no less than euro120–180 billion for all ten candidate countries for EU membership. Such a sum exceeded the resources of the Commission and of the candidate countries for EU membership alike, and it could only be hoped, somewhat optimistically, that the greater part could be raised from private investment. The challenge was equally great for the EU, but of a different nature. If it insisted on compliance with its own high environmental standards as a precondition of membership, which many including its own environment commissioner wanted, it ran the risk of delaying to an unacceptable degree its commitment to accepting the candidate countries as new members. If on the other hand it accepted them as members on the basis of lower standards, it would be destroying the level playing field for business competition which was the cornerstone of the key concept of the single market. The answer in practice was likely to be the compromise of long-term transition periods ('derogations') running from an adherence date now most plausibly put at 2005.

The Czech Republic, Hungary, Poland and Slovenia (together with Estonia and Lithuania) have now successfully completed their negotiations with the

EU on the environment chapter of the accession process on that basis. The negotiations with Slovakia (and Latvia) are, as of 2001, still in progress but those with Bulgaria and Romania have not yet started. The cost of Poland's adoption of EU environmental standards is, however, placed by the Polish government at euro30 billion even with derogations lasting up to the year 2015.

The EU and the candidate countries have faced comparable challenges over nuclear power, further complicated by the decision of some existing states, notably Germany, to phase out their own capacity. The EU has always insisted that the most hazardous plant in central and eastern Europe, including some of the reactors at Kozloduy in Bulgaria and Ignalina in Lithuania, must be decommissioned as an absolute precondition of EU membership, and has offered financial help to that end. It has, though, had to accept that energy shortages are such that many reactors of Soviet design with less than ideal safety provisions will have to remain in service for a considerable time to come.

Greater controversy has actually surrounded the completion of new nuclear plant to much safer Russian designs. Austria, which is strongly anti-nuclear, has strongly opposed the commissioning by Slovakia of Mochovce in Slovakia and by the Czech Republic of the new power station at Temelin, 60 kilometres from the Austrian border, despite assurances from international inspectors that it fully complies with western standards. Austria has gone so far as to threaten to veto the Czech Republic's admission to the EU if it is not fully satisfied.

The new non-Communist governments had their own disputes. Hungary and Slovakia inherited a large hydro-electric dam project at Nagymaros on the Danube which Slovakia was anxious to continue, but which Hungary strongly opposed on account of its feared environmental impact. The increasingly acrimonious dispute defeated EU mediators and eventually had to be referred to the International Court of Justice in The Hague, which found in favour of a reduced scheme.

It must also be admitted that, although western countries have certainly introduced advice and investment, not least through the EU's Phare programme, they have also introduced some less conscientious plant operators. The poor management of the Romanian Baia Mare gold mine led in January 2000 to the collapse of a retaining dam, releasing 120 tons of cyanide into the tributaries of the Danube and threatening the water supplies of cities far downstream. Disaster was narrowly averted, but the management of 23 other plants in the region remains a subject of major concern.

Part 7

HUMAN STATISTICS

7.1 POPULATION STATISTICS

	1921	1939	1946–48	1991
Albania	831 877	1 003 124	1 120 522	3 303 000*
Austria	6 428 000	–	7 062 942	7 800 000
Bulgaria	4 910 000	6 077 939	7 022 026	8 798 000
Czechoslovakia	13 610 000	9 807 096	12 164 661	15 567 666
Czech Republic				–
Slovakia				–
Hungary	7 945 878	11 137 993		10 500 000*
Poland	27 092 025	32 106 400	23 929 757	38 337 000*
Romania	17 303 149	19 585 398	16 409 367	23 276 000*
Yugoslavia	12 017 323	15 630 000	15 751 938	–
Bosnia–Hercegovina				4 366 000
Croatia				4 760 300
Macedonia				2 038 047**
Serbia and Montenegro				10 500 000**
Slovenia				1 962 000

* estimated
** 1992 figure

7.2 ETHNIC MINORITIES

Ethnic Bulgarians

	1921	1930/31
Romania	–	361 058

Ethnic Byelorussians

	1921	1930/31
Poland	–	989 900

Ethnic Germans

	1921	1930/31
Czechoslovakia	3 122 892	3 231 688
Hungary	–	478 630
Poland	–	741 000
Romania	–	740 169

Ethnic Hungarians

	1921	1930/31	2001
Austria			70 000
Czechoslovakia	746 809	691 923	
Romania	–	1 426 178	2 000 000
Slovakia			600 000
Ukraine			200 000
Yugoslavia			345 000

Jews by nationality

	1921	1930/31
Czechoslovakia	180 337	186 642

Jews by religion

	1921	1930/31
Austria	–	191 481
Bulgaria	–	48 398
Czechoslovakia	353 644	356 830
Poland	–	2 732 600*
Romania	834 344	900 000
Yugoslavia	64 159	68 405

* Yiddish and Hebrew speakers in the December 1931 census

Ethnic Poles

	1921	1930/31
Czechoslovakia	75 705	

Ethnic Russians

	1921	1930/31
Romania	–	415 217

Ethnic Ruthenians

	1921	1930/31
Romania	–	577 693

Ethnic Slovaks

	1921	1930/31
Hungary	–	104 819

Ethnic Ukrainians

	1921	1930/31
Poland	–	3 222 000

7.3 WAR LOSSES

(1939–45)

Albania: 22,000.

Czechoslovakia: about 200,000.

Germany: estimated 3 million killed and 3.4 million permanently wounded as of 1945, many of whom had died prematurely by 1950, together with 1,148,000 soldiers and 190,000 civilians still missing in 1950. Perhaps 6 million in all.

Hungary: 500,000.

Poland: nearly 3 million.

Romania: 500,000.

Soviet Union: precise figures are unobtainable, but estimates of some 25 million killed are generally accepted.

Yugoslavia: 1,685,000 killed, representing more than 10 per cent of the population. More than 75 per cent had been shot or lost their lives in concentration camps or death chambers, and the average age of those killed or missing was 22.

(**Jews** from central and eastern Europe as a whole: perhaps 4 million.)

(1992–95)

Bosnia–Hercegovina: about 200,000.

7.4 THE POST-WAR MIGRATIONS

7.4.1 THE EVICTION OF THE GERMANS

1945–46

from Czechoslovakia:	3 million	(the Sudeten Germans)
from East Prussia:	2 million	(from the detached area of pre-war Germany centred on Königsberg, annexed by Poland and the Soviet Union jointly in 1945)
from Hungary:	0.5 million	
from Poland:	7.5 million	(2m from pre-war Poland, and 4.5m from Silesia and 1m from East Pomerania, both annexed by Poland in 1945 in compensation for her loss of territory in the east to the Soviet Union)
from Romania:	300,000	

1978–83

from Romania:	55,000 voluntary emigrants

7.4.2 THE EVICTION OF THE HUNGARIANS

1945–46

from Slovakia:	100,000

7.4.3 THE MIGRATION OF THE POLES

1945–46

from the eastern territories ceded to the Soviet Union and mostly to the new western territories transferred from Germany:	2–3 million

7.4.4 DISPLACED AND RESETTLED PERSONS

1944–46

Total:	15–17 million

7.5 REFUGEES WITHIN YUGOSLAVIA

Macedonia

Contains some 60,000 refugees from Bosnia (1992).

Serbia

Contains 400,000 Serb refugees from Bosnia and Croatia, and 230,000 from Kosovo (2001).

Part 8

CULTURE

8.1 COSMOPOLITANISM AND CULTURAL NATIONALISM

The popular image of the Austro-Hungarian Empire and of its twin capitals of Vienna and Budapest was one of gaiety: of Viennese waltzes, operetta and cream cakes. It was summarised in the familiar Austrian comment that 'the situation is critical but not serious'. That image persists and is valid on its own terms, but it concealed the empire's darker side – its grimly repressive prisons such as the Spilberk in Brno, the grinding poverty of many of its workers which made Vienna 'Red Vienna' at an early date and its anti-Semitism. It also did Vienna a grave disservice by distracting attention from the reality that it was one of the most creative cities of the early twentieth century. Indeed it can be plausibly argued that, as home to Freud, Adler and Jung, Schoenberg, Webern and Berg, Musil, Kokoschka and Wittgenstein, it was a more vibrant centre than London, Paris or Berlin. Moreover, Freud largely created the science of psychology, just as Schoenberg created the 'modern' music which continues to inspire some of music's most original minds. Although Musil is less well known, his work is compared with that of the great French literary innovator, Marcel Proust. This powerful artistic and scientific tradition not only survived the First World War, but peaked in the new Austrian republic established in 1919. Indeed some of its greatest achievements immediately preceded the republic's very darkest years. It was a tradition which was cosmopolitan in its outlook but German-speaking and to no small degree Jewish. It was suspect on all counts. It was out of step with a Europe organised on the nationality prin-ciple, with an Austria rendered 'German' by the loss of its Imperial territories, and with a public opinion which was minded to see Austria's future as lying in union with Germany. It was a tradition which was faltering throughout the 1930s, and which died in 1938 when the victorious Nazis, Austrian and German alike, suppressed 'degenerate' art and science and persecuted and ultimately eliminated that part of the Jewish population which had not already fled. It was a tradition which was not to be reborn in 1945, because too many of its supports had been destroyed. Cosmopolitanism in central and eastern Europe was no more and, more fundamentally, the wealth which had flowed into Vienna from the far corners of the empire and sustained its administra-tive, merchant and military classes was no more. Defeat in 1918 had rendered Austria marginal and Vienna provincial, and the cultural and intellectual Indian Summer of the following twenty years had masked, but could not alter, that underlying reality.

Budapest and Prague had formed part of that intellectual world, but were increasingly centres of a specifically national culture. As early as 1867, Liszt had captured national and nationalist sentiment with his Coronation Mass for the Habsburg emperor, now declared king of Hungary. A rich vein of genius, including Bartók in Hungary and Janáček in Czechoslovakia, built on these foundations. Warsaw was, perhaps, less obviously creative, but all in the longer term were to face the continuing challenge of sustaining creativity within what had become a very much narrower environment.

8.2 THE ARTS UNDER FASCISM AND COMMUNISM

Not surprisingly, official art and architecture between the wars reflected the nationalistic strivings of politics and social life. They also reflected, however, an urge to achieve a style which was modern and appropriate for a nation which was seeking to establish itself in the post-war world. These twin urges discouraged work which was individual or experimental in favour of a more conformist approach. Academism prevailed over innovation. In practice this meant a pared down classical style, paralleled in the celebrated town hall of Stockholm and municipal buildings in Britain, including Norwich, Southampton and Walthamstow (London).

In central and eastern Europe, it did not usually mean the grandiloquent monumentalism of Mussolini's Italy, of which Milan Central Station remains the most evocative memorial. Even when the classicism of its new public buildings approached the monumental, it did not verge on the imperial. It also did not mean the sheer scale of Nazi architecture, starting with Berlin's 1936 Olympic Stadium, partly because their inspiration came too late and partly because they were too extravagantly expensive.

Such work was not necessarily bad. It could have qualities of balance and proportion, but it usually lacked inspiration. It did not share the dauntingly inhuman mass of such Nazi buildings as Berlin's Air Ministry (now the Federal Finance Ministry), but its modernism was symbolic. The option of questioning orthodoxy, particularly if it related to fundamentalist nationalism, was excluded. Personal creativity, and the anxieties it addresses, were out of fashion.

These same trends were reflected in the more private arts, although literature and music are harder to control. The nationalist impulse had proved intensely stimulating to composers such as Bartók. Predecessors such as Smetana, Dvořák and Liszt had after all played a major role in the nineteenth century in crystallising the spirit of Czech and Hungarian nationalism. Bartók, however, had been able to marry his national melodies with very un-national Viennese modernism and a high level of personal experimentation. Nevertheless even he found the political climate in Hungary increasingly oppressive and ultimately opted to emigrate to the United States. Vienna itself, as already noted, had turned its back on Berg, well before the Nazis suppressed all experimental work as 'degenerate'.

It was logical that it was only in liberal Czechoslovakia that the creative theatre flourished. Karel Čapek enjoyed a European reputation for his avant-garde dramas which could not be matched elsewhere. Lyric poetry was similarly rich and the achievement of Jaroslav Seifert was belatedly recognised in the award of the Nobel prize for literature in 1984. Budapest could retain its polish and style with the later operettas of Franz Lehar, but they did not aspire to be high art.

The Communist approach to the arts was in some respects very similar to the Fascist approach. There was the same fondness for the heroic and the monumental, for the public against the private. In the one spot where there was ever a direct confrontation between the two, the 1937 Paris exhibition, the German and Soviet pavilions mirrored each other. Profound differences in philosophy could generate comparable results. Lenin had taught that all endeavour, including artistic endeavour, had to serve the people and their revolution. Fascism maintained that all endeavour was for the good of the corporate state. Neither left any room for 'art for art's sake'.

Communist art and architecture, though, was a much more complex subject than Fascist art and architecture. It was inspired by Soviet art, itself rooted in a revolution initially as radical artistically as it was politically. The Soviet poster was to retain some of that artistic radicalism until 1990, and it inspired imitation throughout Communist central and eastern Europe. Soviet influence after 1945, however, was also much more tangible. Wartime devastation demanded urgent repair and rebuilding, and austere office and apartment blocks born of necessity were a common European response. They were, though, not the only response. The reconstruction of historic cities is discussed in the next section, but the surprising response was the widespread adoption of the lavish palatial style associated with Stalin himself and sometimes dubbed 'wedding cake' style. It could even perhaps be described as 'Moscow Metro' style. The best known example in central and eastern Europe is probably the 'Palace of Culture' in Warsaw, presented by Stalin as an (unwanted) gift to Poland in the early 1950s, which gives part of the Warsaw skyline a decidedly Soviet feel – no doubt the intention. The same style was favoured for the early reconstruction of the centre of Magdeburg in East Germany. The most remarkable example, though, remains the development of Stalinallee, now Karl-Marx-Allee, in East Berlin. The new East German state, declared in 1949, planned and executed the total redevelopment of some 2.5 kilometres of the humble Frankfurter Allee with mansion blocks which truly deserved the description of 'people's palaces'. Some of the detailing is undoubtedly Russian in inspiration, as is the choice of road width, but the supervising architect was Hermann Henselmann, the Berlin city architect. It was widely derided by the west at the time, largely for political reasons, but is now officially recognised as one of Europe's most significant building ensembles. Recently rehabilitated with the aid of finance from the EU Regional Development Fund, it can reveal vistas of real urban beauty.

The more personal arts were kept under strict control, particularly after the notorious Soviet Zhdanov decree of 1948 insisting on socialist realism. Although it provoked a great deal of poor work, it was also bypassed to a remarkable degree by more independent spirits and was also very erratically applied both in time and place. Ludmilla Zhivkova, as minister of culture, introduced considerable artistic freedom in Bulgaria. Poland was always regarded as extremely liberal by East German standards, although writers like East Germany's Christa

Wolf succeeded in producing excellent work. Nevertheless, the works of the émigré Polish poet, Professor Czeslaw Milosz, were only officially published in Poland after he had been awarded the Nobel prize for literature in 1980. Dissidents everywhere, like Václav Havel in Czechoslovakia, seemed to feel restraint almost as a stimulus. Nevertheless both he and Kundera saw their works banned after 1968.

Communist rule, though, had its positive side. Wider educational opportunities produced a much larger audience for literature and stimulated writers, particularly in the Balkans, in a way that had not previously been the case.

8.3 POST-WAR REBUILDING OF THE NATIONAL HERITAGE

One of the most remarkable features of post-war rebuilding was the willingness of the new Communist regimes to restore, and even rebuild from nothing, historic buildings and centres with which, in some cases, they could have felt only limited sympathy.

The most celebrated example is the historic centre of Warsaw which was rebuilt with the aid of paintings by the eighteenth-century Venetian painter, Bellotto. Little less remarkable, though, was the recreation one by one of most of the devastated monuments of Dresden in East Germany, which long remained isolated from each other in a wasteland of destruction.

It was a reaction which gained a further impetus from German unification. After considerable controversy it was decided to reconstruct the great *Frauenkirche* in Dresden, rather than leave the rubble as a permanent war memorial. It is a reaction, also, which has not yet run its course. The media conglomerate, Bertelsmann, is building headquarters offices on the Unter den Linden, which was Berlin's, and then East Berlin's, and now reunited Berlin's grandest street, and building anew from original drawings and photographs the splendid neo-classical façade. Most remarkable, and most open to criticism, of all, is the serious objective of many to rebuild from nothing the whole of the royal palace in eastern Berlin which was totally demolished by the Soviet occupation authorities after heavy damage in the Second World War. The only preserved fragment is the balcony from which Karl Liebknecht (qv) declared the German Communist Republic after the First World War, now in the (currently closed) East German Palace of the Republic (*Palast der Republik*).

8.4 LINGUISTIC POLITICS

The concept of linguistic politics may have an unfamiliar sound to English readers, but will be much more familiar to any reader from an ethnically contested region. It is the process whereby language is self-consciously used to assert and to cultivate national identity, often in the face of assimilation by a larger or more dominant adjacent group. Linguistic assimilation is associated with cultural and political assimilation, and to be countered and, if possible, reversed accordingly as one facet of national self-determination.

The first stage in the process has to be codification of a standard language with a reasonably common grammar, pronunciation and vocabulary out of a number of conflicting dialects which may be mutually incomprehensible. It will co-exist with dialects, and will probably be rooted in one, but will usually have more prestige as the speech of the better educated and increasingly of literature. It is a process which had been completed in England and France by the early seventeenth century, if not before, but which had to wait until the nineteenth century in parts of central and eastern Europe, and remains incomplete in Albania. It is, though, an ambiguous process. If the creation of a common language facilitates the process of nation building, then the corollary is also true. The existence of a common language hinders the pursuit of different national aspirations within the same language area. What this means in practice is that dialects are promoted to languages, and languages demoted to dialects, to fit changing political circumstances. Europe has a range of examples. Croatian nationalists, including the later president, Franjo Tudjman, sought to establish from the 1970s onwards that Croatian was a specific language and not just a national variant of the Serbo-Croat shared with Serbia. The slav speech of the Czech Republic and of Slovakia is sufficiently similar for it to have been customary to speak until 1992/93 of a Czechoslovak language, but that is now very much less the case. Languages like Byelorussian, Polish, Ruthenian and Ukrainian merge into each other and are defined by cultural and historic considerations as much as by linguistics. Similarly, languages can be deliberately distinguished from one another in an attempt to justify a particular political allegiance. The former Yugoslavia described Macedonian as a distinct language, as does the current FYROM, but many would argue that Macedonian is only a Bulgarian dialect. Likewise, the former Soviet Union insisted that Moldavian was a separate language rather than a dialectal version of Romanian. Such disputes can be very bitter. It was not until February 1999, for example, that the Bulgarian government first recognised Macedonian as a separate language. Some five years before, on 13 April 1994, the Bulgarian minister of science and education, Marko Todorov, had broken off his visit to Macedonia, having refused to acknowledge the existence of Macedonian as a separate tongue. Similar motives can affect spelling. Romania's post-war allegiance to the Soviet Union was reflected in a spelling reform which emphasised the slav elements in the Romanian language. Its reassertion of independent nationalism was then followed by a further reform which emphasised the language's Romance roots.

Above all, though, linguistic politics is about the promotion of the 'national' language at the expense of the 'imperial' language, on the one hand, and of minority languages on the other. The former process can prove the simpler. It is difficult to remember now, for example, that Prague in the middle of the nineteenth century was a German-speaking city. The Germans in Poland during the Second World War attempted to reverse the process. The Poles were deprived of education in the belief that an illiterate people ceased to exist as a nation. The exclusion of minority languages, though, is a much more sensitive issue. It raises issues of human rights, like the right to education in one's own language, the possibility of pressures for frontier changes, and the advance of a multiculturalism which may be seen as threatening and divisive.

At the time of writing (2001) the issue of language appears to be at its most sensitive in the Former Yugoslav Republic of Macedonia, but the greater potential problems lie with the large Hungarian diaspora in Romania, Slovakia and Yugoslavia. The use of Hungarian for official purposes, including higher education, seems likely to remain subject to repeated challenge.

BIOGRAPHIES

Adler Alfred: born 7 February 1870, Penzing, Austria. One of the fathers of modern psychology, associated in particular with the concept of the inferiority complex. Initially closely associated with Sigmund Freud (qv), but disagreed with him over the role of sexuality in human personality, and severed ties after 1911. Established his first child-guidance clinic in Vienna, 1921, which was soon followed by a further 30. Visiting professor, Long Island College of Medicine, New York, 1932. His clinics were closed by the Austrian government, 1934. Died Aberdeen, Scotland, 28 May 1937.

Alexander I (Alexander Karađorđević), King: born Cetinje, Montenegro, 16 December 1888. Second monarch of the Triunine Kingdom of Serbs, Croats and Slovenes and, from 1929, of Yugoslavia. Spent his youth with his exiled father at the Russian imperial court in St Petersburg. Returned to Serbia as heir apparent in 1909, a noted commander in the Balkan Wars 1912–13, and commander-in-chief of the Serbian Army throughout the First World War. He retained complete control of the army throughout his reign. Able to mix with his countrymen at all levels, but autocratic in personality and lacking patience with parliamentary procedure and democratic methods. Finding his country virtually ungovernable, he proclaimed a royal dictatorship in January 1929. Assassinated by Croat *Ustaša* extremists, Marseilles, 9 October 1934.

Antonescu Ion, General: born Pitesti, Romania, 15 June 1882. Pro-German Romanian dictator (*conducator*) during the Second World War. Minister of defence, 1937–38, but dismissed for his Iron Guard sympathies. Appointed prime minister, 4 September 1940, following Romania's substantial territorial losses to the Axis powers and the Soviet Union. His domestic reforms and declaration of war on the Soviet Union brought him initial support, but the tide of war turned and he was ousted in a *coup d'état* led by King Michael in August 1944. Executed by Romania near Jihlava as a war criminal, 1 June 1946.

Bartók Béla: born Nagyszentmiklós, then Hungary, now Sînnicolau Mare, Romania, 25 March 1881. One of the greatest of twentieth-century composers. An ethnic Hungarian, he was inspired by the historic folk music of Hungary, rather than by the Gypsy music which had been popularised by Liszt, as well as by the folk music of Slovakia and of Romanian Transylvania which was part of Hungary until 1920. The nature of the tunes he collected, in collaboration with Zoltán Kodály (qv), as well as the inspiration of the Viennese twelve-note school, led him to largely abandon traditional harmonies in his own compositions. He is particularly famous for his works for strings, of which the violin concerto (1938) may be the greatest, and his works for the piano, notably *Mikrokosmos* (1926–39), which progressively spans the range from the very easy to the very difficult. His most popular work, however, is the concerto for orchestra of 1944, written in a more traditional style. Emigrated to America in 1940. Died New York, 26 September 1945.

Beneš Edvard: born Kozlany, then Austria–Hungary, now Czech Republic, 28 May 1884. A founder, and in due course president, of the Czechoslovak state. Doctor of laws, 1908, and a lecturer at the Czech University of Prague before 1914. Followed Tomáš Masaryk (qv) to Switzerland during the First World War, and a co-organiser of the Czechoslovak National Council. Foreign minister 1918–35, and six times chairman of the council of the League of Nations. Opposed Austro-German unification in 1919 and again in 1931, as a threat to Czechoslovak independence. President 1935–5 October 1938, when he resigned and went into exile. Established a Czechoslovak National Committee in Paris in 1939 and then in London in 1940. Re-elected president, 1945, but refused to sign the new 1948 constitution and resigned, 7 June 1948. Died Sezimovo Ustí, Czechoslovakia, 3 September 1948.

Berg Alban: born Vienna, 9 February 1885. A major composer of the atonal, twelve-note school associated primarily with Schoenberg (qv) of whom he was a pupil. His operas *Wozzeck* (1925) and *Lulu* (perf. 1937), and his violin concerto (perf. 1936) are among the greatest compositions in twentieth-century music, but his work was dismissed as 'degenerate' by the Nazis in Germany and denied performance there. Despite his residence in Vienna throughout his life, his work was little appreciated by his fellow Austrians. Died Vienna, 24 December 1935.

Boris III King (Tsar): born Sofia, 30 January 1894. Ascended the Bulgarian throne on 4 October 1918, following the abdication of his father. An opponent of the authoritarian Aleksandŭr Stamboliyski (qv), leader of the Agrarian Party and possibly involved in the coup which displaced him in June 1923. The object of a number of assassination attempts. His marriage to an Italian princess symbolised Bulgaria's links with Italy. Progressively reasserted his personal power after the formation of the military dictatorship in 1934 and installed his personal favourite, Kiosseivanov, as prime minister in 1935. Effectively dictator from 1938 onwards.

A political opportunist but also a man of considerable and varied talents. A brilliant linguist, a keen naturalist and botanist, and a highly enthusiastic engine driver, who was a member of the Bulgarian Railwaymen's Union and frequently drove the Royal Train in his own country. Despite earlier seeking better relations with Yugoslavia, he aligned Bulgaria with Germany and took his country into the Second World War on the German side in March 1941. He nevertheless refused to declare war on the Soviet Union and was not totally subservient to Hitler. He may have been assassinated. Died Sofia, 28 August 1943.

Brancusi (Romanian Brîncusi) Constantin: born Hobiţa, Romania, 21 February 1876. Major Romanian sculptor and a pioneer of abstraction. His marble *The Beginning of the World* in the shape of an egg, described by Brancusi as 'sculpture for a blind man' (1924), is considered by many to be his greatest achievement. His career was international, although he was often inspired by his earlier life in Romania, and he became a French national in 1952. Died Paris, 16 March 1957.

Brătianu Constantin: born Florica, Romania, 13 January 1866. Brother of Ionel (qv, following). Leader of the Romanian Liberal Party after the assassination of Ion G. Duca in December 1933, and an opponent of King Carol's growing authoritarianism. At first supported war against the Soviet Union, but opposed the Antonescu regime after the recovery of Romanian territory from the Soviet Union. A conspirator in the successful anti-fascist plot of August 1944, and a member of two liberation cabinets. Adopted a pro-western and anti-Soviet position, and declined to join Petru Groz(e)a's left-wing government in March 1945. Imprisoned without trial 1950, and died in prison, probably in 1952.

Brătianu Ionel: born Florica, Romania, 20 August 1864. Six times Romanian prime minister, son of the co-founder of modern Romania, and champion of the concept of a greater Romania at the post-First World War peace negotiations. The concept was realised with the transfer of Bessarabia and Transylvania. Responsible 1922–26 for Romania's new constitution and for agrarian reform. Died Bucharest, 24 November 1927.

Čapek Karel: born Malé Svatoňovice, then Austria–Hungary, now Czech Republic, 9 January 1890. Leading Czech avant-garde writer, probably most remembered for his plays *R.U.R. Rossum's Universal Robots* (1920), which gave the world the word 'robot', and, with his brother Josef, *Ze života hmyzu* (The Insect Play) (1921) with its celebrated lines:

> Big fleas have little fleas
> Upon their backs to bite 'em,
> And little fleas have smaller fleas,
> And so ad infinitum.

His play *Věc Makropoulos* (The Makropoulos Case) forms the basis of the opera by Janáček (qv) of the same name. Died Prague, 25 December 1938.

Carol II King of Romania: born Sinaia, Romania, 15 October 1893. His colourful life as crown prince in which he successively contracted a morganatic marriage with a commoner, an unhappy marriage with the daughter of King Constantine I of Greece and a liaison with a Jewish adventuress, Magda Lupescu (whom he finally married in 1947), obliged him to renounce his claim to the throne in 1925 and contributed in no small degree to the western perception of the Balkans as a latter-day Ruritania. He nevertheless returned in 1930 to become king, ruling for the next ten years in an increasingly authoritarian style modelled on that of Mussolini. He declared a corporatist dictatorship in February 1938 in an attempt to counter the growing power of the fascist Iron Guard (see Glossary) and in the December created the *Frontul Renaşterii Naţionale* (Front of National Rebirth) led by himself to replace the dissolved political parties. Following the extensive losses of Romanian territory to the Axis powers (see Vienna Settlement in Glossary) and the Soviet Union at the beginning of the Second World War, he was forced to abdicate in favour of his son, Michael, on 6 September 1940. Died in exile, Estoril, Portugal, 4 April 1953.

Ceauşescu Nicolae: born Scornicesti, Romania, 26 January 1918. Romanian Communist leader. Joined the party's youth movement in the early 1930s. Imprisoned 1936 and 1940 for Communist activities, where he was a cell mate of Gheorghe Gheorghiu-Dej (qv). Escaped 1944, secretary of the Union of

Communist Youth, 1944–45, and minister of agriculture, 1948–50. Deputy minister of the armed forces, 1950–54. Rose through the Politburo to succeed Gheorghiu-Dej as First Secretary of the Romanian Communist Party in 1965, a post he held till his death. President of the State Council, 1967–74, and President, 1974 till his death. Pursued a highly nationalistic and independent policy which led to tension with the Soviet Union but to warmer relations with the western nations. He condemned both the 1968 invasion of Czechoslovakia by the Warsaw Pact and the 1979 invasion of Afghanistan by the Soviet Union. He strictly suppressed dissent, but was primarily undone by his decision to repay at any price the large foreign debt incurred through ill-considered industrialisation during the 1970s. Romania almost came to a standstill and starved as all production was diverted to export. Disposed to large and extravagant schemes, he proposed to demolish thousands of villages and urbanise their inhabitants, and was in the course of creating a vast palace for himself and his wife in Bucharest as part of their personality cult. Their personal tastes nevertheless remained modest. Overthrown in the uprising of December 1989, and tried and shot with his wife, 25 December 1989.

Codreanu Corneliu Zelea: born Iaşi, Romania, 13 September 1899. Founder and leader of the Romanian Iron Guard (qv). Helped establish the Association of Christian Students, 1922, affiliated, 1923–27, with the anti-Semitic League of National Christian Defence. Imprisoned, 1923, for threats to kill 'traitors', and accused of murder, 1925, but acquitted. Founded the Legion of the Archangel Michael, later the Guard, 1927. Garrotted and/or shot near Bucharest, 30 November 1938.

Curie Marie Skłodowska: born Warsaw, Russian Poland, 7 November 1867. The first great woman scientist, and the daughter of a professor of physics at Warsaw. Wife of Pierre Curie (1859–1906), professor of physics at the Sorbonne in Paris, with whom she collaborated to discover radium, sharing with him in consequence the Nobel prize for physics in 1903. Received the Nobel prize for chemistry in 1911. Although her most creative period preceded the creation of the Polish state in 1919, her achievements were a matter of great national pride. She was appointed to the International Commission on Intellectual Cooperation by the council of the League of Nations and her sister, Bronia, became director of the Radium Institute in Warsaw on its inauguration in 1932. Her daughter, Irène Joliot-Curie, shared with her husband the 1935 Nobel prize for chemistry for their discovery of new radioactive elements prepared artificially. Died near Sallanches, France, 4 July 1934.

Dimitrov Georgi Mikhailovich: born Kovachevtsi, Bulgaria, 18 June 1882. Bulgarian Communist leader. A printer and trade union leader, who was secretary of the Bulgarian Trades Union Federation from 1905 until its dissolution in 1923, and a co-founder of the Bulgarian Communist Party in 1919. Elected to the *Sobranje*, 1913, and conducted a violent anti-nationalist and anti-militarist campaign during the First World War for which he was twice court-martialled. Deprived of his seat in the *Sobranje* by the Stamboliyski regime. Elected to the executive committee of the Comintern (Communist International), Moscow, 1921. Leader of the 1923 Bulgarian Communist uprising for which he was sentenced to death in absentia. Head of the central European section of the Comintern in Berlin from 1929. Accused by the Nazis of conspiring with other Communist leaders to burn down the Reichstag on 27 February 1933, but acquitted after a brilliant self-defence. Adopted Soviet citizenship, 1934. Secretary-general of the executive committee of the Comintern in Moscow, 1935–43, from where he encouraged the formation of popular front governments. Directed resistance to Bulgaria's pro-German government, 1944, returning to Bulgaria, 1945, where he reassumed Bulgarian nationality and immediately became prime minister in the Fatherland Front government. Presided over Bulgaria's transformation into a People's Republic. Died near Moscow, Soviet Union, 2 July 1949. His funeral in Sofia on 10 July was attended by some 500,000 people.

Dohnányi Ernő (Ernst von): born Bratislava, then Hungary, now Slovakia, 27 July 1877. Hungarian composer, particularly for the piano, in the more traditional style. His *Variations on a Nursery Song* for piano and orchestra is well known. He left Hungary as a political exile in 1948, settling in America the following year, and his music was banned in Hungary for more than ten years. Died New York, 9 February 1960.

Dollfuss Engelbert, Dr: born Texing, Austria–Hungary, 4 October 1892. A leading member of the conservative and clerical Austrian Christian Social Party. Austrian Chancellor, 1932–34. Increasingly authoritarian under the influence of Mussolini, whom he saw as a defender against Nazi Germany, and absolute fascist dictator from May 1934. Assassinated in the Chancellery, Vienna, by the Austrian Nazis, 25 July 1934.

Dubček Alexander: born Uhrovec, Czechoslovakia, now Slovakia, 27 November 1921. Czechoslovak reformist Communist Party leader. Educated in Kyrgyzstan, then Soviet Central Asia, but returned to Czechoslovakia with his parents, 1938. A member of the wartime resistance. A Communist Party official, and chief secretary of the Bratislava regional committee and a member of the Central Committee of both the Czechoslovak and Slovak Communist Parties, 1958. A full member of the presidium, 1962. Led the economic and political reformers as well as the Slovak nationalists to replace Antonin Novotný as First Secretary of the party on 5 January 1968. Granted greater press freedom and pursued the rehabilitation of victims of the purges. Responsible for the reform programme entitled 'Czechoslovakia's Road to Socialism', better known as 'socialism with a human face', which alarmed the leaderships of both the Soviet Union and the other neighbouring Communist states. Proved unable to reassure the Soviet leaders at Cierna, Slovakia, between 29 July and 2 August, and the other leaders at subsequent meetings, that he was in control of the situation. Following the invasion by the 'Group of Five' on 20–21 August, forcibly taken to Moscow, and obliged on his return to withdraw many of his reforms. Progressively marginalised and replaced as First Secretary of the party, 17 April 1969. Initially president of the Federal Assembly, and ambassador to Turkey, January 1970, but later expelled from the party and appointed an inspector of the forestry administration. Returned to influence in 1989 with his election on 28 December as chairman of the Federal Assembly. Leader of Slovakia's Social Democratic Party, 1992. Died from a car accident, Prague, 7 November 1992.

Enesco Georges (Romanian, Enescu, George): born Liveni, near Dorohoi, Romania, 19 August 1881. Romania's only composer with a European reputation. Also a celebrated virtuoso violinist. Died Paris, 4 May 1955.

Freud Sigmund: born Freiberg, Austria–Hungary, now Příbor, Czech Republic, 6 May 1856. Effectively the creator of the modern science of psychology. First stimulated by working with the French neurologist, Jean-Martin Charcot, in Paris, he pioneered the concept that mental disease could be caused by totally non-organic factors. Back in Vienna, he developed theories of the subconscious, the nature of neuroses and of human sexuality and the creation of the Oedipus complex, which have profoundly changed modern man's perception of the human condition. He also pioneered the technique of psychoanalysis. Died London, 23 September 1939.

Gheorghiu-Dej Gheorghe: born Birlad, Romania, 8 November 1901. Romanian Communist leader. Joined the outlawed Communist Party, 1930, and sentenced to twelve years' hard labour for his involvement in the Grivița railwaymen's strike, 1933. Escaped from prison, August 1944, with the aid of Ion Gheorghe Maurer, later Romanian prime minister. Secretary-General of the party, virtually immediately. Minister of communications, 1944–46, and effective in securing a government dominated by the Communists and their allies by 1945. Thereafter promoted governmental economic planning and the development of industry. Prime minister, 1952, having ousted rivals identified with the interests of the then Soviet leadership. Pursued policies deemed to promote Romanian rather than Soviet interests, but in a manner which threatened neither the loss of Communist Party control nor the danger of Soviet intervention. Resigned as prime minister, 1955, but returned in the equivalent role of president of the State Council, 1961. Pursued an increasingly independent course and overrode the objections of the other members of the Soviet bloc to make Romania an increasingly industrialised, rather than an essentially agricultural, country. Also successfully courted both China and countries outside the Soviet bloc from the mid-1960s. Died Bucharest, 19 March 1965.

Gierek Edward: born Porabka, Austrian Poland, 6 January 1913. First Secretary of the Polish United Workers (Communist) Party, 1970–80. Emigrated to France with the rest of his family following the death of his father in a mining accident, 1923. First an agricultural labourer and then a miner. Joined the French Communist Party, 1931, but deported for organising a sit-down strike. Undertook his military service in Poland, and then worked again as a miner near Limburg, Belgium. Active in the Resistance during the war, becoming by 1945 the head of the special Polish section of the Belgian Communist Party.

Returned to Silesia, Polish from 1945, and First Secretary of the Communist Party Committee in Katowice, south-western Poland, 1951. Obtained an engineering degree, and head of the heavy industry section of the Central Committee in Warsaw, 1954. Recognised as a brilliant industrial organiser. Chaired the commission of inquiry into the 1956 Poznan riots, concluding that the party had failed to keep in touch with the workers. Briefly a member of the Politburo, 1956, and then again from 1959. A highly successful regional leader of Silesia, and elected First Secretary of the Polish United Workers Party, 1970, largely for that reason and for his considerable personal popularity in the country. Although he is remembered positively for the much greater social and political liberalism he introduced, for his willingness to adapt the Soviet party line to national circumstances, and for the new stress on consumer goods, he was hindered by a conservative party machine. Essentially, though, he was undermined by his policy of 'kick-starting' the economy with huge investment in industry financed by western loans. A high-risk strategy even in favourable times, it proved disastrous in the worldwide recesssion of the 1970s ultimately attributable to the dramatic increases in the price of oil imposed by OPEC. Attempts to cope with Poland's spiralling mountain of debt quickly eroded his popularity, and he was removed as party leader on 5 September 1980. Expelled from the party and interned for one year under the Jaruzelski regime. Subsequently retired to Silesia, where he died, 29 July 2001.

Gomulka Władysław: born Bialobrzegi, near Krosno, then Austrian Poland, 6 February 1905. First Secretary of the Central Committee of the Polish Communist Party, 1956–70. A locksmith by trade. Joined the underground Polish Communist Party, 1926, and thereafter a professional trade union organiser. Seriously wounded in the leg by police during a textile strike at Łódź in 1932. Sentenced to four years' imprisonment, but released, 1934, on medical grounds. Student at the International Lenin School, Moscow, 1934–35. Returned to Poland as a revolutionary agitator in Silesia, and sentenced to seven years' imprisonment, 1936. Released in 1939 and joined in the defence of Warsaw. Resumed political activity on the German invasion of the Soviet Union, first in Krosno and then in Warsaw, where he became district secretary and a member of the Central Committee of the *Polska Partia Robotnicza (PPR)* (Polish Workers' Party), as well as an organiser in the anti-Nazi resistance movement. General Secretary of the PPR from November 1943, and deputy prime minister in the Communist-dominated provisional Polish government in Lublin from January 1945. Assumed responsibility for all Polish lands acquired from Germany in June 1945. Elected to the Politburo, December 1945. Determined to ensure Communist domination, he led the attack on the Polish Peasant Party (PSL) and strongly supported the merger of his PPR with the Polish Socialist Party in 1948 to create the *Polska Zjednoczona Partia Robotnicza (PZPR)* (Polish United Workers' Party). Nevertheless, independent in his thinking and opposed both agricultural collectivisation and the formation of the Cominform in October 1947. Consequently distrusted by Stalin as a Titoist, he was deposed as General Secretary of the PPR, September 1948, dropped from the Politburo,

December 1948, dismissed from his ministerial posts, January 1949, expelled from the PZPR, November 1949, and finally arrested, July 1951. Released, late 1954, politically rehabilitated, 1956, and readmitted to the PZPR in the August. Reelected to the Politburo, and First Secretary of the Central Committee, October 1956. Soon thereafter also elected to the collective presidency. Despite initially enjoying almost total popular backing, his failure to execute sufficiently radical reforms until too late a stage, particularly in the economic and intellectual spheres, progressively reduced his support. He was ousted as First Secretary on 20 December 1970 following workers' riots in Gdánsk, Gdynia and Szczecin. Died Warsaw, 1 September 1982.

Gottwald Klement: born Dědice, then Austria–Hungary, now Czech Republic, 23 November 1896. Czechoslovak Communist prime minister and president. Trained as a carpenter and cabinet maker in Vienna, and a socialist at sixteen. Deserted to the Russians from the Austro-Hungarian army during the First World War. Joined what became the Czechoslovak Communist Party, 1918, soon editor of the party newspapers, *Hlas Ludu* (Voice of the People) and *Pravda* (Truth). Member of the Party Central Committee, 1925, and secretary-general, 1927. Member of the Czechoslovak parliament, 1929. Left Czechoslovakia for Moscow after Munich. Deputy prime minister in the 1945 provisional government. Chairman of the Czechoslovak Communist Party, March 1946, and prime minister, 3 July 1946. Led a purely Communist government from 1948. The successful rival of Rudolf Slánský (qv), the First Secretary of the Party. Caught a chill at Stalin's funeral in Moscow on 9 March 1953 and died of pneumonia, Prague, 14 March 1953.

Grotewohl Otto: born Brunswick, 11 March 1894. A printer by trade. Joined the German trade union movement and the SPD in 1912. Active in the province of Brunswick after 1918 as a journalist, deputy, minister and regional chairman of the SPD. Elected to the Reichstag, 1925. Persecuted and imprisoned by the Nazis on several occasions. Chairman of the SPD Central Committee after the war. Joint chairman of the SED, 1946–54. Head of the constitutional committee of the German People's Council, 1947, a member of the SED Politbüro and Chairman of the East German Council of Ministers (prime minister), 1949–64. Signatory of the 1950 Görlitz agreement between East Germany and Poland, recognising the Oder–Neisse line as their mutual frontier. Intelligent and a good speaker, he probably anticipated that the SPD element in the SED would play a more positive role than proved possible in the Cold War climate of the late forties and the fifties. Died 21 September 1964.

Havel Václav: born Prague, Czechoslovakia, 5 October 1936. Czech playwright, dissident and politician. Of middle-class parentage. Initially a stagehand, but by 1968, resident playwright at Prague's Theatre of the Balustrade. Prominent in the liberal climate of the 1968 'Prague Spring', which led after the Soviet invasion to the banning of his plays and the withdrawal of his passport. Thereafter repeatedly arrested and imprisoned, 1979–83, for his dissident promotion of human rights. His best-known play, *Vyrozumeni* (The Memorandum) of 1965, explores the breakdown of human relationships in the face of bureaucratic artificiality, and contains echoes of Kafka. Later plays explore the self-delusions and moral compromises induced by totalitarianism.

Returned to political prominence in the demonstrations of 1989 and became the leader of the umbrella grouping, Civic Forum, which entered into an interim coalition government with the Communists. Elected interim president, 29 December 1989, and re-elected as president, July 1990. Resigned as the Czechoslovak state approached voluntary dissolution, 1992, but elected president of the new Czech Republic on its inception in 1993. His political skills in office have been the subject of criticism from some.

Henlein Konrad: born Maffersdorf bei Reichenberg, then Austria–Hungary, now Liberec, Czech Republic, 6 May 1898. Leader of the Sudeten German Home Front (*Sudetendeutsche Heimatfront*) from 1935. Formerly a bank clerk and head of the German gymnastics movement (*Deutsche Turnbewegung*) in Czechoslovakia, 1923–33. Unsuccessfully demanded Sudeten autonomy, 24 April 1938, and following a later demand for cession of the Sudetenland to Germany fled there to escape arrest, his party having been suspended for treasonable activities. Founded a Sudeten German legion (*Freikorps*) and, following the cession of the Sudetenland to Germany at Munich, appointed *Reichskommissar* for the territory, 1 October 1938, and subsequently *Gauleiter* and *Reichsstatthalter* of Sudetenland. Committed suicide in Allied custody, Plžen, Czechoslovakia, 10 May 1945.

Hlinka Andrej, Father: born Stará Černová, then Austria–Hungary, now Slovakia, 27 September 1864. Leader of the movement for Slovak autonomy within Czechoslovakia in the inter-war years. Roman Catholic priest of Ružomberok from 1905. As leader of the clerical Slovak People's Party supported union with the Czechs in 1918 but soon cooled and entered into opposition to the Prague government in 1922, alleging in the Žilina Memorandum that the Czechs had denied the Slovaks their autonomy. His relations with the Czechs fluctuated, but were characterised in his last years by an intense hostility which was exploited by the Germans and the Hungarians and which made a considerable contribution to the destruction of Czechoslovakia in 1939. Died Ružomberok, then Czechoslovakia, now Slovakia, 16 August 1938.

Honecker Erich: born Neunkirchen, Saarland, 25 August 1912. A roof tiler by trade. Joined KPD, 1929. In Moscow, 1930–31. An official of the Young Communist League of Germany from 1931. Imprisoned, 1935–45. Chairman of the Free German Youth (FDJ), 1946–55. An alternate member of the Politbüro, 1950, and full member, 1958. First Secretary of the SED, 1971–76, and General Secretary, 1976–89. Chairman of the Council of State, 1976–89. Directly involved in the erection of the Berlin Wall in 1961, he was also believed to be a key figure in the fall of Dubček in Czechoslovakia in 1968.

Although intolerant and narrow in outlook, and little loved, he was in some respects a genuinely tragic figure. Proud of his creation and blind to its deficiencies, he lived to see it disintegrate around him in the events of 1989/90. He moved initially to the Soviet Union, but with its collapse he took refuge in the Chilean Embassy in Moscow in December 1991 to avoid extradition. On his returning to Germany he was charged with manslaughter in May 1992. He made just one statement to the court on 3 December 1992 denouncing the proceedings, which had opened on 12 November 1992, as a political spectacle and defending the decision to build the Berlin Wall. He accepted political responsibility for the killings at the border, although he regretted them, but felt no 'legal and moral guilt'. Following criticism of his detention by the Constitutional Court, the charges against him were dropped on 13 January 1993 and he was allowed to join his wife in Chile. That decision was itself annulled by a higher court on 27 January, before the charges were definitively suspended on 7 April 1993. There was widespread suspicion that the government did not wish the trial to proceed because it feared embarrassing revelations about the intimacy of earlier inter-German relations. He had claimed to be looking forward to it. Died in exile in Chile, 29 May 1994.

Horthy Miklós (Nagybányai), Admiral: born Kenderes, Hungary, 18 June 1868. Of Protestant, aristocratic origin. Trained as a naval officer at the Austro-Hungarian naval academy at Fiume, now Rijeka, Croatia. Aide-de-camp to Emperor Franz Josef, 1909–14, and a successful naval commander in the First World War. Admiral, 1918. Supervised the transfer of the Imperial fleet to Yugoslavia, October 1918. Raised an army to defeat the Communist regime of Béla Kun (qv) 1919, at the request of the counter-revolutionary government based in Szeged. Elected regent of Hungary, March 1920, by the Parliament elected that January, which had opted for the restoration of the monarchy. Nevertheless prevented his king, Karl IV, from ever ascending the throne. Hungarian head of state until 1944, but did not run the government until the 1930s and in particular after 1937 when his powers were considerably extended. Personally antipathetic to Hitler, but took Hungary into the Second World War on the German side to help the 'crusade against Bolshevism'. Later attempts to take Hungary out of the war resulted in his compulsory abdication, and detention by the Germans in 1944. Released by the Allies, May 1945, and in exile in Portugal until his death. One of the few captured collaborators with the Germans never to face war crimes charges. Died Estoril, Portugal, 9 February 1957.

Hoxha Enver: born Gjirokastër, Albania, then Turkish Empire, 16 October 1908. Communist ruler of Albania. Of Muslim middle-class origin. Studied in the French school at Korçë, and then in France and Belgium, where he read law. Professor of French at his former school in Korçë, 1936. Organised resistance to the Italians, who sentenced him to death in absentia, after 1939, and then to the Germans. Helped found the Albanian Communist Party (later Party of Labour) and the 1942 Peza Convention, where he was placed in charge of all military and political activities. First Secretary of the Communist Party's Central Committee, 1942 until his death, and prime minister, 1944–54. A lifelong admirer of Stalin. His rule made Albania largely self-sufficient in agricultural products and achieved much progress in education, health and industrial development, but at the expense of making Albania a closed society characterised by government brutality and control and increasing isolation from the rest of the world. Died Tiranë, 11 April 1985.

Husák Gustav, Dr: born Bratislava, then Austria–Hungary, now Slovakia, 10 January 1913. Czechoslovak Communist Party leader. Joined the Communist Party, 1933. A lawyer. Imprisoned by the wartime Slovak government, 1940–43. A member of the Central Committee of the Slovak Communist Party and an organiser of the Slovak national uprising, 1944. Interior minister and then chairman of the Slovak Board of Commissioners, 1945–50. Purged, 1950, and detained, 1951, as a member of an 'organised anti-party gang' plotting to establish a separate Slovak republic. Imprisoned, 1954–60. Rehabilitated, 1963. Attacked the party's prevalent neo-Stalinism and a deputy prime minister, April 1968, under the liberalising Alexander Dubček. Alarmed by Dubček's liberalism, however, he increasingly urged caution and, after the 1968 Soviet invasion, a reversal of policy. Leader of the Slovak Communist Party, 28 August 1968, and First Secretary (after 1971 General Secretary) of the Czechoslovak Communist Party, April 1969. President 1975–89. An outwardly dour and humourless figure, who firmly suppressed dissent and who neither won nor seemed to seek popularity. Nevertheless a competent manager under whom Czechoslovak prosperity grew steadily though slowly. It was almost the only Soviet bloc country in the late 1980s not to be burdened by external debt. Unsympathetic to the mood of reform launched by Gorbachev in the Soviet Union, he retired as Communist Party General Secretary, 1987. Resigned as president, 1989. Died Bratislava, 18 November 1991.

Janáček Leoš: born Hukvaldy, Moravia, then Austria–Hungary, now Czech Republic, 3 July 1854. Celebrated Czech composer, he remained closely associated with the area of his birth, settling in the city of Brno at the age of 30 and concentrating his activities there until his death. His creative genius reached its peak when he was in comparatively advanced years, perhaps inspired by his passion for Kamilla Stösslová, a married woman thirty-eight years his junior whom he met in 1917. His music is strongly influenced by the rhythms of Czech speech and he is particularly celebrated for his operas *Jenůfa* (1916), *Kat'a Kabanová* (1921), *Příhody Lišky Bystroušky* (The Cunning Little Vixen) (1923), *Věc Makropulos* (The Makropulos Affair) (1925), *Z Mrtvého Domu* (From the House of the Dead) (1928) and for his *Mša Glagolskaja* (Glagolitic Mass) (1927), which uses an Old Slavonic text. His stature has been rising steadily in recent decades and he is now esteemed by many as one of the greatest of twentieth-century composers. Died Ostrava, Czechoslovakia, 12 August 1928.

Jaruzelski Wojciech Witold, General: born Kurow, Poland, 6 July 1923. Polish military and Communist Party leader. Deported with his family to the Soviet Union on the outbreak of the Second World War. Joined the Polish Army established in the Soviet Union, 1943, and graduated from the Polish General Staff Academy. Joined the Polish Workers' Party, 1947. Steadily advanced to become a member of the party's Central Committee, 1964, minister of defence, 1968, and a member of the Politburo, 1971. Prime minister, February 1981, and First Secretary of the Polish United Workers' (Communist) Party, October 1981, against a background of unrest associated with *Solidarność* (Solidarity). Declared martial law, 13 December 1981, almost certainly to avert the threat of Soviet invasion. Lifted martial law in July 1983. Resigned as prime minister, to become chairman of the Council of State, 1985. Executive president, July 1989–December 1990. Resigned all his senior party posts, July 1989, and transferred the vestiges of Communist power to the new government, December 1990. A skilful and flexible politician but unable to surmount Poland's economic difficulties. Since charged at law with responsibility for the deaths of anti-government protesters while minister of defence. Possibly saved many more lives through his declaration of martial law.

John Paul II, Pope: born Karol Wojtyla, Wadowice, Poland, 18 May 1920. Studied Polish literature in the University of Kraków before the war, briefly a worker in the chemicals industry, and ordained, 1 November 1946. Doctor in ethics of the Angelicum University in Rome, and professor of philosophy at the Catholic University, Lublin, and at Kraków. Auxiliary bishop of Kraków, 1958, archbishop, 1964, and cardinal, 1967. Fluent in English, French, German, Italian, Portuguese and Spanish, as well as in Latin and his native Polish. Elected Pope, 16 October 1978, the first Polish Pope, and the first non-Italian Pope for 456 years. The victim of an assassination attempt in 1981. Celebrated for his charisma, his pioneering missionary journeys pursued into his eighties despite his suffering from Parkinson's Disease, and his dedication, but also strongly criticised for his doctrinal conservatism and authoritarianism, particularly on such subjects as abortion and contraception.

He has also courted controversy with his declaration of 447 saints, more than declared by the total of all his predecessors. The process shows no sign of slowing down. Another 1,237 candidates have been beatified, which is the first step to sainthood, and the official count of twentieth-century martyrs to totalitarianism published in 2000 includes 13,000 names, although not all would be candidates for sainthood. The merits of some are contested. Moves to canonise Pope Pius XII have faltered under outside criticism of his failure to condemn the Nazis and the persecution of the Jews, and Bishop Voytassak of Slovakia had been implicated in wartime Nazi administration.

Kádár János: born János Czermanik (Csermanek), Fiume, then Austria–Hungary, now Rijeka, Croatia, 26 May 1912. Hungarian Communist leader. A skilled mechanic by training. Joined the then-illegal Hungarian Communist Party, 1931. A member of its Central Committee, 1942, and its Politburo, 1945. Minister of the interior, 1949, but expelled from the party by its Stalinist faction and imprisoned, 1951–53, when he may have suffered torture. Rehabilitated, 1954, and appointed First Secretary of the Hungarian Socialist Workers' (Communist) Party, 25 October 1956. A member of Imre Nagy's brief liberalising government, but left him on 3 November 1956 to establish a new government friendly to the Soviet Union. Served as prime minister until 1958 and then again from 1961–65. His motivation seems to have been primarily a sense of duty. He was to write later: 'I have been working as an organised Communist since 1931 . . . I have been working ever since that time, because it is the rule for man to work. Yet I feel that, if you have nothing else to say for yourself except that in 1956, in a critical period, and in the following few years, you were of some use – you can say you have not lived in vain.' Allegedly asked Khrushchev somewhat despairingly in 1956 what he should do and was told 'make yourself popular'. Apocryphal or not, it was what after an initial period of repression he set out to do on the basis that 'he who is not against us is with us'. He proved remarkably successful, achieving in due course a real measure of public esteem and genuine popularity. Comparatively liberal and pragmatic approaches in all fields and economic liberalisation in the form of the New Economic Mechanism, introduced in 1968, generated a Hungary conspicu-ously more buoyant than its orthodox neighbours. 'Goulash Communism' was a force to be reckoned with. Progress faltered, however, and in 1988 Kádár was ousted as First Secretary, as the Hungarian Socialist Workers' Party em-barked on a programme of reform which was to turn it the next year into the modern Hungarian Socialist Party: an evolution he strenuously opposed. Party president until May 1989. Died Budapest, 6 July 1989.

Kafka Franz: born Prague, then Austria–Hungary, now Czech Republic, 3 July 1883. Great German-language novelist, most of whose work was neither finished nor published at his death. A nominal Jew, whose three sisters were to die in the concentration camps. His famous novels *Der Prozess* (The Trial) (1925), *Das Schloss* (The Castle) (1926) and *Amerika* (America) (1927) foreshadow both the rise of European totalitarianism and the sense of alienation and help-lessness widely experienced by twentieth-century man. His work has exercised extensive influence particularly on the surrealists. Virtually unknown in his lifetime, he had instructed that all his unpublished work be destroyed. It was, however, edited and published after his early death from tuberculosis by his friend and biographer Max Brod, who also corresponded regularly with Janáček (qv). Died Kierling, near Vienna, Austria, 3 June 1924.

Kodály Zoltán: born Kecskemét, Hungary, 16 December 1882. Hungarian com-poser and a collaborator with Bartók (qv) in the collection of Hungarian folk tunes. Similarly national in inspiration and modern in harmony. Probably his finest work, the sonata for unaccompanied cello (1915), predates our period, but he is more popularly known for the choral *Psalmus Hungaricus* (1923) and in particular for the *Háry János* suite (1927), the Dances of Marosszék (1927) and the Dances of Galanta (1933). Died Budapest, 6 March 1967.

Kun Béla: born Szilágycseh, Transylvania, then Hungary, now Romania, 20 February 1886. Of Jewish origin. Prisoner of war in Russia, 1916, where he joined the Bolsheviks and attracted Lenin's attention. Trained in revolutionary tactics and returned to Hungary after the war where he founded the Hungar-ian Communist Party on 20 December 1918. Imprisoned by Count Károlyi's government in February 1919, but remained politically active. Released 20 March 1919, to become next day commissar for foreign affairs and effective leader of a new Communist–Social Democrat coalition government. His government won considerable support for its creation of a national Red Army which reconquered substantial tracts of national territory lost to Czechoslovakia and Romania, but then lost support for its suppression of its less revolutionary elements, its failure to secure promised military help from the Russian Red Army, and its nationalisation rather than redistribution of the landed estates. Fled to Vienna, August 1919, and then Russia, from where, as a leader of the Third International, he sought to provoke revolution in Germany and Austria. Ultimately succumbed to one of Stalin's purges. Energetic and a good organiser, but skilled in neither the arts of government nor the tactics of survival within the wider Communist movement. Died Soviet Union, about 30 November 1939.

Kundera Milan: born Brno, Czechoslovakia, 1 April 1929. Celebrated Czech writer in a range of genres. Although generally a member of the Communist Party, his works were always subject to political criticism and suppression. His finest work may be his first novel, *Žert* (The Joke) of 1967, which explores with comic irony Czech lives in the Stalinist years. Active in the 'Prague Spring' of 1968, after which his works were banned and he was expelled from the Communist Party. Allowed to emigrate to France, 1975, but stripped of his Czechoslovak citizenship, 1979. He has remained a profilic writer.

Lehár Ferenc (Franz): born Komarno, then Hungary, now Slovakia, 30 April 1870. Perhaps the most successful of all operetta composers, works such as *Die lustige Witwe* (The Merry Widow) (1905) complemented the Viennese waltzes of the Strauss family to define the popular image of the Austro-Hungarian Empire in its final phase. He remained highly productive after 1919, and his work is influenced in part by the folk music of what had become Yugoslavia. Died Bad Ischl, Austria, 24 October 1948.

Liebknecht Karl: born Leipzig, 13 August 1871. German Social Democrat who with Rosa Luxembourg (qv) founded the revolutionary *Spartakusbund* (Spartacus League) which was to become the German Communist Party (KPD). He had been the first deputy in the Reichstag to vote against war credits. Sought to turn the German revolution of November 1918 into a Bolshevik revolution along Soviet lines but was soon arrested by counter-revolutionary volunteers and, with Rosa Luxembourg, summarily shot. Both were to become icons of the East German state founded in 1949. Died Berlin, 15 January 1919.

Ligeti György: born Diciosânmartin (now Tirñaveni), Transylvania, Romania, 28 May 1923. Leading avant-garde composer. An ethnic Hungarian, he taught there until 1956, after which he moved to western centres of musical experimentation such as Cologne, Darmstadt, Stockholm and Vienna. Some of his music is electronic, and in general he obliterates traditional harmonies, rhythms and intervals, and the difference between vocal and instrumental sounds. His work attracts respectful attention, but any consensus on its true musical value seems unlikely for a considerable time.

Luxembourg Rosa: born Zamość, Russian Poland, 5 March 1871. A founder of both the Polish Social Democratic Party, which was to become the Polish

Communist Party, and of the Spartacus League which was to become the German Communist Party. Her emphasis on democracy and revolutionary mass action rather than Lenin's tight party discipline and democratic centralism made her a heretical figure in Marxist circles, but also gave her a sympathetic image, aided by her good looks, which contributed to her lasting influence. Like her associate Liebknecht (qv) she tried to turn the German revolution of November 1918 to the left, when she was known as *die blutige Rosa* (bloody Rosa), but was soon arrested with him by counter-revolutionary volunteers and summarily shot. They were to become icons of the East German state founded in 1949. Died Berlin, 15 January 1919.

Masaryk Jan (Garrigue): born Prague, then Austria–Hungary, now Czech Republic, 14 September 1886. Son of Professor Tomáš Masaryk (qv, following). Foreign minister in the Czechoslovak émigré government in London during the Second World War, and in the restored Czechoslovak government, 1945–48. Sought to retain the friendship of both the Soviet Union and the West. Remained in office after the Communists assumed power until his death shortly afterwards. It has never been satisfactorily established whether he committed suicide or whether he was murdered by either the Czech or the Soviet secret service. Died Prague, 10 March 1948.

Masaryk Tomáš (Garrigue), Professor: born Hodonin, then Austria–Hungary, now Czech Republic, 7 March 1850. 'The father of Czechoslovakia.' Son of a Slovak father and a Germanised Czech mother, both of humble origin. Appointed professor of philosophy at the Czech university of Prague, 1882. Entered into politics, 1889, by editing a political review, and a member of the Austro-Hungarian Reichsrat 1891–93 for the Young Czech Party. Founded his own Realist Party, 1890, and a leading figure of the left-wing Slav opposition in the reformed Reichsrat. Escaped Austria, 1914, to become a professor at King's College, University of London, and to agitate for the Czechoslovak idea in western Europe and then in America during the First World War. Sentenced to death by the Austrians in absentia for his nationalist activities, but returned 1918 to become president of the new Czechoslovak Republic. Re-elected 1920, 1927 and 1934, benefiting from the constitutional provision that he alone could serve more than one presidential term. Widely admired as a humanist and a democrat in a continent and period when both were under savage attack, he must nevertheless bear some responsibility for the new state's failure to meet its promises to its Slovak inhabitants. Died Lány, Czechoslovakia, 14 September 1937.

Milošević Slobodan: born Pozarevac, Yugoslavia, 22 August 1941. President of Serbia, 1989–97, president of Federal Yugoslavia, 1997–2000. Son of an Orthodox priest, who like his mother committed suicide. Joined Communist Party, 1959, and married Mira Marković, the daughter of Tito's mistress, 1965. President of the United Bank of Belgrade, 1978–83. President of the Serbian regional Communist Party from 1986, and president of Serbia from 1989. Stepped down in 1997 to become Federal Yugoslav president. Indicted by the International

Tribunal for the Former Yugoslavia as a war criminal, 27 May 1998, and handed over by the Yugoslav government on 28 June 2001 in return for a promise of international aid which was described as substantial but bore little relationship to the cost of the damage caused by NATO bombing. Unquestionably autocratic and intransigent, but never quite the dictator he is often painted.

Musil Robert: born Klagenfurt, Austria, 6 November 1880. Austrian novelist, whose best-known, but unfinished, novel, *Der Mann ohne Eigenschaften* (The Man Without Qualities), describing life in the Austro-Hungarian Empire, has been compared with the work of the great French novelist, Proust. The First Book of the novel was published 1930, part of the Second Book 1933, and a further part of the novel after his death, 1943. Fled to Switzerland after the 1938 *Anschluss*. Died Geneva, Switzerland, 15 April 1942.

Nagy Imre: born Kaposvár, Hungary, 7 June 1896. Hungarian Communist leader. Captured as an Austro-Hungarian soldier by the Russians in the First World War and became a Communist, fighting with the Soviet Army. Lived in Moscow, 1929–44, as a member of the Institute for Agrarian Sciences. Returned to Hungary at the end of 1944, and repeatedly a government minister before becoming prime minister, 1953. Forced to resign because of his independent line, 1955, but returned to power in the October 1956 uprising. Captured, tried and executed after its suppression, but posthumously rehabilitated by the Hungarian Supreme Court, 1989. Died Budapest, 16 June 1958.

Paderewski Ignacy Jan: born Kuriłówka, Podolia, Russian Poland, 18 November 1860. A dazzling pianist with an audience appeal akin to that of Liszt and, like his father who had been exiled to Siberia, an ardent Polish nationalist. A member of the Polish National Committee during the First World War and their representative in the United States, where he worked to secure President Woodrow Wilson's support for Polish independence. His lasting achievement was to see it included as the 13th of the president's 14 Points on 8 January 1918. Called upon by Piłsudski (qv), as provisional head of state after the war, to form a government of experts free from party affiliation, which was duly established on 17 January 1919. He served as his own foreign minister and represented 'Poland' at Versailles. Accustomed as a pianist to adulation and resentful of criticism, however, he proved a failure as prime minister and resigned on 27 November 1919. Similarly unsuccessful in his desire to be elected president, for which he lacked the support of any political party, he returned to Switzerland never to revisit Poland. That did not, however, prevent his being offered the chairmanship of the Polish National Council by the Polish government-in-exile in Paris in October 1939. That council met under Paderewski in Angers but on the fall of France in 1940 he moved to the United States. Died New York, 29 June 1941.

Pašić Nikola: born Zaječar, Serbia, 31 December 1845. Five times prime minister of Serbia up to 1918 and one of the founders of the Kingdom of Serbs, Croats and Slovenes in 1918–19. Responsible as prime minister of the new kingdom, 1918, 1921–24, and 1924–26 for the unitary constitution of 1921 which entrenched Serb supremacy and a powerful monarchy. Until his resignation in March 1926 he pursued policies of increasing centralisation in a none too scrupulous manner. Died Belgrade, 10 December 1926.

Paul (Pavle Karađorđević), Prince: born St Petersburg, Russia, 27 April 1893. Regent of Yugoslavia from the assassination of Alexander I in October 1934 until his deposition by the Yugoslav military on 27 March 1941, but almost pathologically ill at ease with all but the most cultivated and westernised of his fellow countrymen. Allegedly pro-British and French, he nevertheless allied Yugoslavia with the Axis powers. Fled to Greece following his deposition in 1941 where he was ultimately captured by the British and for a time interned in Kenya. He had been deprived of membership of the Yugoslav royal family in January 1942. Settled thereafter in Paris. Died Paris, 14 September 1976.

Pavelić Ante, Dr: born Bradina, Bosnia, then Turkish Empire, 14 July 1889. Croat fascist leader. A lawyer. An early member of the nationalist Croatian Party of Rights and a member of the Yugoslav *Skupština*, 1927–29. Fled to Italy in 1929 where he founded the Croat terrorist movement, *Ustaša* (Insurgence), which developed its own terrorist training centres in Italy and Hungary. The movement was responsible for King Alexander's assassination in 1934. Installed by the Axis powers as *poglavnik* (head) of the new independent Croat state, which also included all Bosnia–Hercegovina and some of Serbia, in 1941. His regime was responsible for a degree of oppression of Serbs, Jews and Gypsies which appalled even the Germans and provoked intermittent Italian intervention. His reputation did not prevent him from being received by the Pope. Fled Croatia in 1945, and reached Argentina in 1948 via Austria and Italy. A failed assassination attempt in 1957 led him to move to Paraguay and ultimately Spain. Died Madrid, 28 December 1959.

Penderecki Krzysztof: born Debica, Poland, 23 November 1933. Acclaimed Polish composer. His advanced style features the use of quarter-tone clusters, glissandi and whistling harmonics as well as other radical innovations, and is well to the fore in his impressive opera, *The Devils of Loudun* (1968). His best known works however, the Stabat Mater (1962) and the Passion according to St Luke (1963–66), are somewhat more traditional in their approach.

Peter I (Petar Karađorđević), King: born Belgrade, 11 July 1844. King of Serbia from 1903 and a strong advocate of constitutional government. Declared the first monarch of the Kingdom of Serbs, Croats and Slovenes (later Yugoslavia) on 1 December 1918. Died Topcider, near Belgrade, 16 August 1921.

Peter II (Petar Karađorđević), King: born Belgrade, 6 September 1923. Nominally monarch of Yugoslavia at the age of 11 on the assassination of his father Alexander I in 1934, but only ruled in practice for the few weeks in 1941 between the deposition of the regent, his uncle Paul (qv) and the Axis invasion. Fled to London, where he led the émigré government until the abolition of the monarchy by Tito in 1945, and then settled in America. Died Los Angeles, 3 November 1970.

Piłsudski Józef, Marshal: born Zułow, Russian Poland, now Lithuania, 5 December 1867. First head of state of the independent Poland declared in November 1918. In exile in Siberia, 1887–92, on the unfounded charge that he had plotted the assassination of Tsar Alexander III. On his return, joined and soon became a leader of the Polish Socialist Party, and was again imprisoned by the Russians, first in Warsaw, then in St Petersburg. Sought to secure Japanese assistance for a Polish uprising during the Russo-Polish War of 1904–5. Organising the nucleus of a future Polish army, initially financed by robbery, 1908 onwards. Following the proclamation of Polish independence by Austria–Hungary and Germany on 5 November 1916, appointed head of the military department of the Polish council of state. Again imprisoned in 1917, this time by the Germans, for refusing to agree that the Polish military units swear 'fidelity in arms with the German and Austrian forces'. Released at the armistice and unanimously chosen as Polish head of state and commander-in-chief of the Polish Army in Warsaw on 14 November 1918. Renounced any party affiliation. Dreamed of a Polish–Lithuanian–Ukrainian federal state, and disappointed that his counter-attack against the Soviet Army in 1920 was not allowed to continue much further east. Relinquished the post of president in 1922, but remained chief of the general staff until the assumption of power by a right-wing government in 1923. Disillusioned with parliamentary democracy, he led the march by military units on Warsaw, May 1926, which brought down the government and led to his being elected president by parliament. Although he declined the post in favour of another associate, Ignacy Móscicki, he became minister of defence and effectively directed Polish foreign and military policy until his death in 1935. Intolerant of opposition from the left-wing circles with which he had originally been associated, and who mounted a campaign against his alleged dictatorship in 1930, he temporarily arrested the leaders, although he did not suspend the parties. His protégés, notably Colonel Jozef Beck, foreign minister from 1932, were to dominate Polish politics until 1939 and beyond. Reminiscent in his charisma and romanticism of Garibaldi in nineteenth-century Italy, the course of his career more nearly paralleled that of Mussolini. In essence, he remained a revolutionary conspirator, impatient of compromise, reckless and unpredictable. For all his achievements, his lack of attention to economic problems, including the proper equipping of the Polish Army, and his inability to come to terms with either of his great neighbours, lent a certain inevitability to Poland's second partitioning in 1939–40. Died Warsaw, 12 May 1935, and buried among Polish kings in Wawel Cathedral, Kraków.

Radić Stjepan: born Trebarjevo, then Austria–Hungary, now Croatia, 11 July 1871. Co-organiser of the Croat Peasant Party from 1904 and cooperated with the National Council in Zagreb from March 1918 to found a Yugoslav union with equal rights for Croats and Serbs and with recognised autonomy for Croatia. Imprisoned by Belgrade 1919–20, and again in 1924–25. Unsuccessfully sought foreign support for a Croat peasant republic, 1923–24. Accepted the centralist 1921 Yugoslav constitution, 1925, and participated in government until 1927. Ebullient in personality, he was known to describe his govern-mental colleagues as 'tyrants, gangsters and swine'. Shot during a heated debate in the *Skupština*, 20 June 1928. Died Zagreb, 8 August 1928.

Rákosi Mátyás: born Ada, Serbia, 14 March 1892. Hungarian Communist leader of Jewish origin. A Communist on his return to Hungary in 1918 after a spell as a prisoner of war in Russia, and commissar for socialist production in Béla Kun's (qv) brief Communist government. Fled to Moscow, but returned, 1924, to reorganise the Hungarian Communist Party. Arrested, 1925, and re-arrested on his release in 1934 to be sentenced to life imprisonment. Nevertheless per-mitted to go to Moscow, 1940. Returned, 1944, to become First Secretary of the Hungarian Communist Party until 1948. A convinced Stalinist and among the shrewdest and least scrupulous of the party leaders in the Soviet bloc. The term 'salami tactics' to describe the progressive exclusion of elements hostile to the Communists is his invention. First Secretary of the Hungarian United Workers' Party, 1948–53, and prime minister, 1952, which post he was obliged to relinquish to Imre Nagy (qv) in 1953 following the death of Stalin. Remained party First Secretary until 1956, and ousted Nagy in 1955, but was then him-self removed by the Soviet Union at the behest of Marshal Tito. Particularly unpopular for his Stalinist policies and unquestioning loyalty to Moscow, as well as for his personal qualities, he fled to Moscow when the Hungarian revolt broke out in October 1956. Died Gorky, Soviet Union, 5 February 1971.

Schœnberg Arnold: born Vienna, 13 September 1874. The creator of the twelve-note school of musical composition, and as such one of the most influential figures in twentieth-century music. A number of his better known works pre-date the First World War, including the *Gurrelieder* (first performed 1913) which with Mahler's Eighth Symphony, or Symphony of a Thousand, represent the culmination and the conclusion of the Austro-German monumental musical tradition. Totally broke with that tradition by creating the twelve-note style of composition which dispenses with harmony and the familiar scales, 1921, and achieved wide recognition, being based in Berlin from 1925. As a Jew and pro-moter of 'degenerate' music, however, he lost his post in 1933 and emigrated to America the same year. His impressive, but incomplete, opera, *Moses and Aaron*, dates from 1930–32. Died Los Angeles, 13 July 1951.

Schuschnigg Kurt von: born Riva del Garda, Trento, then Austria–Hungary, now Italy, 14 December 1897. Austrian Chancellor prior to the *Anschluss* (qv, in Glossary). A member of the Christian Social Party, and minister of justice, 1932, and of education, 1933, in the cabinet of Dr Dollfuss (qv). Appointed Chancellor on the assassination of Dollfuss. Asserted his authority with the ousting in May 1936 of the vice-Chancellor, Prince von Starhemberg, the leader of the paramilitary *Heimwehr*, and the dissolution of the *Heimwehr* itself in October.

Proved unable, however, to mount an effective resistance against Hitler, capitulating to him at Berchtesgaden in February 1938. His final attempt to reassert Austrian independence by a plebiscite scheduled for 13 March 1938 was overtaken by the *Anschluss*. Imprisoned by the Nazis until 1945. Lecturer in America, 1948–67, when he returned to Austria. Died Mutters, Austria, 18 November 1977.

Slánský Rudolf: born Nezvestice, near Plzeň, then Austria–Hungary, now Czech Republic, 31 July 1901. Communist leader and victim of one of the most notable 'show trials'. Of Jewish origin. Member of the Czechoslovak Communist Party, 1921, and editor of its newspaper, *Rudé Právo*, 1924. Member of the party's Central Committee, 1929, and elected to the National Assembly, 1935. In Moscow during the war, but also served on the Ukrainian front and in the 1944 Slovak uprising. Secretary-general of the Czechoslovak Communist Party, 1945, and a Czechoslovak vice-premier, 1948. Dismissed from the Party Secretariat, September 1951, and arrested, November 1951, on charges of espionage. Tried with thirteen others, November 1952, in a markedly anti-Semitic atmosphere. Pleaded guilty and quickly executed. Posthumously exonerated, 1963, and restored to party membership, 1968. Died Prague, 3 December 1952. (See 'Show Trials' in Part 3.6.3.)

Stamboliyski Aleksandŭr: born Slavovitsa, Bulgaria, 1 March 1879. Reformist Bulgarian prime minister and leader of the Agrarian Party after the First World War, in which he had supported the Allies. Sentenced to life imprisonment in 1915 for threatening the life of his pro-German king. Freed in September 1918, he led a rebellion which forced the king's abdication and proclaimed a republic. He nevertheless joined the government on the restoration of the monarchy under Boris III (qv), becoming prime minister in October 1919. A political firebrand, he favoured the agricultural over the urban and industrial interests and his regime has been described as a peasant dictatorship. He once maintained that 'city people live by deceit, by idleness, by parasitism, by perversion', and on another occasion that they were 'verminous parasites'. He redistributed land to the peasantry, reformed the legal system, promoted universal suffrage and democratisation, and favoured peasant cooperatives. His hopes of creating a peasant 'Green International' to oppose the Communist 'Red International' were, however, disappointed, as were his hopes of establishing a South Slav federation with 'Yugoslavia'. Nevertheless he remains a hero figure to many. Both his domestic and foreign policies were opposed by the army, and although he won the 1923 elections triumphantly he was deposed in a military coup on 9 June 1923. He was arrested near his home village of Slavovitsa and executed there, 14 June 1923. Konstantin Muraviev, Bulgarian prime minister in 1944, was his nephew and former secretary.

Stojadinović Milan, Dr: born Čačak, Serbia, 23 July 1888. Prime minister and foreign minister of Yugoslavia, 1935–39. Reorientated Yugoslav foreign policy away from France and Czechoslovakia and towards Germany. Negotiated treaties with Bulgaria and Italy in 1937 with German support. Mistrusted by the Croats. Arrested in 1940 among fears that he was about to establish a pro-German puppet regime. Smuggled out of Yugoslavia, 1941, and resident in Argentina from 1949. Died Buenos Aires, 24 October 1961.

Teresa Mother of Calcutta: born Agnes Gonxha Bojaxhu, Skopje, then Turkish Empire, now Macedonia, 27 August 1910. Ethnic-Albanian nun celebrated for her work with the poor of India. Joined the Institute of the Blessed Virgin Mary in Ireland, 1928, and sent to India as a teacher six weeks later. Following nursing training, established her own Order of the Missionaries of Charity in the slums of Calcutta, 1948, which soon acquired its own dispensaries and schools. Adopted Indian citizenship. Her Order, which became subject only to the Pope in 1965, maintained a wide range of facilities for the old and the disabled and for lepers and the dying. Awarded the 'Padmashri' by the Indian government for her services to the people of India, 1963, the first Pope John XXIII Peace Prize, 1971, and the Nobel Peace Prize, 1979. By that date, her Order comprised more than 1,000 nuns, focused on Calcutta but also operating worldwide. Fervently admired by many for her compassion, she was also savagely criticised for the impact on India's poor of her total hostility to birth control. She is likely to be declared a saint. Died, Calcutta, 5 September 1997.

Tiso Jozef, Monsignor: born Velká Bytča, then Austria–Hungary, now Slovakia, 13 October 1887. Slovak dictator 1939–45. A priest like his mentor Father Hlinka (qv), a member of the Czechoslovak government 1927–29, and Hlinka's successor as leader of the clerical Slovak People's Party from 1938. Prime minister of autonomous Slovakia in the newly federated Czechoslovakia from 6 October 1938 and Slovak president on independence under German auspices from 1939. His government enjoyed a modest freedom of manoeuvre, but collapsed with the Soviet liberation of Czechoslovakia in April 1945. Convicted of treason, the suppression of freedom and crimes against humanity, he was executed Bratislava, Slovakia, 18 April 1947.

Tito Marshal: born as Josip Broz, Kumrovec, near Zagreb, then Austria–Hungary, 7 May 1892, of a Croat father and Slovene mother, both of peasant stock. Yugoslav Communist statesman. Trained as a locksmith. Joined the Social Democratic Party of Croatia–Slavonia in Zagreb, 1910. Served in the Austro-Hungarian Army on first the Serb and then the Russian front in the First World War. Seriously wounded and a prisoner of war of the Russians, 1915–17, whereafter he participated in the Revolution, joining the Red Guards in Omsk. Returned to the new Kingdom of the Serbs, Croats and Slovenes, October 1920, and joined the Communist Party of Yugoslavia. Operated underground after the banning of the party in December 1920, becoming political secretary of its Zagreb branch, 1929. Arrested and sentenced to five years' imprisonment, 1928, for planning insurrection and possessing bombs. A member of the Yugoslav party Politburo in exile in Vienna on his release and adopted the pseudonym of Tito by which he was later always to be known, although it was but one of his pseudonyms. With the Comintern in Moscow, 1935–36, and its choice as the Yugoslav party's new Secretary-General, 1939. He held the post, later known as the party presidency, till his death. Shot to fame as the inspired guerrilla leader of the Yugoslav Communist Partisans following the German/Hungarian/Italian invasion of 1941, who were the only group with the discipline and organisation to mount uncompromising resistance across the whole country. Assumed the title Marshal and recognised by the western Allies, 1943, as their wartime partner in preference to the compromised Mihajlović and the ineffectual royal government-in-exile. Effectively prime minister, 1943, and formally in office, 1945–53, when he became president until his death.

Pursued orthodox Communist policies at home after 1945, but increasingly annoyed Stalin even during the war by his pursuit of foreign policies tailored to Yugoslavia's perceived needs rather than to those of the Soviet Union. His assertive nationalism, bolstered by his international prestige and personal popularity well beyond Yugoslavia's borders, led the Soviet Union to break off relations and have Yugoslavia expelled from the Cominform in 1948. Tito's response was complex. Initially he made overtures to the west which received a ready response in the climate of fear of Russian expansionism of the time. These were balanced, though, by a willingness to build bridges to the new Soviet leadership of Nikita Khrushchev following the death of Stalin in 1953. These bore fruit in Khrushchev's visit of apology to Belgrade in 1955, a highlight in Tito's already remarkable career. His thirst for real independence, though, left him dissatisfied with a position of rather negative equidistance from both power blocs, and he initiated a foreign policy of active non-alignment which sought, with the cooperation of kindred spirits like Nasser in Egypt and Nehru in India, to promote a constructively different third way. Even more creatively original in his domestic policy, the break with Stalin was followed by a complete break with the orthodox Communist policies pursued in the immediate post war years. Central planning was abolished in favour of a system of direct worker management and control, which attracted international interest (see Titoism, Part 3.8). A man of enormous courage, charisma and originality as well as a showman who revelled in his public image, he was arguably the most remarkable of all the European statesmen of the twentieth century, not least for the length of time over which he held power. Perhaps he stayed in power too long: for certain he proved indispensable. His funeral in Belgrade was attended by an almost unparalleled galaxy of world leaders. Died Ljubljana, Yugoslavia, now Slovenia, 4 May 1980.

Tsankov Aleksandŭr, Professor: born Oriakhova, Bulgaria, 1879. An opponent of Aleksandŭr Stamboliyski (qv) and his successor as Bulgarian prime minister after the military coup of 1923, until 1926. Leader of the Bulgarian fascist movement in the 1930s and head of a Bulgarian government in exile in Austria under German auspices following the Soviet entry into Bulgaria in 1944. Temporarily interned by the Americans in 1945, after which he emigrated to Argentina. Died Belgrano, Argentina, 17 July 1959.

Tudjman Franjo: born Veliko Trgovisce, then Yugoslavia, now Croatia, 14 May 1922. A Communist Partisan during the war, after which he attended the Yugoslav Higher Military Academy in Belgrade. His father, a firm nationalist and previously a local leader of the Croat Peasant Party, was shot dead in 1946 in suspicious circumstances. A general in the Yugoslav National Army before the age of 40, but left it, 1961, to obtain a doctorate in Croatian history from the University of Zadar. It has been alleged that it was largely plagiarised.

Abandoned Communism in the late 1960s and embraced a Croatian interpretation of recent history which partly rehabilitated the *Ustaša*, and maintained that the number of Jews and Serbs killed in the notorious Jasenovac concentration camp was far lower than the official Yugoslav figure of 700,000. Expelled from the Yugoslav League of Communists for maintaining that Croatian was a language separate from Serbo-Croat. Sentenced to two years' imprisonment, 1971, for anti-Yugoslav activity in that year's expression of Croat national sentiment, later commuted to nine months. Again imprisoned, 1981, for three years for nationalist agitation but again released, after less than nine months. Founded the nationalist Croatian Democratic Union (HDZ), 1989, and established links with the Croatian diaspora, particularly in Australia and Canada, aided by Gojko Susak, incongruously the owner of a pizza bar in Toronto, whom he later appointed as minister of defence. Swept to power as president of Croatia, 1990, following an election campaign in which the HDZ had adopted an openly secessionist stance. Persecuted Croatia's Serb minority who, having become second-class citizens under a new constitution and in many cases lost their jobs, responded by declaring their loyalty to Belgrade. Nevertheless won the media battle in the west against Serbia's Slobodan Milošević (qv), and was rewarded with EU recognition of Croatian independence at German insistence in December 1991. Enjoyed American assistance in training his army to recover Western Slavonia in May 1995 and the Krajina in August 1995 despite UN appeals, which resulted in the flight of up to 300,000 Serb refugees. Failed, however, to realise his dream of incorporating the Croats of Bosnia–Hercegovina in his own state. Corrupt and personally vain, he ruled autocratically, playing down the unsavoury nature of Croatian nationalism under Dr Pavelić (qv), whose remains he considered bringing back from Argentina for state burial, and guilty of a nepotism which engendered growing public resentment. He reversed some of his more extreme opinions under American pressure in his last years. Died in office, Zagreb, 10 December 1999. His state funeral was attended by some 100,000 Croat mourners, but shunned by virtually all world leaders.

Ulbricht Walter: born Leipzig, 30 June 1893. A carpenter. Joined SPD, 1912, served in the war, 1915–18, a Spartacist, then a member of the KPD. KPD official, 1921–23. Studied, Moscow, 1924. Member of the Reichstag, 1928–33. In exile in Paris, 1933–38, and in Moscow, 1938–45. Returned to Berlin to organise the KPD, 1945. Elected SED deputy chairman, 1946. General Secretary of the SED from July 1950, a deputy chairman of the Council of Ministers, 1949–55 and First Deputy Chairman, 1955–60. First Secretary of the SED, July 1953 – May 1971. Chairman of the SED, May 1971 – August 1973. Chairman of the Council of State, 1960–73. An orthodox Stalinist with a talent for organisation, but neither an orator nor a theoretician, he appears to have triumphed over his more liberal rivals in 1957 by persuading Khrushchev after the 1956 Hungarian revolt that he was both totally in control of East Germany and totally committed to the interests of the Soviet Union. His fall came when he tried to discourage the rapprochement between West Germany and the Soviet

Union by asserting East German interests. A dour and seemingly humourless figure, he appears to have been increasingly deceived by his own propaganda, losing much of his contact with reality in the process. This was not perhaps totally surprising in view of his life history. Even his beard was alleged by some to be modelled on Lenin's. Little was known of the private man except for his enthusiasm for amateur sport including table tennis. He enjoyed a muted state funeral after his death. Died East Berlin, 1 August 1973.

Vaida-Voevod Alexandru, Dr: born Olpret, then Austria–Hungary, now Romania, 1872. Romanian prime minister 1919–20, 1932, and 1933, and a proponent before 1919 of the union of Transylvania with the 'Old Kingdom' (Regat) of Romania, comprising Moldavia and Walachia. Entered the Hungarian parliament in 1906 where he was one of the leading opponents of the Magyarisation of national minorities. A member in December 1918 of the Transylvanian directing council which united the province with Romania. Following his final dismissal from office, he founded the ultra-nationalist, semi-fascist Romanian Front. Died Bucharest, 19 March 1950.

Waldheim Kurt: born Sankt Andrä-Wördern, Austria, 21 December 1918, of an ethnic Czech father and Austrian mother. Austrian diplomat and president. A German Army officer in the Balkans, 1942–45. A professional diplomat from 1945, Austrian ambassador to the United Nations, 1964–68 and 1970–71, and Austrian foreign minister (People's Party), 1968–70. UN secretary-general, 1972–81, where he was seen as remote, and Austrian president, 1986–92. Dogged from the campaign onwards and throughout his presidency by revelations, previously denied, that he had been deeply involved in reprisals against Yugoslav Partisans and in the deportation of Greek Jews to German concentration camps. Accusations of specific war crimes, however, remained unproven. The end of his presidency was met with a measure of national and international relief.

Wałęsa Lech: born Popowo, near Wloclawek, Poland, 29 September 1943. Polish trade union leader and politician. Initially an electrician in the Lenin Shipyard in Gdánsk. A union activist in the 1976 anti-government riots, which cost him his job. Nevertheless, joined the 14 August 1980 protests in the shipyard and elected leader of a negotiating strike committee. Although the shipyard strikers' demands were met within three days, maintained his strike as leader of the Interfactory Strike Committee covering all enterprises in the Gdánsk–Sopot–Gdynia region. The Committee claimed and won on 31 August the right for workers to organise themselves freely and independently. When the committee was formed into a national trade unions' federation as *Solidarność* (Solidarity) he became its chairman and leading negotiator, but was arrested and imprisoned for nearly a year when martial law was declared and *Solidarność* banned on 13 December 1981. Remained leader of the underground movement and regained open influence when *Solidarność* was again legalised in 1989. Elected president, 1990, by a large margin in direct elections, but his confrontational style and reluctance to compromise, notably over abortion, fitted ill with the presidential role. Defeated, 1995, and again in 2000. His poor show-ing led him to withdraw from politics on 15 October. Awarded the Nobel Prize for Peace, 1983.

Webern Anton von: born Vienna, 3 December 1883. A leading composer of the atonal school associated with his teacher Schoenberg (qv) and his friend Berg (qv). Largely neglected in an increasingly right-wing Austria, the pub-lication of his works was banned after the *Anschluss* in 1938. They have never-theless been claimed as an inspiration by later advanced composers such as Boulez and Stockhausen. Accidentally killed by a soldier of the American occupation forces in the village near Salzburg in which his family had taken refuge. Died Mittersill, Austria, 15 September 1945.

Zhivkov Todor: born Pravets, near Botevgrad, Bulgaria, 7 September 1911. Bulgarian Communist Party leader. Of poor peasant origin. Joined the youth league of the outlawed Communist Party in the late 1920s and helped organ-ise the People's Liberation Insurgent Army during the Second World War. After the Communist assumption of power, commanded the People's Militia. A full member of the Politburo, 1951, and First Secretary of the Communist Party Central Committee, 1954. As such, the youngest national leader in the Soviet bloc. A protégé of Khrushchev. Prime minister, 1962–71, and President of the State Council, established under the new constitution, 1971–89. Sur-vived an attempted coup, unique in the Soviet bloc, 1965. Loyal to the Soviet line throughout, but an able manager under whom Bulgarian living standards improved substantially. Gorbachev described him as the Chinese Emperor of Bulgaria. Resigned, November 1989, to make way for a more moderate Com-munist leadership, expelled from the Bulgarian Communist Party in the December, and sentenced to seven years' imprisonment for the misappropria-tion of state funds and embezzlement, 1992. Reportedly released from house arrest, January 1997. Died 6 August 1998. His daughter, Ludmilla, was a not-able minister of culture.

Zog I (Ahmed Bey Zogu, previously Zogolli), King of Albania: born Castle Burgajet, Albania, then Turkish Empire, 8 October 1895. A supporter of Austria–Hungary during the First World War, and thereafter leader of the reformist Popular Party. Exiled in June 1924, but returned with Yugoslav help in December, and elected president on 1 February 1925. Proclaimed king on 1 September 1928. His rule was characterised by comparative stability and ever closer links with Italy. Despite his efforts after 1932 to restrain it, Italian influence grew ever more pervasive and he was ousted by Mussolini in 1939. Formally abdicated, 2 January 1946. Died Suresnes, France, 9 April 1961.

Part 10

GLOSSARY

10.1 BRIEF HISTORIES OF THE STATES AND REGIONS OF CENTRAL AND EASTERN EUROPE PRIOR TO 1919. SOME CHARACTERISTICS AND POPULAR PERCEPTIONS

ALBANIA

Little is known of the early history of what is now Albania, but its people comprise a distinct ethnic group speaking a language of the Indo-European family but distinct from Greek or Slavonic. They may, or may not, be identifiable as the Illyrians of Roman times. The Albanians came under Turkish rule in 1431 and remained so except between 1443 and 1468 under Prince Gjergj Kastrioti, surnamed Skanderbeg, a national hero, and again briefly in the eighteenth century. Ambitious Albanians, not unlike their peers from the Baltic States in the Russian Empire, were prominent in the administration of the Turkish Empire. The nineteenth-century khedives of Egypt were of Albanian stock. Although an Albanian League was founded in 1880 and ruled for two years, attempts to obtain independence were unsuccessful, and Albania was to be the last European nation to be carved wholly out of the Turkish Empire. Its independence was proclaimed at Vlorë on 28 November 1912 and the principle of autonomy agreed at the London Ambassadorial Conference on 20 December 1912 when the new country's frontiers were also approximately determined. Prince Wilhelm of Wied accepted the crown on 21 February 1914, and the power of government was vested in him and an International Commission of Control.

Both, however, left after the outbreak of the First World War in 1914, when Albania descended into anarchy, being invaded by the forces of Greece, Italy, Montenegro and Serbia, with the Italians occupying Vlorë. The more remote areas remained under the suzerainty of tribal chieftains. Austro-Hungarian troops overran the country in 1916, but the Italian commander proclaimed Albania independent on 3 June 1917 and a provisional government was established at Durrës. Suggestions made prior to Versailles that the new state should become an Italian protectorate were, however, opposed in Albania and were specifically rejected at the 1918 Lushnje Conference, which established a government of four regents: two Muslim, one Orthodox and one Roman Catholic. Italian forces were promptly withdrawn except from Saseno, off the harbour of Vlorë. The boundaries of the new state were part determined by an International Commission in 1922.

It was exceptionally undeveloped, economically, politically and socially. It had just 310 miles of road, no railways, no industry not related to agriculture, no banks and no national currency. The period of Italian domination was to enjoy considerable popular support as it progressively remedied many of these deficiencies. The Ghegs in the north were divided into clans or tribes and the second main group, the Tosks, in the south took their lead from beys or chiefs. The tradition of hostility to any form of central authority ran deep and it remains an important factor in contemporary Albanian politics.

Albania was the only part of the Turkish Empire in Europe where the majority of the population converted to Islam, and modern Albania is Europe's sole primarily Islamic state.

AUSTRIA

The creation of an Austrian nation state was to be the logical, but probably least thought through, consequence of the application of the principle of ethnic self-determination to the peoples of the former Austro-Hungarian Empire. Equally it was testimony to the inconsistency of the Allies at Versailles and the subsequent treaty conferences, who applied the nationality principle when it suited them but ignored it when it did not.

The new state was to inherit no meaningful sense of identity, not least because the preceding Austro-Hungarian Empire had had no common identity. It had not even had a formal name other than 'The kingdoms and territories represented in the Reichsrath'. The western province of Vorarlberg, centred on Bregenz, tried to join Switzerland. Moreover, virtually all Austrians were agreed that the new state was not economically viable, a perception which had much truth in the circumstances of the time, but which also tended to be self-fulfilling. These problems were to be exacerbated by the gulf in outlook between the social democrats of Vienna and the catholic socialists dominant in the rest of the country; a gulf which was not to be bridged until after the Second World War. A token legacy of Austria's early revolutionary socialism is the hammer and sickle still held in the Austrian eagle's talons on the national coat of arms. Nazism and anti-Semitism blossomed at an equally early date.

Austria after 1919 was to form an interesting contrast with the new Turkey, the other core nation state resulting from the dismemberment of a multi-national empire at the end of the First World War. In Kemal Atatürk, though, the Turks had a general and leader of genius, who was able both to defeat the ambitions of the Allies on Turkey itself and to cultivate and harness Turkish ethnic nationalism for the creation of a new nation state on western, secular lines. Such options were not open to Austria. The Austrians could only be defined as the German-speaking rump of the former Habsburg Empire. The ambition of their most celebrated leader, Adolf Hitler, working in and through Germany, was to fuse the two states, an ambition he was to achieve with the *Anschluss* of 1938.

278

BESSARABIA

That part of the former autonomous principality of Moldavia lying to the east of the River Prut. Ceded to Russia by the Turkish Empire in 1812, and regarded by Romania as *terra irridenta* after the realisation of national independence until its transfer in 1918. A Romanian census of 1930 gives the population as 2,864,000, of whom 1,611,000 were ethnic Romanians. The territory was claimed back by the Soviet Union in 1940 and the central part and a strip of the Ukrainian SSR east of the River Dniestr were declared the constituent Moldavian SSR, with its capital at Kishnev, now Chisinau.

It became the independent republic of Moldova in 1991.
(See Part 10.2.)

BOSNIA–HERCEGOVINA

The rugged core of the Balkans which had never enjoyed a national identity. As in Albania, a significant proportion of the population converted to Islam while under Turkish rule, and some intermingled with Turkish settlers. The rebellion against Turkish imperial rule opened with the slavs of Hercegovina in July 1875, followed shortly after with those of Bosnia.

The province, however, changed one imperial master for another when Austria–Hungary occupied it as a result of the Congress of Berlin in 1878. The climate was created in which a Bosnian Serb could assassinate the heir to the imperial throne in 1914 and set the First World War in motion.

Bosnia–Hercegovina was incorporated in Yugoslavia in 1918, and formed part of Dr Ante Pavelić's Croat state during the Second World War. That experience of persecution was a major contributor to the Serb minority's decision to try to establish a state of its own when Bosnia–Hercegovina declared independence in 1992.

BUKOVINA

Originally the core of the later autonomous principality of Moldavia, but ceded to Austria by the Turkish Empire in 1775. Its transfer to Romania in 1918 was recognised by the Treaty of Saint-Germain in 1919, but the northern part, including the capital, Chernivtsi, was transferred to the Ukrainian SSR under the 1947 peace treaty with the Soviet Union, where it remains.

The mainly fifteenth-century churches of Romanian Bukovina, characterised by unique weather-resistant external frescos, are the finest known examples of Romanian art and architecture and comprise a UNESCO World Heritage Site.

BULGARIA

The Bulgarians are the slav people with the oldest historic identity, and they can be traced back as settlers on the Danube estuary to about AD 650. They are recorded as crossing the Danube from north to south between AD 679 and 681. They were soon a threat to the Byzantine Empire and by the ninth century had established their own first empire, which extended over much of modern Albania and Macedonia as well as Bulgaria. Converted to Christianity in the same century. The second empire succumbed with Serbia to the Turks in the fourteenth century.

Modern Bulgaria re-emerged with the 1877 war of liberation. It was recognised as an autonomous and tributary principality under the sovereignty of the Sultan of Turkey, but with a Christian government, under the Treaty of Berlin in 1878. The same treaty created a territory of Eastern Rumelia, now southern Bulgaria, under Turkish military and political rule but with administrative autonomy. Following a rebellion, it pronounced its union with Bulgaria in 1885, to which the Sultan effectively agreed in the following year. Bulgaria declared her total independence on 5 October 1908.

Bulgaria allied herself with Serbia, Greece and Montenegro to wrest virtually all the remaining European territory of the empire (essentially Macedonia and Thrace) from Turkey in the First Balkan War of 1912–13. Dissatisfied with her territorial share under the Treaty of London of 30 May 1913, however, she went to war with her former allies on 29 June 1913 in the Second Balkan War, provoking intervention from Romania on 10 July. She recognised defeat under the Treaty of Bucharest of 10 August (26 July under the old-style calendar) 1913, but entered the First World War on the side of the central powers in an unsuccessful attempt to improve her position.

For all its subsequent history of military and royal autocracy, Bulgaria was much more egalitarian in its traditions than its neighbours. The division between rulers and ruled was political, much more than economic or social.

CROATIA

The Croats moved with the other southern slavs ('yugoslavs') into the Balkan peninsula in the sixth century and, like the Slovenes, but unlike the Serbs, were converted to Roman Catholicism. Croatia was united with Hungary by a personal union of the crowns in 1091 but was conquered by the Turks in 1463. It later returned to Hungarian rule. In 1918 it joined the new Kingdom of the Serbs, Croats and Slovenes and its history became that of Yugoslavia until 1991 when it declared its independence.

CZECHOSLOVAKIA

The state of Czechoslovakia, declared in 1918 and confirmed in 1919, attempted to bring together for the first time two closely related slav peoples, the Czechs and the Slovaks, as well as the Ruthenes (see separate entry), in a single nation. Both Czechs and Slovaks had been subject to the Austro-Hungarian Empire, but the Czech territories had comprised the medieval kingdom of Bohemia until 1526.

In that year, however, the Habsburgs had been elected to the Bohemian throne, creating the dynastic link which lasted until 1918. The Habsburgs had suppressed both national traditions and the religious reform movement inaugurated by Jan Hus, provoking the revolt of 1618 which marked the beginning of the Thirty Years War, when Catholics and Protestants struggled for supremacy across Germany and central Europe. Although the Czech revolt itself was completely crushed at the White Mountain near Prague in 1620, the questioning Hussite spirit resurfaced to some extent within Czech Catholicism to give national life and politics in later centuries a flavour distinct from that of neighbouring states.

The Slovaks in contrast had remained deeply, even narrowly, Catholic and the clergy exercised substantial influence over a largely peasant population which was poorly educated. Slovak nationalism was little developed, and positive support for the Czechoslovak idea came mainly from the Lutherans and from some American Slovaks. In broad terms, the Czech lands in 1919 were comparable with western Europe, and the Slovak lands with Poland and the Balkans. The tension between the liberal and prosperous Czechs and the conservative and devout Slovaks, who suffered severe disadvantage from the loss of their economic links with Hungary, was to remain a source of grave weakness to the Czechoslovak state until its dismemberment by the Germans in 1939.

Although Czechoslovakia was to be reconstituted by the Allies in 1945, less Ruthenia which was absorbed by the Soviet Union, the tension was not to disappear. It was to lead first, after some years of Communist rule, to a federal constitution, and ultimately in 1993 to voluntary dissolution into the Czech Republic, with its capital in Prague, and Slovakia, with its capital in Bratislava, which we know today.

Perhaps because of their history and small size, the Czechs and Slovaks have sometimes been perceived by their neighbours as being too ready to accommodate, rather than resist, superior force. The duplicitous Švejk (Schweik) of Jaroslav Hašek's celebrated twentieth-century novel, *The Good Soldier Švejk* is the (in)famous exponent of that alleged characteristic. The traditionally more romantic and less realistic Poles used to joke maliciously that the Czechoslovak Army's marching exercise was 'hut-two-three-I-give-up (etc.)'!

Be that as it may, and with full regard to its deficiencies, Czechoslavakia in its 67-year history did little, if anything, of which its successors need feel ashamed. That could not be said of any of its neighbours.

HUNGARY

The Hungarians enter European history as the Magyars who raided Europe as far west as southern France in the tenth century, before settling in broadly their present home in the eleventh, when they were converted to Christianity. Their leader, later canonised as St Stephen, became the national patron saint. His coronation crown, returned to Hungary by the Americans in the 1960s amid national rejoicing, is one of the greatest treasures of the National Museum in Budapest. The Magyars were ultimately a Mongol people, and the modern, notoriously difficult Hungarian language is unrelated to any others in Europe except Finnish and perhaps Turkish.

The medieval Hungarian kingdom reached its zenith under King Matthias Corvinus (1459–90), whose court was at Visegrád on the Danube above Budapest, but in 1526 Hungary fell to the Turks at the Battle of Mohács, and remained under Turkish rule until the Treaty of Karlovci of 1699. The most lasting legacy of Turkish rule was probably in the kitchen. Gifted cooks themselves, the Turks introduced the sweet paprika pepper, which the Hungarians subsequently developed the art of drying. Its use as a powdered condiment gives so many Hungarian meat and fish dishes, notably the famous gulyás (goulash), their characteristic red appearance. The combination of traditional, Turkish, and aristocratic influences has raised Hungarian cuisine to a pre-eminent position in central and eastern Europe. Under the terms of the Karlovci Treaty, Hungary became a part of the Austrian Empire, which it remained until 1918, but did not recover its independence. Nationalist agitation did, however, secure the *Ausgleich* (compromise) of 1867 whereby the Austrian Empire became the dual Austro-Hungarian Empire and Hungary assumed control of its own affairs other than foreign policy and trade, and the military. Hungary also returned to its previous frontiers, which meant that the Croats, Slovaks, Transylvanian Romanians and Ruthenian Ukrainians passed under specifically Hungarian imperial rule.

Hungary remained essentially a country of great estates and, although its parliament dated back to 1222, the franchise remained too restricted to modify significantly the power traditionally exercised by the aristocracy, the gentry and the Roman Catholic Church. The concentration of developed industry around Budapest was not on the whole in Magyar Hungarian hands prior to 1919.

Although aristocratic domination weighed heavily on the peasantry, it made Budapest eastern Europe's most elegant and glamorous capital, and no doubt contributed to the Hungarian's ready charm and ease of manner. Despite their comparatively small number, Hungarians were to make a disproportionate contribution to twentieth-century life whether in music with Bartók, Dohnányi and Ligeti, in British politics with Harold Wilson's famous 'two Hungarians' (his economic advisors Balogh and Kaldor) and with George Soros, the international financier credited with forcing the £ sterling out of the European Exchange Rate Mechanism (ERM) in 1992, or in invention with the ubiquitous 'Biro' pen and 'Rubik' cube.

They were also to show considerable adaptability. For all its unhappy beginnings, Kádár's Communist regime was to acquire genuine popularity and Hungary was to witness economic experimentation unparalleled in the Soviet bloc. Budapest had its Hilton Hotel long before the fall of communism and serious thought was being given before 1990 to the introduction of full convertability of the national currency, the forint.

KOSOVO

The heartland of medieval Serbia, which returned to Serbia from Turkish rule after the Balkan Wars in 1913 in recognition of its historic importance. It contains some of Serbia's greatest cultural monuments, including the churches at Pec, one-time seat of the Serbian Patriarchate, and Prizren, internationally celebrated for their Byzantine wall paintings.

By 1990 the province was 90 per cent ethnically Albanian, partly as a result of the highest birth rate in Europe, and pressures intensified for renewed autonomy or union with Albania, pressures which the Serbs determinedly resisted.

The NATO campaign of 1999 was intensely controversial and is likely to remain so. Those in favour, led by the British prime minister, Tony Blair, argued that the moral duty to resist ethnic cleansing was paramount. Those against noted that the scale of Serb persecution had been greatly increased as a consequence of NATO pressure, and doubted the likelihood of bombing assisting in the reconciliation of the two peoples. They were also concerned that the attacks were not approved by the United Nations and were indeed contrary to its charter.

The campaign was preceded by pressure on Yugoslavia which can only be described as 'gun at the head' diplomacy. Some considered that the judgement of the Czech-born American secretary of state, Madeleine Albright, was distorted by memories of the western failure to resist Hitler at Munich. True or false, Yugoslavia was presented with a NATO ultimatum such as no country would freely accept and which Yugoslavia was perhaps not meant to. Many in the west were profoundly unsympathetic to a country which remained Communist and had bolstered its case with intransigence rather than flexibility. Yugoslavia was to give NATO 'unrestricted passage and unimpeded access throughout federal Yugoslavia' and immunity from all legal process 'whether civil, administrative or criminal'. Its personnel were to have the right to bivouac and use local facilities free of charge.

The result of the campaign was acclaimed as a success by NATO, but is open to conflicting interpretations. Most of the ethnic-Albanian refugees returned, but their return provoked a flood of perhaps 150,000 Serb refugees. The prospect of peaceful co-existence appears remote as ethnic-Albanians dominate Kosovo institutions, notably the courts, and the international institutions are hampered by an acute shortage of finance. It was noted in 2000 that the annual budget of the UN administrator was the equivalent of less than the 1999 cost of half a day's bombing. The consequence is an explosion of crime across the province, ranging from internal disorder to the smuggling of drugs, prostitutes and refugees from further afield. Ethnic-Albanian Muslims are applying pressure on ethnic-Albanian Catholics. NATO policy is also determined by strategic considerationa which do not necessarily correspond to the interests of Kosovo. Communal separation is opposed because of its implications first for Bosnia and now for Macedonia, not to mention regions further away. The corollary is the somewhat desperate support of arrangements which can only be described as artificial.

MACEDONIA

Despite its fame as the homeland of the Greek conqueror, Alexander the Great, whose empire extended as far east as modern Pakistan, it is a territory which never subsequently developed a real political identity. Settled extensively by slavs during the sixth and seventh centuries, but with constantly fluctuating borders, it formed at differing times part of the Byzantine, Bulgarian, Serbian and ultimately Turkish Empires. The motivation of the Balkan Wars of 1912–13 (see Bulgaria) which resulted in the predominantly Greek-speaking southern part, focused on Thessaloniki, being awarded to Greece, and almost all the predominantly slavonic-speaking north, focused on Skopje, to Serbia with a small portion to Bulgaria.

The north, which had been incorporated in Yugoslavia between 1918 and 1991, proclaimed its independence in 1992 but its use of the name 'Macedonia' has been bitterly contested by Greece, which deems it a Greek name. International recognition has been achieved under the uneasy compromise formula of 'Former Yugoslav Republic of Macedonia'.

MONTENEGRO

The only Balkan state never to have been part of the Turkish Empire. Ethnically and religiously closely akin to the Serbs, its people were traditionally loyal to their clan rather than to any central government and this social pattern has by no means disappeared. Montenegro was doubled in size and recognised internationally as independent at the Congress of Berlin in 1878. Its leader pronounced himself King Nicholas in 1910, but was deposed in 1918 when a national assembly under Serb influence merged the country with Serbia.

It regained autonomy within Yugoslavia in 1946, partly in recognition of the contribution made by its Communist partisans to Yugoslav liberation.

POLAND

The Poles have a long history as an identifiable west slavonic ethnic group, but their territorial boundaries have changed drastically over the last thousand years. Slavs colonised the area of what became Berlin in the eleventh century until displaced by Germans, and the frontier between the two peoples stabilised on roughly the present Oder–Neisse line for some centuries, until the Germans started their long movement of eastwards expansion.

In the Middle Ages, much of modern Poland, the Baltic States, Belarus and Ukraine fell within a Polish–Lithuanian Empire, which was a rival to Russia but whose boundaries changed repeatedly.

That Polish Commonwealth nevertheless succumbed, and was divided between Prussia, Russia and Austria in the partitions of 1772, 1793, and 1795. Only Austrian Poland enjoyed a measure of autonomy in the form of the Galician Diet at Lwow. National sentiment nevertheless remained strong.

The recovery of independence in 1918–19 posed the problem of boundaries in its most acute form. Some Poles sought to re-establish the former empire, and the final eastern frontier, as determined by the Treaty of Riga, brought many non-Poles within the new Poland. The frontier of 1945 was much more faithful to ethnic principles.

The Poles have a reputation as an emotional and idealistic people, whose relations with their neighbours have been summed up in the adage that every Pole keeps two bullets left in his gun – one for the German to be shot out of duty, one for the Russian to be shot for pleasure! Poland has engendered similarly powerful emotions among outsiders. Norman Davies, a warm admirer, quotes the famous economist, J. M. Keynes's description of pre-war Poland as 'an economic impossibility whose only interest is Jew-baiting'. The inter-war military caste did little to develop the habits of compromise and restraint on which a modern democracy depends, and the deep Catholic faith of the majority of the population was similarly unhelpful. The fall of communism has been followed by disputes over abortion and religious education more intense than elsewhere. Nevertheless both democracy and the habit of compromise appear to have taken root more effectively than many observers anticipated in 1990.

ROMANIA

Romania, as its name implies, is the only part of the Roman Empire in central or eastern Europe to have retained its Latin speech, although much altered both by internal developments and external influences. Among the more striking of the former are the tendency to replace the classical Latin consonants 'k' and 'g' by 'p', 'b' or 'm'. Hence Latin *quattuor* (four) has become *patru* and *octo* (eight) has become *opt*. On the other hand, *mensa* (table), declined as their first task by countless generations of Latin scholars, has remained little altered as *masă*.

Romanians trace themselves back to the Dacians, who were closely related to the better-known Thracians, an Indo-European people valued as mercenaries by both the Macedonian Greeks and the Romans. They passed under Roman rule in AD 106, but the Romans left as early as the late third century, making the local retention of Latin speech all the more remarkable. The Latin poet, Ovid, had regarded his banishment to Dacia's Black Sea coast as banishment to the end of the earth.

The area was subject to repeated conquest and settlement, and eastern Orthodoxy was introduced during the eighth–tenth centuries, when much of the present Romania formed part of the First Bulgarian Empire. The first properly Romanian state was Wallachia, established south of the Carpathian mountains in the early fourteenth century, followed by Moldavia in the Prut Valley east of the Carpathians in 1349. They became vassal states of the Turkish Empire in the late fourteenth century and in 1455 respectively.

Modern Romania dates back to 1856 when the Turks first recognised the autonomy of the two principalities, and their full independence followed in 1878. Until the outbreak of the First World War the Romanian national movements outside Romania only sought autonomy within the Austro-Hungarian Empire. As late as 1911, Alexandru Vaida-Voevod, a future prime minister, descibed the union of all Romanians as a 'beer table fantasy'. In reality, though, the 'old kingdom' (*regat*) was to be greatly enlarged in 1918 by the progressive transfer of Bessarabia from Russia, Bukovina from Austria, and Transylvania and most of the Banat from Hungary, the former two being recognised by the Treaty of Saint-Germain in 1919 and the latter two by the Treaty of Trianon in 1920.

The transfer of Bessarabia was never recognised by the Soviet Union, which had not, as Bolshevik Russia, been a party to the Saint-Germain treaty. It was reclaimed in 1940.

(See also Bessarabia and Bukovina in this chapter, Moldova in Part 10.2 and Vienna Award in Part 10.3.)

RUTHENIA (SUB-CARPATHIAN)

A traditionally backward area, also known as Transcarpathian Ukraine and Sub-Carpathian Russia, immediately to the east of modern Slovakia. Ethnically slav, and speaking a range of dialects akin to the neighbouring slavonic languages. Divided religiously between the Orthodox and Uniate denominations. Prior to 1919 the commercial and educated classes were almost all Jewish or Hungarian, and both the small number of educated Ruthenes and the Uniate clergy were Hungarian in sympathy. The goal of independence from Hungary was promoted almost exclusively by emigrants to America who successfully urged Masaryk to incorporate Ruthenia in the new Czechoslovak republic.

Despite a 1918 promise of autonomy, the inter-war years were to see a Czech dominance which was administratively beneficial but economically harmful. The earlier Hungarian sympathies of the Uniate clergy transferred to the Ukraine, and the Communists were the largest political party.

Following the liberation of Czechoslovakia by the Soviet Army in 1945, the province was annexed by the Soviet Union and joined to the Ukraine, where it remains.

SERBIA

The Serbs, like the other southern slav peoples, appear to have entered the Balkans in the sixth–seventh centuries AD, but they became prominent in the first half of the fourteenth century under Stefan Dušan, whose rule extended from the Danube to central Greece. Defeated by the Turks, first at Chernomen in 1371 and then more decisively at Kosovo Polje on 15 June 1389, the Serbs had succumbed completely by 1459.

The three centuries of Turkish rule saw major emigration out of the Serbian heartland in Kosovo and southern Serbia northwards into central Serbia, the Vojvodina and Croatia. Those Serbs resident north of the Danube, however, passed under Habsburg rule in 1699 under the Treaty of Karlovci, marking the beginning of the progressive expulsion of the Turks from Europe other than from the region of Istanbul, which remains a key part of modern Turkey.

Modern Serbia dates from the rebellions of 1804 onwards under Karađorđe Petrović, the ancestor of the twentieth-century Yugoslav monarchs, and Miloš Obrenović. Its autonomy within the Turkish Empire was recognised after the Russo-Turkish War of 1828–29, but full independence had to wait until 1878, when Serbia also gained additional territory.

Serbia was on the winning side in the two Balkan Wars of 1912 and 1913, but the assassination of Crown Prince Franz Ferdinand of Austria–Hungary by a Bosnian Serb on 28 June 1914 impelled the Austro-Hungarian government to make punitive demands on Serbia, which its government under Nikola Pašić (qv) effectively met. The Austro-Hungarian government, however, was still not satisfied and declared war, thus setting the First World War in motion.

Serbia was defeated by Austria–Hungary in 1915 and its king and forces retreated to Corfu leaving the country to be occupied by Austro-Hungarian and Bulgarian troops. The end of the First World War, however, saw a complete reversal of fortune and the declaration in December 1918 of the Triunine Kingdom of Serbs, Croats and Slovenes with the Serb monarch as the new king. The history of Serbia then becomes the history of Yugoslavia until 1990.

SLAVONIA

A region of Croatia. Not to be confused with either Slovakia (Czechoslovakia) or Slovenia (qv).

SLOVENIA

The north-westernmost republic of the former federal Yugoslavia, and the most western in orientation.

The Slovenes can trace themselves back to the sixth century, and in the seventh their territory extended as far north as the modern Leipzig. Neverthe-less the kingdom succumbed to German rule, and its more northern part was permanently Germanised. The area of the modern Slovenia passed progress-ively under Habsburg rule from the thirteenth century onwards, and remained there until December 1918 when it became part of the new Kingdom of the

Serbs, Croats and Slovenes. It was the first of the federal Yugoslav republics to declare its independence in 1991.

The Slovene language is closely related to Serbo-Croat and, although the standard language is clearly distinct, the dialects of the one merge into those of the other.

SUDETENLAND

The border regions to the north-west and south-west of what is now the Czech Republic which were included within the new state of Czechoslovakia established by the Treaty of Versailles in 1919. They were included so as to give the new state defensible frontiers, but were predominantly German in population. These so-called Sudeten Germans were the subject of suspicion at best and discrimination at worst in inter-war Czechoslovakia, and were highly responsive to Hitler's extreme nationalism. Powerful Nazi pressures both from Germany itself and from the Sudetenland, which the British and the French were unwilling to help the Czechoslovak government to withstand, culminated in the Munich Agreement of 1938 which transferred the regions to Germany.

They reverted to Czechoslovakia with the defeat of Germany in 1945 and the Potsdam Agreement endorsed the expulsion of the Sudeten Germans from Czechoslovakia 'in an orderly manner'. In practice, however, the passions engendered by the war made the expulsions summary and brutal.

10.2 BRIEF HISTORIES OF THE COUNTRIES OF 'FURTHER' EASTERN EUROPE

ARMENIA

The Armenians are an ultimately Indo-European people with an ancient history, who are first identifiable in the sixth century BC in the ruins of the kingdom of Urartu around Lake Van in what is now north-eastern Turkey. Their most dramatic historical era was the first century BC, when they resisted the eastwards spread of the Roman Empire, in association with Mithridates the Great of Pontus, and formed a valuable buffer state between Rome and Parthia during the struggles for power between Mark Antony, Cleopatra and Octavius Caesar (later Augustus). Christianity was recognised as the state religion in AD 300 and the Armenian Church centred in Etchmiadzin is the world's oldest established Christian church. The unique Armenian alphabet was derived from the Aramaic by St Mesrop in the early fifth century. Traditionally skilled in commerce and with a wide diaspora, not least in the United States, they are considered by some to be an even more truly cosmopolitan people than the Jews.

Although the area of the modern Armenian state fell within the Russian Empire, very many Armenians lived in the Turkish, where they were feared as potentially disloyal. The massacres of Armenians by Turks in the years before and during the First World War have been compared qualitatively if not quantitatively with the genocide of the Jews by the Nazis in the Second. Moreover, some 1,750,000 Armenians were deported by the Turks from Turkish Armenia in 1915 to Syria and the then Mesopotamia, and in consequence many businesses across modern eastern Turkey, Syria and the Lebanon, and Iraq are in Armenian hands.

The two most famous twentieth-century Armenians, both from Soviet Armenia, were probably Aram Khachaturian, the composer, whose *Gayaneh* and *Spartacus* suites are very well known, and Anastas Mikoyan, the wily, long-serving Soviet trade minister.

Armenia formed part of the Transcaucasian Soviet Federal Socialist Republic between 1922 and 1936, when it was proclaimed a constituent republic of the Soviet Union in its own right. It declared its full independence in September 1991, but became a member of the Commonwealth of Independent States (CIS) in December.

The years of independence have been marked by violence, both internal and in warfare with Azerbaijan over the disputed enclave of Nagorno–Karabakh. An armistice was signed under Russian auspices on 18 February 1994. The prime minister, the parliamentary speaker, and six officials were assassinated by a gunman during a televised debate on 27 October 1999.

BELARUS

Russian Byelorussia or White Russia. Its inhabitants should not be confused with the 'Whites' or White Russians opposed to the Bolshevik 'Reds' in the Russian civil war. Closely related to the Russians and with a historically non-literary language little more than a Russian dialect, their sense of individual identity has traditionally been very limited. During the Middle Ages the area formed part of the Polish–Lithuanian Empire. Like the Ukraine, it had its own seat on the United Nations as a Soviet Republic, after 1945. Independence was declared under the internationally unfamiliar name of Belarus in August–September 1991 and it became a member of the Commonwealth of Independent States (CIS) in December.

The powers of the president, Alyaksandr Lukashenka, were substantially extended in a referendum in November 1996, of contested validity. President Lukashenka has consistently pursued policies of closer economic and political relations with Russia, and a union between the two countries was signed on 21 February 1995.

ESTONIA

The smallest of the Baltic States and with no history as a state prior to its declaration of independence from the Russian Empire in May 1919. Its capital, Tallinn, was the easternmost member of the medieval German Hanseatic trading League. Like the other Baltic states, it had provided many of the Russian Empire's administrators and during the Soviet period was a centre of sophisticated industries. It became an authoritarian and increasingly fascist state under Konstantin Päts after 1934. A secret protocol to the German–Soviet neutrality (non-aggression) pact of 23 August 1939 allocated Estonia to the Soviet sphere of interest, and a Soviet ultimatum of 16 June 1940 led to the formation of a government sympathetic to the Soviet Union. Soviet forces entered the country the next day and Estonia joined the Soviet Union on 6 August. Independence was again declared on 20 August 1991 and conceded by the Soviet Union on 6 September.

The Estonians have close ethnic and linguistic ties with the Finns, whom they traditionally regarded as their cultural inferiors. Since 1990 trade has been totally reorientated towards the west and the Scandinavian nations have taken the lead in establishing new commercial, cultural and communications links. Estonia is likely to be in the next wave of new members to join the EU, before Latvia or Lithuania.

The strategic sensitivity of the country, however, remains. There are fewer than 1 million ethnic Estonians in a small country of only some 1.6 million, and it dominates the sea approaches to St Petersburg. More than 30 per cent of the population is Russian, and Estonian citizenship is dependent on competence in the Estonian language. The Organisation for Security and Cooperation in Europe (OSCE) opposed in December 1998 an Estonian law requiring all elected officials to speak Estonian. The Organisation claimed that it was contrary to the Estonian constitution and Estonia's international commitments.

GEORGIA

The traditionally colourful and passionate Georgians are a distinctive ethnic group of the western Caucasus, speaking an Indo-European language written in a unique alphabet derived from the Aramaic by St Mesrop in the early fifth century AD. Georgians take great pride in their early conversion to Christianity in AD 337. Many also take great pride in their most famous son, Josef Djugashvili, better known as the Soviet leader, Josef Stalin, who to the end of his days spoke Russian with a thick Georgian accent. Statues to him remained in place when they were removed elsewhere in the Soviet Union after 1956.

Despite their long history of national identity, the Georgians have remained divided along clan lines and the creation of a nation state in any modern sense has proved difficult. Association with Russia has often been seen as a necessary framework for longer-term stability.

Georgia had become part of the Russian Empire in 1806 and independence was first proclaimed on 26 May 1918 and recognised by Bolshevik Russia on 7 May 1920. Following an uprising in 1921, however, Georgia was drawn back into the Russian orbit and was merged with Armenia and Azerbaijan to form the Transcaucasian Soviet Federal Socialist Republic on 15 December 1922. It became a constituent republic of the Soviet Union in its own right in 1936. Full independence was again declared on 9 April 1991, but Georgia joined the Commonwealth of Independent States (CIS) in October 1993.

Civil war racked the country between 1991 and 1993 but a measure of stability has been achieved under the presidency of Eduard Shevardnadze, formerly Soviet foreign minister under Gorbachev. He has escaped several assassination attempts.

The country's future is likely to be closely bound up with the strategic rivalry between America and Russia over the routeing of gas and oil pipelines from Central Asia to the west.

LATVIA

Successively under Germanic, Polish, Swedish and, from 1721, Russian rule. Like the other Baltic states, it had provided many of the Russian Empire's administrators and during the Soviet period was a centre of sophisticated industries. Pro-Bolshevik in 1917 and again in 1919, but the Bolshevik regime was overthrown by the British and the Germans acting in concert the same year. The subsequent liberal democratic government was overthrown in a fascist coup in 1934, when Karlis Ulmanis seized power and remodelled Latvia on specifically Italian lines.

A secret protocol to the German–Soviet neutrality (non-aggression) pact of 23 August 1939 allocated Latvia to the Soviet sphere of interest, and a Soviet ultimatum of 16 June 1940 led to the formation of a government sympathetic to the Soviet Union. It enjoyed significant, if minority, support. Soviet forces entered the country the next day and Latvia joined the Soviet Union on 5 August. Independence was again declared on 21 August 1991 and conceded by the Soviet Union in September.

The Latvian language (Lettish) belongs with Lithuanian to the Baltic grouping of the Indo-European family, and the Latvians are primarily of the 'Baltic' physical type found along the coast from Denmark to Russia.

Only just over 50 per cent of the population is ethnically Latvian, and Russians form the majority of the population in the capital, Riga. Isolated clashes have occurred, notably on the occasion of a march in Riga by Latvian SS veterans, many in their old uniforms, in March 1998, but have been contained. A much greater threat to the country may though be represented by the declining overall trend in a population which already numbers under 2.5 million.

Trade, as elsewhere in the Baltic States, has been reorientated towards the west and close links established with Scandinavia in particular.

LITHUANIA

The largest of the Baltic States and the only one with a national history prior to 1919. It was united with Poland dynastically in 1385 and politically in 1569 and the fourteenth-century Lithuanian Empire included Belarus and large areas of Russia and the Ukraine. It nevertheless succumbed in its turn and was absorbed into the Russian Empire in 1795. Like the other Baltic States it provided many of the Russian Empire's administrators and during the Soviet period was a centre of sophisticated industries.

It was occupied by Germany during the First World War, and then invaded first by Bolshevik Russia and second by Poland before a liberal democratic national government was established in 1919. The capital, Vilnius was, however, seized for Poland in 1920 and incorporated in it in 1923. The liberal democratic regime was overthrown in 1926 in a coup led by the Nationalist Party and right-wing army officers. The new constitution of 1928 introduced a presidential dictatorship under Antanas Smetona, supported by the army and the increasingly fascist Nationalists.

A secret protocol to the German–Soviet neutrality (non-aggression) pact of 23 August 1939 allotted most of Lithuania to the Soviet sphere of interest, and a Soviet ultimatum of 16 June 1940 led to the formation of a government sympathetic to the Soviet Union. Lithuania joined the Soviet Union on 5 August.

A newly elected Lithuanian Supreme Soviet declared independence on 11 March 1990 but the declaration was not initially recognised by the Soviet Union. A period of disorder and some casualties ensued before total independence was conceded on 6 September 1991.

The Lithuanian language belongs with Latvian to the Baltic grouping of the Indo-European family, and the Lithuanians are primarily of the 'Baltic' physical type found along the coast from Denmark to Russia. Some 80 per cent of the national population is ethnically Lithuanian, which may make long-term internal stability easier to achieve than elsewhere in the Baltic region. The Russian enclave of Kaliningrad (qv) between Lithuania and Poland could, however, always prove a bone of contention as the enclave of Memel (Klaipeda) was with Germany between the wars.

Trade, as elsewhere in the Baltic States, has been reorientated towards the west and close links established with Scandinavia in particular. The reformed former Communist Party returned to power as the Homeland Union in 1996.

MOLDOVA

The former Soviet republic of Moldavia formed out of the greater part of Bessarabia (see Part 10.1) and a strip of the Ukraine in 1940. It became independent in August 1991 and a member of the Commonwealth of Independent States (CIS) in December.

Fighting broke out in 1992 between government forces and separatists in the largely Russian-speaking areas east of the River Dniestr, which had been declared the Republic of Transdniestria in September 1991. The dispute was calmed by a Russo-Moldovan agreement on 21 July 1992 which guaranteed self-determination for Transdniestria in the event of any union of Moldova with Romania. The Moldovan language is Romanian in all but name.

RUSSIAN ENCLAVE OF KALININGRAD

The northern half of German East Prussia, divided between Poland and the Soviet Union at Potsdam in 1945 and focused on the city of the same name, formerly Königsberg. It is probably the sole remaining European city to be named after a Communist revolutionary.

Its future as a detached Russian enclave on the coast between Poland and Lithuania is problematic. It has been suggested that it might become a commercial 'free city', but its current difficulties are substantial.

UKRAINE

The Ukrainians are a slav people closely related ethnically and linguistically to the Russians. Although the Ukraine enjoyed a period of independence in the seventeenth century, it became a part of the Russian Empire and Ukrainians in the eastern part of the country were extensively Russianised, Khrushchev, the former Soviet leader, being a notable example. The Ukrainians were trusted by the Russians as natural allies in the Imperial and Soviet periods alike.

There are significant differences in outlook between the Russianised, Orthodox eastern part of the country and the more westernised part, which are at their most marked in the regions transferred from Poland in 1945, where Roman Catholicism is strong. Such differences could prove a problem for the country's longer-term stability.

The Ukrainian Soviet Socialist Republic was established in December 1919, and it joined the future Soviet Union as an independent state in December 1920. It had its own seat in the United Nations from 1945. Total independence was again declared on 5 December 1991, but the Ukraine joined the Commonwealth of Independent States (CIS) the same month.

The years since independence have been chequered, both economically and politically. President Kuchma was accused in 2000 of complicity in the murder of a journalist critic, and on 26 April 2001 an alliance of Communists and business oligarchs in the Ukrainian parliament passed a vote of no confidence in the market-orientated reformist government of Viktor Yushchenko. It was anticipated that the vote would be followed by the gradual return of the Ukraine to the Russian sphere of influence and perhaps the extension to the Ukraine of the 1995 union between Belarus and Russia. America would probably try to counter such a development.

10.3 GLOSSARY OF SPECIALIST TERMS

Charter 77: the petition signed by Czechoslovak intellectuals in January 1977 expressing their grievances against the Communist regime of President Gustav Husák.

Curzon Line: the line proposed by the British foreign secretary, Lord Curzon, in 1919, as the eastern frontier of Poland. Although the border had been some 150 miles further east between 1920 and 1939, the Line was agreed by the Allies at the 1943 Tehran Conference as the frontier of post-war Poland. With some adjustments, it was adopted in 1944–45 and has remained the border ever since.

Fourteen Points: the Fourteen Points formulated the ideas of President Woodrow Wilson of America on the proper nature of a post-First World War settlement, and were first announced in his address to the joint session of the US Congress on 8 January 1918. Those points of particular relevance to central and eastern Europe were number 3 urging the removal of national economic barriers and the establishment of equal international trade conditions, number 6 urging the evacuation of all Russian territory, number 9 accepting a readjustment of Italy's borders in accordance with the nationality principle, number 10 urging autonomous development for the peoples of Austria–Hungary, number 11 requiring the evacuation of Romania, Serbia and Montenegro, and the provision for Serbia of free and secure access to the sea, number 13 requiring the establishment of an independent Poland and number 14 arguing for an international association to guarantee independence and security. A general point number 1 on the need for open diplomacy ran counter to the numerous private understandings and undertakings entered into during the war.

Internal Macedonian Revolutionary Organisation (IMRO): a terrorist organisation originally founded in 1893 to free Macedonia (qv) from the Turks. It opposed the inclusion of (northern) Macedonia within Yugoslavia, but functioned almost as a state within a state in Bulgaria, where it was for a time used as an agent of the government prior to being forcibly crushed. It maintained shadowy relations with Mussolini's Italy and the Croat *Ustaša*.

Its most prominent victim was Aleksandŭr Stamboliyski, the Bulgarian prime minister, whom it bloodily executed in association with the Bulgarian military. It sent his decapitated head to Sofia in a box.

Iron Guard (*Garda de Fier*): the pre-war Romanian fascist organisation. Founded as the Legion of the Archangel Michael in 1927 by Corneliu Codreanu and later known as the Legion or Legionary Movement, the Iron Guard was 'Christian', anti-Semitic, racist and mystically nationalistic in its outlook. Its concept of the nation included 'the souls and tombs of the dead', and the organisation regarded the resurrection from the dead as the nation's highest and most sublime goal. Although the name of 'Iron Guard' was popularly applied to the movement as a whole, it strictly applied only to its armed wing. The Guard was responsible for campaigns of murder and terror, and received funds from Germany after the Nazi accession to power. Banned in December 1933, it reappeared as *Totul Pentru Țara* (All-for-the-Fatherland) and enjoyed some support for a time from King Carol. It was nevertheless again banned in December 1938 when the king proclaimed a royal dictatorship, but promptly resurfaced. In 1940–41 it split between the extreme Romanian nationalist faction and the faction supporting General Antonescu and cooperation with Germany and Italy. The movement came to an end when the former rebelled against General Antonescu in January 1941 and was suppressed with German assistance.

Magyar: the Hungarians' own word to identify themselves and their culture, and more widely used to distinguish between ethnic Hungarian and Gypsy, Jewish or other strands in Hungarian life and culture.

Oder–Neisse Line: the line formed by the courses of the Rivers Oder and Neisse which in 1945 became the provisional German–Polish border. It was accepted with some reluctance as the permanent border by the German government in the 'Treaty on the Final Settlement with respect to Germany', signed on 12 September 1990.

Orszagyüles: the unicameral Hungarian National Assembly.

Orthodox Church: the eastern branch of the Christian faith, the identity of which dates back to the fourth-century administrative division of the Roman Empire into a western half dependent on Rome and an eastern half dependent on Byzantium, later Constantinople, now Istanbul. The eastern half of the empire had Greek as its lingua franca as against the Latin of the western half. Roman Catholicism and Orthodoxy saw themselves as rivals from the beginning, and totally split asunder in the Great Schism of 1054. The division was reinforced by the western crusaders pillaging Constantinople on their return from the unsuccessful Fourth Crusade in 1204. The great carved horses now in front of St Mark's Basilica in Venice are their best-known trophy.

The eastern half of the Roman Empire, or the Byzantine Empire as it came to be known after the fall of Rome in the fifth century, steadily shrank in size under Muslim attack first from the Arabs and then from the Turks, and disappeared totally in the fifteenth century, but its practices and thinking strongly influenced the Orthodox churches which survived in Bulgaria, Greece, Romania, Serbia and, most important of all, Russia. Devout Russians considered Moscow the 'Third Rome'. The most important of those influences was the absence of the distinction between church and state which developed in the west. There was no eastern equivalent of Thomas à Beckett. Organisationally, the different Orthodox churches were 'autocephalous', the Greek expression for 'having its own head' or being self-governing. There was no equivalent of the Pope, although the patriarchs of Athens and Istanbul enjoy historic prestige and rivalry.

The schism between Orthodoxy and Roman Catholicism is healing – slowly. Pope John Paul II in visiting Romania in May 1999 made the first papal visit to a primarily Orthodox country since 1054. Many Orthodox clergy, however, remain deeply suspicious of western ideas and intentions.

pyramid scheme: a finance scheme based on informal deposit taking, and much favoured in the less developed Balkan countries, particularly Albania, in the early 1990s. A pyramid scheme compensated for the lack of a formal banking system by absorbing without undue scrutiny legitimate personal savings and remittances from expatriates, proceeds from smuggling and other forms of crime, and 'dirty money' from anywhere in the world. They were subject to manipulation and sudden collapse, and in the Albanian case their dramatic collapse early in 1997 led to enormous losses for large sectors of the population.

Sabor: the Croat diet 1918, and the lower house of the Croat parliament since 1990.

salami tactics: the term coined by Mátyás Rákosi, the Hungarian Communist Party leader, to describe the squeezing out (like a salami in a sandwich) of elements in a coalition grouping hostile to the Communists.

Sejm: the lower house of the Polish parliament.

Siebenburgen Saxons: a community of some half a million ethnic Germans at the beginning of the twentieth century who had colonised a part of Transylvania in the twelth century and established the seven fortified towns which gave the community its name. Ion Gheorghe Maurer, Romanian prime minister, 1961–74, was of Siebenburgen stock on his father's side.

The community has now shrunk to 15,000 and western foundations are attempting to help preserve its medieval villages.

Skupština: the lower house of the Yugoslav parliament.

Sobranje: the unicameral Bulgarian parliament and, since 1990, the Macedonian parliament.

Teschen (Polish Cieszyn, Czech Těšín): an area of some 350 square miles and with a population of some 227,000 centred on the town of the same name, best known under its German form. The area, which was important for its coal mines and as a communications centre, was bitterly contested between Czechoslovakia and Poland in the inter-war years. The Conference of Ambassadors on 28 June 1920 had awarded the greater part of the area including the town to Poland, but the railway station, on the vital route from Bohemia–Moravia to Slovakia, to Czechoslovakia. The whole area was occupied by Poland following Munich, and remained Polish in 1945 despite Czechoslovak objections.

velvet revolution: the name given to the bloodless revolution in Prague in December 1989, whereby the Czechoslovak Communist Party agreed to share governmental power with the Civic Forum.

'Vienna Award' (first): the 'Award' was an adjustment of the Czechoslovak/ Hungarian border imposed on Czechoslovakia by the German and Italian foreign ministers, Joachim von Ribbentrop and Count Ciano, on 2–3 November 1938, following the Munich conference in September. A strip of southern Slovakia of some 12,000 square kilometres with a mainly ethnic Hungarian population was returned to Hungary. Neither the British nor the French (nor the Soviet Union) was represented, and Italian influence may have made the Award more favourable to the Hungarians than it would otherwise have been.

'Vienna Award' (second): the 'Award' was the settlement of the Hungarian/ Romanian border question imposed by the Axis powers in 1940. Ever since the Treaty of Trianon on 4 June 1920, Hungary had bitterly resented the total loss of Transylvania to Romania, and all Hungarian parties had the national slogan of *Nem, nem, sohar!* (no, no, never!) to the whole post-war settlement. Hungary had allied itself with Italy and then Germany in an attempt to secure its ultimate reversal. According to the Romanian census of 1930, the population of Transylvania was 48 per cent Hungarian, 43 per cent Romanian, 2.5 per cent German and 6.5 per cent other. Direct negotiations between the two parties failed in mid-August 1940, following which their prime and foreign ministers were summoned to Vienna on 27 August. Hitler and Mussolini, together with their foreign ministers, Joachim von Ribbentrop and Count Ciano, there effectively imposed the Award, which transferred most of Transylvania and 2,370,000 Romanian nationals, more than a million of them ethnic Romanians, to Hungary. Hungary recovered all of northern Transylvania including the city of Cluj (Hungarian Kolozsvar), with its Romanian university, and Oradea Mare, and the three Szekler provinces which had been almost solely Magyar populated for more than a thousand years. The Axis powers guaranteed Romania's new frontiers and the security of the Romanian minority in Hungary.

Demonstrations and protests erupted across Romania, in which Dr Maniu, the National Peasant Party and Transylvanian leader, played an important role, but Romania could not go against the will of its German ally.

The Award was reversed by the Hungarian armistice agreement of January 1945.

Zveno Group: Bulgarian military and political group. Responsible for the *coup d'état* of May 1934 which installed Colonel Kimon Georgiev as prime minister until 1935. He was later arrested. The group was initially dictatorial and militaristic in temper, although fundamentally republican and in favour of a sincere understanding with Yugoslavia, particularly on the Macedonian question. The group later veered to the Left and formed the *Otechestven* (Fatherland) Group with other parties, Colonel Georgiev again becoming prime minister, 1944–46.

10.4 MAJOR ASSASSINATIONS, SUICIDES AND POLITICAL EXECUTIONS

16 December 1922	President Gabriel Narutowicz of Poland (A)
18 February 1923	Finance minister Alois Rašin of Czechoslovakia (A)
14 June 1923	Prime minister Alexandŭr Stamboliyski of Bulgaria (E)
29 December 1933	Prime minister Ion G. Duca of Romania (A)
15 June 1934	Interior minister Colonel Pieracki of Poland (A)
25 July 1934	Chancellor Dr Engelbert Dollfuss of Austria (A)
9 October 1934	King Alexander of Yugoslavia (A)
10 October 1938	Major-General Jordan Peeff, Chief of the General Staff of the Bulgarian Army (A)
30 November 1938	Corneliu Zelea Codreanu, leader of the Romanian Iron Guard (A)
21 September 1939	Prime minister Armand Calinescu of Romania (A)
27 November 1939	General Argescanu and Professor Iorga, former Romanian prime ministers (A)
3 April 1941	Prime minister Count Teleki of Hungary (S)
28 August 1943	King Boris III of Bulgaria (S perhaps)
1 February 1945	Prince Kiril, Professor Filov and General Mikhov, former Bulgarian regents, together with subsequently Dr Bojilov and Ivan Bagrianov, former Bulgarian prime ministers, and twenty other ministers (E)
10 May 1945	Konrad Henlein, former Sudeten German leader (S)
7 June 1945	Dr Nikola Mandić, former Croatian prime minister (E)
10 January 1946	Laszlo de Bardossy, former Hungarian prime minister (E)
6 February 1946	General Milan Nedić, former prime minister of Serbia (S)
28 February 1946	Béla de Imredy, former Hungarian prime minister (E)
12 March 1946	Ferenc Szálassi, former Hungarian prime minister and leader of the Arrow Cross, together with subsequently nine members of his cabinet including Dr Sandor Csia, former member of the Regency Council (E)
22 May 1946	Karl Hermann Frank, former Reichs-Protector of Bohemia and Moravia (E)
1 June 1946	General Ion Antonescu, former *conducator* of Romania (E)

17 July 1946	Colonel Draža Mihajlović, former leader of the Četniks (E)
16 October 1946	Dr Arthur Seyss-Inquart, leader of the Austrian Nazi Party (E)
18 April 1947	Former President Mgr Jozef Tiso of Slovakia (E)
23 September 1947	Nikola Petkov, leader of the Bulgarian Agrarian Party (E)
10 March 1948	Jan Masaryk, Czechoslovak foreign minister (S/A)
15 October 1949	Laszlo Rajk, former Hungarian foreign minister (E)
16 December 1949	Traicho Kostov, former Secretary-General of the Bulgarian Communist Party (E)
3 December 1952	Rudolf Slánský, Former Secretary-General of the Czechoslovak Communist Party (E)
	Vladimir Clementis, former Czechoslovak foreign minister (E)
·14 April 1954	Lucretiu Patrascanu, former Romanian minister of justice (E)
18 December 1981	Mehmet Shehu, Albanian prime minister (S)
25 December 1989	President Nicolae Ceauşescu of Romania and his wife Elena (E)
25 June 1998	Marek Papala, former head of the Polish police (probably A, by criminal interests)
12 September 1998	Azem Hajdari, a leading member of the Albanian opposition (A)
11 January 1999	Jan Ducky, former Slovak economics minister (A)
15 January 2000	Arkan, Serbian warlord (A)
8 February 2000	Pavle Bulatović, Yugoslav defence minister (A)

BIBLIOGRAPHICAL ESSAY

The student of central and eastern Europe in the twentieth century tends to be faced with the problem of too few books in some directions and almost too many in others.

The number on the region as a whole is comparatively limited. Among the most useful are: Joseph Held (ed.), *The Columbia History of Eastern Europe in the Twentieth Century* (New York: Columbia University Press, 1992) and Philip Longworth, *The Making of Eastern Europe: From Prehistory to Postcommunism* (Basingstoke and London: Macmillan, 2nd edn, 1997). The latter follows the distinctive approach for a history of starting with the present and explaining its problems by working backwards, and successively repeating the exercise. Despite its title, it gives very full coverage to the twentieth century. Robert Bideleux and Ian Jeffries, *A History of Eastern Europe: Crisis and Change* (London: Routledge, 1998) is less helpful in that particular respect.

The seminal work for the inter-war period is probably Hugh Seton Watson, *Eastern Europe 1918–41* (Hamden, CT: Archon Books, an updating of the second edition of the original, Cambridge University Press, 1946). It is not always dispassionate, but it reflects the perspectives of the time. Ivan T. Berend, *Decades of Crisis: Central and Eastern Europe before World War II* (Berkeley, Los Angeles and London: University of California Press, 1998) is somewhat wider in scope and more academic in its analysis, but very accessible. J. Rothschild, *East Central Europe between the two World Wars* (Seattle, WA, 1975) is also very useful, but has a narrower focus.

There is a wider range on the Communist period. Martin McCauley (ed.), *Communist Rule in Europe 1944–49* (London, 1977) concentrates on the initial assumption of power. Jerzy Tomaszewski, *The Socialist Regimes of Eastern Europe* (London and New York: Routledge, 1989) reviews the whole period. Zbigniew Brzezinski, *The Soviet Bloc: Unity and Conflict* (Cambridge, MA, 1960) considers the 1950s while Stephen Fischer-Galati (ed.), *Eastern Europe in the 1980s* (Boulder, CO: Westview Press; London: Croom Helm, 1981) is self-explanatory. Ben Fowkes, *Eastern Europe 1945–69* (Harlow: Longman, 2000) is an up-to-date assessment. George Klein and Milan J. Reban (eds), *The Politics of Ethnicity in Eastern Europe* (New York: Columbia University Press, 1981) is a necessary reminder that communism did not depose nationalism. Students with a particular interest in the economy are referred to M. Kaser and J. G. Zielinski, *Planning in Eastern Europe* (London, 1970).

The collapse of communism and the following decade generated a plethora of books. Among the best are Misha Glenny, *The Rebirth of History* (Harmondsworth: Penguin, 1990) and Sten Berglund and Jan Åke Dellenbrant (eds), *The New Democracies in Eastern Europe* (Aldershot: Edward Elgar, 2nd edn, 1994). Michael Mandelbaum (ed.), *Post Communism: Four Perspectives* (New York: The Council on Foreign Relations Inc., 1996) opposes some very differing interpretations of what has, and will, happen. Bulent Gokay, *Eastern Europe, 1970–96* (Harlow: Longman, 2001) puts transition in a longer timescale.

Barry Turner (ed.), *Central Europe Profiled* (London: Macmillan, 2000) captures the present moment.

Turning to ideologies and philosophies, Roger Eatwell, *Fascism: A History* (London: Vintage, 1996) is accessible but focuses on Germany and Italy and therefore has to be interpreted somewhat for the different world of central and eastern Europe. John Hutchinson and Anthony D. Smith (eds), *Nationalism* (Oxford: Oxford University Press, 1994) is much more comprehensive. Studies on communism are voluminous but students should not overlook some of the original sources which are both short and lively. They include Karl Marx and Friedrich Engels, *Manifesto of the Communist Party* (originally written, 1848, translated and published by, among others, Lawrence & Wishart, London, 1983) and V. I. Lenin, *What is to be done?* (Moscow: Progress Publishers, 1963).

If books on the whole region are few, there are more on certain zones, particularly the Balkans. Among them are Misha Glenny, *The Balkans 1804–1999* (London: Granta, 1999) and Stevan K. Pavlowitch, *A History of the Balkans 1804–1945* (Harlow: Longman, 1999). Books on individual countries are in some cases sparse and in others plentiful. Works on individual countries include:

Albania

Miranda Vickers, *The Albanians: A Modern History* (London and New York: I. B. Tauris, 1999) has no real rival. Bemd Fischer, *Albania at War 1939–45* (London: Hurst, 1999) is self-explanatory.

Bosnia–Hercegovina

The only general history in English appears to be N. Malcolm, *Bosnia: A Short History* (2nd edn, London: Macmillan, 1996). Ivan Lovrenovic, *Bosnia: A Cultural History* (translated Bosnian Institute, London, London: Saqi Books, 2001) has a self-evidently different focus.

There are far more books on the three-year war, some polemical. They include: Steven L. Borg and Paul S. Shoup, *The War in Bosnia–Hercegovina* (New York, 1999); N. Cigar, *Genocide in Bosnia: The Policy of Ethnic Cleansing* (Texas University Press, 1995); J. V. A. Fine and R. J. Donia, *Bosnia–Hercegovina, a Tradition Betrayed* (London: Hurst, 1994); F. Friedman, *The Bosnian Muslims: Denial of a Nation* (Boulder, CO: Westview Press, 1996); E. O'Balance, *Civil War in Bosnia 1992–94* (London: Macmillan, 1995); D. Rieff, *Slaughterhouse: Bosnia and the Failure of the West* (New York, 1997); and M. A. Sells, *The Bridge Betrayed: Religion and Genocide in Bosnia* (California University Press, 1996).

Bulgaria

The obvious work is Richard Crampton, *A Concise History of Bulgaria* (Cambridge: Cambridge University Press, 2001) which updates the 1997 edition and the author's *A Short History of Modern Bulgaria* (Cambridge: Cambridge University Press, 1987).

Books on specific periods include: Marshall Lee Miller, *Bulgaria during the Second World War* (Stanford, CA, 1975); Nissan Oren, *Bulgarian Communism: The Road to Power, 1934–44* (New York, 1971); J. F. Brown, *Bulgaria under*

Communist Rule (London: Pall Mall, 1970); and Hristo Devedjiev, *Stalinisation of Bulgarian Society 1949–53* (Philadelphia, PA, 1978).

The Bulgarian economy is discussed in John R. Lampe, *The Bulgarian Economy in the Twentieth Century* (London, 1986) and the problems of transition from capitalism in Mito Isusov (ed.), *Problems of Transition from Capitalism to Socialism* (Sofia, 1975).

Croatia

The only readily available history of Croatia is M. C. Tanner, *A Nation Forged in War* (New Haven, CT: Yale University Press, 1997).

Czechoslovakia

Somewhat surprisingly, no general full-length histories of the Czechoslovak state ever seem to have been written either in English or in any other western European language. The nearest equivalents are: William V. Wallace, *Czechoslovakia* (1976); Norman Stone and Eduard Strouhal (eds), *Czechoslovakia: Crossroads and Crises 1918–88* (1989); Jaroslav Krejčí, *Czechoslovakia at the Crossroads of European History* (1990); and Jaroslav Krejčí and Machonin Pavel, *Czechoslovakia 1918–92: A Laboratory for Social Change* (London: Macmillan, 1996). The pre-war period is covered in R. W. Seton-Watson, *A History of the Czechs and Slovaks* (1943, reprinted 1965) and S. Harrison Thomson, *Czechoslovakia in European History* (2nd edn, enlarged, 1953, reprinted 1965), but both, naturally, show their age.

The standard work on the Sudeten issue is Elizabeth Wiskemann, *A Study of the Struggle in the Historic Provinces of Bohemia and Moravia* (2nd edn, 1967). Also valuable are: J. W. Bruegel, *Czechoslovakia before Munich: The German Minority Problem and British Appeasement Policy* (1973); F. Gregory Campbell, *Confrontation in Central Europe: Weimar Germany and Czechoslovakia* (1975); Radomir Luza, *The Transfer of the Sudeten Germans: A Study of Czech–German Relations 1933–62* (1964); Ronald M. Smelser, *The Sudeten Problem, 1933–38, Volkstumspolitik and the Formulation of Nazi Foreign Policy* (1975); C. S. Leff, *National Conflict in Czechoslovakia: The Making and Remaking of a State 1918–87* (Princeton, NJ, 1988) is more broadly based.

The 1968 'Prague Spring' and its antecedents, however, are extensively covered in: Galia Golan, *The Czechoslovak Reform Movement: Communism in Crisis 1967–68* (1971) and *Reform Rule in Czechoslovakia: The Dubček Era, 1968–69* (1973); Zdeněk Mlynár, *Nightfrost in Prague: The End of Humane Socialism* (translated 1980); Hans Renner, *A History of Czechoslovakia since 1945* (1989); H. Gordon Skilling, *Czechoslovakia's Interrupted Revolution* (1976); L. William Zartman, *Czechoslovakia: Intervention and Impact* (1970); and Z. A. R. Zeman, *Prague Spring* (1969).

The subsequent period and the transition to liberal democracy are described in Vladimir V. Kusin, *From Dubček to Charter 77: A Study of Normalisation in Czechoslovakia 1968–78* (1978) and Bernard Wheaton and Zdeněk Kavan, *The Velvet Revolution: Czechoslovakia, 1988–91* (Boulder, CO: Westview Press, 1992).

The most extensive work on the economy is Alice Teichova, *The Czechoslovak Economy 1918–80* (1988) but the specific problems of reform are the focus of John N. Stevens, *Czechoslovakia at the Crossroads: The Economic Dilemmas of Communism in Postwar Czechoslovakia* (1985) and Martin Myant, *The Czechoslovak Economy, 1948–88: The Battle for Economic Reform* (1989).

East Germany

The most comprehensive book on East Germany probably remains David Childs, *The GDR, Moscow's German Ally* (London: Allen & Unwin, 1983). Martin McCauley's *The German Democratic Republic since 1945* (London and Basingstoke: Macmillan, 1983) focuses more on the specifically historical and has a detailed chronology. It is usefully read in conjunction with David Childs (ed.), *Honecker's Germany* (London: Allen & Unwin, 1985) which ranges more widely. Mary Fulbrook, *Anatomy of a Dictatorship. Inside the GDR 1949–89* (Oxford: Oxford University Press, 1995) contains much valuable information, but is not really a history in the narrower sense. Heinz Heitzer, *GDR: An historical outline* (Dresden: Verlag Zeit im Bild, 1981) presents the official SED view. The definitive history of East Germany in the historical context is probably yet to be written.

Hungary

The most recent history is Miklos Molnár, *A Concise History of Hungary* (translated Anna Magyar, Cambridge: Cambridge University Press, 2001). Earlier histories include: Jorg K. Hönsch, *A History of Modern Hungary 1867–1994* (translated Kim Traynor, Harlow and London: Longman, 2nd edn, 1996); C. A. Macartney, *Hungary: A Short History* (London, 1962); and P. F. Sugar (ed.), *A History of Hungary* (London, 1991).

The period from 1919 to 1945 is covered in: C. A. Macartney, *October Fifteenth: A History of Modern Hungary 1929–45* (2 vols, 2nd edn, Edinburgh: Edinburgh University Press, 1961); Thomas L. Sakmyster, *Hungary, the Great Powers, and the Danubian Crisis 1936–39* (1980); and Gyula Juhász, *Hungarian Foreign Policy 1919–45* (1979).

Miklos Molnár, *A Short History of the Hungarian Communist Party* (1978) and Bennett Kovrig, *Communism in Hungary: From Kun to Kádár* (1979) focus on the communist period. The 1956 revolt is covered by: Charles Gati, *Hungary and the Soviet Bloc* (1986); William F. Robinson, *The Pattern of Reform in Hungary: A Political, Economic and Cultural Analysis* (1979); Peter A. Toma and Ivan Voloyes, *Politics in Hungary* (1977); Ferenc A. Vali, *Rift and Revolt in Hungary: Nationalism versus Communism* (Cambridge, MA: Harvard, 1961); and Paul E. Zinner, *Revolution in Hungary* (New York and London: Columbia University Press, 1962, re-issued 1972).

The transition from communism and the history of the last decade are discussed in: A. Bozoki (ed.), *Post-Communist Transition: Emerging Pluralism in Hungary* (London, 1992); T. Cox and A. Furlong (eds), *Hungary: The Politics of Transition* (London, 1995); András Gerő, *Modern Hungarian Society in the*

Making: the Unfinished Experience (translated James Patterson and Enikö Koncz, Budapest, London and New York: Central European University Press, 1995); and András Körösenyi, *Government and Politics in Hungary* (Central European Press, 1999).

Economic reform is discussed in J. Batt, *Economic Reform and Political Change in Eastern Europe: a Comparison of the Czechoslovak and Hungarian Experiences* (Basingstoke: Macmillan, 1988).

Macedonia

The question of identity is central to L. M. Danforth, *The Macedonian Conflict: Ethnic Nationalism in a Transnational World* (Princeton, NJ: Princeton University Press, 1996) and James Pettifer (ed.), *The New Macedonian Question* (Basingstoke: Palgrave, 1999).

Poland

The standard work is probably Norman Davies, *God's Playground: A History of Poland* (Oxford: Oxford University Press, 1981). More recent, however, is Jerzy Lukowski and Hubert Zawadski, *A Concise History of Poland* (Cambridge: Cambridge University Press, 2001). W. F. Reddaway (ed.), *The Cambridge History of Poland* (2 vols, reprinted 1971) remains authoritative although somewhat out of date. Other sources include: O. Halecki and A. Polonsky, *A History of Poland* (translated from the Polish, 1983); R. F. Leslie (ed.), *The History of Poland since 1863* (Cambridge: Cambridge University Press, 1980); R. Sikorski, *The Polish House: An Intimate History of Poland* (London, 1997); and J. Wedel, *The Unplanned Society, Poland during and after Communism* (New York: Columbia University Press, 1992).

More specialist books covering particular periods include: Anthony Polonsky, *Politics in Independent Poland 1921–39: The Crisis of Constitutional Government* (Oxford: Oxford University Press, 1972); R. Debicki, *Foreign Policy of Poland 1919–32* (New York, 1962); Jósef Garlinski, *Poland in the Second World War* (1985); Michael Checinsky, *Poland: Communism, Nationalism, Anti-Semitism*; Abraham Brumberg (ed.), *Poland, Genesis of a Revolution* (1983); B. Kaminski, *The Collapse of the State of Socialism: the Case of Poland* (Princeton, NJ: Princeton University Press, 1981); Peter Raina, *Poland, 1981: Towards Social Renewal* (1985); Jadwiga Stanisykis, *Poland's Self-Limiting Revolution* (1984) and Lawrence Weschler, *The Passion of Poland: From Solidarity through the State of War* (1984).

Closer, perhaps, to journalism (and that is not meant pejoratively) are: Neal Ascherson, *The Polish August: The Self-Limiting Revolution* (1982); Timothy Garton Ash, *The Polish Revolution: Solidarity 1980–82* (1983); Adam Bromke, *Eastern Europe in the Aftermath of Solidarity* (1985); and John Rensenbrink, *Poland Challenges a Divided World* (1988). Such books have inevitably been somewhat overtaken by events.

The history of Polish Jewry is discussed by Bernard Weinryb, *The Jews of Poland* (Philadelphia, PA, 1973).

Studies of the transition to liberal democracy include: K. D. Mitchell (ed.), *Political Pluralism in Hungary and Poland, Perspectives on the Reforms* (New York, 1992); R. F. Staar (ed.), *Transition to Democracy in Poland* (New York, 1993); and J. Stanisykis, *The Dynamics of the Breakthrough in Eastern Europe: the Polish Experience* (California University Press, 1991).

The standard work on economic questions is probably Zbigniew Landau and Jerzy Tomaszewski, *The Polish Economy in the Twentieth Century* (translated 1985) but more recent, although more limited in scope, is B. Slay, *The Polish Economy Crisis, Reform and Transformation* (Princeton, NJ: Princeton University Press, 1994). G. R. Feiwel, *Problems in Polish Economic Planning: Continuity, Change and Prospects* (London, 1971) gives an earlier perspective.

Romania

Histories of Romania are limited in number and scope. Dennis Deletant, *Romania under Communist Rule* (Oxford and Portland, OR: Centre for Romanian Studies, Iaşi, 1999) is authoritative on its period. Professor Andrei Otetea (ed.), *A concise history of Romania* (London: Robert Hall, 1985) presents the story from a Romanian perspective. M. Rady, *Romania in Turmoil: A Contemporary History* (London, 1992) and N. Ratesh, *The Entangled Revolution* (1991) study the process of transition, while T. Gallagher, *Romania after Ceauşescu: the Politics of Intolerance* (Edinburgh: Edinburgh University Press) brings the story more up to date.

Slovenia

The two main volumes are J. Benderly and E. Kraft (eds), *Independent Slovenia: Origins, Movements, Prospects* (London, 1995) and James Gow and Cathie Carmichael, *Slovenia and the Slovenes* (London: Hurst, 2000).

Yugoslavia

Yugoslavia has sadly but inevitably generated a vast output of books, of variable quality. Some have a discernible bias against one or other ethnic group or cultural tradition.

The most authoritative on the disintegration of the former federation is probably Misha Glenny, *The Fall of Yugoslavia* (Harmondsworth: Penguin, 1992). Other valuable perspectives are provided by: C. Bennett, *Yugoslavia's Bloody Collapse: Causes, Course and Consequences* (Farnborough, 1995); L. J. Cohen, *Broken Bonds: the Disintegration of Yugoslavia* (Boulder, CO, 1993); Mihailo Crnobrnja, *The Yugoslav Drama* (London: I. B. Tauris, 1994); D. Dyker and I. Vejvoda (eds), *Yugoslavia and After: a Study in Fragmentation, Despair and Rebirth* (Harlow: Longman, 1996); J. Udovicki and J. Ridgeway (eds), *Burn this House: The Making and Unmaking of Yugoslavia* (Durham, NC: Duke University Press, 1997); and S. L. Woodward, *Balkan Tragedy: Chaos and Dissolution after the Cold War* (Washington DC: Brookings Institution).

Books specifically on Serbia include Branimir Anzulovic, *Heavenly Serbia: From Myth to Genocide* (London: Hurst, 1999) and Tim Judah, *The Serbs* (New Haven, CT and London: Yale University Press, 2nd edn, 2000). Those on its Kosovo province include: Tim Judah, *Kosovo* (New Haven, CT and London: Yale University Press, 2000); Noel Malcolm, *Kosovo: A short history* (Basingstoke: Macmillan, 1998); and M. Vickers, *Between Serb and Albanian: A History of Kosovo* (London: Hurst, 1998). *One Woman's War* by Eve-Anne Prentice (London: Duck Editions, 2000) gives the individual perspective of a British journalist married to a Serb.

Books on the former federation written while it was still in existence include: V. Dedijer, *History of Yugoslavia* (New York, 1974); H. Lydall, *Yugoslavia in Crisis* (Oxford: Oxford University Press, 1989); B. McFarlane, *Yugoslavia: Politics, Economics and Society* (London, 1988); C. Prout, *Market Socialism in Yugoslavia* (Oxford: Oxford University Press, 1985); and F. Singleton, *Twentieth Century Yugoslavia* (London, 1976).

Biographies

Biographies are a valuable source although, like autobiographies, they sometimes have to be treated with discretion. They include:

István Bethlen: A great conservative statesman of Hungary by Ignác Romsics (translated Mario D. Fenyo, distributed Columbia University Press, New York, 1995) gives a sympathetic, revisionist view.

Dubček by William Shawcross (revised and updated, 1990).

Václav Havel by John Keane (London: Bloomsbury, 1999) is extremely comprehensive and at times critical of both the man and his policies, possibly unfairly.

Mussolini by Denis Mack Smith (London: Weidenfeld & Nicolson, 1981) is the standard biography.

Tito: A Pictorial Biography by Fitzroy Maclean (Basingstoke: Macmillan, 1980) is an intimate non-academic portrait by a Briton who observed Tito at first hand in the midst of the war.

Tito by Stephen K. Pavlowitch (London: Hurst, 1992) is an academic assessment benefiting from a longer perspective.

Lech Wałęsa by Roger Boyes (London: Secker & Warburg).

Essays, Speeches and Writings

Erich Honecker, *From My Life* (Oxford: Pergamon Press, 1981)
János Kádár, *On the Road to Socialism* (Budapest: Corvina, 1965)
Imre Nagy on Communism (London: Thames & Hudson, 1957)
J. B. Tito, *The Essential Tito* (New York, 1970)
Todor Zhivkov, *Selected Works* (Oxford: Pergamon Press, 1985)

MAPS

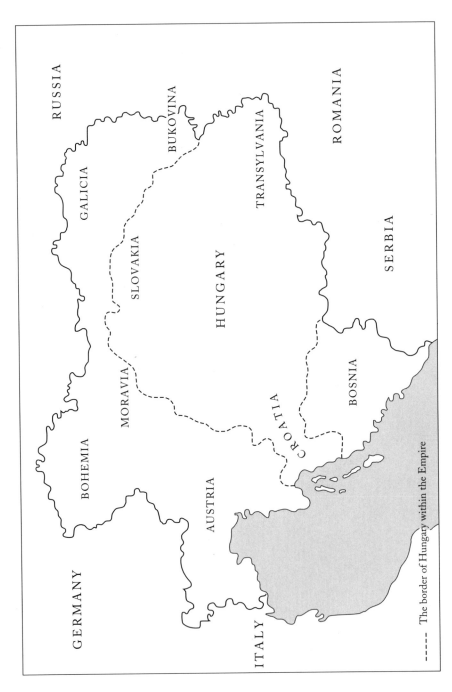

Map 1 The Austro-Hungarian Empire in 1914

- - - - The border of Hungary within the Empire

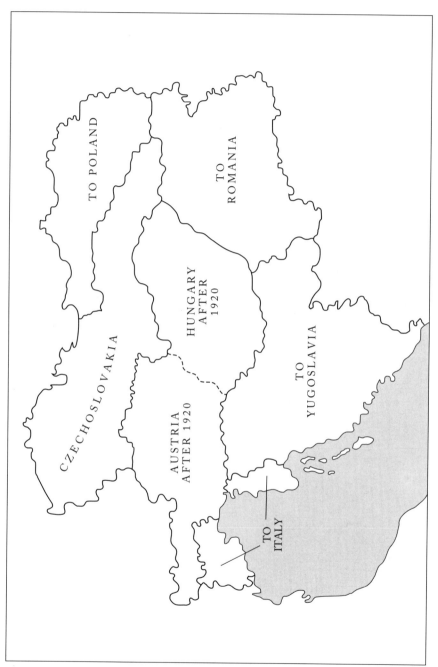

Map 2   The dismemberment of the Austro-Hungarian Empire

Map 3   Central and Eastern Europe in 1942

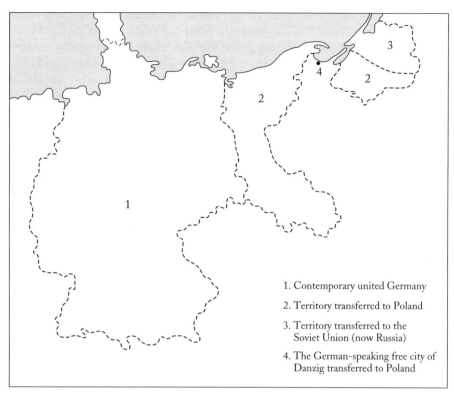

1. Contemporary united Germany

2. Territory transferred to Poland

3. Territory transferred to the
   Soviet Union (now Russia)

4. The German-speaking free city of
   Danzig transferred to Poland

Map 4   Germany within its 1937 boundaries and the territory lost in 1945

INDEX